AF619216

Data Mining and Computational Intelligence

Studies in Fuzziness and Soft Computing

Editor-in-chief
Prof. Janusz Kacprzyk
Systems Research Institute
Polish Academy of Sciences
ul. Newelska 6
01-447 Warsaw, Poland
E-mail: kacprzyk@ibspan.waw.pl
http://www.springer.de/cgi-bin/search_book.pl?series=2941

Further volumes of this series can be found at our homepage.

Vol. 46. J.N. Mordeson and P.S. Nair
Fuzzy Graphs and Fuzzy Hypergraphs, 2000
ISBN 3-7908-1286-2

Vol. 47. E. Czogała† and J. Łęski
Fuzzy and Neuro-Fuzzy Intelligent Systems, 2000
ISBN 3-7908-1289-7

Vol. 48. M. Sakawa
Large Scale Interactive Fuzzy Multiobjective Programming, 2000
ISBN 3-7908-1293-5

Vol. 49. L.I. Kuncheva
Fuzzy Classifier Design, 2000
ISBN 3-7908-1298-6

Vol. 50. F. Crestani and G. Pasi (Eds.)
Soft Computing in Information Retrieval, 2000
ISBN 3-7908-1299-4

Vol. 51. J. Fodor, B. De Baets and P. Perny (Eds.)
Preferences and Decisions under Incomplete Knowledge, 2000
ISBN 3-7908-1303-6

Vol. 52. E.E. Kerre and M. Nachtegael (Eds.)
Fuzzy Techniques in Image Processing, 2000
ISBN 3-7908-1304-4

Vol. 53. G. Bordogna and G. Pasi (Eds.)
Recent Issues on Fuzzy Databases, 2000
ISBN 3-7908-1319-2

Vol. 54. P. Sinčák and J. Vaščák (Eds.)
Quo Vadis Computational Intelligence?, 2000
ISBN 3-7908-1324-9

Vol. 55. J.N. Mordeson, D.S. Malik and S.-C. Cheng
Fuzzy Mathematics in Medicine, 2000
ISBN 3-7908-1325-7

Vol. 56. L. Polkowski, S. Tsumoto and T.Y. Lin (Eds.)
Rough Set Methods and Applications, 2000
ISBN 3-7908-1328-1

Vol. 57. V. Novák and I. Perfilieva (Eds.)
Discovering the World with Fuzzy Logic, 2001
ISBN 3-7908-1330-3

Vol. 58. D.S. Malik and J.N. Mordeson
Fuzzy Discrete Structures, 2000
ISBN 3-7908-1335-4

Vol. 59. T. Furuhashi, Shun'Ichi Tano and H.-A. Jacobsen (Eds.)
Deep Fusion of Computational and Symbolic Processing, 2001
ISBN 3-7908-1339-7

Vol. 60. K.J. Cios (Ed.)
Medical Data Mining and Knowledge Discovery, 2001
ISBN 3-7908-1340-0

Vol. 61. D. Driankov, A. Saffiotti (Eds.)
Fuzzy Logic Techniques for Autonomous Vehicle Navigation, 2001
ISBN 3-7908-1341-9

Vol. 62. N. Baba, L.C. Jain (Eds.)
Computational Intelligence in Games, 2001
ISBN 3-7908-1348-6

Vol. 63. O. Castillo, P. Melin
Soft Computing for Control of Non-Linear Dynamical Systems, 2001
ISBN 3-7908-1349-4

Vol. 64. I. Nishizaki, M. Sakawa
Fuzzy and Multiobjective Games for Conflict Resolution, 2001
ISBN 3-7908-1341-9

Vol. 65. E. Orłowska, A. Szalas (Eds.)
Relational Methods for Computer Science Applications, 2001
ISBN 3-7908-1365-6

Vol. 66. R.J. Howlett, L.C. Jain (Eds.)
Radial Basis Function Networks 1, 2001
ISBN 3-7908-1367-2

Abraham Kandel
Mark Last
Horst Bunke
Editors

Data Mining and Computational Intelligence

With 90 Figures
and 45 Tables

Springer-Verlag Berlin Heidelberg GmbH

Dr. Abraham Kandel
Computer Science and Engineering
University of South Florida
4202 E. Fowler Ave., ENB 118
Tampa, Florida 33620
USA
kandel@csee.usf.edu

Dr. Mark Last
Information Systems Engineering
Ben-Gurion University of the Negev
Beer-Sheva 84105
Israel
mlast@csee.usf.edu

Dr. Horst Bunke
Department of Computer Science
University of Bern
Neubruckstrasse 10
CH-3012 Bern
Switzerland
bunke@iam.unibe.ch

ISSN 1434-9922

Cataloging-in-Publication Data applied for
Die Deutsche Bibliothek – CIP-Einheitsaufnahme
Data mining and computational intelligence: with 45 tables / Abraham Kandel ... ed.
(Studies in fuzziness and soft computing; Vol. 68)

DOI 10.1007/978-3-7908-1825-3

Originally published by Physica-Verlag Heidelberg New York in 2001
MyCopy version of the original edition 2001

Hardcover Design: Erich Kirchner, Heidelberg

SPIN 10793207 88/2202-5 4 3 2 1 0 – Printed on acid-free paper
www.springer.com/mycopy

Preface

Many business decisions are made in the absence of complete information about the decision consequences. Credit lines are approved without knowing the future behavior of the customers; stocks are bought and sold without knowing their future prices; parts are manufactured without knowing all the factors affecting their final quality; etc. All these cases can be categorized as *decision making under uncertainty*.

Decision makers (human or automated) can handle uncertainty in different ways. Deferring the decision due to the lack of sufficient information may not be an option, especially in real-time systems. Sometimes expert rules, based on experience and intuition, are used. *Decision tree* is a popular form of representing a set of mutually exclusive rules. An example of a two-branch tree is: *if a credit applicant is a student, approve; otherwise, decline*. Expert rules are usually based on some hidden assumptions, which are trying to predict the decision consequences. A hidden assumption of the last rule set is: *a student will be a profitable customer*.

Since the direct predictions of the future may not be accurate, a decision maker can consider using some information from the past. The idea is to utilize the potential similarity between the patterns of the past (e.g., "most students *used to be* profitable") and the patterns of the future (e.g., "students *will be* profitable"). The problem of inference from data is closely related to the old and the well-established area of *statistics*. According to (Mendenhall et al. 1993), modern statistics is concerned with "examining and summarizing data to predict, estimate, and, ultimately, make business decisions." Statisticians have a variety of tools at their disposal. These include linear and nonlinear *regression models*, which produce mathematical equations for estimating the value of a dependent variable. Regression models, like other statistical methods, are based on restricting assumptions regarding the type and the distribution of the analyzed data. Thus, the linear regression model requires all the model variables to be continuous. This requirement is not necessarily satisfied in every real-world dataset. The assumption regarding the "normality" of the data distribution is also very common in statistics, though the actual distribution of the real variables may be completely different. As indicated by (Elder and Pregibon 1996), statisticians are more interested in the interpretability of their results, rather than in the classification/estimation performance of the statistical models. The distinction between the real patterns and the "noise" is another important consideration in statistics: the sample data is assumed to include some amount of noise and a confidence interval is associated with every statistical conclusion.

The increasing availability of electronic information has accentuated the limitations of the classical statistical models. On one hand, most statisticians still adhere to simple and global models (Elder and Pregibon 1996), and, on the other hand, today's computers have enough memory and computational power to find the best, though not necessarily the simplest models in a complex hypothesis space within minutes or even seconds. Alternative model representations include neural networks, decision trees, Bayesian networks, and others. Algorithms for computationally efficient search in a large set of models, specified by a given representation, have been developed by statisticians as well as by researchers from the artificial intelligence, the pattern recognition, and the machine learning communities (see Mitchell, 1997).

A book by Fayyad et al. (1996) has defined *data mining* as "the application of specific algorithms for extracting patterns from data." According to the same book, data mining is a step within the process of *knowledge discovery in databases*, which starts with pre-processing the raw data and ends up with business-oriented interpretation of data mining results. Fayyad et al. (1996) present a list of data analysis methods (decision tree learning, clustering, regression, etc.) that can be used at the data mining step.

Most research challenges for knowledge discovery and data mining have not changed much during the last five years. The list of research topics raised by Fayyad et al. (1996) includes the following issues.

Understandability of patterns. Classification/prediction accuracy is still the most common criterion for comparing the performance of data mining algorithms. However, the *knowledge discovery* means that the user gets a better insight into a specific domain or problem. Improving the interpretability of the discovered patterns is a major concern for most papers in this volume, especially Chapters 1-6 and 9. Since the discovered knowledge may include certain amount of uncertainty and imprecision, *fuzzy sets* (see below) can be used to represent the extracted patterns in more understandable, linguistic form.

Complex relationships between attributes. Several data mining methods (e.g., decision trees and association rules) automatically produce sets of rules of the form *if condition then consequence*. The task of learning rules from attribute-value records has been extensively studied in machine learning (see Mitchell, 1997). Though in simple systems the cause-effect relationships may be straightforward, automated rule induction from data representing complex phenomena should be done with caution. Extraction of complex relationships by using a two-phase approach to data mining is covered in Chapter 2. Chapters 3 and 7 handle the problem of finding complex associations in relational and transactional data. Discovering complex relationships in other types of data (e.g., financial and image data) is covered by Chapters 10 and 12.

Missing and noisy data. Business databases suffer from high rates of data entry errors. Moreover, to avoid operational delays, many important attributes are defined as optional, leading to a large number of missing values. Alternative techniques for dealing with missing and noisy data are described in Chapters 1, 4 and 8 of this book.

Mining very large databases. The UCI Machine Learning Repository (Blake and Merz 1998) has been recognized as a benchmark for evaluating performance of data mining algorithms. The repository is a collection of flat tables, having mostly fewer than 1,000 rows (records) and 50 columns (attributes). This is much less data than one can find in a typical commercial database application, where multi-gigabyte tables are commonplace. When dealing with large volumes of data, the loading of complete tables in the computer's main memory becomes impractical. A scalable data mining algorithm, which requires a single scan of a database is presented in Chapter 7. Another problem associated with large databases, high dimensionality, is handled by the Fuzzy-Rosa method in Chapter 6.

Changing data The original versions of many data mining methods assume the patterns to be static (time-invariant). The time dimension is absent from most benchmark datasets of the UCI Repository. However, modeling the dynamic behavior of non-stationary time series is very important for analyzing different types of financial data, like exchange rates and stock indices. Chapter 13 of this book is concerned with the problem of detecting changes in nonlinear time series.

Integration with database systems Since most business information is stored by database management systems (DBMS), an interface between DBMS and data mining tools might very useful. Chapter 5 of this book presents a fuzzy querying interface, which can support a specific data mining technique, called "linguistic summaries."

As shown by several chapters in this book, the fuzzy set theory can play an important role in the process of knowledge discovery. Central to the fuzzy set theory, introduced by Lotfi A. Zadeh (1965), is the concept of *fuzzy sets*, which are sets with imprecise boundaries. The membership of an object in a fuzzy set is a matter of a degree: for example, two persons of different height may belong to the same set of *tall people*, but their membership degree may be different. In the above example, *tall* is an imprecise linguistic term, which can be used by humans for communication and even for decision-making. This view of uncertainty is different from the probabilistic approach used by most data mining methods, since the calculation of membership grades is based on user-specific understanding of the domain (expressed mathematically by *membership functions*) rather than on purely statistical information.

Knowledge discovery in databases can be seen as a process of *approximate reasoning*, since it is concerned with inferring imprecise conclusions from imprecise (noisy) data. Traditionally, the data mining methods have been optimized along a single dimension, namely classification or estimation accuracy. However, business users are aware of the inherent uncertainty of the decision-making process and they may prefer comprehensible models that do not achieve the best classification performance. As demonstrated by this book, the fuzzy set theory provides an efficient tool for representing the trade-off between good performance and high comprehensibility of data mining methods.

The areas in which the chapters of this volume are contributing can be categorized in more detail as follows.

Rule extraction and reduction. A neuro-fuzzy method for rule learning in presented by Klose et al. in Chapter 1. The emphasis of the method is on producing a set of interpretable rules, which may be examined by a human expert. Pedrycz (Chapter 2) proposes a two-phase approach to the rule induction process: first, associations are built and scored by their relevancy and, in the second phase, some associations can be converted into production (direction-driven) rules. According to Pedrycz's approach, associations are relations between two or more *information granules*. An information-theoretic fuzzy approach to reducing dimensionality of a rule set, without disclosing any confidential information to the users, is presented by Last and Kandel in Chapter 3. As demonstrated by Chan and Au (Chapter 4), fuzzy rules may be particularly useful for mining databases, which contain both relational and transactional data. A fuzzy querying interface and procedure for mining fuzzy association rules in a Microsoft Access™ database are presented by Kacprzyk and Zadrozny in Chapter 5. Chapter 6 by Slawinski et al. describes the Fuzzy-ROSA method for data-based generation of small rule bases in high-dimensional search spaces. Ben Yahia and Jaoua (Chapter 7) introduce a new efficient algorithm, called FARD, for mining fuzzy association rules in transaction databases.

New data mining methods and techniques. Two Dimensional Partitioning Techniques (DPT1 and DPT2) are applied by Chang and Halgamuge (Chapter 8) to the problem of mining labeled data with missing values. In Chapter 9, Alahakoon et al. present a method for automated identification of clusters using a Growing Self Organizing Map (GSOM). Shnaider and Schneider (Chapter 10) have developed a fuzzy analog of the traditional regression model, called "soft regression," that evaluates the relative importance of each explanatory variable related to the dependent variable.

Mining non-relational data. Chapters 11 and 12 are concerned with mining image databases, while Chapter 13 deals with time series analysis. Nguyen et al. (Chapter 11) apply a combination of data mining and soft computing techniques to classification of dynamically changing images. A new FFT-based mosaicing algorithm is developed and implemented by Gibson et al. (Chapter 12) for finding common patterns in several images. The algorithm is applied to two problems: mosaicing satellite photos and searching images stored on the web. In Chapter 13, Wu employs a genetic-based approach for modeling time-series data. The genetic modeling is used to detect a change period and/or change point in a nonlinear time series.

The methods and application results presented in this volume suggest many promising directions for the future research in data mining, soft computing, and related areas. Some of the main problems and challenges remaining in this field are covered below.

Generalization and overfitting. Statistical techniques (e.g., regression and analysis of variance) provide clear relationship between the distribution of noise and the significance of simple data models. Applying the standard statistical approach to more complex models, like a decision tree, has been unsatisfactory (see Quinlan 1993, p. 37). Reliable assessment of model generalization (with and without the time factor) is one of the most important research challenges for the data mining community.

Use of prior knowledge. The expert knowledge is usually expressed in linguistic terms, while most of business data is still stored in a numeric format. As demonstrated by neuro-fuzzy methods, fuzzy sets are a natural tool for combining the available prior knowledge with the patterns discovered in data. New methodology should be developed for enabling the integration of fuzzy set technology with additional data mining algorithms (e.g., C4.5 or CART).

New forms of data. The last three chapters in this volume elucidate the problems associated with mining non-relational data. With multimedia databases becoming the main source of information in the 21st century, the existing data mining methods need a thorough revision to make them applicable to new types of data. The capability of a data mining method to quickly identify the most important features in a high-dimensional data set is crucial for mining text, image, and video databases.

Publication of this book was possible due to the enthusiastic response of all the contributors. We would like to thank them for their effort and for their constructive cooperation and support. We would also like to acknowledge the partial support by the USF Center for Software Testing (SOFTEC) under grant No. 2108-004-00. We hope the book will promote future research and development in data mining, computational intelligence and soft computing.

Tampa, Florida, USA

December 2000

Abraham Kandel

Mark Last

Horst Bunke

References

[1] C.L. Blake & C.J. Merz (1998). *UCI Repository of machine learning databases* [http://www.ics.uci.edu/~mlearn/MLRepository.html].

[2] J.F. Elder IV and D. Pregibon (1996). A Statistical Perspective on Knowledge Discovery in Databases. In U. Fayyad, G. Piatetsky-Shapiro, P. Smyth, and R. Uthurusamy, editors, *Advances in Knowledge Discovery and Data Mining*, pages 83-113. AAAI/MIT Press.

[3] U. Fayyad, G. Piatetsky-Shapiro, and P. Smyth (1996a). From Data Mining to Knowledge Discovery: An Overview. In U. Fayyad, G. Piatetsky-Shapiro, P. Smyth, and R. Uthurusamy, editors, *Advances in Knowledge Discovery and Data Mining*, pages 1-30. AAAI/MIT Press.

[4] W. Mendenhall, J.E. Reinmuth, R.J. Beaver (1993). *Statistics for Management and Economics*. Duxbury Press.

[5] T.M. Mitchell (1997). *Machine Learning*. McGraw-Hill.

[6] J. R. Quinlan (1993). *C4.5: Programs for Machine Learning*. Morgan Kaufmann.

[7] L. A. Zadeh (1965). Fuzzy Sets. *Information and Control*, 8 (3): 338-353.

Contents

Data Mining with Neuro-Fuzzy Models

A. Klose[1], A. Nürnberger[1], D. Nauck[2], R. Kruse[1]

[1] Department of Computer Science, University of Magdeburg, Germany

[2] British Telecom, Ipswich, UK

Abstract. Data mining is the central step in a process called knowledge discovery in databases, namely the step in which modeling techniques are applied. Several research areas such as statistics, artificial intelligence, machine learning, and soft computing have contributed to the arsenal of methods for data mining. In this paper, however, we focus on neuro-fuzzy methods for rule learning. In our opinion, fuzzy approaches can play an important role in data mining, because they provide comprehensible results. This goal often seems to be neglected – possibly because comprehensibility is sometimes hard to achieve with other methods.

Keywords. Data mining, neuro-fuzzy models, fuzzy classification, fuzzy rules

1 Introduction

Due to modern information technology, which produces ever computers that are more powerful every year, it is possible today to collect, store, transfer, and combine huge amounts of data at very low cost. Thus, an ever-increasing number of companies and scientific and governmental institutions can afford to build up large archives of documents and other data like numbers, tables, images, and sounds. However, exploiting the information contained in these archives in an intelligent way turns out to be difficult. In contrast to the abundance of data, there is a lack of tools that can transform this data into useful information and knowledge. Although a user often has a vague understanding of his data and their meaning, and can usually formulate hypotheses and guess dependencies, he rarely knows where to find the "interesting" or "relevant" pieces of information, whether these pieces of information support his hypotheses and models, whether (other) interesting phenomena are hidden in the data, which methods are best suited to find the needed pieces of information in a fast and reliable way, and how the data can be translated into human notions that are appropriate for the context in which

they are needed. In reply to these challenges, a new area of research has emerged, which has been named "knowledge discovery in databases" or "data mining".
In [7] the following definition is given:

> Knowledge discovery in databases (KDD) is a research area that considers the analysis of large databases in order to identify valid, useful, meaningful, unknown, and unexpected relationships.

Some well-known analysis methods and tools that are used in data mining are, for example, statistics (regression analysis, discriminant analysis etc.), time series analysis, decision trees, cluster analysis, neural networks, inductive logic programming, and association rules.

Classical models usually try to avoid *vague, imprecise* or *uncertain* information, because it is considered to have a negative influence in an inference process. Fuzzy systems, on the other hand, deliberately make use of this kind of information. This often leads to simpler, more suitable models, which are easier to handle and are more familiar to human thinking. In this paper we concentrate on combinations of fuzzy methods with neural networks (the so-called neuro-fuzzy methods) in data mining and show where and how they can be used.

In Sect. 2, we will briefly review the key concepts of neural networks and fuzzy systems, as well as the symbiosis resulting from their combination. Furthermore, we present our view of *data mining* and stress those aspects that we consider important in this context. We will show how neuro-fuzzy systems can be applied to data mining, and what makes this field especially suited for the application of neuro-fuzzy methods. Furthermore, Sect. 2.1 gives an overview of techniques – apart from neuro-fuzzy – that allow to induce fuzzy rules from data and in Sect. 2.2, we discuss which class distributions can be represented by fuzzy rules. Sect. 3 covers the theoretical aspects of neuro-fuzzy architectures (Sections 3.1 and 3.2), describes concrete implementations of neuro-fuzzy models (Sections 3.3, 3.4 and 3.5) and describes recent developments to improve the applicability of neuro-fuzzy models in data mining (Sect. 3.6). Applications of these neuro-fuzzy methods are illustrated in Sect. 4. Finally, some comments and conclusions are given in Sect. 5.

2 Neuro Fuzzy Systems and Data Mining

Over the last few decades, neural networks and fuzzy systems have established their reputation as alternative approaches to information processing. Both have certain advantages over classical methods, especially when vague data or prior knowledge is involved. However, their applicability suffered from several weaknesses of the individual models. Therefore, combinations of neural networks with fuzzy systems have been proposed, where both models complement each other. These so-called *neural fuzzy* or *neuro-fuzzy systems* allow to overcome some of the individual weaknesses and offer some appealing features.

Neural networks, also known as *connectionist models,* are systems that try to make use of some of the known or expected organizing principles of the human brain. They consist of a number of independent, simple processors - the *neurons.* These neurons communicate with each other via weighted connections - the *synaptic weights.* At first, research in this area was driven by neurobiological interests. The modeling of single neurons and the so-called „learning rules“ for modifying synaptic weights were the initial research topics. Modern research in neural networks, also called *connectionism,* considers the development of architectures and learning algorithms, and examines the applicability of these models to information processing tasks. Although there are still many researchers who devote themselves to modeling biological neural networks by artificial neural networks to learn more about the structure of the human brain and the way it works, we will restrict ourselves to the problem of information processing with artificial neural networks, and do not claim biological plausibility. What these models have in common is that they are based on rather simple processing units or neurons exchanging information via weighted connections. Different types of neural networks can solve different problems, like pattern recognition, pattern completion, determining similarities between patterns or data - also in terms of interpolation or extrapolation - and automatic classification (see, for example, 14). Learning in neural networks means to determine a mapping from an input to an output space by using example patterns. If the same or similar input patterns are presented to the network after learning, it should produce an appropriate output pattern.

We can use neural networks if we have training data. We do not need a mathematical model of the problem of interest, and we do not need any form of prior knowledge. On the other hand, we cannot interpret the solution obtained from the learning process. The neural network is a black box, and we cannot usually check whether its solution is plausible, i.e. its final state cannot be interpreted in terms of rules. This also means that we cannot initialize a neural network with prior knowledge if we have any. The network usually must learn from scratch. The learning process itself can take very long, and we have no guarantee of success.

Fuzzy systems. Fuzzy set theory provides excellent means to model the "fuzzy" boundaries of linguistic terms by introducing gradual memberships. In contrast to classical set theory, in which an object or a case either is a member of a given set (defined, e.g., by some property) or not, fuzzy set theory makes it possible that an object or a case belongs to a set only to a certain degree 24. Interpretations of membership degrees include similarity, preference, and uncertainty 6: They can state how similar an object or case is to a prototypical one, they can indicate preferences between sub optimal solutions to a problem, or they can model uncertainty about the true situation, if this situation is described in imprecise terms. In general, due to their closeness to human reasoning, solutions obtained using fuzzy approaches are easy to understand and to apply. Due to these strengths, fuzzy systems are the method of choice, if linguistic, vague, or imprecise information has to be modeled 23.

The fuzzy systems we consider in this context are based on if-then rules. The antecedent of a rule consists of fuzzy descriptions of input values, and the consequent defines a - possibly fuzzy - output value for the given input. The benefits of these fuzzy systems lie in the suitable knowledge representation. However, problems arise when fuzzy concepts have to be represented by concrete membership degrees, which guarantee that a fuzzy system works as expected. The determination of concrete membership degrees between 0 and 1 to specify the extent to which an object fulfils a concept, is a general problem in fuzzy systems. However, the determination of the membership degrees influences the behavior of a fuzzy system to a large extent.

A fuzzy system can be used to solve a problem if we have knowledge about the solution in the form of linguistic if-then rules. By defining suitable fuzzy sets to represent linguistic terms used within our rules, we can create the fuzzy system from these rules. We do not need a formal model of the problem of interest, and we also do not need training data. On the other hand, we are lost without if-then rules.

Neuro-fuzzy systems. Intuitively, the basic idea of combining fuzzy systems and neural networks is simple: We use a fuzzy system to represent knowledge in an interpretable manner and borrow the learning ability of neural networks to determine membership values. The drawbacks of both of the individual approaches - the black box behavior of neural networks, and the problems find suitable membership values for fuzzy systems - could thus be avoided. A combination can constitute an interpretable model, which is capable of learning and can use problem-specific prior knowledge.

A typical task of fuzzy data analysis is to discover rules in large sets of data. The rules found can then be used to describe the dependencies within the data and to classify new data. The task of pattern classification is a typical domain of neural networks, but of course, classical statistical methods like cluster analysis, discriminant analysis, and regression analysis are also applied 1]. If there are already a number of powerful methods, what additional benefit can be offered by a fuzzy approach?

We conceive neural networks and fuzzy systems as convenient tools for solving a problem without having to analyze the problem itself in detail. By gathering data or linguistic rules from experts, we can concentrate on the solution. We are usually content to obtain a rough solution, if we can obtain it quickly, easily and at low cost. If we are, however, in need of an exact solution no matter the cost, then traditional approaches that model the nature of the problem, and derive a solution from that is our premier choice. It does not make sense to substitute neural or fuzzy solutions for a working solution just for the sake of using such an approach.

If we use neuro-fuzzy classifiers, we have to keep in mind that we are using a (self optimizing) fuzzy classifier. In general, fuzzy classifiers cannot be meant to outperform other classification approaches. This is mainly prevented by the usually small numbers of linguistic terms that are shared by all rules. The benefit gained by using a fuzzy classifier lies in interpretability and readability of the rule base. This is widely considered more important than the 'last percent' increase in classification performance.

Fuzzy classification. The fuzzy rules used in pattern classification are of the form

$$\mathrm{R}_r : \text{if } x_1 \text{ is } \mathrm{A}_{j_1}^{(1)} \text{ and} \ldots \text{and } x_n \text{ is } \mathrm{A}_{j_n}^{(n)} \text{ then } (x_1, \ldots, x_n) \text{ in } \mathrm{C}_j$$

where $\mathrm{A}_j^{(1)}, \ldots, \mathrm{A}_{j_n}^{(n)}$ are linguistic terms, which are represented by fuzzy sets $\mu_{j_r}^{(1)}, \ldots, \mu_{j_n}^{(n)}$. $\mathrm{C_j} \subseteq \mathrm{IR}^n$ is a pattern subset and represents class j. The patterns are vectors $\boldsymbol{x} = (x_1, \ldots, x_n)$ in IR^n, and we assume that they are divided into m disjunct classes, i.e. each pattern can be mapped to exactly one class $\mathrm{C_j}$. Each feature x_i is partitioned by q_i fuzzy sets $(\mu_1^{(i)}, \ldots, \mu_{q_i}^{(i)})$, and the classification is described by a rule base of k fuzzy rules $(\mathrm{R}_1, \ldots, \mathrm{R}_k)$.

Learning fuzzy classification rules. We are looking for a procedure that can create suitable fuzzy rules of the above-mentioned form. The elements of the learning problem are pairs $(\boldsymbol{x}, \boldsymbol{c})$ with

$$\boldsymbol{c} = (c_1, \ldots, c_m) \text{ and } c_j = \begin{cases} 1 & \text{if } \mathbf{x} \text{ in } \mathrm{C_j} \\ 0 & \text{otherwise.} \end{cases}$$

The procedure should be able to create fuzzy rules, and adapt the fuzzy sets appearing in the rules to the learning problem.

2.1 Approaches to the Induction of Fuzzy Rules

Sect. 3 delivers a detailed description of how neural networks and fuzzy systems can be coupled to derive fuzzy rules from data. Aside from neuro-fuzzy systems, there are other approaches to induce fuzzy rules. Some of the more common approaches – namely fuzzy cluster analysis, decision trees and evolutionary algorithms – will be presented in the following, since they may be combined with neuro-fuzzy models or used to generate initial rule bases.

- **Fuzzy Cluster Analysis**

Cluster analysis is also known as unsupervised classification. It tries to find groups in the data such that objects in the same group are similar to each other. The clustering is called *unsupervised* as it does not use any class information of the training data, and thus can be applied to unlabeled data. In fuzzy cluster analysis 16 the prototypes of each cluster are multidimensional fuzzy sets on the pattern space. The fuzzy sets define hyperspheres or hyperellipsoids and may partially overlap.

By using fuzzy clustering methods it is possible to learn fuzzy *if-then* rules from data 20. Every cluster represents a fuzzy *if-then* rule. The fuzzy sets in the single dimensions are derived by projecting the clusters to the specific dimensions. A fuzzy rule base can be obtained by projecting all clusters. Usually the projection is approximated by triangular or trapezoidal fuzzy sets. Due to this approximation and the projection of the clusters, the generated fuzzy rules only roughly represent the original clusters. This error can be reduced if the cluster search is restricted to axes parallel clusters. It is also possible to improve the classification rules by fine tuning them with a neuro-fuzzy approach.

A further problem of fuzzy rules obtained from cluster analysis methods is that these rule bases are sometimes hard to interpret, since the contained fuzzy sets are not restricted to match any semantic interpretation.

- **Tree Oriented Approaches**

Decision trees are a popular classification method. Their tree-like classification structures can efficiently be induced from data by a greedy divide-and-conquer heuristic. The extraction of rules from the decision trees is relatively simple [3] [36]. As these approaches considered only crisp rules, several extensions to generate fuzzy rules can be found in the literature.

Two basic approaches are proposed: The first group softens the thresholds used in decision trees. This leads to partial memberships of example objects to several branches in the tree, and therefore specialized fuzzy information theoretic measures are necessary for induction [42] [44]. The approaches of the second group use standard decision trees to induce crisp rules. These rules are then transformed into fuzzy rules. Eventually post-processing steps, like merging, pruning or shifting, are applied afterwards [4] [18] [26].

- **Evolutionary Algorithms**

Apart from the other approaches, *genetic or evolutionary algorithms* 9 are often discussed for optimizing or creating fuzzy systems. The advantage of evolution strategies is the ability to modify and optimize model *structure*, whereas most optimization strategies can only adapt model *parameters*. Thus a unified optimization of rule base and membership functions can be performed. This comes at the cost of an (possibly drastically) enlarged search space. Discussions of evolutionary algorithms can for example be found in [15], [19], [25] and [41].

2.2 Capabilities of Fuzzy Rules

When a fuzzy classifier is applied to data, usually a winner takes all principle is used to determine a single class to which the applied data is most similar. Therefore, there are always crisp borders between regions of different predicted classes.

In this section, we discuss the shape of these borders and thus show which class distributions can be represented by such a system. This section shall mainly give the potential user an intuition of what a fuzzy classifier can do and cannot do, for which kind of datasets fuzzy classifiers are suited and what should be considered when one is created. More detailed discussion can be found in [34] and [35].
As a simple example of a fuzzy classification system in a two dimensional domain we consider the following rule base consisting of three fuzzy rules:

R_1: If x is A_1 and y is B_1 then (x, y) in C_1
R_2: If x is A_2 and y is B_2 then (x, y) in C_2
R_3: If x is A_3 and y is B_3 then (x, y) in C_3

The fuzzy sets A_i and B_i are defined by triangular membership functions depicted in Figure 1. The pyramids R_1, R_2, and R_3 represent the membership degrees of each data point (x, y) to the respective classes C_i, obtained by use of the *min* t-norm. In Figure 1b, the resulting class borders and the contour lines of equal membership values are represented in a projection to the (x, y)-data space.

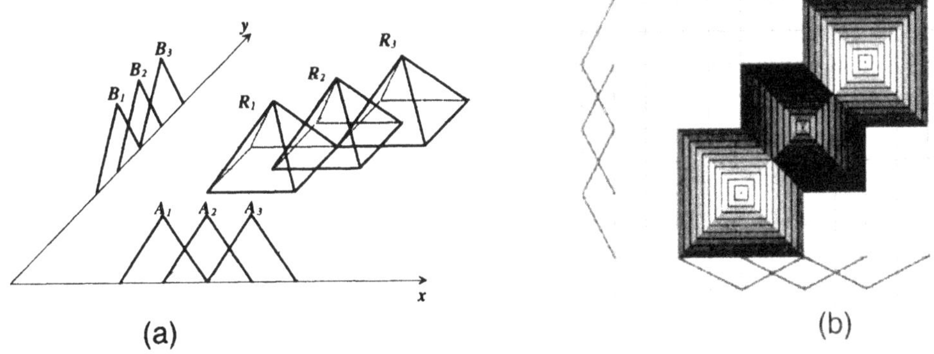

Figure 1. Representation of three fuzzy rules

If we consider more complex rule bases, we can mainly distinguish between *full* and *sparse* rule bases. We call a rule base a *full rule base* when it contains rules with all possible combinations of fuzzy sets in the antecedents, as depicted in Figure 2a. Full rule bases often result from neuro-fuzzy learning approaches without pruning. The classification obtained by evaluating the rule base is arranged in a regular grid – independent of the used t-norm (Figure 2a). The same holds for the higher dimensional case [35].

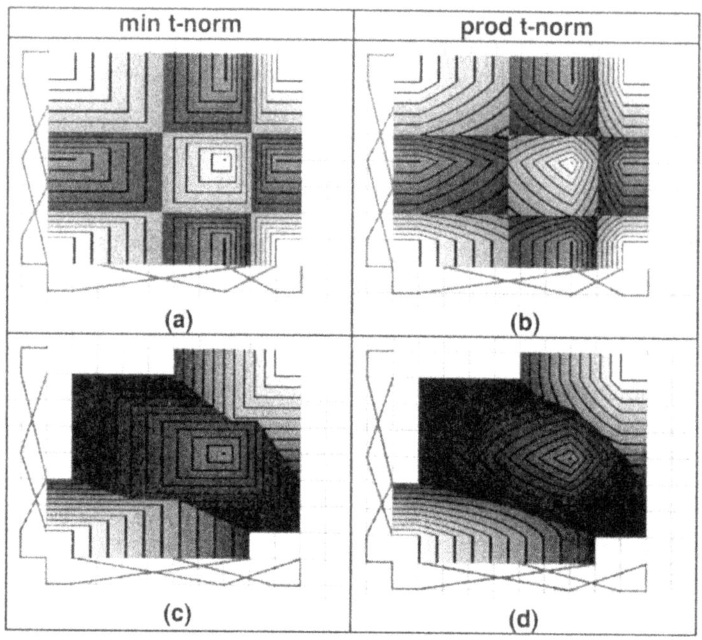

Figure 2. 2D cluster shapes

A *sparse rule base* is usually obtained if neuro-fuzzy learning methods with pruning techniques or fuzzy clustering techniques were used, or specific clusters were defined manually. In this case, specific classes are described by individual but mostly overlapping areas defined by individual fuzzy rules. Hereby, the resulting borders between two classes have more flexibility and strongly depend on the t-norm used as depicted in Figure 2c and d. The cluster shape obtained by use of the algebraic product t-norm (*prod*) is much smoother than the shape obtained by use of the minimum t-norm (*min*). Nevertheless, in both cases the border to the 'undefined' data space is the same.

If the t-norm *min* is used, then the class borders can be described – assuming no enclosing fuzzy sets – by at most three lines (see Figure 1b and Figure 2c). If the *prod* t-norm is used, the borders can be described by hyperbola sections (see Figure 2d).

To obtain usable diagrams of three-dimensional fuzzy clusters we omit the (direct) representation of the membership degrees. The clusters were shown by plots of the outer cluster surfaces in the 3D data space. To improve our visualization of the plots, they have been rotated. Nevertheless, all single clusters created by fuzzy classifiers are spanned by the fuzzy sets in the antecedents of the rule. Therefore, the axes of the spanning system are always parallel to the axes of the data space. The presented plots in Figure 3 were obtained by use of two fuzzy rules.

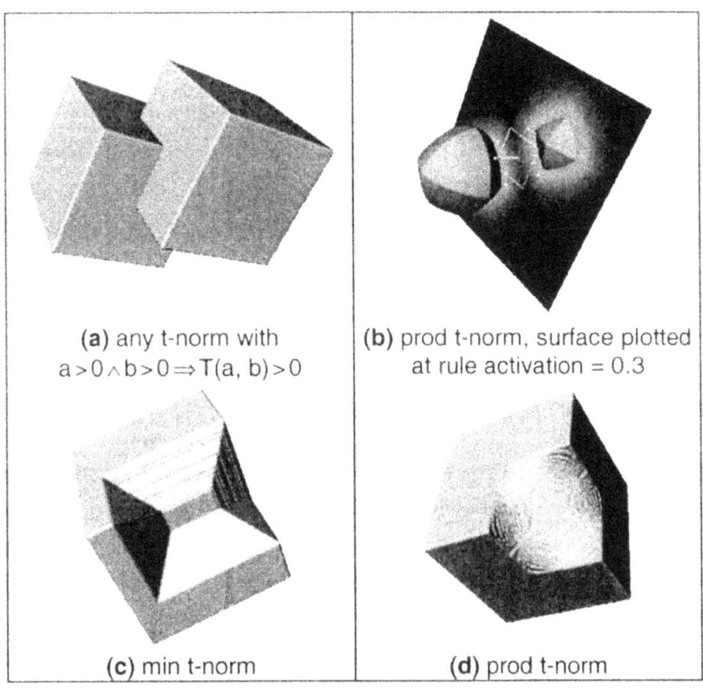

Figure 3. 3D Cluster Shapes

As for most of the commonly used t-norms $(a>0 \wedge b>0) \Rightarrow T(a, b)>0$ is valid, and so the outer shape of the cluster is usually defined by an axes parallel hyper box (see 3a). An example of the distribution of membership degrees is depicted in 3b. If a sparse rule base is used, the cluster forms depend on the used t-norm if two clusters overlap or a threshold value is used – as in the two dimensional case. If overlapping clusters define different classes, the class borders depend on the t-norm used: plane sections if *min* (see 3c), or hyperboloid sections if *prod* is used (see 3d).

If a sparse rule base is used in higher dimensional data space, cluster forms and borders can be derived as presented above. Unfortunately, in higher dimensional data space the *prod* t-norm results in a very low rule activation at the cluster borders, since the activation of a rule R depends exponentially on the number of antecedents. If a rule base with fuzzy rules consisting of different numbers of antecedents is used – which usually occurs if pruning techniques were applied – the *prod* t-norm can lead to different cluster sizes even if the same fuzzy sets were used (i.e. in overlapping areas) to represent linguistic terms. If a threshold value is used it will be nearly impossible to define such classifiers manually. Even the interpretability of learned classifiers usually will be poor. These effects do not occur if the t-norm *min* is used. It is rather insensitive to the number of dimensions, as it is the only absorbing t-norm. This allows pruning techniques that reduce the number of antecedents in the individual rules. Other t-norms cause the average activation to decrease rapidly with a growing number of antecedents. So, the advantages and disadvantages of specific t-norms should be carefully considered if a fuzzy classification system is created.

Furthermore, it should be considered that full rule bases – or fully covered parts of rule bases – can only represent axes parallel class borders, due to the partitioning induced by the fuzzy sets as shown above. Thus, fewer rules can give more flexibility and may enable the classifier to represent the actual class distribution of the data.

3 Neuro-Fuzzy Architectures

Most of the existing neuro-fuzzy models were motivated by fuzzy control systems. The main idea of fuzzy control is to build a model of a human control expert, who is capable of controlling a plant without thinking in terms of a mathematical model. The control expert specifies control actions in the form of linguistic rules. These control rules are translated into the framework of fuzzy set theory, providing a calculus, which can simulate the behavior of the control expert. However, due to uncertainties in specifying fuzzy controllers a manual tuning process is often necessary to overcome the initial design errors. Therefore, a neural component was incorporated to ease and automate the tuning procedure.

There are also a number of neuro-fuzzy approaches in data analysis, a domain with different characteristics. The learning can mostly be done off-line, as the data is generally not process data, but available from a database. Efficient learning from scratch is more frequent than in control applications, and requires special attention. The interpretability of the resulting rule base, which allows the user to learn more about the domain, is often more important than in control, where one is often satisfied with a working controller. However, the motivation to combine the human accessible fuzzy rule approach and the learning capabilities from neural networks are similar.

The term *neuro-fuzzy systems* is often used to refer to all kinds of combinations of neural networks and fuzzy systems. Our understanding of neuro-fuzzy systems is more specific. We use the following taxonomy to differentiate between combinations of neural networks and fuzzy systems [31]:

Fuzzy neural networks: Fuzzy methods are used to enhance the learning capabilities or the performance of a neural network. This can be done by using fuzzy rules to change the learning rate [12] or by creating a network that works with fuzzy inputs [17] [28]. These approaches are not to be confused with neuro-fuzzy approaches in a narrower sense.

Concurrent "neural/fuzzy systems": A neural network and a fuzzy system work together on the same task, but without influencing each other, i.e. neither system is used to determine the parameters of the other. Usually the neural network preprocesses the inputs to, or post-processes the outputs from, the fuzzy system. These kinds of models are strictly speaking neither real neuro-fuzzy approaches nor fuzzy neural networks.

Cooperative neuro-fuzzy models: A neural network is used to determine the parameters (rules, rule weights and/or fuzzy sets) of a fuzzy system. After the learning phase, the fuzzy system works without the neural network. These are simple forms of neuro-fuzzy systems, and the simplest form - determining rule weights by neural learning algorithms - is widely used in commercial fuzzy development tools, even though semantic problems can arise [30]. Cooperative models can be further divided into approaches that: a) learn fuzzy sets offline, b) learn fuzzy rules offline, c) learn fuzzy sets online, d) learn rule weights.

Hybrid neuro-fuzzy models: A neural network and a fuzzy system are combined into one homogeneous architecture. The system may – before, during and after learning – be interpreted either as a special neural network with fuzzy parameters, or as a fuzzy system implemented in a parallel distributed form.

Most modern neuro-fuzzy approaches are hybrid neuro-fuzzy models. In data analysis, this architecture is especially predominant. In the next sections, we will describe in detail how fuzzy rule systems can be transformed into this architecture and how they can be induced (learned) from data.

3.1 Mapping Fuzzy Rules to a Network Structure

To be able to transform fuzzy rules to a neural network and vice versa, an explicit mapping of the elements of the rule system to elements in the network is usually chosen. The usual approach is a feed-forward network with at least three layers. The domain attributes are mapped to the units of the input layer. The output layer contains one unit for each possible value of the class attribute. The fuzzy rules are represented in a hidden layer, where each rule has a corresponding unit. The antecedents of the rules are modeled as connections from the input to the rule layer, the consequents as connections from the rule layer to the output layer. Depending on the model, the membership functions are represented either as fuzzy valued weights, or as additional layers with special activation functions and parameterizing weights.

In this structure, a given input tuple is classified by propagation through the net, which comprises the following steps:

- Setting the *input unit* values according to the tuple values
- Determine *membership* values of the inputs to the fuzzy sets (either in the hidden layer or by applying fuzzy weights)
- These membership values are used in the *rule layer*. The rule units combine their participating inputs to common rule activation. This represents conjunction or disjunction of the antecedents.

- Each class unit in the *output layer* aggregates the activations from the corresponding rules. The output class is the unit with the highest activation (winner-takes-all).

The models usually represent Mamdani type fuzzy rule systems. From a given network, we can directly derive rules and fuzzy membership functions.

3.2 Learning From Data

"Learning" in this context means to create and optimize a fuzzy classification system from sample data. This usually implies two phases: induction of the structure (rule base) and adaptation of the connection weights (fuzzy sets).

If a rule base is set up from prior knowledge, the structure can be derived in advance. However, neuro-fuzzy systems should also be able to adapt the (initial) rule base to the data, and even create a network structure from scratch. Furthermore, in some cases it may be necessary to have methods to identify and change structures that have missing, wrong, or superfluous rules. Unfortunately, structural modifications are still a challenging topic in neural network theory. However, this problem must be addressed in neuro-fuzzy systems. Fortunately, it is usually possible to find heuristic solutions, when assumptions on the shape of the fuzzy partitions can be used to restrict the search space. Since the inputs and outputs are fixed during learning, and the partitions are initially given, inducing the structure is reduced to the problem of finding the number of units in the rule layer and its connections to the other layers. One of the first working heuristics is described in [43].

Learning or optimizing membership functions is usually less complex than the adaptation of the rule base. Membership functions can easily described by parameters, which can be optimized with respect to a global error measure. Adaptation of parameters is a standard task for neural networks. There are some problems, however. Neural network learning algorithms are usually gradient descent methods like error backpropagation. They cannot be applied directly to a standard fuzzy system that uses non-differentiable functions (like min and max) in the inference process. The solution is to either replace the functions by differentiable functions with similar characteristics, or replace the gradient-based neural learning algorithm by a better-suited procedure. Another problem is that default learning techniques do not take into account the semantics of the underlying fuzzy system. Therefore, suitable constraints must be used to guarantee certain properties of the membership functions and thus their semantic meaning. For example, membership functions of neighboring linguistic terms must not change position and must overlap to a certain degree. In addition, some neuro-fuzzy models make use of rule weights. This can be realized with relatively simple learning procedures. However, rule weights may destroy the semantics of a fuzzy system, and thus can make the interpretation of the system difficult or impossible [29] [30].

In the following sections, we present three neuro-fuzzy methods that have been proposed in the literature and applied to data analysis. For the NEFCLASS model and its implementations there are some recent extensions of special interest for data analysis. Therefore, these are described in more detail.

3.3 The FuNe Model

The neuro-fuzzy model FuNe-I [11] [13] is based on the architecture of a feed-forward neural network (Figure 4) with five layers. The first layer contains a unit for each input variable and propagates the input values unchanged via weighted links to the second layer. This layer consists of units with sigmoid activation functions that are used to create membership functions. Membership functions like medium that are not located at the boundaries of the domain, are represented by superimposing two sigmoid functions. Therefore, their outputs are multiplied by +1 or -1 and added in the units of the third layer.

The third layer contains specialized units that are only used to represent fuzzy sets that do not touch the domain boundaries (see below). The units of the second and third layer propagate their activations via unweighted links to the fourth layer. Units from the second layer that have connections to the third layer are not connected to the fourth layer. The fourth layer consists of units that represent fuzzy rules.

Compared to other neuro-fuzzy approaches, the FuNe-I model is special because it uses three kinds of rules: the antecedents can be conjunctions or disjunctions, and there are rules with only one variable as antecedent (simple rules). A unit computes its activation – depending on the kind of rule, it represents – by a "soft minimum" (conjunction), a "soft maximum" (disjunction), or the identity function. The "soft" versions of minimum and maximum are differentiable, so gradient based learning can be used [13]. The fifth layer contains the output units that compute their input by a weighted sum and their activation by a sigmoid function.

FuNe-I only uses rules with one or two variables in the antecedent. To build up a rule base, rules with two variables are separately considered for conjunctive and disjunctive antecedents. The learning procedure is based on a special *training network* that differs only in the rule layer from the original FuNe-I network. In the following, we describe the procedure for creating a rule base.

At the beginning of rule, learning initial fuzzy sets must be specified for the input values by providing suitable sigmoid functions. Next, for each input variable three conjunctive and three disjunctive rule units are created within the training network. Each conjunctive rule unit and each disjunctive rule unit is connected to all output units via randomly initialized weights. After a FuNe-I training network has been created this way, it is trained under supervision. During the learning procedure, only the weights between rule units and output units are modified, hence algorithms such as the delta rule can be used, for example. After training, the weights are interpreted to create the final structure of the FuNe-I network (*target network*).

The FuNe-I network is then trained with the same fixed learning problem that was used to create the rule base. In this phase, the rule weights and the weights between input layer and second layer are modified. The usual neural network backpropagation algorithm (i.e. gradient descent) may be used as a learning procedure, because all functions within a FuNe-I network can be differentiated. At this time, the network can contain many rules, perhaps more than a user wants to have. It is therefore possible to delete rule units with very small weights.

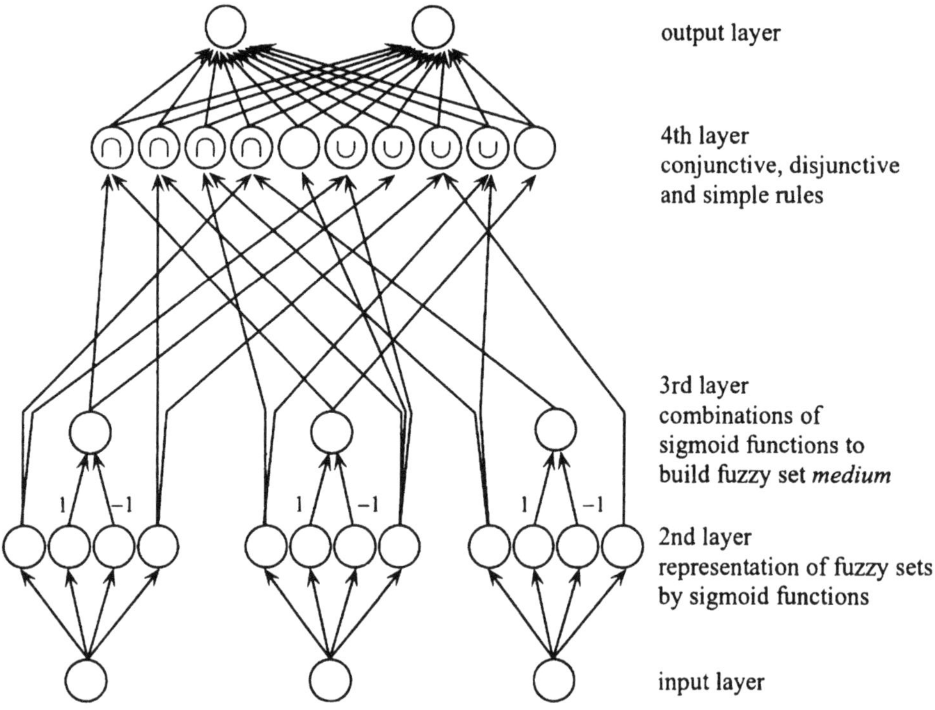

Figure 4. The architecture of a FuNe-I system

The resulting FuNe-I network contains conjunctive, disjunctive, and simple rules. It uses rule weights to obtain exact values in the output units, and therefore the weights can assume any value. FuNe-I also permits negative rule weights. The rule weights are interpreted as the rule's influence on an output variable. Rules with negative weights are interpreted as negations "**if** ... **then not** ...". By this, the weight has an inhibitive influence on the selection of a certain class. This use of rule weights is intuitively clear. However, the use of rule weights, especially with negative values and values above 1, violates the usual calculus of fuzzy systems. This can have side effects that make semantic interpretation difficult [29] [30].

Another important point for the interpretation of the model is to suitably restrict the modifications of the fuzzy sets during learning. Because the membership functions as well as the activation functions can be differentiated, it is possible to train FuNe-I by gradient descent. When the procedure is implemented, the changes applied to the membership functions must be properly restricted. This is especially important for fuzzy sets like *medium* that are combined from two sigmoid functions.

FuNe-I uses only rules with one or two variables in the antecedents. This restriction reduces the complexity of structure identification and the resulting rules are easier for humans to understand. However, the representation capabilities of this network are limited, and may not yield good results if the patterns in the data are more complex.

Applications and modifications of FuNe-I are described in [11] and [13]. A rule structure with one or two inputs was important for the hardware implementation of FuNe-I. This network has successfully been applied to classify faulty solder joints. To solve fuzzy control problems FuNe-II was derived from FuNe-I by adding a new output layer that is connected to the previous output layer. On the connections, discrete samples of fuzzy sets are stored to represent control values. The activations of the new output units represent points in the support of a fuzzy set that must be defuzzified to obtain the final control value.

3.4 A Sugeno-Type Neuro-Fuzzy System

In [39] a neuro-fuzzy system is described that was especially designed to predict the German DAX stock index (cf. illustrative applications in Sect. 4). The system can be interpreted as a special RBF network. The network structure encodes weighted fuzzy rules whose consequents are single crisp numbers. The fuzzy sets in the antecedents are modeled by Gaussian or logistic (sigmoidal) functions, and the degree of fulfillment of a rule is determined by multiplying the membership degrees in its antecedent. The overall output value is computed by a weighted sum. This fuzzy system can therefore be seen as a simple Sugeno-type system of weighted rules.

The learning algorithm is based on backpropagation (gradient descent) and a fixed learning problem. The algorithm modifies parameters of the membership functions, the consequent values, and the rule weights. The sum of the rule weights remains constant during learning, i.e. rules compete with each other for high rule weights. This is done to identify superfluous rules, which ideally should have rule weights near zero after learning. The learning algorithm tries to preserve the semantics of the rule base. A user can specify constraints that ensure that certain modifications are not allowed. For example, fuzzy sets of the same variable must keep their relative positions, or some fuzzy sets must always be identical. After training, standard pruning algorithms for neural networks can be used to delete complete rules or variables from the antecedents of the rules.

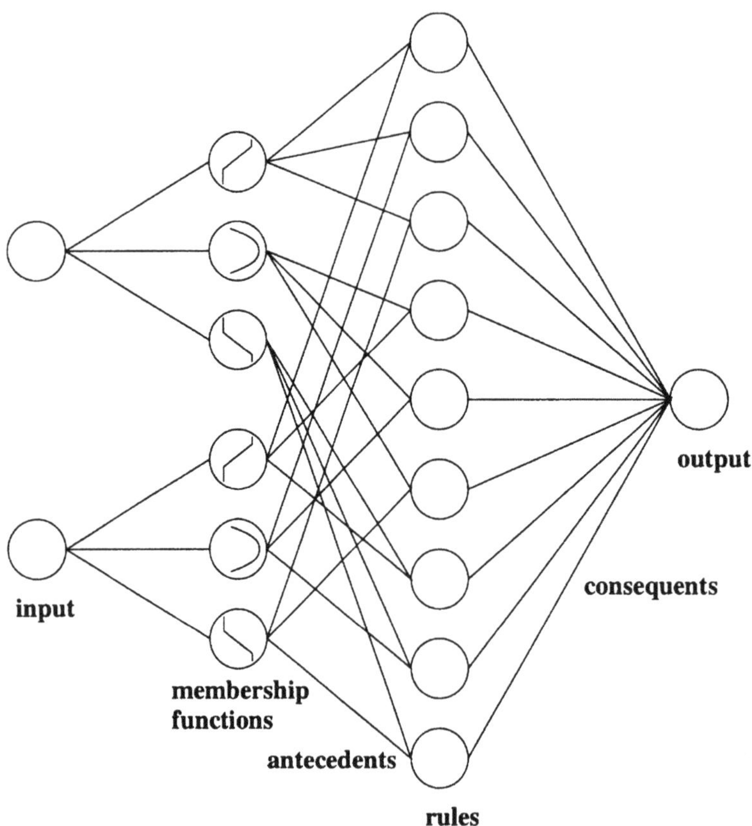

Figure 5. A neuro-fuzzy model that implements simple Sugeno-type fuzzy systems with weighted rules

This neuro-fuzzy system is one of the first commercially available approaches that consider the semantics of the underlying fuzzy system during training. However, it uses weighted fuzzy rules, which can cause problems in interpretation. The approach is implemented in the commercial neural network development environment SENN from Siemens Nixdorf Advanced Technologies.

3.5 NEFCLASS

In Figure 6a, NEFCLASS system is shown that maps patterns with two features (first layer) into two distinct classes (third layer) by using five linguistic rules (second layer). The membership functions are represented by fuzzy valued weights on the connections between the first and second layers. Instead of the product of the weight and output of the previous unit, the membership value of the output is propagated to the input of the next layer. To ensure that linguistic values of an input variable are represented by the same fuzzy set NEFCLASS uses coupled weights. These weights are treated as one in all modifications.

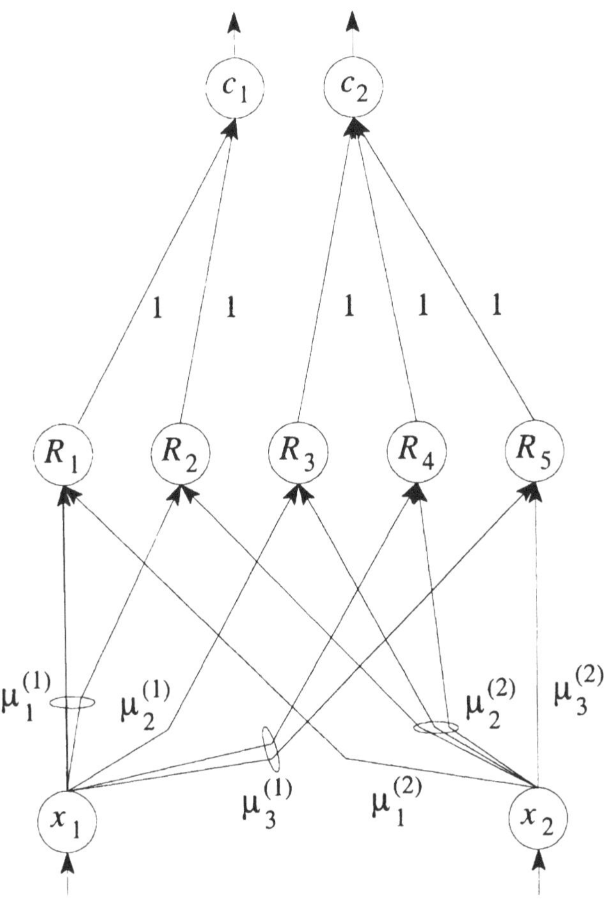

Figure 6. A NEFCLASS system with two inputs, five rules and two output classes

A NEFCLASS system can be built from initial expert knowledge or from scratch by learning. The structural learning is a modification of the method from Wang and Mendel [43]. The user must first define initial fuzzy sets that partition the domains of the input features. The created rules have all inputs in their antecedents. Thus, all possible fuzzy rules form a grid in the data space, i.e. the rules would be regularly overlapping hyper boxes in the input space. In the structural learning stage, the training data are processed, and those hyper boxes that cover areas where data is located are added as rules into the rule base of the classifier. After creation the rules are evaluated, i.e. the performance of the rule is determined to assign the best consequent to each rule. The performance measure is also used to restrict the number of rules by choosing an appropriate subset.

After the rule base has been learned, the fuzzy sets are fine-tuned. By default, NEFCLASS uses min and max as inference functions (see the discussion in Sect. 2.2) and triangular or trapezoidal membership functions. As these are not differentiable, gradient descent cannot be applied. Instead, the learning procedure for the fuzzy sets is a simple heuristic. The algorithm seeks to increase the activation of a rule unit for correct classifications and decrease it for wrong classifications. It identifies the fuzzy set that delivered the smallest membership degree for the current pattern and that is therefore responsible for the current rule activation (because of the min conjunction). This fuzzy set is shifted, and its supports is enlarged or reduced (see Figure 7). The shifting procedure obeys the usual restrictions on maintaining the semantics of the fuzzy system. Rule weighting can be done, but is not recommended. A detailed description of the learning algorithm can be found in [31].

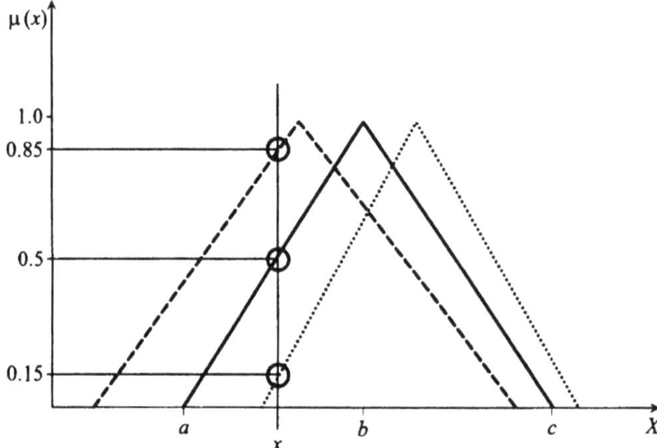

Figure 7. The adaptation of a fuzzy set is carried out by simply changing the parameters of its membership function such that the membership degree for the current feature value is increased or decreased (middle: initial situation, left: increase situation, right: decrease situation)

3.6 NEFCLASS-J: Implementing and Extending the NEFCLASS Model

There are several implementations of the NEFCLASS model for different machine platforms. The most recent version – NEFCLASS-J – has been implemented in Java, which allows platform independence to a large extent. The implementation allows very flexible choices, for instance, of the shape of fuzzy sets or the inference functions (conjunction, disjunction) to be used [33]. Additionally, many of the current extensions of the NEFCLASS model are included in this implementation. Most of these extensions address the specific characteristics and problems of real world data and its analysis. The extensions – namely methods to prune rule bases and to treat symbolic, missing, and unbalanced data – will be introduced and outlined in the next few sections. The program is – like the previous versions – publicly available from http://fuzzy.cs.uni-magdeburg.de.

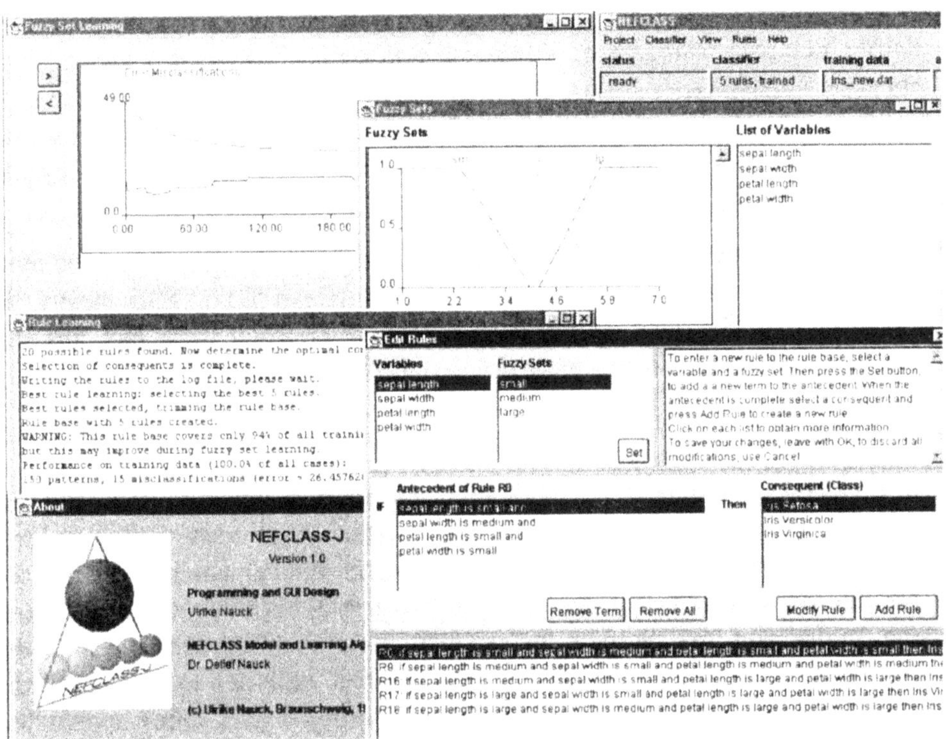

Figure 8. Screen shot of a NEFCLASS-J session

3.6.1 Symbolic Values

Symbolic information is often contained in real world data and it is usually transformed to artificial metric scales. However, it would be useful to be able to create fuzzy rules from data that contain symbolic variables without converting them. NEFCLASS can now deal with symbolic data by using *mixed* fuzzy rules.

Let us consider two attributes x and y, where $x \in X \subseteq \mathbb{R}$ is continuous and $y \in Y = \{A, B, C\}$ is symbolic (categorical). In a fuzzy rule, we describe values of x by linguistic terms. We use *lvalue* to denote any such linguistic term (*lvalue* may be a term like *small*, *approximately zero*, *large*, etc.). In a mixed fuzzy rule using two variables, we can have the following situations:

fuzzy-exact: if x is *lvalue* and y = A then ...
fuzzy-imprecise: if x is *lvalue* and $y \in \{B, C\}$ then ...
fuzzy-fuzzy: if x is *lvalue* and y is $\{(A, \mu(A)), (B, \mu(B)), (C, \mu(C))\}$ then ...

In the first two cases, the symbolic variable y has a "switching function" for a rule. If y does not assume one of the values noted in the respective y-term of the antecedent, the rule is not applicable at all. However, if y does assume any of these values, the applicability of the rule is not restricted by this argument, and the degree of fulfillment only depends on the value for x.

In the third situation, we use a fuzzy set to describe the value that y may assume, by simply attaching a degree of membership to each element of Y using some membership function μ: Y $\rightarrow$ [0, 1]. By giving some value to μ (y), we can now restrict the applicability of the rule to any degree between 0 and 1. Obviously case (i) and (ii) are just special cases of case (iii), because we can replace y = A by y is {(A, 1), (B, 0), (C, 0)} and y $\in$ {A, B} by y is {(A, 1), (B, 1), (C, 0)}.

Because the elements of Y are not ordered, we cannot easily use a linguistic term to label fuzzy sets like {(A, μ (A)), (B, μ (B)), (C, μ (C))}. This means the interpretability of the rules is restricted compared to fuzzy rules that just use variables on metric scales. For a more detailed discussion, see [32].

3.6.2 Missing Values

Missing values are common in many applications. It is not always possible to observe all features of a pattern. This can be due to high costs, faulty sensors, errors in recording, etc. If a feature is sometimes measured and sometimes not, we can use the cases for which it has been measured to predict its values when it is missing. In decision tree learning, for example, the probability distribution of the feature is used when a value is missing [36]. Another approach to learning in the presence of unobserved variables is the EM algorithm [5] [27]. Other approaches [10] are

- to use only cases with complete data
- to delete cases and/or variables with missing data with excessive levels
- to use imputation methods that replace missing values with a constant,
- the mean, a value computed by regression, etc.

For NEFCLASS we use the following simple strategy [33]. If a feature is missing, we do not make any assumptions about its value but assume that any value may be possible. Based on this assumption we do not want to restrict the application of a fuzzy rule to a pattern with missing features. This means a missing value will not influence the computation of the degree of fulfillment of a rule. This can be done by assigning 1.0 as the degree of membership to the missing feature [2], i.e. a missing value has a degree of membership of 1.0 with any fuzzy set. A pattern where all features are missing would then fulfill any rule of the fuzzy rule base with a degree of 1.0, i.e. any class would be possible for such a pattern. We denote a pattern with missing values by **p** = (**x**, ?). According to [2], we compute the degree of fulfillment μ_r of some rule R_r by

$$\mu_r(\mathbf{x}, ?) = \min_{x_i}\{\mu_r^{(i)}(x_i), 1\} = \min_{x_i}\{\mu_r^{(i)}(x_i)\}$$

In NEFCLASS, we must consider three stages where missing values must be considered:

- learning fuzzy rules
- training membership functions
- classification of patterns

Item (iii) was just considered above. In [2], it is suggested to complete an input pattern with missing values by using the fuzzy rule base of the classifier during training. We will not use this approach here, because it cannot be used for rule learning, and we want to use the same technique in all three stages.

Rule learning in NEFCLASS consists of three steps:

- determine all possible antecedents,
- create an initial rule base by finding an appropriate consequent for each antecedent,
- select a final rule base from the initial rule base by computing the performance of each rule.

Step (i) is implemented by the Wang/Mendel approach [43]. This means antecedents are created by selecting hyperboxes from a structured data space (structure-oriented approach [31]). If we encounter a missing value, any fuzzy set can be included in the antecedent for the corresponding variable. Therefore, we create all combinations of fuzzy sets that are possible for the current training pattern. In step (ii) of the rule learning algorithm, appropriate consequents will be determined for these antecedents, depending on all training patterns. In step (iii), the rules with the highest performance will be selected.

After a rule base was created, the membership functions are trained by NEFCLASS. If a missing value is encountered, then for the corresponding fuzzy set no training signal will be generated from this pattern.

3.6.3 Pruning Techniques

In learning fuzzy rule bases, the number of fuzzy rules must often be given in advance. NEFCLASS can now find a minimal number of the best fuzzy rules that cover all training data. The new pruning strategies of NEFCLASS-J also support this approach, by identifying rules that can be removed from the rule base, if they cover only few data that is also sufficiently covered by other rules. The new rule learning and pruning features are discussed in [33].

Rule learning in NEFCLASS previously required that the users specify a maximum number of rules to be included in the rule base. NEFCLASS at first creates an initial rule base consisting of all rules that are supported by the training data. This is a very fast procedure and requires two cycles through the training set (numerical attributes only). In the first cycle, all antecedents are identified, and in the second cycle, the best consequent for each antecedent is determined and performances values for the rules are computed. We use μ_r to denote the antecedent of rule R_r. With

$$\mu_r(\mathbf{p}) = \min_{x_i}\left\{\mu_r^{(1)}(x_1),\ldots,\mu_r^{(n)}(x_n)\right\}$$

we denote the degree of fulfillment of a rule given input pattern **p**. The consequent is a class label c_r. Let class (**p**) denote the class of **p**. The performance of a rule $R_r = (\mu_r, c_r)$ is defined as

$$\text{perf}_r = \frac{1}{|\tilde{L}|} \left(\sum_{\substack{(p,t)\in\tilde{L} \\ class(p)=c_r}} \mu_r(p)\cdot t_{c_r} - \sum_{\substack{(p,t)\in\tilde{L} \\ class(p)\neq c_r}} \mu_r(p)\cdot(1-t_{c_r}) \right).$$

For the performance $-1 \leq \text{perf}_r \leq 1$ holds, where $\text{perf}_r = 1$ if all training patterns are correctly classified by the rule and each training pattern **p** is assigned to exactly one class by its target vector **t**. If a rule classifies all patterns perfectly wrong, $\text{perf}_r = -1$ holds. For perf_r = zero the rule either covers no patterns or causes as many errors as correct classifications.

The goal of the rule learning algorithm is to construct a rule base consisting only of rules with large positive performance values. The final rule base can be created by one of two evaluation procedures - *best* or *best per class* selection. The first option orders the rules by their performance and selects the best rules. This can result in a rule base that does not cover all classes if the number of rules is fixed. The second selection scheme avoids this by selecting an equal number of rules for each class according to the performance values.

The problem of rule learning is to specify a suitable rule base size. The new rule learning algorithm can automatically determine the size of the rule base by continuing to select rules by one of the two selection schemes until all training patterns are covered by at least one rule. If the rule base becomes too large, it can be reduced by applying the automatic pruning strategies after training the membership functions.

The creation of the rules begins with the creation of initial antecedents that contain only numerical attributes using the Wang/Mendel procedure 43. After the training data is processed once, we have found all antecedents that are supported by the numerical data. If there are also symbolic attributes, we continue as follows.

To reduce the rule base, NEFCLASS uses pruning methods based on a simple greedy algorithm that does not need to compute complex test values as it is sometimes required in neural network pruning methods. For pruning a rule base NEFCLASS-J uses four heuristic strategies that were already defined for previous implementations [31]. Pruning is now done in an automatic fashion without the necessity of user interaction. The pruning strategies are given in the following list.

- **Pruning by correlation:** The variable that has the smallest influence on the classification is deleted. To identify this variable statistical measures like correlations and χ^2 tests or information theoretic measures like information gain can be used.
- **Pruning by classification frequency:** The rule that yields the largest degree of fulfillment in the least number of cases is deleted.

- **Pruning by redundancy:** The linguistic term that yields the minimal degree of membership in an active rule in the least number of cases is deleted.
- **Pruning by fuzziness:** The fuzzy set with the largest support is identified and all terms that use this fuzzy set are removed from the antecedents of all rules.

After each pruning step, the membership functions are trained again. Each of these four pruning strategies is iterated until a pruning step fails. Then the next pruning strategy is selected. If the rule base becomes inconsistent during pruning (which may happen in steps (i), (iii), (iv)), the inconsistencies are automatically resolved by deleting contradictory rules or generalizations/specializations of rules according to their performance values until the rule base is consistent again. Pruning will not remove the last rule for a class. A pruning step fails if the error has increased after training the membership functions, or if the rule base cannot be made consistent again. In this case, the pruning step is undone.

3.6.4 Learning from Unbalanced Data

In many practical domains, the available training data is more or less unbalanced, i.e. the number of cases of each class varies. This causes problems for many classification systems and their associated learning algorithms. This is especially obvious if the classes are not well separated. A typical example is a marketing database, where the task of the classifier is to identify 'good' customers, e.g. to focus mailing activities. A classifier is trained from historical data of 'good' and 'bad' customers. As response rates of mailings are typically very small, there are only few positive examples. Moreover, these can be very similar to the negative cases and proper separation is not possible. In such cases, classifiers tend to predict the majority class. This is completely reasonable to minimize the error measure, but does not take into account the special semantics of the problem: It is not the same if a good customer is classified as bad or vice versa. A mailing to a bad customer costs merely more than the postage, while ignoring a good customer means a bigger financial loss. A straightforward way to model this asymmetry would be to directly specify the costs of every possible misclassification. This has become possible with NEFCLASS with the introduction of a matrix **m** containing the misclassification costs. This is an n by (n + 1) matrix, where the M_{ij} represent the costs caused if the system classifies a pattern of class i as class j, or as *ambiguous* (j = n + 1). The diagonal elements M_{ii} are usually equal to 0, all other elements are set to 1 by default. If the domain bears asymmetries of the classes, this matrix allows rather fine and intuitive specification of the errors.

The next paragraphs outline the necessary modifications to the original NEFCLASS model, a detailed description can be found in [22].

In the **first learning phase,** the input dimensions are partitioned and basic rules are created. The class labels of the points and the cost matrix must be used to determine the correct consequents. The original NEFCLASS system uses a heuristic evaluation measure, which supports patterns lying closer to the centers of the fuzzy rules by weighting them with their activations. We modified this to a heuristic estimation of the misclassification costs that would occur if the consequent were changed to a class c. The costs are calculated as

$$V_{r,c} = \sum_{p \in L} a_r^{(p)} M_{c_p c}$$

and the consequent of rule r is set to the class that minimizes this term.

For the **second learning phase,** the back-propagation-like algorithm was replaced by one that allows easier utilization of the cost matrix. We implemented a kind of evolutionary strategy, known as (1+1)-strategy. This algorithm is one of the earliest and probably one of the simplest evolutionary strategies known in literature, with a population of only one individual and exactly one offspring per generation 0. Actually, this means that random changes (*mutation*) are applied to the fuzzy sets and are tested on the learning data. The changes are established if the offspring's rule base performs better than its parent's, otherwise the unmodified rule base is kept (*selection*). As in the original backpropagation algorithm, constraints are imposed on the changes to maintain the semantics of the fuzzy rules.

The cost matrix can directly be used by the learning procedure if an appropriate error measure is specified. We implemented two different measures, which are analogous extensions of the misclassification rate and the error rate in the original NEFCLASS system. The former is calculated from the crisp classifications and reflects the borders between the fuzzy rules, whereas the latter uses the activations and reflects ambiguousness and the position of the fuzzy sets in relation to the classes. The misclassification rate is extended to an estimation of classification costs by summing up the cost matrix elements given by the actual class c_p of a pattern and the decision of NEFCLASS n_p for this pattern:

$$E_{cost} = \sum_{p \in L} M_{c_p n_p} .$$

The main aim of the learning phase is to minimize this error measure. This measure depends on the crisp classification and not directly on activations of the rules. If during learning the crisp classification does not change (e.g. if changes of the rule base are small or in sparsely covered regions), the error does not change and thus gives no feedback whether the change is desirable. To direct the learning in these situations the second measure is used, which directly uses the activations a_c of the output layer for class c and prefers unambiguous classifications. The exact definition is

$$E_{pos} = \sum_{p \in L} \sum_{c \in C} M_{c_p c} (f - a_c^{(p)})^2, \text{ with } f = \begin{cases} 1 & \text{for } c = c_p \\ 0 & \text{otherwise.} \end{cases}$$

Intuitively the first measure adjusts the borders between classes, and the second measure fits (the centers of) the fuzzy sets to the data. Although the new learning algorithm is relatively simple, it produces quite satisfactory results. The need for sophisticated search algorithms is not so apparent, as the second learning phase of NEFCLASS does only fine-tune the fuzzy sets.

A basic set of the most important pruning techniques from NEFCLASS have been modified to incorporate the misclassification cost matrix. These are input pruning, rule merging and rule evaluation, which are normally applied in that order. Input pruning tries to find a discriminant subset of the inputs. By deleting inputs, several rules can be projected onto one, and thus the rule base consists of a smaller total number of merged rules. The resulting loss of accuracy was originally estimated used a measure based on minimum description length [21]. This has been replaced by an estimation of the misclassification costs using the given matrix. This is done by determining which cases of the data will be classified by a merged rule. The consequent of the rule is chosen to minimize the costs given the misclassification cost matrix. The increase of the sum of the costs over the data is used as a measure to decide which inputs may be deleted. Rule merging is similar to input pruning, except that it removes inputs from the antecedents of individual rules instead from the whole data set.

Rule evaluation is normally used as a final clean up. As fuzzy rules partially overlap, some rules may be superfluous and can be deleted from the rule base. To find a minimal set of rules that covers all data points, a performance measure is specified. According to this measure, a subset of the rules is chosen as the new rule base. The performance measure determines, for every rule, the increase in costs that would result from deletion of that single rule. The more a rule contributes to correct classification, the higher the aggregated performance will be. Low performance can result from rare activations of rules that are too specific, or from rules that lie between classes and thus should be removed.

4 Illustrative Applications

In the following a benchmark of classifiers and two examples of successful applications of neuro-fuzzy classification models are given. The first example describes how NEFCLASS was applied to an image processing problem. The second example describes the application of the model from Sect. 3.4 to financial data.

4.1 Comparison of the NEFCLASS Model with Other Classifiers

Model	Tool	Remarks (): mean	Error (on test set)	Validation
Discriminant Analysis	SPSS	linear model, 9 variables	3,95%	1-leave-out
Multilayer Perceptron	SNNS	4 inner units, RPROP	5,18%	50% test set
Decision Tree	C4.5	31 (24.4) node, pruned	4,9%	10-fold
Decision Tree Rules	C4.5rules	8 (7.5) rules with 1-3 variables	4,6%	10-fold
NEFCLASS (metric variables)	NEFCLASS-X (Unix-Version)	2 (2.1) rules with 5-6 variables	4,94%	10-fold
NEFCLASS (2 symbolic variables)	NEFCLASS-J (Java-Version)	2 (2.1) rules with 1-3 variables	3,95%	10-fold

Table 1. Comparison of the NEFCLASS model with other classifiers

To obtain a comparison of classification systems a benchmark on the "Wisconsin breast cancer data set" (WBC data) from the UCI Machine Learning Repository was performed 32. The results are depicted in Table 1. Of course, as common to benchmarks, the results of a single benchmark cannot be generalized to other data sets. Nevertheless, our experience shows that the performance of neuro-fuzzy models like NEFCLASS can mostly compete with other models.

4.2 Analysis of Image Processing Data

The automatic analysis of man-made objects in remotely sensed images is a challenging task. In the framework of structural analysis of complex scenes, a blackboard-based production system (BPI) is presented in [40]. In this system, transformations of the simple objects extracted from SAR (synthetic aperture radar) images into more complex objects are given by productions (e.g. extracted edges $\Rightarrow$ lines $\Rightarrow$ long-lines $\Rightarrow$ parallel-lines $\Rightarrow$ runways). A production net proceeds stepwise according to a model, and produces intermediate results with an increasing degree of abstraction [37 - 38].

Figure 9a shows the extracted edge segments, Figure 9c shows the detected runway as a result of the production system. The analysis of the process for this image shows that only 20 lines of about 37,000 are used to construct this stripe. However, the analyzing system has to take all of the lines into account and time consumption is typically at least $O(n^2)$.

The production process could significantly be sped up if only the most promising primitive objects are identified and the analysis is started with them. The idea is to extract features from the image that describe the primitive objects and train NEFCLASS to decide which lines can be discarded. Experiments showed that the regions next to the lines bear useful information. For each line, a set of statistical (e.g. mean and standard deviation) and textural features (e.g. energy, entropy, etc.) was calculated from the gray values next to that line.

In the study described in [22], a set of 17 images depicting five different airports was used. Each of the images was analyzed by the production net to detect the runway(s) and the lines were labeled as *positive* if they were used for runway construction or *negative* else. Four of the 17 images form the training dataset used to train NEFCLASS. The training set contains 253 runway lines and 31,330 negatives.

A classifier has to take into account the special semantics of the task. The positive lines are the minority class and thus easily ignored by a classifier. However, every missed positive can turn out to be very expensive, as it can hinder successful object recognition. Misclassifying negative lines just increases processing time. With NEFCLASS, this could be considered by specifying asymmetric misclassification costs (Sect. 3.6.4). Thus, the costs of false negatives have empirically been set to 300 times the costs of false positives. After learning, the NEFCLASS pruning techniques were used to reduce the number of rules from over 500 to fewer than 20. The best result was obtained with 16 rules.

The lines from the remaining 13 images were used as test data The quality of the result could be characterized by a detection and a reduction rate: The detection rate is defined as the ratio of correctly detected positives to all positives. The higher this value is, the higher the probability for a successful recognition is. The average detection rate on the unseen images was 84%, and varied from 50% to 100%. The second measure is the reduction rate, which is defines as the ratio of lines classified as positive to the total number of lines. The lower this value is, the shorter the processing time will be. The average reduction rate on the unseen images was 17%. For most of the images – even with lower detection rates – the image analysis was successful, as the missed lines are mainly shorter and less important. Figure 9b shows the lines NEFCLASS classified as positive in the example image, which was one of the unseen images. On this image, the number of lines was reduced to one tenth, which means a reduction of processing time to under 1%.

(a) 37,659 lines (edge segments) extracted from SAR image.

(b) Lines from NEFCLASS result (3,281 lines ⇒ reduction rate for this image is 8.7%).

(c) Runway constructed by production net, build from 20 lines from (a). As all 20 lines are also contained in (b), the detection rate is 100%.

Figure 9: Images and results

4.3 Prediction of the German Stock Index DAX

The neuro-fuzzy model described in Sect. 3.4 was used to predict the DAX stock index 3947. The task was to predict the daily returns (i.e. relative day-to-day differences) of the DAX using other time series as inputs. Based on previous investigations, the time series given in Table 2 have been chosen to model the DAX. The data is available on a daily basis and the numbers of national and international variables are balanced. From these inputs the relative differences were calculated:

$$\Delta DAX_t = \left(\frac{DAX_t}{DAX_{t-1}} - 1 \right) \cdot 100\%$$

DAX	Composite DAX	German 3 month interest rates
Return Germany	Price earning ratio	Morgan Stanley index Europe
US-$ / DM	Nikkei index Japan	Morgan Stanley index Germany
Gold price	US treasury bonds	Dow Jones industrial index

Table 2. Inputs for DAX prediction

Fuzzy membership functions for the linguistic terms *decreasing, stable,* and *increasing* were derived from statistical analysis of the time series. For the linguistic term *stable* a Gaussian membership function is chosen, the other linguistic terms have logistic membership functions.

The initial rule base is generated by creating rules with two antecedents. These were the relative change of the DAX itself (ΔDAX) combined with each of the other attributes. For each pair of attributes there are 3 x 3 different combinations of linguistic terms. Thus, 99 = 11 x 3 x 3 rules were generated. Due to the semantic properties of the domain, the number of different membership functions could be limited to 36.

The given data was partitioned into a training set (~ 67%), a cross-validation set (~ 10%), and a test set (~ 23%). The cross-validation set was used to prevent over-fitting [8].

Model Evaluation. The resulting neuro-fuzzy models was used on the test data with a trading strategy, to buy if the network prediction is positive and sell if the prediction is negative. The performance was compared with the following trading systems:

- *Buy&Hold:* buy the DAX at the beginning of the test set and sell it at the end. This strategy assumes an efficient capital market that does not allow excess return because the conditional expectation of the returns is zero. The Buy&Hold strategy gains only by exploiting the market trend.
- *Naive prediction:* Buy or hold the DAX if the last difference is positive and sell otherwise. The naive prediction assumes that the market behaves like a random walk.
- *Linear model:* A linear model with 36 inputs.
- *Multi-Layer Perceptron (MLP):* A state of the art neural network with 36 inputs, 40 hidden units, and pruned to an optimized model with 12 inputs and 27 weights 45.

The performance of the strategies are compared by computing the profit and loss curves (P&L) on the test set. The P&L curve measures the return of a trading system by adding up the gains from the transactions. To measure the accuracy of the predictions, the mean squared error (MSE) is given.

The optimized neuro-fuzzy model consists of 31 rules and 22 membership functions. A further pruning to 21 rules and 20 membership functions was reported, when stable conclusions and small rule weights were pruned. The resulting model has no significant decrease of the performance. Figure 10 shows the performance of the benchmarks and the different models without transaction costs, as well as taking into account costs of 0.1% costs per transaction. The values are shown in Table 3.

Both the MLP and our neuro-fuzzy approach achieve a significantly higher profit than the other benchmarks. The performance of the neuro-fuzzy approach is comparable to that of the MLP, although the latter had more flexibility. The neuro-fuzzy approach has the significant advantage of interpretable rules, which may be examined by a human expert.

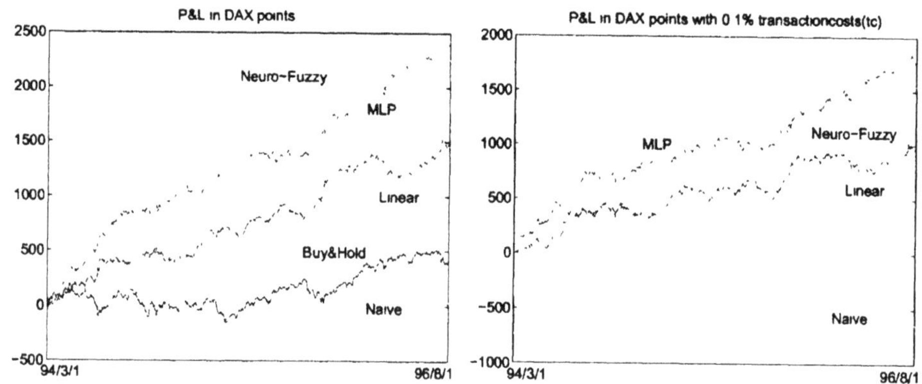

Figure 10: Comparison of P&L-curves of different models

Model	MSE	profit	in %	profit (0.1% tc)	in %
Buy & Hold	-	45.74	2.21	43.67	2.11
naive prediction	-	441.59	21.36	-626.01	-30.19
Linear	0.81	1516.20	73.35	943.05	45.62
Neuro-Fuzzy	0.72	2272.63	109.95	1567.82	75.85
MLP	0.55	2426.61	117.39	1792.97	86.74

Table 3. Results of the compared models in numbers

5 Conclusions

The state of the art in data mining, which is the core step in knowledge discovery in databases, is dominated by purely data-driven approaches. Model-based approaches are rare and mostly used in the refinement phases. These, however, are often skipped in industry, where quick solutions are desired and often the first successful approach wins. Nevertheless, exploiting background knowledge and other sources of – in general non-numeric – information, and concentrating on comprehensible models can turn out to be a great benefit. When choosing models, we often have the trade-off between (often quantitative) methods that achieve good performance and (often qualitative) models that give insights into a specific domain or problem. L. A. Zadeh formulated this dilemma as the principle of the incompatibility of precision and meaning [45].

The problem can certainly not be solved generally in the near future. However, fuzzy set theory provides a method to formulate knowledge in a way that is interpretable to humans, and still allows efficient computations. Intuitively speaking, precision and meaning can be compatible, if a problem has a certain "robustness", and in that case, it may be suited for neuro-fuzzy solutions. As we know from fuzzy control and as shown in Sect. 4 for data analysis, many practical problems have this robustness and can thus be addressed with neuro-fuzzy models. For the user this means that he might find it reasonable to sacrifice some performance for the sake of understandable models.

Bibliography

1. Berry, M. J. A., G. Linoff, and S. Gordon (1997). Data Mining Techniques: For Marketing, Sales and Customer Support, New York, Chichester et. al.: John Wiley & Sons.
2. Berthold, M., and Huber, K.-P. (1998). Tolerating Missing Values in a Fuzzy Environment, In: Mares et al. (eds.), Proc. Seventh International Fuzzy Systems Association World Congress IFSA'97, I:359-362, Academia, Prague.
3. Breiman, L., Friedman, J. H., Olshen, R. A., and Stone, C. J. (1984). Classification and Regression Trees. Wadsworth, Belmont, Ca.
4. Chi, Z., and Yan, H. (1996). ID3-derived fuzzy rules and optimal defuzzification for handwritten numeral recognition. IEEE Trans. Fuzzy Systems, 4(1):24-31.
5. Dempster, A.P., and Laird, N.M., and Rubin, D.B. (1997). Maximum Likelihood from Incomplete Data via the EM algorithm, Journal of the Royal Statistic Society, Series B, 39(1):1-38.
6. Dubois, D., Prade, H., and Yager, R.R. (1996). Information Engineering and Fuzzy Logic. Proc. 5th IEEE International Conference on Fuzzy Systems (FUZZ-IEEE'96, New Orleans, LA, USA), 1525-1531. IEEE Press, Piscataway, NJ, USA.
7. Fayyad, U., Piatetsky-Shapiro, G., Smyth, P., and Uthurusamy, R. eds. (1996). Advances in Knowledge Discovery and Data Mining. MIT Press, Menlo Park, CA, USA.
8. Finno, W., Hergert, F., and Zimmermann, H. G. (1992). Improving Generalization by Nonconvergent Model Selection Methods. Neural Networks 6.
9. Goldberg, D. (1989). Genetic Algorithms in Search, Optimization and Machine Learning, Addison-Wesley, Reading, MA.
10. Hair, J. F., Anderson, R. E., Tatham, R. L., and Black, W. C. (1998). Multivariate Data Analysis, Fifth Edition, Prentice-Hall,Upper Saddle River, NJ.
11. Halgamuge, S. K., and M. Glesner (1994). Neural networks in designing fuzzy systems for real world applications. Fuzzy Sets and Systems 65: 1-12.
12. Halgamuge, S. K., Mari, A., and Glesner, M. (1994). Fast Perceptron Learning by Fuzzy Controlled Dynamic Adaption of Network Parameters, In: Kruse, R., Gebhardt, J. and Palm, R. (eds.), Fuzzy Systems in Computer Science, pp. 129-139, Vieweg, Braunschweig.
13. Halgamuge, S. K. (1995). Advanced Methods for Fusion of Fuzzy Systems and Neural Networks in Intelligent Data Processing, PhD Thesis, Technische Hochschule Darmstadt.
14. Haykin, S. (1994). Neural Networks, Prentice-Hall Inc., New Jersey.

15. Hopf, J., and Klawonn, F. (1994). Learning the Rule Base of a Fuzzy Controller by a Genetic Algorithm, In: Kruse, R., Gebhardt, J. and Palm, R. (eds.), Fuzzy Systems in Computer Science, pp. 63-73, Vieweg, Braunschweig.
16. Höppner, F., Klawonn, F., and R. Kruse (1999). Fuzzy Clusteranalysis. John Wiley & Sons Ltd., Chichester.
17. Ishibuchi, H., Morioka, K., and Turksen, I. B. (1995). Learning by Fuzzified Neural Networks, Int. J. Approximate Reasoning, 13(4), pp. 327-358.
18. Jäkel, J., Gröll, L., and Mikut, R. (1999). Automatic generation and evaluation of interpretable rule bases for fuzzy systems. In Computational Intelligence for Modelling, Control and Automation CIMCA'99, pages 192-197. IOS Press, Amsterdam.
19. Kinzel, J., Klawonn, F., and Kruse, R. (1994). Modifications of Genetic Algorithms for Designing and Optimizing Fuzzy Controllers, In: Proc. IEEE Conference on Evolutionary Computation, pp. 28-33, IEEE, Orlando, FL.
20. Klawonn, F., and R. Kruse (1997). Constructing a Fuzzy Controller from Data. Fuzzy Sets and Systems, 85:177-193.
21. Klose, A., Nürnberger, A., and Nauck, D. (1998). Some Approaches to Improve the Interpretability of Neuro-Fuzzy Classifiers, In: Proc. 6th European Congress on Intelligent Techniques and Soft Computing (EUFIT98), pp. 629-633, Aachen.
22. Klose, A., Nauck, D., Schulz, K., and Thönnessen, U. (1999). Learning a Neuro-Fuzzy Classifier from Unbalanced Data in a Machine Vision Domain, In: Fuzzy-Neuro Systems 1999 – Computational Intelligence (FNS'99), pp. 23-32, G. Brewka, R. Der, S. Gottwald, and A. Schierwagen, Leipziger Universitätsverlag, Leipzig.
23. Kruse, R., Borgelt, C., and Nauck, D. (1999). Fuzzy Data Analysis: Challenges and Perspectives. Proc. 8th IEEE International Conference on Fuzzy Systems (FUZZ-IEEE'99, Seoul, Korea). IEEE Press, Piscataway, NJ, USA.
24. Kruse, R., Gebhardt, J., and Klawonn, F. (1994). Foundations of Fuzzy Systems, John Wiley & Sons, Inc., New York, Chichester.
25. Lee, M. and Takagi, H. (1993). Integrating Design Stages of Fuzzy Systems Using Genetic Algorithms, In: Proc. IEEE Int. Conf. on Fuzzy Systems 1993, pp. 612-617, San Francisco.
26. Maher, P. E., and St. Clair, D., (1993). Uncertain reasoning in an ID3 machine learning framework. In Proc. 2nd IEEE Int. Conf. on Fuzzy Systems, pages 7-12, San Francisco.

Michalewicz, Z. (1996). Genetic Algorithms + Data Structures = Evolution Programs, Springer-Verlag, Berlin.

27. Mitchell, T. M. (1997). Machine Learning, McGraw-Hill, New York, NY.
28. Narazaki, H., and Ralescu, A. L. (1991). A Synthesis Method for Multi-Layered Neural Network Using Fuzzy Sets, In: Proc. of IJCAI-91: Workshop on Fuzzy Logic in Artificial Intelligence, pp. 54-66, Sydney.

29. Nauck, D., and Kruse, R. (1992). Interpreting Changes in the Fuzzy Sets of a Self-Adaptive Neural Fuzzy Controller, In: Proc. Second Int. Workshop on Industrial Applications of Fuzzy Control and Intelligent Systems (IFIS'92), pp. 146-152, College Station, Texas.
30. Nauck, D., and Kruse, R. (1994). Choosing Appropriate Neuro-Fuzzy Models, In: Proc. Second European Congress on Fuzzy and Intelligent Technologies (EUFIT'94), pp. 552-557, Verlag und Druck Mainz, Aachen.
31. Nauck, D., Klawonn, F., and Kruse, R. (1997). Foundations of Neuro-Fuzzy Systems. John Wiley & Sons Inc., New York.
32. Nauck, D., and Kruse, R. (1999). Fuzzy Classification Rules Using Categorical and Metric Variables, In: Proc. 6th Int. Workshop on Fuzzy-Neuro Systems 1999 (FNS'99), pp. 133-144, Leipziger Universitätsverlag, Leipzig.
33. Nauck, D., Nauck, U., and Kruse, R. (1999). NEFCLASS for JAVA - New Learning Algorithms, In: Proc. 18th International Conf. of the North American Fuzzy Information Processing Society (NAFIPS'99), pp. 472-476, IEEE, New York, NY.
34. Nürnberger, A., Klose, A., and Kruse, R. (2000). Analyzing Borders Between Partially Contradicting Fuzzy Rules. In Proc. of the 19th International Conference of the North American Fuzzy Information Processing Society (NAFIPS'2000), NAFIPS, Atlanta.
35. Nürnberger, A., Klose, A., and Kruse, R. (1999). Discussing Cluster Shapes of Fuzzy Classifiers. In Proc. of the 18th International Conference of the North American Fuzzy Information Processing Society (NAFIPS'99), NAFIPS, New York, June 10-12.
36. Quinlan, J. R. (1993). C4.5: Programs for Machine Learning, Morgan Kaufman, San Mateo, CA.
37. Schärf, R., Schwan, H., and Thönnessen, U. (1998). Reconnaissance in SAR Images,In: Proc. of the European Conference on Synthetic Aperture Radar, Berlin, Offenbach, pp. 343-346.
38. Schwan, H., Schärf R., and Thönnessen, U. (1998). Reconnaissance of extended targets in SAR image data, In: Proc. of the European Symposium on Remote Sensing, Barcelona, September 21th-24th.
39. Siekmann, S., Kruse, R., Neuneier, R. and Zimmermann, H. G. (1997). Advanced Neuro-Fuzzy Techniques Applied to the German Stock Index DAX, In: Proc. Second European Workshop on Fuzzy Decision Analysis and Neural Networks for Management, Planning, and Optimization (EFDAN'97), pp. 170-179, Dortmund.
40. Stilla, U., Michaelsen, E., and Lütjen, K. (1996). Automatic Extraction of Buildings from Aerial Images, Mapping Buildings, Roads and other Man-Made Structures from Images, Leberl F, Kalliany R, Gruber M (eds.), Proceedings IAPR-TC7 Workshop, Graz, pp. 229-244, R. Oldenbourg, München.

41. Takagi, H., and Lee, M. (1993). Neural Networks and Genetic Algorithms, In: Fuzzy Logic in Artificial Intelligence (FLAI93), pp. 68-79, Springer-Verlag, Berlin.
42. Wang, C.-H., Liu, J.-F., Hong, T.-P., and Tseng, S.-S. (1999). A fuzzy inductive learning strategy for modular rules. Fuzzy Sets and Systems, 103:91-105.
43. Wang, L., and Mendel, J. M. (1992). Generating fuzzy rules by learning from examples, IEEE Trans. Syst., Man, Cybern., 22(6):1414-1427.
44. Yuan, Y., and Shaw, M. J. (1995). Induction of fuzzy decision trees. Fuzzy Sets and Systems, 69(2):125-139.
45. Zadeh, L. (1973). Outline of a new approach to the analysis of complex systems and decision processes, IEEE Trans. SMC, SMC-3 (1), January, 1973, pp. 28-44.
46. Zimmermann, H. G., and Weigend, A. (1996). A new architecture for time series analysis, NNCM.
47. Zimmermann, H. G., Neuneier, R., Dichtl, H., and Siekmann, S. (1996). Modeling the German Stock Index DAX with Neuro-Fuzzy, In: Proc. Fourth European Congress on Intelligent Techniques and Soft Computing (EUFIT'96), Verlag und Druck Mainz, Aachen.

Granular Computing in Data Mining

Witold Pedrycz

Department of Electrical & Computer Engineering, University of Alberta, Edmonton, Canada (pedrycz@ee.ualberta.ca) and Systems Research Institute, Polish Academy of Sciences, 01-447 Warsaw, Poland

Abstract. In this study, we are concerned with the role of information granulation in data mining in databases. By their nature, data mining pursuits are very much oriented towards end-users and imply that any results need to be easily interpretable. Granulation of information promotes this interpretability and channels all pursuits of data mining (that are otherwise computationally intensive and thus highly prohibitive) towards more efficient and feasible processing. First, we discuss the essence of information granulation and afterwards elaborate on the main approaches to the design of information granules. We distinguish between user-driven, data-driven and hybrid methods of information granulation. Several main classes of membership functions of information granules-fuzzy sets are investigated and contrasted in terms of some selection criteria such as parametric flexibility and sensitivity of the ensuing information granules. We propose two fundamental concepts in data mining: associations and rules. Associations are direction-free constructs that capture the most essential components of the overall structure in database. The relevance of associations is expressed by the cardinality of the data embraced by the Cartesian products of the information granules contributing to the construction of the associations. The proposed methodology of data mining comprises two phases. First, associations are built and the most essential (relevant) ones are collected in the form of a data mining agenda. Second, some associations can be converted into direction-driven constructs (rules). The idea of consistency of the rules is discussed in detail.

Keywords. Data mining, information granularity, granulation, associations, rules, fuzzy sets, associations versus rules, directionality, attributes

1 Introduction

Succinctly put, data mining in databases tries to make sense of raw data by revealing meaningful and easily interpretable relationships (see [1] [3][4][8][18][21][24]). This research goal, in spite of many existing variations, permeates the entire area. The domain of data mining is highly heterogeneous embracing a number of well-established information technologies including statistical pattern recognition, neural networks, machine learning, knowledge-based systems, etc. [2][6][9][10][11][14][22][23][25][28]. The synergistic character of data mining is definitely one of its dominant and visible features that make this pursuit to emerge as a new area of research and applications. The ultimate goal of data mining is revealing patterns that are easy to perceive, interpret, and manipulate. One may ask, in turn, what makes necessary to develop such patterns. To address this essential question, we should revisit what makes humans so superb at perceiving, understanding, and acting in complex situations and yet so limited in basic arithmetic operations, manipulating numbers, etc. The cornerstone of human cognition is the concept of information granules and information granulation. Information granules help us cope with an abundance of detailed numeric data. Numbers are important, yet humans tend to produce abstractions that are more tangible and easy to deal with. Abstractions manifest themselves in the form of information granules -- entities that encapsulate a collection of fine grain entities (in particular, numbers) into a single construct thus making them indistinguishable. The level of detail retained depends on the size of the information granules and is directly implied by the problem at hand. Information granulation makes all data mining pursuits more user-oriented, and allows the user to become more proactive in the overall process.

Granulation and information granules are found in many different frameworks, such as set-based environments and their generalizations (fuzzy sets, rough sets, shadowed sets, random sets, etc.) [15][13][19][20][29][30][31][17][16], as well as probabilistic frameworks (subsequently leading to probabilistic information granules). In this study, we concentrate on the use of fuzzy sets regarded as a conceptual environment of information granulation.Nevertheless, this environment of data mining along with the ensuing methodology is valid for some other scenarios of information granulation.

The study is organized into a number of sections. First, in Section 2, we concentrate on the very idea of information granulation, formal models of information granules and various algorithms leading to information granulation. Section 3 describes the development side by proposing the design of data-legitimate information granules (fuzzy sets). Such fuzzy sets are then used as building blocks to design associations (Section 4). The paper makes a strong distinction between associations and rules: rules are regarded as directional constructs resulting from associations. The discussion on this matter is presented in several ensuing sections (Section 5, 6, and 7). The notion of consistency of rules is introduced and studied in detail along with some computational details (Section 8). Conclusions are discussed in Section 9.

2 Granulation of Information

In this section, we concentrate on the essence of information granulation and the role of information granules in a spectrum of perception processes carried out by humans. Then our focus moves into the construction of information granules in the setting of fuzzy sets. In particular, we distinguish between major design avenues pursued in information granulation and contrast their performance.

2.1 Prerequisites: the Role of Information Granulation in Data Mining

The essence of information granulation lies in a conceptual transformation in which a vast amount of numbers is condensed into a small number of and meaningful entities - information granules [16][29][31]. Information granules are user-oriented. They are easily comprehended, memorized and used as building blocks helpful when perceiving more complex concepts. Information granules are manifestations of *abstraction*. The level of such abstraction depends upon the objective of a perception process carried out by humans. This, in turn, is implied by the goal of data mining and a level of the related decision - making processes. Strategic, long-term decision processes invoke the use of coarse and more stable information granules. Short-term decision-making processes involving immediate actions require another look at the same database that requires fine grain information granules. In this way, the size of information granule becomes crucial to the successful process of data mining. So far, we have not defined information granules and their "size" (granularity) in any formal fashion. As a matter of fact, such a definition has to be linked with the formal framework in which such information granules are constructed (one should emphasize that fuzzy sets form one among possible formal environments of information granulation). This means that when using, for instance, fuzzy sets, the size of the granules needs to be expressed in terms of the language of fuzzy set theory. Another way of expressing granularity should hold for probabilistic granules. Nevertheless, on the intuitive side, we can envision the general relationship: the larger the number of elements embraced by the information granule, the lower the granularity of such construct. And conversely, the lower the number of elements in the information granule, the higher its granularity. We can also use the term specificity as being the inverse to the notion of granularity.

2.2 Information Granulation with the Aid of Fuzzy Sets

In this study, we concentrate on the use of fuzzy sets as a vehicle of information granulation. There are three main ways in which information granules - fuzzy sets or fuzzy relations can be constructed

User-oriented. It is a user or designer of the system who completely identifies the form of the information granules. For instance, they could be a priori defined as a series of triangular fuzzy numbers. Moreover, the number of these terms as well as their parameters are totally specified in advance.

Algorithmic approach to information granulation. In this case, information granules are determined as a result of optimization of a certain performance index (objective function). Clustering algorithms are representative examples of such algorithms of unsupervised learning that lead to the formation of information granules. Quite commonly, the granules are fuzzy sets (or fuzzy relations) when using FCM and similar algorithms or sets (or relations) when dealing with the methods such as ISODATA [5][12]

A combination of these two. The methods that fall under this category are a hybrid of user-based and algorithmic driven methods. For instance, some parameters of the information granulation process can be set up by the user while the detailed parameters of the information granules can be determined (or refined) through some optimization mechanism during the second phase. The influence of the user versus the influence of data varies from case to case

One should become aware of the advantages and potential drawbacks of the two first methods (the third one is a compromise between the user and data-driven methods and as such may reduce the disadvantages associated with its components). The user-based approach, even quite appealing and commonly used, may not reflect the specificity of the problem (and, more importantly, the data to be granulated). There could be a serious danger of forming fuzzy sets not conveying any experimental evidence. In other words, we may end up with a fuzzy set whose existence could hardly be justified in light of the currently available data. The issue of the experimental legitimization of fuzzy sets along with some algorithmic investigations has been studied in detail in [15]. On the other hand, the algorithmic-based approach might not be able to reflect the semantics of the problem. Essentially, the membership functions are built as constructs minimizing a given performance index. This index itself may not capture the semantics of the information granules derived in this fashion. Moreover, the data-driven information granulation may be computationally intensive, especially when dealing with large sets of multidimensional data (that are common to many tasks of data mining). This may eventually hamper the usage of clustering as a highly viable and strongly recommended option in data mining.

Bearing in mind the computational facet of data mining, we consider a process of granulation that takes place for each variable (attribute) separately. There are several advantages to follow this approach. First, the computational aspect of data mining pursuits are addressed. Second, there is no need for any prior normalization of the data that could eventually result in an extra distortion of relationships within the database; this phenomenon has been well known in statistical pattern recognition [10]. The drawback of not capturing the relationships between the variables can be considered minor in comparison to the advantages of this approach. In building a series of information granules we follow the hybrid approach, namely we rely on data but provide the number of the linguistic terms in advance along with their general form (type of membership function).

Before proceeding with the complete algorithm, it is instructive to elaborate on different classes of membership functions, and analyze their role in information granulation as it applies to data mining.

2.3 Classes of Membership Functions and their Characterization

There is an abundance of classes of membership functions encountered in the theory and applications of fuzzy sets. In general, their intent is to model linguistic concepts. When it comes to data mining, several useful guidelines as to a suitable selection may be sought

Information granules need to be flexible enough to "accommodate" (reflect) the numeric data. In other words, they should capture the data quite easily so that the granule become *legitimate* (viz. justifiable in the setting of experimental data). This implies parameterized membership functions (so that these parameters could be adjusted when required). The experimental justification of the linguistic terms can be quantified with the aid of probabilities, say the probability of a fuzzy event [29][30]. Given a fuzzy set A, its probability computed in light of experimental data $\mathbf{X} = \{x_1, x_2, ..., x_N\}$ originates as a sum of the membership values

$$Prob(A) = \sum_{k=1}^{N} A(x_k)$$

We say A is *experimentally justifiable* if the above sum achieves or exceeds a certain threshold value γ.

Information granules need to be "stable" meaning that they have to retain their identity in spite of some small fluctuations occurring within the experimental data. This also raises a question of sensitivity of the membership functions and an issue of their distribution vis-à-vis specific values of the membership grades. We claim that the sensitivity of the membership values should be more evident for higher membership grades and decay for lower membership grades. This is intuitively appealing: we are not concerned that much about the lower membership values while the values close to 1 are of greater importance as those are the values that imply the semantics of the information granule. The quantification of this property can be done by the absolute value of the derivative of the membership function A regarded as a function of the membership grade (u), that is

$$s(A)(u) = \left|\frac{dA(x)}{dx}\right| = \varphi\ (u)$$

In what follows, we analyze three classes of membership functions (triangular, parabolic, and Gaussian fuzzy sets) by studying the two criteria established above.

The triangular fuzzy sets are composed of two segments of linear membership functions, (see Figure 1(a)). The membership function is

$$\mathrm{T}\,(x;\, a,\, m,\, b) = \begin{cases} \dfrac{x-a}{m-a} & x \in [a, m] \\ 1-\dfrac{x-m}{b-m} & x \in [m, b] \end{cases}$$

(for all other x, the membership values are equal to zero).

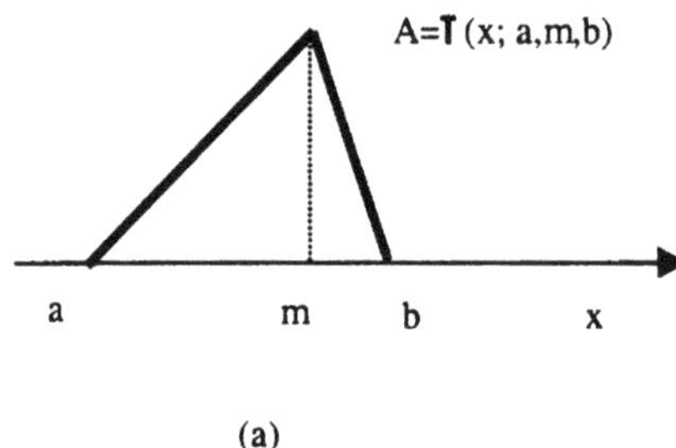

(a)

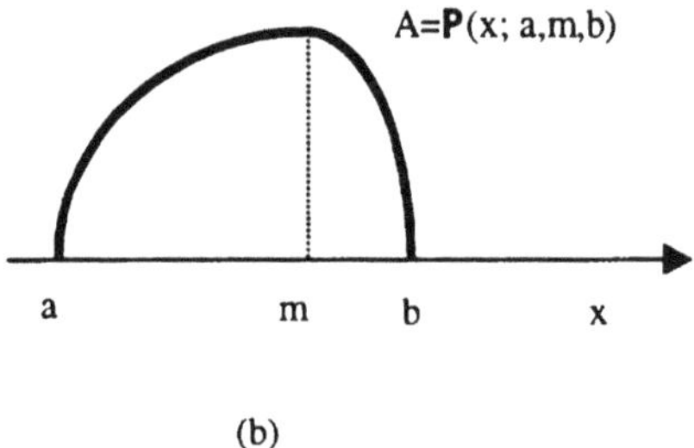

(b)

Fig. 1. Two general classes of triangular (a) and parabolic membership functions (b)

They are defined by three parameters: a modal value (m) and two bounds (a and b). The left-hand and right-hand sides of the fuzzy set are determined separately. Thus the parametric flexibility is available in the design of the information granule. The sensitivity of A is constant and equal to the increasing or decreasing slope of the membership function. The sensitivity does not depend on the membership value and does not contribute to the stability of the fuzzy set.

The parabolic membership functions are defined by three parameters (a, m, and b), Fig 1(b)

$$P(x; a, m, b) = \begin{cases} 1-\left(\dfrac{x-m}{m-a}\right)^2, & x \in [a, m] \\ 1-\left(\dfrac{x-m}{b-m}\right)^2, & x \in [m, b] \\ 0, \text{otherwise} \end{cases}$$

These parameters can make the fuzzy set asymmetrical and help adjust the two parts of the information granule separately. The sensitivity Figures an interesting pattern; it achieves the lowest values around the membership value equal to 1 and increases when the membership values approach zero. In this sense, the range of high membership values of the granule becomes emphasized as being more stable, see Figure 2. The direct computations clearly reveal this. Consider, for instance, the increasing portion of the membership function of the parabolic membership function. Its derivative is equal to

$$\frac{dP(x; a, m, b)}{dx} = 1 - 2\frac{(x-m)}{(m-a)^2} \quad \text{for } x \in [a, m]$$

Let x = a. Then the derivative is equal to $1 + \dfrac{2}{(m-a)}$. For x = m we obtain

$$\frac{dP(x; a, m, b)}{dx}_{|x=m} = 1 - 2\frac{(m-m)}{(m-a)^2} = 1.$$

The Gaussian membership function is governed by the expression

$$A(x) = \exp(-(x - m)^2 / \sigma^2)$$

and includes two parameters (m and σ). The first one (m) determines the position of the fuzzy set. The second parameter (σ) controls the spread of the information granule. Gaussian fuzzy sets are symmetrical. This may be a problem when the data Figure a significant asymmetry that cannot be easily coped with. The sensitivity pattern Figures its maximum around the membership value equal to 0.5, see Figure 3.

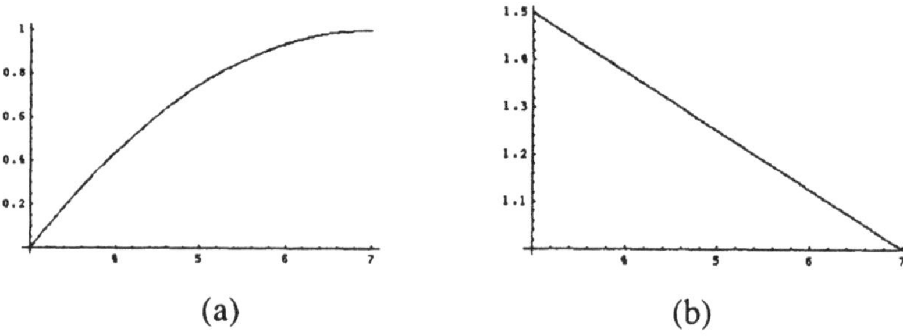

Fig. 2. Sensitivity pattern of the parabolic membership function with m = 7; a = 3; shown is an increasing portion of the membership function (a) and its derivative (b)

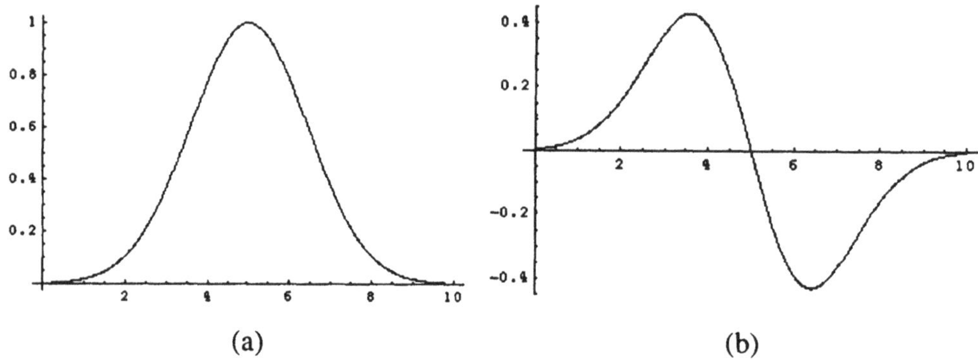

Fig. 3. Sensitivity pattern of the Gaussian membership function with m = 5; s = 2; membership function (a) and its derivative (b)

3. The Development of Data-Justifiable Information Granules

Our objective is to construct fuzzy sets that are legitimized by data. The problem is posed in the following way: We are given is a collection of numeric one-dimensional data $\mathbf{X} = \{x_1, x_2, \ldots, x_N\}$ where x_k is a real number. Form a collection of fuzzy sets $A_1, A_2, \ldots, A_c$ coming from a certain family of fuzzy sets $\mathcal{A}$ (triangular, parabolic, etc.) so that each of fuzzy set carries the same level of experimental evidence. In other words, its probability (as a fuzzy event) is the same and equal to 1 / c. Moreover assume that any two adjacent fuzzy sets in $\mathcal{A}$ satisfy the condition of zeroing at the modal value of the individual fuzzy set as illustrated in Figure 4 (this requirement prevents us from dealing with fuzzy sets with excessively "long" tails overlapping some other fuzzy sets).

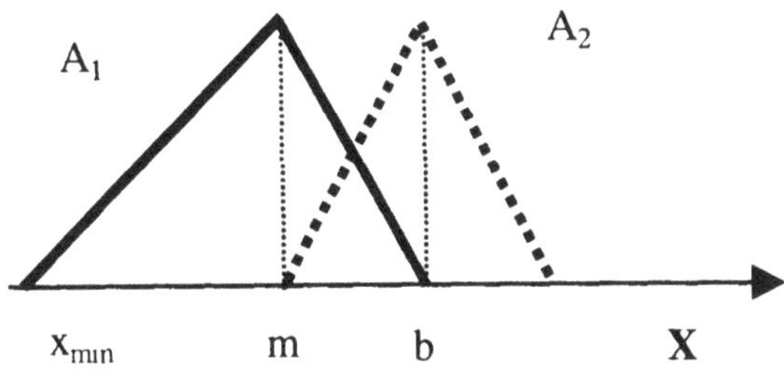

Fig. 4. A collection of fuzzy sets with the parameters to be determined

The above formulation of the problem has a strong intuitive underpinning: by defining each element of $\mathcal{A}$ to be supported by the same amount of data, we construct information granules that will Figure the same level of evidence, no matter what the details of the ensuing data mining method could be. Similarly, these information granules are detail-neutral, that is, independent of the data mining architecture.

The algorithm of building fuzzy sets of $\mathcal{A}$ could be quite straightforward: we scan the universe of discourse $\mathbf{X}$ from left to right and allocate the characteristic points of the fuzzy sets in such a way so that we reach the required level of experimental evidence. Getting into details, let us illustrate how the algorithm works by constructing a family of parabolic fuzzy sets. The increasing and decreasing parts of the membership functions are determined independently from each other. Regarding the first fuzzy set, its lower bound is equal to the lowest value in $\mathbf{X}$, a = arg min $\mathbf{X}$. The modal value of A is determined by moving towards higher values of $\mathbf{X}$, computing the accumulated values of the sum

$$\sum_{i:\, x_i \leq m} A_1(x_i) \tag{1}$$

and terminating the search at the value of "x" for which the above sum attains the value equal to N / 2c (or meets it at some given tolerance level), Figure 5.

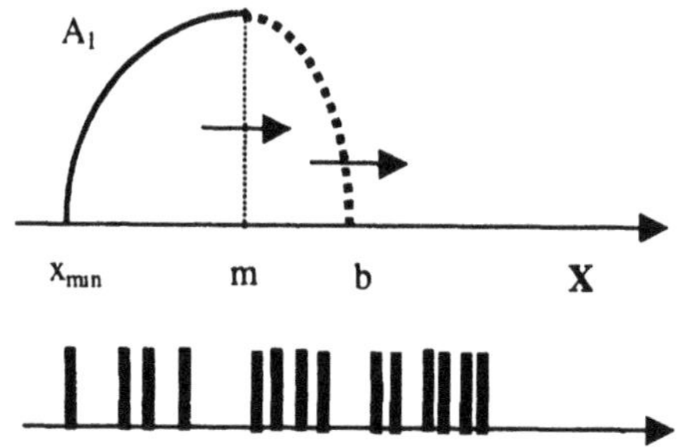

Fig. 5. Determination of the membership function of A_1; see description in text

This particular value of x is then a modal value of A_1 equal to m. Then the inclusion of farther values continues, and the overall process is monitored by the value of the sum

$$\sum_{i:\, m \leq x_i \leq b} A_1(x_i) \tag{2}$$

As before, it should reach the value approximately equal to N / 2c (this, as pointed out by the above sum, is achieved for x = b). Summing (1) and (2), the total evidence supporting A_1 is equal to N / c. Proceeding with the construction of A_2, we note that the determination of the increasing portion of the membership function has been already done, see Figure 5. We have to compute the experimental evidence behind the increasing part of A_2; this, in general, may not necessarily be equal to N / 2c. Denote this value by q. The difference

N / 2c - q is then used to determine the decreasing part of the membership function of A_2. In this case the mechanism is the same as already described. The remaining elements of this family of information granules A are computed in an analogous manner.

There are several parameters of the algorithm one may refine in order to carry out the entire construction. In particular, this concerns the aggregation steps across the universe of discourse and the tolerance level at which the thresholds of the evidence have to be determined. One should be vigilant as to the difference

$$N / 2c - q \tag{3}$$

that is used to construct the decreasing portion of the membership functions. It could well be that this expression could be zero or even negative. This prevents us from building the remaining portion of the fuzzy set. The reason behind this deficiency is linked with the distribution of the experimental data, which may Figure quite substantial "jumps". To avoid this problem, one has to reduce the number of information granules. This would increase the value of the experimental evidence (N / 2c), thus making the final value of (3) positive.

4 Building Associations in Databases

Once the information granules have been constructed for each variable in the database separately, they need to be combined. The aggregated (composite) granule

$$\text{granule } A_i \text{ and granule } B_j$$

is a fuzzy relation defined as a Cartesian product of the corresponding coordinates

$$A_{ij} = A_i \times B_j$$

The membership function is defined by taking the and-combination (aggregation) of the contributing membership functions, namely

$$(A_i (x) t B_j (y))$$

with "t" denoting the triangular norm. The definition easily extends to any number of the information granules defined in the corresponding universes of discourse, say

$$A_{ij\ldots l} = A_i \times B_j \times \ldots \times \ldots Z_l$$

that is

$$A_{ij\ldots l}(\mathbf{x}) = A_{ij\ldots l}(x_1, x_2, \ldots, x_n) = A_i(x_1) \, t \, B_j(x_2) \ldots t \ldots Z_l(x_n) \quad (4)$$

with "n" being the number of the attributes (variables) encountered in the problem. Assume that for each coordinate (variable, attribute), we have constructed "c" granules. With the fixed number of attributes equal to "n", we come up with c^n different Cartesian products. Only a certain fraction of these combinations would be legitimate in light of the experimental data available in the database. Each Cartesian combination of the information granules as outlined above is quantified by computing its σ-count. The information granules are then ranked according to the values of their σ-counts. We can form an agenda **D** of the most significant Cartesian products that is those ones characterized by the highest values of the σ-counts. The construction of the agenda of size "p" can be characterized as follows:

- cycle through all Cartesian products and retain those characterized by the highest values of σ-counts

With an increasing number of attributes existing in databases, there is an explosion in the number of combinations. Say, for c = 7 (which could be a fairly typical value of the number of the information granules) and n = 40, we end up with possible combinations of 7^{40} composite granules (Cartesian products). Subsequently, if an exhaustive search is out of question, one may consider various evolutionary techniques as a viable alternative. With the increasing number of information granules defined for each attribute, the likelihood of having strongly supported Cartesian products may be lower. Larger information granules promote Cartesian products described by higher values of the experimental evidence, that is, higher values of the corresponding σ-counts.

4.1. Determining Links Between Multidimensional Information Granules

Once we have derived a collection of associations, one may be interested in revealing whether these associations are linked together and if a certain association is strongly tied with some other. As associations are manifestations of some patterns in data, the relationships between them could be regarded as a certain type of high-level data analysis. More descriptively, we start with a collection of the associations (elements of the already developed agenda, **D**) and build a web of links between them. This is graphically depicted in Figure 6, where the strength of an individual link is reflected by some numeric value (the values of which are usually confined to the interval [-1, 1]). What has been shown in Figure 6 is an undirected graph whose nodes are the associations and the edges represent the level of bonding (influence) occurring between the nodes.

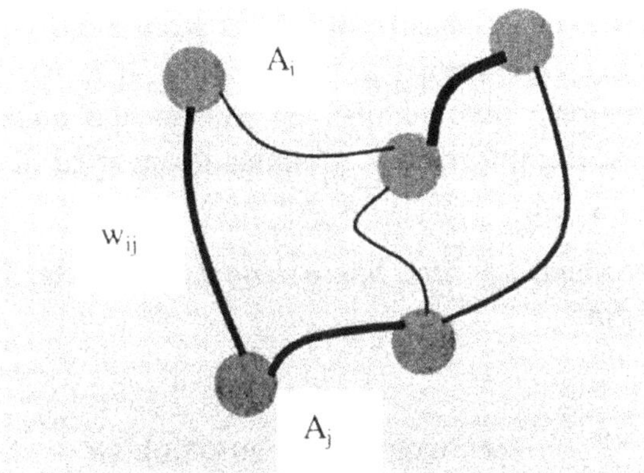

Fig. 6. A web of associations; the strength of the bonding is reflected by the width of the link occurring between the corresponding associations

The values associated with the edges can be determined in many different ways. The Hebbian learning is a plausible option. Denote by w_{ij} a level of bonding between association A_i and A_j, i, j = 1, 2, ..., p. Hebbian learning is an example of unsupervised correlation-driven learning where the values of w_{ij} are updated as follows

$$w_{ij}(new) = w_{ij} + \alpha\, A_i(\mathbf{x}_k)A_j(\mathbf{x}_k)$$

where α is a learning rate, $\alpha > 0$. The updates are affected by individual elements of the database (more specifically, their manifestations through the information granules formed at the very beginning of the data mining process). The initial values of the links are set to small random numbers. Notice that, if both manifestations $A_i(\mathbf{x}_k)$ and $A_j(\mathbf{x}_k)$ are substantial, then the value of w_{ij} increases. For previous values of the connections close to zero, the changes in the value of the corresponding bonding are negligible.

5 From Associations to Rules in Databases

The Cartesian products constructed in the previous section, are associations - basic entities that are the tangible results of data mining. The agenda **D** retains the most significant (that is, data legitimate) findings in the database. It captures the most essential dependencies. It is important to stress that associations are *direction free*. They do not commit to any causal link between the variables, or more specifically, between the information granules. In this sense, associations are general constructs. One may even emphasize that these are the most generic entities to be used in mining static relationships in data mining. It is needless to say that the form of the associations, their number as well as the underlying experimental evidence, hinges on the information granules being used across all activities of data mining.

Rules, on the other hand, are *direction-oriented* constructs. They are conditional statements of the form

- if condition(s) then action(s)

The form of the rule clearly stipulates the direction of the construct: the values of the conditions stipulate certain actions. The direction makes the construct more detailed and fundamentally distinct from associations. All rules are associations but not all associations are rules. This observation is merely a translation of associations and rules in the language of mathematics: all relations (Cartesian products) are functions (rules) but not the other way around.

In data mining, the issue of distinction between associations and rules plays a primordial role. We may not be certain as to the direction between attributes (what implies what). Therefore it is prudent to proceed with a two-phase design: first, reveal associations and then analyze if some of them could become rules. Note that when dealing with rules, they could be articulated once we decide upon the split of attributes (variables) into inputs and outputs. The task looks quite obvious for modeling physical systems (very few variables with an obvious direction between them). In data mining, though, this could be a part of the data mining pursuit. The two-phase process of data mining associations - rules is illustrated in Figure 7.

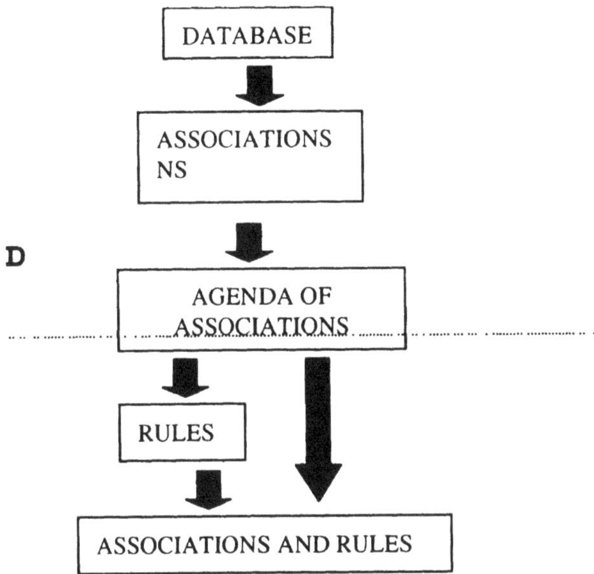

Fig. 7. A two-phase process of data mining: from associations to rules

In the next section, we discuss how to realize the second phase and produce rules. Hopefully, the objective of this pursuit becomes clear: the data mining of rules realized from the very beginning of the process is false and unnecessarily restrictive. This common practice praised and followed by many, could be dangerous from the conceptual point of view: seeing functions where there are only relations is not appropriate.

6 The Construction of Rules in Data Mining

The starting point of this design is a collection of *associations*. Some of them could be recognized as *potential* rules. For the clarity of presentation, we consider only three variables and the associations therein in the form of the following Cartesian products:

$$A_i \times B_l \times C_l \tag{5}$$

I = 1, 2, ..., r. The first step is to split the variables (attributes) into inputs and outputs. For instance, the first two are regarded as inputs, the third one as an output. The potential rules read as follows

- if A_l and B_l then C_l (6)

By taking C_1 as input and retaining the two others as outputs, we get the potential rules.

- if C_1 then (A_1 and B_1) (7)

Obviously, there are far more different arrangements of the variables with respect to their directionality.

In general, when dealing with multivariable associations, numerous potential rules are possible depending on the allocation of the variables. Figure 8 illustrates this by showing the agenda **D** with its entries being identified as inputs or outputs.

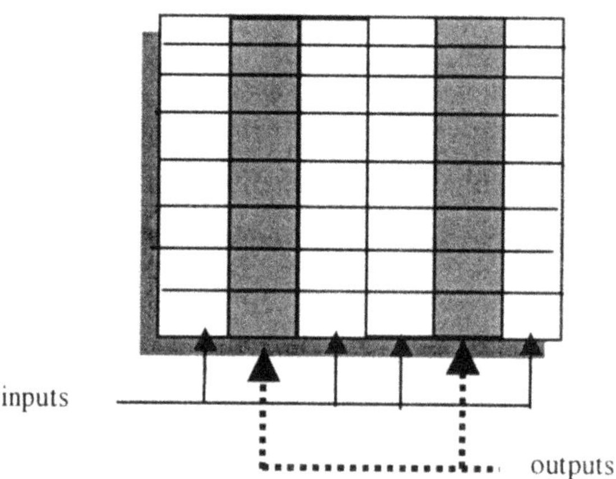

Fig. 8. The agenda of associations in database with the attributes identified as inputs (shadowed entries) and outputs.

The detailed implementation of the rules (involving various models of the implication operator and rule aggregation) were studied in numerous volumes under the banner of fuzzy inference, and is not of particular interest here; the reader may refer to [5][10] as two selected points of reference). The crucial point here is how to identify that some associations are rules. This identification occurs with regard to pairs of associations. The underlying principle is straightforward: the rules obtained from the associations are free of conflict. We say that two rules are conflicting if they have quite *similar* conditions yet they lead to very *different* (distinct) conclusions. The effect of conflict is illustrated succinctly in Figure 9.

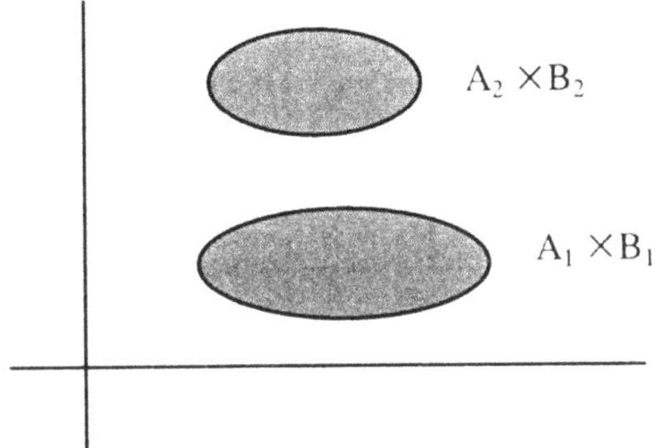

Fig. 9. Two associations and rule induction

Here we have two associations: $A_1 \times B_1$ and $A_2 \times B_2$. When converted into rules of the form if A_i then B_i then these rules are in conflict. Noticeably, the same associations when converted into rules "if B_i then A_i " do not Figure a conflict. To measure the level of conflict, we first have to express similarity (or difference) between two fuzzy relations. There are numerous ways of completing this task. By referring to the literature on fuzzy sets, the reader may encounter a long list of methods. The basic selection criteria would involve efficiency of the method as well as its computational overhead. In what follows, we endorse the possibility measure as a vehicle quantifying the similarity between two fuzzy sets or relations. In essence, the possibility describes a degree of overlap between two fuzzy sets. The computations are direct. For example, while discussing two parabolic fuzzy sets A = P (x; a, m, b) and B = P (x; c, n, d) where m < n, the level of matching is expressed in the form, see also Figure 10.

$$
Poss\,(A, B) = \begin{cases} 0, \text{if } c > b \\ 1, \text{ if } m = n \\ 3/4 \text{ if } m = b \\ 1 - \left(\dfrac{x_0 - b}{m - b}\right)^2 \text{ if } m < c < b; \text{ here } x_0 = \dfrac{n\,(b-m) + b\,(n-c)}{n - m + b - c} \end{cases}
$$

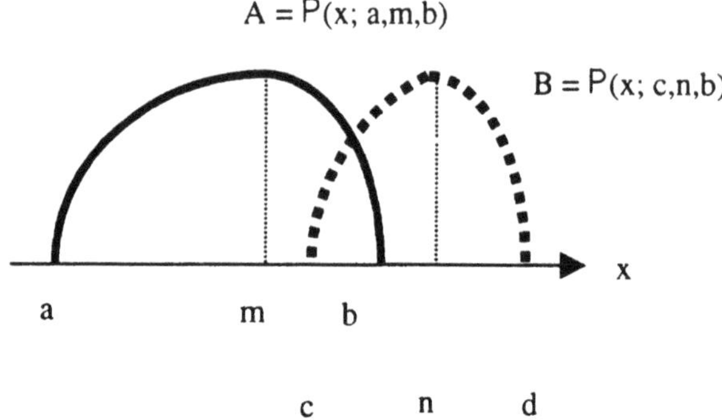

Fig. 10. Computing values of the possibility measure Poss (A, B) for two parabolic fuzzy sets A and B

Subsequently, the possibility of the two fuzzy relations $A_1 \times B_1$ and $A_2 \times B_2$ are

$$Poss\,(A_1 \times B_1, A_1 \times B_1) = (Poss\,(A_1, A_2)\, t Poss\,(B_1, B_2))$$

so the computations are straightforward as we take a t-norm over the coordinates of the fuzzy relation. Now moving to the consistency of the rules, we can distinguish the following general situations as to the similarity of the conditions and the conclusions of some potential rules, see Table 1.

Conditions	Conclusions	Consistency of rules
similar	different	**inconsistent**
similar	similar	consistent
different	similar	consistent
different	different	consistent

Tab. 1. Four general cases of similarity levels between conditions and conclusions of two rules along with their consistency

The above scenarios suggest that a plausible consistency index of the two rules can be based on the fuzzy implication

Cons (rule-1, rule-2) = $Poss\,(A_1 \times B_1, A_1 \times B_1) \Rightarrow Poss\,(C_1, C_2)$ (8)

Where " $\Rightarrow$ " denotes a fuzzy implication (residuation operation) defined in the following way

$$a \Rightarrow b = \sup\{c \in [0,1] \mid atc \leq b\} \tag{9}$$

where "t" stands for some continuous t-norm. Linking the general formula (9) with the qualitative analysis shown before, it becomes apparent that the values of the consistency index, Cons(., .) attains higher values for lower values of the observed possibility for the condition part and higher values for the observed possibility at the conclusion part.

The multidimensional form of the consistency reads as

Cons (rule-1, rule-2) =

= *Poss* (condition part of -1, condition part of -2) $\Rightarrow$ *Poss* (conclusion part -1, conclusion part -2) (10)

where the condition part and conclusion part involve the Cartesian products of the information granules of the attributes placed in the condition and conclusion parts of the rules.

So far, we have investigated a pair of rules. Obviously, when dealing with a collection of associations (and rules afterwards), we would like to gather a global view as to the consistency of the given rule with regard to the rest of the rules. A systematic way of dealing with the problem is to arrange consistency values into a form of a consistency matrix **C** having N rows and N columns (as we are concerned with "N" associations). The (i, j) th entry of this matrix denotes a level of consistency of these two rules. The matrix is symmetrical with all diagonal entries being equal to 1. As a matter of fact, it is enough to compute the lower half of the matrix. The overall consistency of the i-th rule is captured by the average of the entries of the i-th column (or row) of **C**,

$$\text{Cons}\,(\text{i}, \mathbf{D}) = \frac{1}{N}\sum_{j=1}^{N} c_{ij} \tag{11}$$

This gives rise to the linear order of the consistency of the rules. This arrangement helps us convert only a portion of the associations into rules while retaining the rest of them as direction-free constructs. What we end up, is a mixture of heterogeneous constructs as illustrated in Figure 11.

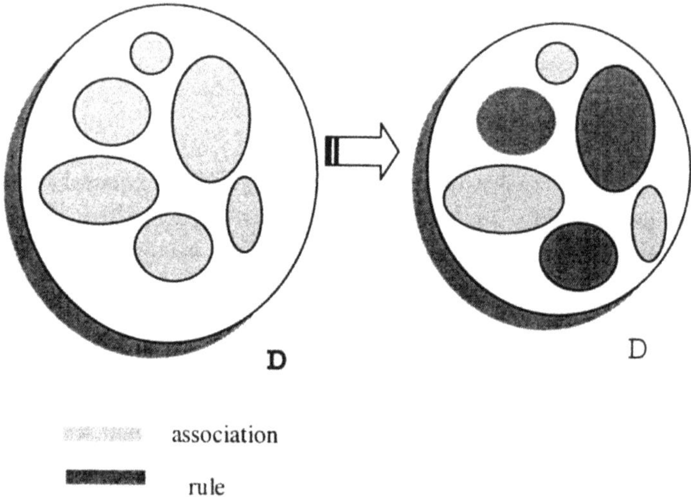

Fig. 11. By selecting highly consistent rules, the result of data mining is a mixture of associations and rules

Obviously, by lowering the threshold level (viz. accepting less consistent rules), more associations can be elevated to the position of rules.

An interesting question arises to the quality of rules, and how a given association could be converted to a rule.

7 Properties of Rules Induced by Associations

How to produce more rules out of associations and make these rules more consistent? There is a lot of flexibility in answering this question. The rules may have a different number of conditions and conclusions. Some attributes can be dropped and not showing up in the rules. To illustrate the point, consider the associations involving four attributes, namely

$$A_i \times B_i \times C_i \times D_i \tag{12}$$

The following are general observations (they come from the interpretation of the consistency index (x) we adhere to).

Increasing the number of attributes in the condition part promotes higher consistency of the rules. That is, the rules

$$\text{- if } A_i \text{ and } B_i \text{ and } C_i \text{ then } D_i$$

are more consistent than the rules in which the first attribute has been dropped, such as

$$\text{- if } B_i \text{ and } C_i \text{ then } D_l$$

This is easy to see in light of the main properties of the implication operation that is

$$atb \Rightarrow c \geq a \Rightarrow c$$

a, b, c $\in$ [0,1].

A drop in the number of attributes in the condition part contributes to rules that tend to be more *general*, i.e., they apply to a broad spectrum of situations. By adding more conditions, we make rules more *specific* (viz. they are appropriate for a smaller number of cases). The increased generality of the rules comes hand in hand with their elevated level of inconsistency.

Interestingly, the analysis of the consistency of the overall set of rules (say, by determining the sum of all entries of **C**, $\Delta = \sum_{i,j} c_{ij}$) brings us to the examination of the relevance of the attributes: if dropping a certain attribute from the condition part does not reduce the values of Δ then the attribute may be regarded as irrelevant. The more evident reduction in Δ linked with the elimination of the given attribute, the more essential this attribute is. This corresponds to the well-known problem of feature selection in pattern recognition [10]. The difference here lies in the fact that the discriminatory properties of a given attribute are quantified not for the attribute itself but a manifestation of this property is determined for the assumed level of granularity (that is the number of fuzzy sets defined there). In other words, if the granularity of the attribute has been changed (say, by increasing the number of information granules therein), it may happen that its discriminatory properties could be affected as well.

By removing attributes from the conclusion part (for a fixed number of attributes in the condition part), the rules become more consistent. Again, by following the definition of inconsistency, this tendency becomes evident as we have

$$atb \Rightarrow ctd \leq a \Rightarrow c$$

The finding concurs with our intuition: by removing more attributes, the conclusions tend to become less "disjoint" thus reducing the level of potential inconsistency. In principle, the rule becomes less specific (viz. it supports more general conclusions).

One should stress that the above analysis is carried out for the fixed associations. In particular, we have not affected the granularity of the original information granules. The size of information granules may substantially affect the consistency of the rules.

8 Detailed Computations of the Consistency of Rules and its Analysis

The way in which information granules have been constructed (the method by which they are organized along each attribute) vastly reduces the necessary computations. First, the possibility measure is computed almost instantaneously for triangular (T) and parabolic (P) membership functions. Consider two triangular fuzzy sets A and B; the following three cases hold

A and B are the same; the possibility is equal to 1

The supports of A and B are disjoint; the possibility is equal to 0

The supports of A and B overlap. Then the overlap is equal to 1 / 2 and the possibility measure equals (1 / 2) t (1 / 2). The result depends on the t-norm being used. For the minimum, *Poss* (A, B) = 1 / 2. The product operator yields a possibility value of 0.25; *Poss* (A,B) = 0.25

Similarly, when dealing with parabolic membership functions, the two first cases are identical as before. For overlapping supports, one can compute that the overlap is equal to 3 / 4. Subsequently, the possibility is equal to (3 / 4) t (3 / 4).

Now, proceeding with "r" dimensional fuzzy relations A and B rather than fuzzy sets, the values of the possibility measure assumes discrete values. The lowest one is equal to zero, the highest is equal to 1. The intermediate values of the possibility measure *Poss* (A, B) are equal to a, ata, at (ata), ..., atat ...ta (r-times). In these cases, for the product t-norm, *Poss* (A, B) = a^r (a = 1 / 2 for the triangular fuzzy sets and a = 3 / 4 for the parabolic fuzzy sets).

Taking these findings into account, the consistency of the rule with "p" condition parts and "r" conclusion parts assumes the following values (here we consider the implication induced by the product t-norm, that is)

$$\{0,\ a^{II},\ 1,\ II = 1, 2, \ldots, p\} \Rightarrow \{0,\ a^{JJ},\ JJ = 1,2,\ldots,r\} = \{0,\ a^{JJ-II},\ 1\}$$

Through the use of the above form of the implication operation, we derive the set of consistency values

$$0, \ldots a^{JJ-II}, \ldots 1$$

It is noticeable that the consistency of the two rules reveals a direct relationship between the level of consistency as a function of the number of condition and conclusion parts. For II = p and JJ = r, the consistency becomes an exponential function of the difference r - p.

9 Conclusions

We have discussed the idea of information granulation realized with the aid of fuzzy sets, and developed a complete algorithmic framework that helps reveal patterns in databases. The study makes a clear distinction between associations and rules by showing that rules are simply directional constructs that originate from associations. More importantly, as any prior commitment to directionality between variables in databases could be too restrictive, the search for associations does make sense while jumping into the formation of rules could be dangerously premature. By the same token, one should beware of exploiting and endorsing standard techniques of model identification and rule-based systems, as the algorithmic skeleton there is too limited and somewhat biased. In simple systems, the direction between variables is in general quite straightforward and could be done up front in the entire design process. When databases include data about phenomena for which the input - output specification is not obvious at all, one should proceed with associations first and then try to refine them in the form of the rules. It is also likely that we may end up with a heterogeneous topology of associations and rules.

Acknowledgment

The support from the Natural Sciences and Engineering Research Council of Canada (NSERC) is gratefully acknowledged.

References

1. R. Agrawal, T. Imielinski, A. Swami, Database mining: a performance perspective, IEEE Transactions on Knowledge and Data Engineering, 5, 1993, 914-925.

2. J. Buckley, Y. Hayashi, Fuzzy neural networks: a survey, *Fuzzy Sets and Systems*, 66, 1994, 1-14.

3. K. Cios, W.Pedrycz, R. Swiniarski, *Data Mining Techniques*, Kluwer Academic Publishers, Boston, 1998.

4. J. Chattratichat, Large scale data mining: challenges and responses, In: *Proc. 3rd Int. Conf. on Knowledge Discovery and Data Mining*, Newport Beach, CA, August, 14-17, 1997, pp.143-146.

5. B.S. Everitt, Cluster Analysis, Heinemann, Berlin, 1974.

6. C.J. Harris, C.G. Moore, M. Brown, *Intelligent Control - Aspects of Fuzzy Logic and Neural Nets,* World Scientific, Singapore, 1993.

7. D.O. Hebb, *The Organization of Behavior: A Neuropsychological Theory*, J. Wiley, N. York, 1949.

8. P.J. Huber, From large to huge: a statistician's reaction to KDD and DM, In: *Proc. 3rd Int. Conf. on Knowledge Discovery and Data Mining*, Newport Beach, CA, August 14-17, 1997, pp.304-308.

9. J. S. R Jang, C.T. Sun, E. Mizutani, *Neuro-Fuzzy and Soft Computing*, Prentice Hall, Upper Saddle River, NJ, 1997.

10. A. Kandel, *Fuzzy Mathematical Techniques with Applications*, Addison-Wesley, Reading, MA, 1986.

11. N. Kasabov, *Foundations of Neural Networks, Fuzzy Systems, and Knowledge Engineering*, MIT Press, Cambridge, MA, 1996.

12. L. Kaufman and P.J. Rousseeuw, Finding Groups in Data, J. Wiley, New York, 1990.

13. Z. Pawlak, Rough Sets: Theoretical Aspects of Reasoning about Data, Kluwer Academic, Dordrecht, 1991.

14. W. Pedrycz, *Computational Intelligence: An Introduction*, CRC Press, Boca Raton, FL, 1997.

15. W. Pedrycz, F. Gomide, *An Introduction to Fuzzy Sets*, Cambridge, MIT Press, Cambridge, MA, 1998.

16. W. Pedrycz, M.H. Smith, Granular correlation analysis in data mining, *Proc. 18th Int Conf of the North American Fuzzy Information Processing Society (NAFIPS),* New York, June 1-12, 1999pp. 715-719.

17. W. Pedrycz, E. Roventa, From fuzzy information processing to fuzzy communication channels, *Kybernetes*, vol. 28, no.5, 1999, 515-527.

18. W. Pedrycz, Fuzzy set technology in knowledge discovery, *Fuzzy Sets and Systems*, 3, 1998, 279-290.

19. W. Pedrycz, Shadowed sets: representing and processing fuzzy sets, *IEEE Trans. on Systems, Man, and Cybernetics, part B*, 28, 1998, 103-109.

20. Pedrycz, W. Vukovich, G. (1999) Quantification of fuzzy mappings: a relevance of rule-based architectures, *Proc. 18th Int Conf of the North American Fuzzy Information Processing Society (NAFIPS),* New York, June 1-12, pp. 105-109.

21. G. Piatetsky-Shapiro and W. J. Frawley, editors. "Knowledge Discovery in Databases", AAAI Press, Menlo Park, California, 1991.

22. J. R. Quinlan, "Induction of Decision Trees", Machine Learning 1, 1, 81-106, 1986.

23. J. R. Quinlan, "C4.5: Programs for Machine Learning", Morgan Kaufmann Publishers, San Mateo, California, 1993.

24. H. Toivonen, Sampling large databases for association rules. In: Proc. 22nd Int. Conf. on Very Large Databases, 1996, 134-145.

25. L.H. Tsoukalas, R.E. Uhrig, *Fuzzy and Neural Approaches in Engineering*, J. Wiley, New York, 1997.

26. R. R. Yager, Entropy and specificity in a mathematical theory of evidence. Int. J. Gen. Syst., 9, 1983, 249-260.

27. K. Yoda, T. Fukuda, Y. Morimoto, Computing optimized rectilinear regions for association rules, In: Proc. 3rd Int. Conf. on Knowledge Discovery and Data Mining, Newport Beach, CA, August 14-17, 1997, pp.96-103.

28. J. Wnek and R. S. Michalski, "Conceptual Transition from Logic to Arithmetic in Concept Learning", Reports of Machine Learning and Inference Laboratory, MLI 94-7, Center for MLI, George Mason University, December 1994.

29. L. A Zadeh, Fuzzy sets and information granularity, In: M.M. Gupta, R.K. Ragade, R.R. Yager, eds., *Advances in Fuzzy Set Theory and Applications*, North Holland, Amsterdam, 1979, 3-18.

30. L. A. Zadeh, Fuzzy logic = Computing with words, *IEEE Trans. on Fuzzy Systems*, vol. 4, 2, 1996, 103-111.

31. L. A. Zadeh, Toward a theory of fuzzy information granulation and its centrality in human reasoning and fuzzy logic, *Fuzzy Sets and Systems*, 90, 1997, 111-117.

Fuzzification and Reduction of Information-Theoretic Rule Sets

Mark Last and Abraham Kandel

Department of Computer Science and Engineering, University of South Florida, 4202 E. Fowler Avenue, ENB 118, Tampa, FL 33620, USA
{mlast, kandel}@csee.usf.edu

Abstract. If-then rules are one of the most common forms of knowledge discovered by data mining methods. The number and the length of extracted rules tend to increase with the size of a database, making the rulesets less interpretable and useful. Existing methods of extracting fuzzy rules from numerical data improve the interpretability aspect, but the dimensionality of fuzzy rulesets remains high. In this paper, we present a new methodology for reducing the dimensionality of rulesets discovered in data. Our method builds upon the information-theoretic fuzzy approach to knowledge discovery. We start with constructing an information-theoretic network from a data table and extracting a set of association rules based on the network connections. The set of information-theoretic rules is fuzzified and significantly reduced by using the principles of the Computational Theory of Perception (CTP). We demonstrate the method on a real-world database from semiconductor industry.

Keywords. Data mining, association rules, fuzzy rules, information-theoretic networks, computational theory of perception.

1 Introduction

As indicated by (Fayyad et al. 1996), discovery of useful and understandable patterns from data is a major goal in data mining. The basic idea of data mining is a computationally efficient search in the infinite space of patterns possibly existing in a database. Patterns and models can be represented in different forms (e.g., neural networks, mathematical equations, etc.), but if-then rules are known as one of the most expressive and human readable representations (Mitchell 1997). Srikant and Agrawal (1996) have suggested a heuristic method for explicit enumeration of association (if-then) rules between database attributes. As opposed to the neural network structure, each association rule is easily interpreted in the natural language. However, a long list of association rules is not much more helpful to the user than the weights of a neural network. Due to the random nature of data, the list may include many meaningless interactions. In addition, the most significant associations (having highest support and confidence) are usually the most trivial and uninteresting ones.

Decision-tree algorithms, like C4.5, suggest a more focused approach to rule extraction (Quinlan 1993). The rule extraction method of C4.5 assumes that the user is interested in only one attribute (called "class") as a consequent of every rule. This assumption significantly reduces the search space vs. the problem of finding association rules between *any* database attributes (see above). A set of mutually exclusive and exhaustive if-then (production) rules can be easily extracted from a decision tree. Quinlan (1993) presents a method for generalizing (simplifying) the rules by removing one or more conditions. The method includes setting a preference ordering for conflicting rules and choosing a default rule. However, these are *decision rules* and not *association rules*: the initial rule set includes only one rule for each tree leaf, which represents the predicted class at that leaf.

The vague nature of human perception, which allows the same object to be classified into different classes with different degrees, is utilized for building *fuzzy decision trees* by Yuan and Shaw (1995). Like in C4.5, each path from root to leaf of a fuzzy decision tree is converted into a rule with a single conclusion. However, the same object may have a non-zero membership grade in more than one rule. If a unique classification is required, the class with the highest membership is selected.

There are many techniques described in the literature for extracting fuzzy rules from raw data. Wang and Mendel (1992) present an algorithm for generating fuzzy rules from numerical attributes. The total size of the fuzzy rule base is exponential in the number of input attributes (n), but, under certain assumptions, the number of active rules for a given input is bounded by 2^n. Au and Chan (1999) describe a genetic algorithm based method, called FARM, for discovering fuzzy associations between linguistic terms. The fitness function (i.e. the "goodness" of a rule) used to evaluate the set of rules is based on a probabilistic approach. Both positive (if-then) and negative (if-then-not) association rules can be discovered by FARM. Slawinski et. al. (1999) use a hybrid evolutionary approach. Here, the fitness of a rule is related to its relevance (a rule is considered relevant if the constrained probability of its conclusion exceeds the unconstrained probability). Fuzzy approach to testing a given set of rules (hypotheses) is presented in (Last and Kandel 1999) and (Last, Schenker, and Kandel 1999).

None of the fuzzy-oriented methods mentioned above attempt to interpret rules extracted by another (possibly "crisp") rule induction algorithm. In this paper, we are applying a fuzzy approach to post-processing a given set of "crisp" association rules extracted from an information-theoretic network (Maimon, Kandel, and Last

1999). The information-theoretic method of knowledge discovery minimizes the dimensionality of extracted rules by using a built-in feature selection procedure. In addition, the algorithm discovers both positive and negative association rules and it is not limited to a single conclusion of each condition. Post-processing of the information-theoretic rules is based on the Computational Theory of Perception (Zadeh 1999) and, as demonstrated by a real-world case study, it results in a small and manageable set of compact linguistic rules.

Section 2 of this Chapter describes the information-theoretic fuzzy approach to knowledge discovery and rule extraction. The process of rule post-processing is presented in Section 3. In Section 4, we proceed with a detailed case study of rule extraction from manufacturing data. The Chapter is concluded by section 5, which reviews the potential of the fuzzy set theory for post-processing of data mining results

2 Information-Theoretic Fuzzy Approach to Knowledge Discovery

The *Info-Fuzzy Network* (IFN) methodology, initially introduced by us in (Maimon, Kandel, and Last, 1999), is a novel and unified approach to automating the process of *Knowledge Discovery in Databases* (KDD). The main stages of the IFN methodology include discretization of continuous attributes, feature selection, extraction of association rules, and data cleaning. The method is aimed at maximizing the *mutual information* (see Cover 1991) between input (predicting) and target (dependent) attributes. The following sub-sections describe the extended data model, used by IFN, the network construction algorithm, and the procedure for extracting information-theoretic association rules from the IFN structure.

2.1 Extended Relational Data Model

We use here the standard notation of the relational data model (see Korth and Silberschatz, 1991). The relational model represents the database as a collection of *relations*, or tables of values. Each table resembles, to some extent, a "flat" file of records.

1) R - a relation schema including n attributes. Each attribute represents a column of the data table. The number of attributes n is called the *degree* of a relation. In our case, $n \geq 2$ (each table is assumed to have at least two columns).

2) A_i - attribute (column) i in the data table. $R = (A_1, ..., A_n)$.

3) D_i - the domain of an attribute A_i. We assume that each domain is a set of M_i discrete values. $\forall i$: $M_i \geq 2$, finite. For numeric attributes having continuous domains, each value represents an interval between two continuous values. The discretization is performed in the process of network construction (see below).

4) V_{ij} - a value j of domain D_i. Consequently, $D_i = (V_{i1}, ..., V_{iM_i})$.

5) $r(R)$ - a relation instance (table) of the relation schema R. This is a set of n-*tuples* (records). Each n-tuple is an ordered list of n values, which represent a row in the data table.

6) m - number of tuples (records) in a relation r. We assume that $m \geq 2$ (each table has at least two rows).

7) $t_k[A_i]$ - value of an attribute i in a tuple (record) k. Each value represents a cell in the data table. Each value is an element of the attribute domain or is null ($\forall k, i$: $t_k[A_i] \in \{D_i, Null\}$). A null value may be *empty* (non-existing in the real world) or *missing* (existing in the real world, but not entered into the data table).

To find a set of association rules in a database, we make the following partition of the relation schema:

1) O - a subset of *target* (classification) attributes ($O \subset R$, $|O| \geq 1$). The values of target attributes will be the *consequents* of association rules.

2) C - a subset of *candidate input* attributes ($C \subset R$, $|C| \geq 1$). The values of candidate input attributes *can be* used as conditions in the *antecedent part* of association rules.

3) I_i - a subset of *input* attributes (features) selected by the algorithm for the target attribute i ($\forall i$: $I_i \subset C$). The antecedent of every rule will include at least one input attribute.

Assumptions:

- $\forall i: I_i \cap O = \emptyset$. An attribute cannot be both an input and a target. This implies that cyclic dependencies cannot be detected by the IFN method.
- $\forall i: I_i \cup O \subseteq R$. Some attributes in a database may be neither input, nor target. These may include identifying (key) attributes and candidate input attributes that were not chosen by the algorithm for the target attribute i.

2.2 Info-Fuzzy Network Structure

An Info-Fuzzy Network (IFN) has the following components:

- $| I_i |$ - total number of hidden layers in a network. Each hidden layer is uniquely associated with an input attribute by representing the interaction of that attribute and the input attributes of the previous layers. The first layer (layer 0) includes only the root node and is not associated with any input attribute. The number of conditions in the antecedent of an association rule cannot exceed the number of network layers.
- L_l - a subset of nodes in a hidden layer l. Each hidden node represents a conjunction
  rule conditions.
- $At\ (l)$ - an input attribute corresponding to the layer l in the network
- K - distinct target nodes V_{ij} for each value j in the domain of the target attribute i. Continuous target attributes are discretized to a pre-defined set of intervals. Each target node represents a consequent of association rules.
- w_z^{ij}- a connection weight between a hidden node z and a target node V_{ij} Each node-target connection is related to a distinct association rule. As we show below, the calculation of the rule weights is based on the information theory.

The network structure, described above, differs from the structure of a standard decision tree (see Quinlan, 1986 and 1993) in two aspects. First, it is restricted to the same input attribute at all nodes of each hidden layer. Second, its node-target connections represent *association rules* between input and target attributes unlike the standard decision trees, which are used to extract *prediction rules* only (e.g., see Quinlan 1993).

2.3 Network Construction Procedure

Without loss of generality, we present here a search procedure for constructing a multi-layered network of a *single* target attribute A_i. In a general case, the network should be re-built (starting with Step 4 below) for every target attribute defined in a database.

Step 1 - Given a relation schema and available domain knowledge, partition the schema into a subset of *candidate input* and a subset of *target* attributes (see the extended relational model above).

Step 2 - Enter a minimum significance level α for splitting a network node (default: $\alpha = 0.001$). High significance levels cause the random ("noisy") rules to be excluded from the network.

Step 3 - Read tuples (records) of a relation. Tuples with non-valid or missing target values are ignored by the algorithm. Missing (null) values of candidate input attributes are ignored too, but without ignoring the other, non-empty attributes in the same tuple. The domain of every attribute may be restricted by the user to a set of pre-defined values or learned by the algorithm from the data itself.

Step 4 - Estimate unconditional (*a priori*) probability of each value of the target attribute by: $P(V_{ij}) = O_{ij}/n$,

where

O_{ij} - number of occurrences of the value j of a target attribute i in the relation

n - number of complete tuples in the relation

Step 5 - Calculate the estimated unconditional entropy of the target attribute (see Cover, 1991) by:

$$H(A_i) = -\sum_{j=1}^{M_i} P(V_{ij}) \cdot \log P(V_{ij}) \tag{1}$$

Where

M_i - domain size of an attribute i (number of distinct values taken by the attribute)

The entropy is a *metric-free* measure of uncertainty. It reaches its highest value ($logM_i$), when the probability of all values is distributed uniformly. If an attribute takes a single value with the probability of 1.0, its entropy is equal to zero. The formula (1) above calculates *unconditional* entropy, since it is not based on the knowledge of values of any other attribute.

Step 6 - Initialize the info-fuzzy network (single root node associated with all tuples, no input attributes, and a target layer for values of the target attribute). An example of the initial network structure for a three-valued target attribute is shown in Figure 1.

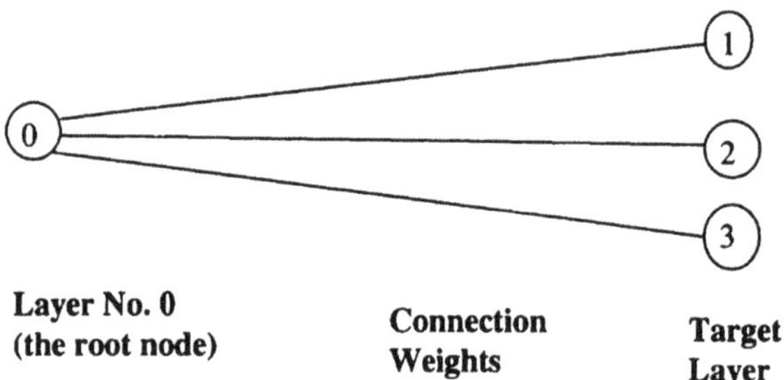

Figure 1. Info-Fuzzy Network: Initial Structure

Step 7 - While the maximum number of layers (equal to the number of candidate input attributes) is not exceeded, do:

Step 8- Repeat for every candidate input attribute $A_{i'}$, *which is not in the network*:

Step 8.1 - Initialize to zero the degrees of freedom and the estimated conditional mutual information of the candidate input attribute and the target attribute, given the final layer of hidden nodes. Conditional mutual information is defined as a decrease in the *conditional entropy*, which represents uncertainty of a random attribute, given values of other attributes. According to (Cover, 1991), the information on more attributes can never increase the entropy. Thus, conditional mutual information is a non-negative variable. As shown below, conditional mutual information can be estimated by using the frequency estimators of conditional and unconditional probabilities of the target attribute values.

Step 8.2 - If $A_{i'}$ is a continuous attribute, then Do:

Step 8.2.1 - Define the boundaries of the interval S, to be partitioned, as the first and the last distinct values of $A_{i'}$.

Step 8.2.2 - Repeat for every distinct value included in the interval S (except for the last distinct value):

Step 8.2.2.1 - Define the distinct value as a partitioning threshold (T). All distinct values below or equal to T belong to the first sub-interval S_1 (sub-interval *1*). Distinct values above T belong to the second sub-interval S_2 (sub-interval 2).

Step 8.2.2.2 - Repeat for every node z of the final hidden layer:

Step 8.2.2.2.1 - Calculate the estimated conditional mutual information between the partition of the interval S at the threshold T and the target attribute A_i, given the node z, by the following formula (based on Cover (1991)):

$$MI\ (T; A_i / S, z) = \sum_{j=0}^{M_i-1} \sum_{y=1}^{2} P(S_y; V_{ij}; z) \cdot \log \frac{P(S_y; V_{ij} / S, z)}{P(S_y / S, z) \bullet P(V_{ij} / S, z)} \qquad (2)$$

where

$P\ (S_y / S, z)$ - an estimated conditional (*a posteriori*) probability of a sub-interval S_y, given the interval S and the node z

$P\ (V_{ij} / S, z)$ - an estimated conditional (*a posteriori*) probability of a value j of the target attribute i given the interval S and the node z.

$P\ (S_y; V_{ij} / S, z)$ - an estimated joint probability of a value j of the target attribute i and a sub-interval S_y, given the interval S and the node z.

$P\ (S_y; V_{ij}; z)$ - an estimated joint probability of a value j of the target attribute i, a sub-interval S_y, and the node z.

Step 8.2.2.2.2 - Calculate the likelihood-ratio test for the partition of the interval S at the threshold T and the target attribute A_i, given the node z, by the following formula (based on Rao and Toutenburg, 1995):

$$G^2(T;A_i/S,z) = 2\sum_{j=0}^{M_i-1}\sum_{y=1}^{2} N_{ij}(S_y,z)\cdot\ln\frac{N_{ij}(S_y,z)}{P(V_{ij}/S,z)\bullet E(S_y,z)} \quad (3)$$

where

$N_{ij}(S_y, z)$ - number of occurrences of a value j of the target attribute i in sub-interval S_y and the node z.

$E(S_y, z)$ - number of tuples in sub-interval S_y and the node z

$P(V_{ij} / S, z)$ - an estimated conditional (*a posteriori*) probability of a value j of the target attribute i, given the interval S and the node z.

$P(V_{ij} / S, z) E \bullet (S_y, z)$ - an estimated number of occurrences of a value j of the target attribute i in sub-interval S_y and the node z, under the assumption that the conditional probabilities of the target attribute values are identically distributed, given each sub-interval.

Step 8.2.2.2.3- Calculate the degrees of freedom of the likelihood-ratio statistic by:

$$DF(T; A_i / S, z) = (NI_{i'}(S, z) - 1)\cdot(NT_i(S, z) - 1) =$$

$$(2-1)\cdot(NT_i(S, z) - 1) = NT_i(S, z) - 1 \quad (4)$$

Where

$NI_{i'}(S, z)$ - number of sub-intervals of a candidate input attribute i' at node z (2)

$NT_i(S, z)$ - number of values of a target attribute i in the interval S at node z.

Step 8.2.2.2.4 - If the likelihood-ratio statistic is significant at the level defined in *Step 2* above, mark the node as "split" by the threshold T and increment the estimated conditional mutual information of the candidate input attribute and the target attribute, given the threshold T; else mark the node as "unsplit" by the threshold T.

Step 8.2.2.2.5 - Go to next node.

Step 8.2.2.3 - Go to next distinct value.

Step 8.2.3 - Find the threshold T_{max} maximizing the estimated conditional mutual information between a partition of the candidate input attribute $A_{i'}$ and the target attribute A_i, given the interval S and the set of input attributes I by:

$$T_{\max} = \arg\max_{T} MI\ (T; A_i / I_i, S) \tag{5}$$

and increment the estimated conditional mutual information between the candidate input attribute $A_{i'}$ and the target attribute A_i by the value calculated in the formula (2) above.

Step 8.2.4 - If the maximum estimated conditional mutual information is greater than zero, then do:

Step 8.2.4.1 - Repeat for every node z of the final hidden layer:

Step 8.2.4.1.1 - If the node z is splitted by the threshold T_{max}, mark the node as splitted by the candidate input attribute $A_{i'}$

Step 8.2.4.2 - Partition each sub-interval of S (go to step *8.2.2).* If the threshold T_{max} is the first distinct value in the interval S, T_{max} is marked as a new encoding interval and only the second sub-interval is partitioned.

Step 8.2.4.3 - EndDo

Else (if the maximum estimated conditional mutual information is equal to zero) Do:

Step 8.2.5 - Create a new encoding interval S and increment the domain size of $A_{i'}$ (number of encoding intervals).

Step 8.2.6 - EndIf

Step 8.2.7 – EndDo

Step 8.3 – Else (if the attribute $A_{i'}$ is discrete), Do

Step 8.3.1 - Repeat for every node z of the final hidden layer:

Step 8.3.1.1 - Calculate the estimated conditional mutual information of the candidate input attribute i and the target attribute i, given the node z, by

$$MI(A_{i'}; A_i / z) = \sum_{j=0}^{M_i-1} \sum_{j'=0}^{M_{i'}-1} P(V_{ij}; V_{i'j'}; z) \cdot \log \frac{P(V_{i'j'}^{ij} / z)}{P(V_{i'j'} / z) \cdot P(V_{ij} / z)} \tag{6}$$

Where

$P\ (V_{i'j'} / z)$ - an estimated conditional (*a posteriori*) probability of a value j' of the candidate input attribute i', given the node z.

$P\ (V_{ij} / z)$ - an estimated conditional (*a posteriori*) probability of a value j of the target attribute i, given the node z.

$P(V_{i'j'}^{ij}/z)$ - an estimated conditional (*a posteriori*) probability of a value j' of the candidate input attribute i' and a value j of the target attribute i, given the node z.

$P(V_{ij}; V_{i'j'}; z)$ - an estimated joint probability of a value j of the target attribute i, a value j' of the candidate input attribute i' and the node z.

Step 8.3.1.2 - Calculate the statistical significance of the estimated conditional mutual information, by using the likelihood-ratio statistic (also based on Rao and Toutenburg, 1995):

$$G^2(A_{i'};A_i/z)=2\sum_{j=0}^{M_i-1}\sum_{j'=0}^{M_{i'}-1} C_{i'j'}^{ij}(z)\cdot\ln\frac{C_{i'j'}^{ij}(z)}{P(V_{ij}/z)\bullet E_{i'j'}(z)} \tag{7}$$

Where

$C_{i'j'}^{ij}(z)$ - number of joint occurrences of value j of the target attribute i and value j' of the candidate input attribute i' in the node z.

$E_{i'j'}(z)$ - number of occurrences of value j' of the candidate input attribute i' at the node z.

$P(V_{ij}/z)\bullet E_{i'j'}(z)$ - an estimated number of joint occurrences of value j of the target attribute i and value j' of the candidate input attribute i' under the assumption that the attributes i' and i are conditionally independent, given the node z.

Step 8.3.1.3 - Calculate the degrees of freedom of the likelihood-ratio statistic by:

$$DF(A_{i'}; A_i/z) = (NI_{i'}(z) - 1)\cdot(NT_i(z) - 1) \tag{8}$$

where

$NI_{i'}(z)$ - number of values of a candidate input attribute i' at node z.

$NT_i(z)$ - number of values of a target attribute i at node z.

Step 8.3.1.4 - If the likelihood-ratio statistic is significant, mark the node as "split" and increment the conditional mutual information of the candidate input attribute and the target attribute, given the final hidden layer of nodes ($MI(A_{i'}; A_i/I_l)$) by the value calculated in the formula (6) above; else mark the node as "terminal".

Step 8.3.1.5 - Go to next node.

Step 8.3.2 - Go to next candidate input attribute.

Step 8.3.3 - EndDo

Step 8.3.4 - EndIf

Step 9 - Find a candidate input attribute maximizing the estimated conditional mutual information ("the best candidate attribute").

Step 10 - If the maximum conditional mutual information is zero, go to Step 13. Otherwise, go to the next step.

Step 11 - Add a new hidden layer to the network: make the best candidate attribute a new input attribute and define a new layer of nodes for a Cartesian product of splitted hidden nodes in the previous layer and the values of the best candidate attribute. A new hidden node is defined if the relation (data table) has at least one tuple associated with it.

Step 12 - EndDo

Step 13 - **Stop** the network construction

Step 14 - Output the network structure which includes the names of the attributes associated with each hidden layer, the ID numbers of hidden nodes related to every value of an input attribute, and the connections between the terminal hidden nodes and the target nodes.

In Figure 2, a structure of a two-layered network (based on two selected input attributes) is shown. The first input attribute has three values, represented by nodes 1, 2, and 3 in the first layer, but only nodes 1 and 3 are split due to the statistical significance testing in Step *8.3* above. The second layer has four nodes standing for the combinations of two values of the second input attribute with two splitted nodes of the first layer. Like in Figure 1, the target attribute has three values, represented by three nodes in the target layer. The network in Figure 2 has five terminal (unsplit) nodes: 2; 1, 1; 1, 2; 3, 1; and 3, 2. The total number of input-target connections in this network is 5 * 3 = 15.

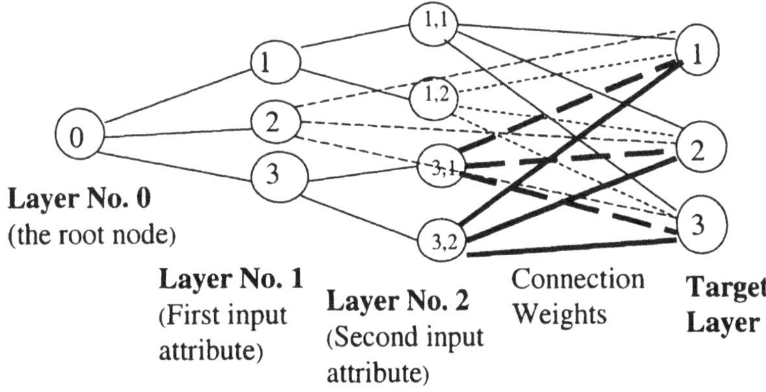

Figure 2. Info-Fuzzy Network: Two-Layered Structure

2.4 Rule Extraction

Each terminal node in an info-fuzzy network represents a conjunction of input attribute values. Thus, a connection between a terminal node and a node of the target layer may be interpreted as a rule of the form *if conjunction of input values, then the value of the target attribute is likely / unlikely to be...* An information-theoretic *weight* is associated with every input-target connection. The general algorithm for extracting association rules from the network connections and evaluating their information-theoretic weights is given below.

Step 1 - Initialize the number of rules r to zero

Step 2 - Repeat for every terminal node z:

Step 2.1 - Repeat for every value j of the target attribute A_i:

Step 2.1.1 - Initialize the hidden layer index l to zero

Step 2.1.2 - While $l <$ {number of layers associated with the node z} Do:

Step 2.1.2.1 - Add new condition to the antecedent part of the rule r, based on the value of the input attribute corresponding to the layer l

Step 2.1.2.2 - Increment l

Step 2.1.2.3 - EndDo

Step 2.1.3 - Make value j the consequent of the rule r

Step 2.1.4 - Calculate the connection weight w_z^j associated with the rule r by:

$$w_z^j = P(V_j; z) \cdot \log \frac{P(V_j / z)}{P(V_j)} \tag{9}$$

Where

$P(V_j; z)$ - an estimated joint probability of the value V_j and the node z

$P(V_j / z)$ - an estimated conditional (*a posteriori*) probability of the value V_j, given the node z

$P(V_j)$ - an estimated unconditional (*a priori*) probability of the value V_j

Step 2.1.5 - Increment the number of rules r by one

Step 2.1.6 - Go to next target value j

Step 2.2 - Go to next terminal node z

Step 3 - End

Each connection weight represents a contribution of a node-pair to the total mutual information between the input attributes and the target attribute. The weight will be positive if the conditional probability of a target attribute value, given the node, is higher than its unconditional probability and negative otherwise. A zero weight means that the target attribute value is independent of the node value. Thus, each positive connection weight can be interpreted as an *information content* of an appropriate rule of the form *if node, then target value*. Accordingly, a negative weight refers to a rule of the form *if node, then **not** target value*. Connections with zero weights can be ignored, since they do not change the conditional probability of the target attribute.

The most informative rules can be found from sorting the rules by their information-theoretic connection weights. Both the rules having the highest positive and the lowest negative weights are of a potential interest to a user. As shown in the proposition below, the sum of connection weights is equal to the estimated mutual information between a set of input attributes and a target attribute. According to the well-known Pareto rule, a small number of informative rules are expected to explain a major part of the total mutual information.

Proposition. The sum of connection weights at all unsplitted and final layer nodes is equal to the estimated mutual information between a set of input attributes and a target attribute:

$$MI(A_i;I_i) = \sum_{z \in F} \sum_{j=0}^{M_i - 1} P(V_{ij};z) \cdot \log \frac{P(V_{ij}/z)}{P(V_{ij})} \tag{10}$$

Where

A_i - target attribute i

I_i - set of input attributes

z - hidden node in the information-theoretic network

F - subset of terminal (unsplit) nodes

$P(V_{ij}; z)$ - an estimated joint probability of the target value V_{ij} and the node z

$P(V_{ij}/z)$ - an estimated conditional (a posteriori) probability the target value V_{ij}, given the node z

$P(V_{ij})$ - an estimated unconditional (a priori) probability of the target value V_{ij}.

Proof. This proposition is directly derived from the definition of mutual information between random variables X and Y (Cover, 1991):

$$MI(X;Y) = \sum_{x \in X} \sum_{y \in Y} p(x,y) \cdot \log \frac{p(y/x)}{p(y)} \tag{11}$$

In the above expression, we have replaced Y with the target attribute A_i and X with the set of input attributes I_i. A node $z \in F$ represents a conjunction of input attribute values. Since the information-theoretic network represents a disjunction of these conjunctions, each conjunction is associated with one and only one node $z \in F$. Consequently, the summation over all unsplitted and final nodes covers all possible values of the input attributes. This completes the proof.

2.5 Computational Complexity of the Algorithm

The computational complexity of the network construction for a single target attribute is calculated by using the following notation:

m - total number of records in a training data set

$|C|$ - total number of candidate input attributes

p - portion of candidate input attributes, selected as inputs by the network construction procedure, $0 \leq p \leq 1$

$|I|$ - number of hidden layers (input attributes), $|I| \leq |C|$

M_C - maximum domain size of a candidate input attribute

M_T - domain size of the target attribute

The computational "bottleneck" of the algorithm is calculating the estimated conditional mutual information between every binary partition of a continuous candidate-input attribute and a target attribute, given a hidden node ($MI(T; A_i / S, z)$). Since each node of l - th hidden layer represents a conjunction of values of l input attributes, the total number of nodes at a layer l is apparently bounded by $(M_c)^l$. However, we restrict defining a new node by the requirement that there is at least one record associated with it (see Step 11 in sub-section 0 above2.3 above). Thus, the total number of nodes at any hidden layer cannot exceed the total number of records (m). In most cases, the number of nodes will be much smaller than m, due to records having identical values of input attributes and the statistical significance requirement of the likelihood-ratio test when splitting a hidden node.

The calculation of the conditional mutual information is performed at each hidden layer of the information-theoretic network for all candidate input attributes at that layer. The number of possible partitions of a continuous attribute is bounded by $m \log_2 m$ (Fayyad and Irani, 1993). For every possible partition, the term $MI(T; A_i / S, z)$ is summed over all nodes of the final layer. This implies that the total number of calculations is bounded by:

$$m \cdot m \cdot \log_2 m \cdot M_T \cdot \sum_{l=0}^{p|C|} (|C| - l) \leq$$

$$\frac{m^2 \cdot \log_2 m \cdot M_T \cdot |C^2| \cdot p \cdot (2-p)}{2} \tag{12}$$

The actual number of calculations will usually be much smaller than this bound, since the number of tested partitions may be less than the number of distinct values (resulting from the likelihood-ratio test). The number of distinct values, in turn, may be much lower than the total number of records (*m)* and some candidate input attributes may not require discretization due to their discrete nature (e.g., nominal attributes). Thus, the run time of the search procedure is quadratic-logarithmic in the number of records and quadratic polynomial in the number of initial candidate input attributes. Moreover, it is reduced by the factor of $p\ (2 - p)$.

3 Post-processing of Association Rules

The number of rules extracted from an information-theoretic network may be quite large. It is bounded by the product of the number of terminal nodes and the number of target nodes (see the algorithm in 0 above), and the previous applications of the algorithm show that this bound is sharp. Although the rules are important for the predictive accuracy of the network, the user may find it difficult to comprehend the entire set of rules and to interpret it in natural and actionable language. As we show in this section, the *fuzzification* of the information-theoretic rules provides an efficient way for reducing the dimensionality of the rule set, without losing its actionable meaning. The process of rule reduction includes the following stages:

Stage 1 - Fuzzifying crisp rules

Stage 2 – Reducing the set of fuzzified rules by conflict resolution

Stage 3 – Merging rules from the reduced set

Stage 4 - Pruning the merged rules

3.1 Fuzzifying Association Rules

Although the boundaries of the discretized intervals are determined by the algorithm of sub-section 0 above 2.3 above to minimize the uncertainty of the target attribute, the user may be more interested in the linguistic descriptions of these intervals, rather in their precise numeric boundaries. Thus, we start with expressing "linguistic ranges" of continuous attributes as lists of terms that the attributes can take ("high", "low", etc.). Then we define membership functions representing the user perception of each term. According to (Zadeh 1999), this is the first stage in an automated reasoning process, based on the Computational Theory of Perception (CTP), which can directly operate on perception-based, rather than measurement-based, information. Subsequent CTP stages include constructing the initial constraint set (ICS), goal-directed propagation of constraints, and creating a terminal constraint set, which is the end result of the reasoning process.

As indicated by (Shenoi 1993), fuzzification of numeric attributes in a real-world database may be used for an additional purpose: *information clouding*. The user may be unwilling to disclose the actual values of some critical performance indicators associated with marketing, sales, quality, and other areas of business activity. In many cases, data security considerations prevent results of successful data mining projects from being ever published. The application part of this chapter also deals with highly sensible data obtained from a semiconductor company. Direct presentation of rules extracted from this data could provide valuable information to the company competitors. However, we are going to "hide" the confidential context of the rules by presenting them in their fuzzified form only.

The terms assigned to each simple condition and to the target (consequence) of the association rule are chosen to maximize the membership function at the middle point of the condition / consequence interval. Thus, we convert a crisp rule into a *fuzzy relation* (Wang 1997). Since a complex condition is a conjunction of simple conditions, an algebraic product is used to find the fuzzy intersection of the simple conditions. Fuzzy implication of Mamdani type (see below) is applied to each rule. Mamdani implication is more appropriate for the fuzzification of the information-theoretic rules due to the local nature of these rules. The informativeness of each fuzzified rule is represented by weighting the implication by the information-theoretic weight of the corresponding crisp rule (see sub-section 2.4 above). If the weight is positive, the rule is stated as "*If <conjunction of terms assigned to rule conditions>, then <term assigned to the rule target >*". If the weight is negative, the rule will be of the form "*If <conjunction of terms assigned to rule conditions>, then* ***not*** *<term assigned to the rule target >*". The expression for calculating the weighted membership grade of an association rule is given below.

$$\mu_R = w \bullet [\prod_{i=1}^{N} \max_j \{ \mu_{A_{ij}}(V_i)\}] \bullet \max_k \{ \mu_{T_k}(O)\} \tag{13}$$

Where
w – information-theoretic weight of the crisp rule
N – number of simple conditions in the crisp rule
V_i – crisp value of the simple condition i in the crisp rule (middle point of the condition interval)
O – crisp value of the rule target (middle point of the target interval)

$\mu_{A_{ij}}(V_i)$ - membership function of the simple condition i w.r.t. term j

$\mu_{T_k}(O)$ - membership function of the target value O w.r.t. term k

3.2 Removing Inconsistent Rules

An information-theoretic ruleset represents association rules between conjunctions of input values and all possible target values. Hence, several rules may have the same IF parts, but different THEN parts. Fuzzification may even increase the number of distinct rules with identical antecedents, since several adjacent intervals may refer to the same linguistic term. This means that the set of fuzzy rules, produced in sub-section 3.1 above, may be *inconsistent*. To resolve the conflicts, we calculate the grade of each distinct fuzzy rule and choose the target value from a conflict group that has a maximum grade. A similar approach is used by (Wang and Mendel, 1992) for resolving conflicts in fuzzy rules generated from data. The reduced set of distinct fuzzy rules is constructed by the following procedure:

Algorithm RESOLVE_CONFLICTS (Set_of_Fuzzified_Rules)

- *Initialize total number of distinct fuzzy rules to zero.*
- *Repeat for every fuzzified rule:*
  - *Find a distinct fuzzy rule with identical linguistic values of input attributes*
  - *If Rule Found,*
    - *Find identical linguistic value of the target attribute in the distinct rule*
  - *If Value Found,*
    - *Increment the grade of the target linguistic value by the grade of the fuzzified rule*
  - *Else (if value not found),*
    - *Update the set of target linguistic values in the distinct rule*
    - *Initialize the grade of the new target value to the grade of the fuzzified rule*
  - *Else (if rule not found)*
    - *Increase number of distinct fuzzy rules*
    - *Update the linguistic values of input attributes in the new rule*
    - *Update the first target linguistic value in the new rule*

- *Initialize the grade of the first target value in the new distinct rule to the grade of the fuzzified rule*

  - *Next fuzzified rule*

- *For each distinct fuzzy rule do*

  - *Find the target linguistic value providing the maximum membership grade for the rule*

  - *Make it the single target value of the rule*

In the above procedure, there is no explicit distinction between positive and negative rule grades. For example, the fuzzified rules of the form *If A then B* and *If A then not B* are associated with the same target value in the same distinct rule. However, their combined grade will be equal to the *difference* of their absolute grades. Eventually the target value with the maximum *positive* grade will be chosen by the above procedure. This closely agrees with the interests of most users, who need to estimate *positively* the expected outcome of each condition.

The computational complexity of the RESOLVE_CONFLICTS algorithm is proportional to the square of the number of fuzzified rules times the average number of rule conditions. This is because the algorithm compares the antecedent conditions of every *fuzzified* rule to the corresponding conditions of every *distinct fuzzy* rule. If the two antecedents are found identical, the grade of the corresponding target linguistic value is updated. If no matching rule is found, a new distinct fuzzy rule is created. Thus, the number of distinct fuzzy rules is bounded by the number of fuzzified rules.

3.3 Merging Reduced Rules

In the previous sub-section, we have shown a method for handling rules having *identical antecedents* and *distinct consequents*. However, the resulting set of conflict-free rules may be reduced by merging the rules having *distinct antecedents* and *identical consequents*. Thus, any two rules (I) and (II) having the form:

I. If *a is A and b is B and c is C, then t is T*

II. *If d is D and e is E and f is F, then t is T*

can be merged into a single rule (III) of the following *disjunctive* form:

III. *If a is A and b is B and c is C* **or** *d is D and e is E and f is F, then t is T*

Using the above approach, we can create a rule base of a minimal size, limited by the number of target values. However, this approach may produce a small number of long and hardly useable rules (like the rule III above). Therefore, we perform the merging of disjunctive values *for the last rule condition only*. The procedure of merging fuzzy conjunctive rules is given below. It is based on the assumption that each fuzzy rule is using the same partial sequence of input attributes, which is true for any rule base extracted from an information-theoretic network (see sub-section 2.3 above).

Algorithm MERGE_RULES (Consistent_Set_of_Fuzzy_Rules)

- *Initialize total number of merged fuzzy rules to zero.*
- *Initialize number of conditions (l) to zero*
- *While (l < total number of input attributes) do*
    - *Repeat for every fuzzy rule having l conditions*
    - *If there are no merged rules having l conditions*
        - *Define the first merged rule with l conditions*
        - *Initialize the rule grade*
    - *Else*
        - *Try to merge with an existing rule (having the same target value and the same input values for (l-1) conditions)*
    - *If merged,*
        - *Update disjunctive condition no. l by a new term*
        - *Update the rule grade by using a fuzzy union ("max" operation).*
    - *Else*
        - *Define a new merged rule with l conditions*
        - *Initialize the rule grade*
- *Increment l*

The computational complexity of the MERGE_RULES algorithm is proportional to the square of the number of distinct fuzzy rules (bounded by the number of information-theoretic rules) times the average number of rule conditions (minus the last condition). This is because the algorithm performs pairwise comparison of all conditions, except for the last one. If the partial antecedents of two rules are found identical and their target values are identical too, the rules are merged. In the end of the process, only the rules, which do not match any other rule, are left unmerged.

3.4 Pruning Merged Rules

The rules merged by the algorithm of sub-section 3.3 above may include several values in the last (disjunctive) condition. The number of values is bounded by the number of fuzzy terms in the attribute corresponding to the last condition. However, if the number of values in a disjunctive condition is *equal* to the number of attribute terms, the condition can be eliminated, since a complete linguistic domain of an attribute represents the entire universe of discourse. In other words, we can *prune* the rule by removing the last condition. The formal algorithm for pruning merged rules is given below.

Algorithm PRUNE_RULES (Set_of_Merged_Rules)

- *Repeat for each layer l in the Info-Fuzzy Network*
    - *Repeat for each merged rule r having l conditions*
        - *If the number of values in the last condition (condition l) is equal to the domain size of the attribute At (l) corresponding to the layer l in the network:*
            - *Decrement the number of conditions in rule r by one*
            - *Remove rule r from the set of rules having l conditions*
            - *Add rule r to the set of rules having (l-1) conditions*
        - *End If*
    - *Next rule r at the layer l*
- *Next layer l*

The computational complexity of the PRUNE_RULES algorithm is proportional to the number of merged rules. The number of merged rules is bounded by the number of information-theoretic rules (see previous sub-sections).

4 Case Study

In this section, we are applying the process of rule extraction, fuzzification, and reduction to a real-world data set provided by a semiconductor company. The semiconductor industry is a highly competitive sector, and the data included in our analysis is considered highly sensitive proprietary information. Consequently, we are forced to omit or change many details in the description of the target data and the obtained results. As indicated in sub-section 3.1 above, fuzzification of continuous attributes has helped us to "hide" the proprietary information from the unauthorized (and, probably, curious) reader.

4.1 The Problem Domain

The Information-Fuzzy Network (IFN) methodology is applied to a real-world database containing typical data from a semiconductor plant. The basic measure of profitability in semiconductor industry is the outgoing *yield* of manufactured batches. Overall, or line yield of a manufacturing process is defined as the ratio between the number of good parts (chips) in a completed batch and the initial number of chips in the same batch. Since capitalization costs constitute the major part of manufacturing costs in semiconductor industry, the *cost* of producing a single batch is almost fixed. However, the *income* from a given batch is equal to the price of one chip times the number of good chips. Thus, there is a direct relationship between the yield and the profits of semiconductor companies, who treat their yield data as "top secret" information.

Controlling and preserving the yield is a complex engineering problem. Both new and mature semiconductor products suffer from variability of yield within and between individual batches and even on specific wafers of the same batch. Improved understanding of this variability can save significant manufacturing costs by focusing on problematic processes and taking appropriate actions, whenever excursion of yield is expected for a given batch, wafer, etc.

Although the amount of manufacturing data collected by semiconductor companies is constantly increasing, it is still hard to identify the most important parameters for yield modeling and prediction. In this study, we are trying to find relationships between the batch yield and two types of available data:

- *Batch-based data* including information about product and process type, batch priority, etc. Different processes are expected to have different yields, depending on their maturity, tool condition, and other factors.
- *WIP (Work-in-Process) data* showing the batch routing (sequence of fabrication steps), the date of completing each fabrication step, quantity transferred to the next step, and other parameters. Multiple records (based on different fabrication steps) may be related to the same batch. The batch yield may depend on the *flow time*, which is the amount of time spent at the same fabrication step. Certain materials used in semiconductor industry are known to be sensitive to the time difference between succeeding operations.

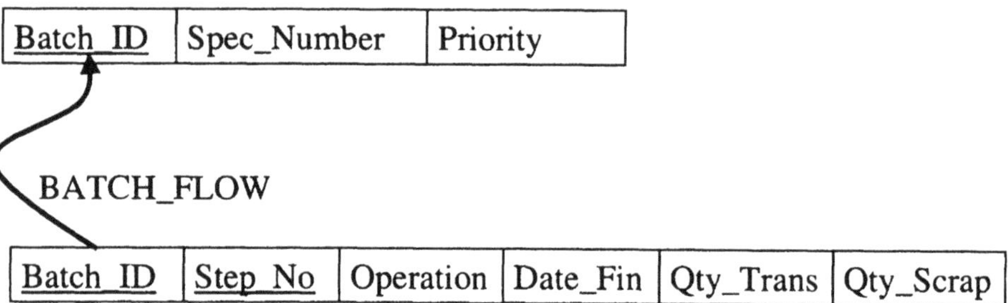

Figure 3. Relational Schema of the Semiconductor Database

The relational schema of the database provided to us by the company is shown in Figure 3 above. Here is a short explanation about each attribute in the schema:

- Table BATCHES
    - *Batch_ID*. This is the identification number of each batch and the primary key of the table.
    - *Spec_Number*. This is a specification (part) number of a batch. It specifies the manufacturing parameters of the batch, like voltage, frequency, chip size, etc.
    - *Priority*. This is the priority rank of a batch, usually assigned by the marketing department.
- Table BATCH_FLOW
    - *Batch_ID*. This is the identification number of a batch. It is a foreign key, since it is related to the primary key of the table BATCHES, but it is also a part of the primary key of this table.
    - *Step_No*. This is the serial number of a fabrication step in the manufacturing process of a given batch. A completed batch has several steps. The attribute *Step_No* is a part of the primary key. Each record in the BATCH_FLOW table is uniquely identified by a combination of values of two attributes: *Batch_ID* and *Step_No*.
    - *Operation*. The code of the operation applied to the batch no. *Batch_ID* at the fabrication step no. *Step_No*.
    - *Date_Fin*. The date when the fabrication step was completed. After completion of a step, the batch is transferred automatically to the next step on its routing list.

- *Qty_Trans*. The quantity of good chips transferred to the next step. If a batch consists of wafers, the number of good chips is calculated automatically from the number of wafers.
- *Qty_Scrap*. This is the number of chips scrapped at the current fabrication step. It is equal to the difference between the number of chips transferred from the previous step and the number of chips transferred to the next step. If entire wafers are scrapped, the number of scrapped chips is calculated automatically.

4.2 Data Preparation

4.2.1 Data Selection

In the original dataset provided by the company, the table BATCHES included 3,129 records. Since the company is manufacturing a variety of semiconductor products, the batches represented by the table records had different electric characteristics and different routings. Consequently, we have decided to focus our analysis on a group of 816 batches related to a single product family. The products of this family have two main parameters (chip size and electric current) and their manufacturing process includes about 30 fabrication steps.

4.2.2 Feature Extraction

The extended relational data model (see sub-section 2.1 above) assumes that the values of all candidate input and target attributes are given in the same record of a relational table. However, the table BATCHES does not include some candidate input attributes (product parameters and flow times between succeeding steps), as well as the target attribute (yield). The product parameters (size and current) were extracted from the attribute *Spec_Number* by using metadata on the attribute's encoding schema. The flow times at each fabrication step (except for the first one) were calculated by taking the difference between the completion dates of the current step and the previous step. The completion dates were given by the attribute *Date_Fin* in the table BATCH_FLOW. The line yield of each batch was found from dividing the value of the attribute *Qty_Trans* in the last fabrication step by its value in the first step. These feature extraction operations have resulted in a new schema of the table BATCHES, which is shown in Figure 4 below.

BATCHES

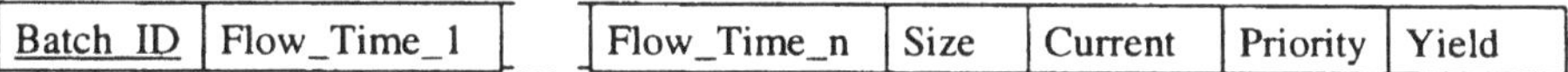

Figure 4. New Relational Schema of the BATCHES Table

4.2.3 Discretization of Target Attribute

The structure of the Info-Fuzzy Network introduced in sub-section 2.2 above requires the target attribute to be a discrete variable. However, yield is a continuous attribute: it can take any value between zero and one. Thus, we have discretized the attribute *yield* to 10 intervals of approximately equal frequency. The resulting entropy of *yield* was 3.32 (very close to $log_2\ 10$).

4.3 Extraction of Information-Theoretic Rules

The Info-Fuzzy Network extracted from the BATCHES table is shown in Figure below. The network includes three hidden layers related to three input attributes selected by the algorithm of sub-section 2.3 above: *Size*, *Current*, and *Flow_Time_29* (flow time at operation 29). *Size* (chip size) was defined as a nominal attribute, since the given product is manufactured in three different sizes only (represented by the three nodes of the first hidden layer). *Current* is a continuous attribute, which was discretized by the algorithm into four intervals resulting in four nodes of the second layer. Another continuous attribute, *Flow_Time_29*, was discretized into two intervals. Hence, the third hidden layer has two nodes. The network has seven terminal (unsplitted) nodes: 1, 2, 5, 6, 7, 8, and 9. Full connections between the terminal and the target nodes are not shown in Figure 5 due to space limitations.

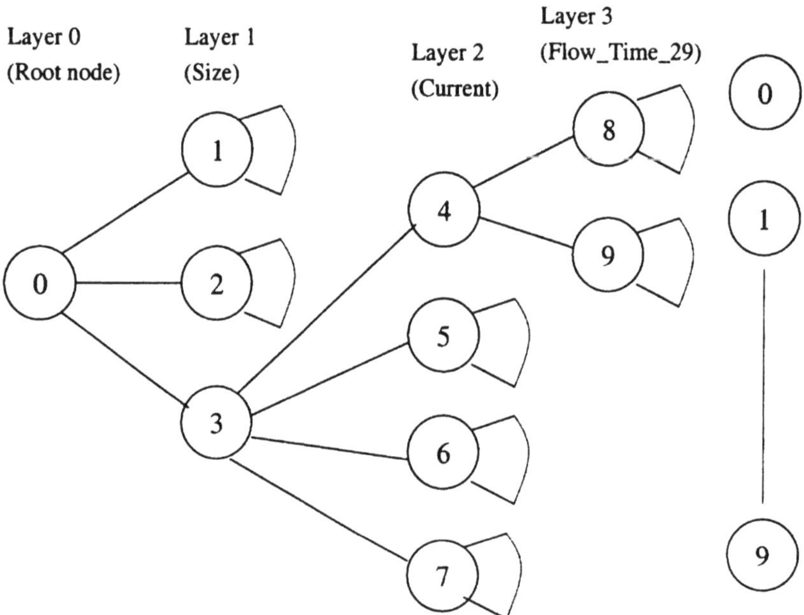

Figure 5. Info-Fuzzy Network (BATCHES Table)

The relative importance of each selected attribute is shown in Table below. The column "Mutual Information" shows the cumulative association between a subset of input attributes, selected up to a given iteration inclusively, and the target attribute. Since the mutual information is defined as the difference between unconditional and conditional entropy (Cover 1991), it is bounded by the unconditional entropy of *yield*, which is 3.32. The estimated net increase in the mutual information, due to adding each input attribute, is presented in the column " Conditional MI ". The last column " Conditional Entropy " is the difference between the unconditional entropy (3.32) and the estimated mutual information.

Iteration	Attribute Name	Mutual Information	Conditional MI	Conditional Entropy
0	Size	0.102	0.102	3.218
1	Current	0.204	0.102	3.116
2	Flow_Time_29	0.255	0.051	3.065

Table 1. Selected Attributes (BATCHES Table)

The network of Figure 5 above can have up to 7 * 10 = 70 connections between its seven terminal nodes and ten nodes of the target layer. The number of connections having non-zero information-theoretic weights is 58. Each connection represents an association rule of the form

If Size $= V_1$ *and Current* $= V_2$, *and Flow_Time_29* $= V_3$ *then Yield is [not]* V_4

where V_1, V_2, and V_3 either represent valid values from the domains of the corresponding attributes, or are equal to "don't care". The consequent V_4 represents one of discretization intervals of the target attribute (*Yield*). The rules having the highest positive and the smallest negative connection weights are given below (confidential information was replaced by meaningless letters).

- **Rule No. 28**: If Size is *Z* and Current is between *C* and *D* then Yield is between *A* and *B* (weight = 0.0737).
- **Rule No. 6**: If Size is *Y* then Yield is not between *E* and *F* (weight = -0.0233).

Though the above rules are expressed in accurate, "crisp" terms defining the exact boundaries of each underlying interval, their representation power is quite limited for the following reasons:

1) The user is more interested in the rules of the form "If current is high, then the yield is low", which is closer to the human way of reasoning. People tend to "compute with words" rather than with precise numbers.

2) The total number of rules, extracted from this dataset, is 58, which is larger than the number of rules generally used by people in their decisions.

3) The rules cannot be presented to outsiders (e.g., representatives of a rival company) without revealing some sensitive information. This may be an obstacle to open exchange of technological information in forums like professional conferences, multi-company consortia, etc.

In the next sub-section, we are going to use the Computational Theory of Perception (Zadeh 1999) for converting the set of "crisp" numeric rules into a reduced set of fuzzy (linguistic) rules.

4.4 Rules Fuzzification and Reduction

We have chosen the following terms (words in natural language) for each type of numerical attribute in the BATCHES table:

- Flow Time: *short, long.*
- Current: *low, medium, high.*
- Yield: *low, normal, high.*

To convert the above attributes into linguistic variables, we have defined triangular membership functions associated with each term (see Figures 6-8 below). Triangular functions are frequently used in the design of fuzzy systems (Wang 1997). To protect the confidentiality of the original data, the membership functions are shown here without the values of the X-axis. The nominal attribute *Size* was not fuzzified.

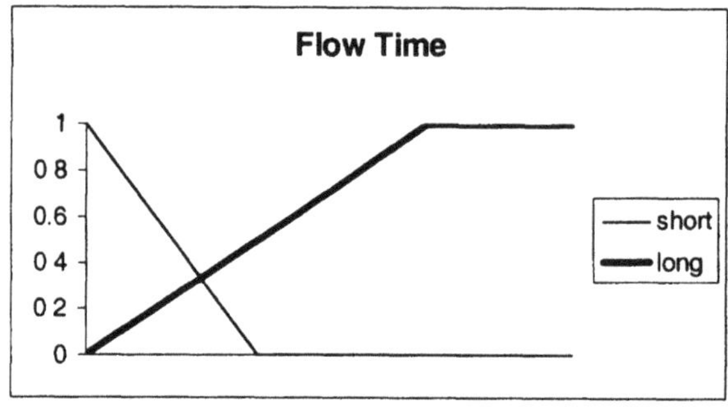

Figure 6. Membership Functions of *Flow Time*

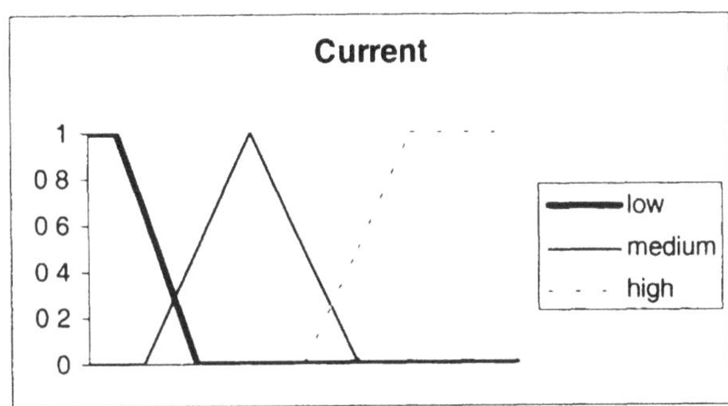

Figure 7. Membership Functions of *Current*

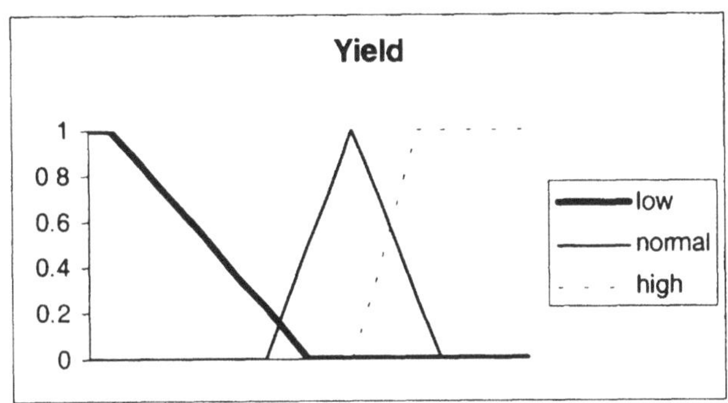

Figure 8. Membership Functions of *Yield*

Applying the fuzzification procedure to the "crisp" rules, shown in the previous sub-section, results in the following fuzzy rules:

- **Rule No. 28**: If Size is *Z* and Current is medium then Yield is normal (grade = 0.0326)
- **Rule No. 6**: If Size is *Y* then Yield is not low (grade = -0.0216)

In Table below, we present the consistent set of fuzzy rules, extracted from the BATCHES table by using the conflict resolution procedure of sub-section 0 above3.2 above. The last column represents the number of original rules (crisp / fuzzified), associated with a given fuzzy rule. As one can see, the size of the fuzzy rule base has been significantly reduced from 58 original rules to six rules only (a decrease of nearly 90%).

Rule No	Rule Text	Grade	Number of Crisp Rules
0	If Size is *X* then Yield is low	0.0522	5
1	If Size is *Y* then Yield is normal	0.0226	10
2	If Size is Z and Current is medium then Yield is normal	0.0395	17
3	If Size is Z and Current is high then Yield is normal	0.0097	8
4	If Size is Z and Current is low and Flow_Time_29 is short then Yield is normal	0.0077	10
5	If Size is Z and Current is low and Flow_Time_29 is long then Yield is low	0.0176	8

Table 2. The Set of Consistent Fuzzy Rules

All the rules in Table above are *conjunctions* of fuzzy and "crisp" conditions. However, rules 2 and 3 can be merged into a *disjunction*, since they have the same consequent (*Yield is normal*). The formal algorithm for merging fuzzy rules was presented in sub-section 3.3 above and the resulting set of 5 merged fuzzy rules is shown in Table below. The merged rule (no. 2) does not include all the terms associated with the attribute *Current*, and, thus, it cannot be pruned by the algorithm of sub-section 3.4.

The users (process engineers) would be particularly interested in the rules describing problematic situations, where the yield is below normal. Thus, Rule 0 indicates that the chips of the size *X* are more problematic, since their yield tends to be low. Corrective actions may include changes of the manufacturing process, purchase of new equipment, and adjustment of chips' prices. Rule 4 says that batches having a different size (Z) and low current suffer from low yield, if the flow time at Operation 29 is long. In this case, the engineers should find the reason why long waiting times at this operation cause the yield to be low. Anyway, the delays may be decreased by the proper changes of the working procedures (assigning higher priority to low-current batches of size Z).

Rule No	Rule Text	Grade
0	If Size is *X* then Yield is low	0.0522
1	If Size is *Y* then Yield is normal	0.0226
2	If Size is *Z* and Current is medium or high then Yield is normal	0.0395
3	If Size is Z and Current is low and Flow_Time_29 is short then Yield is normal	0.0097
4	If Size is Z and Current is low and Flow_Time_29 is long then Yield is low	0.0077

Table 3. The Set of Merged Fuzzy Rules

5 Conclusions

In this paper, we have presented a new approach to extracting a compact set of linguistic rules from relational data. The approach is based on the *Information-Fuzzy Network* (IFN) methodology, which is aimed at maximizing the mutual information between input and target attributes. Post-processing of the IFN output includes information-theoretic fuzzification of numeric association rules, removal of conflicting rules, merging of consistent rules, and pruning of merged rules. As demonstrated by the case study of a semiconductor database, the process results in a small set of interpretable and actionable rules. If necessary, the fuzzification of the rules can also be helpful for hiding confidential information from unauthorized users of the rule set.

The full potential of the fuzzy set theory for efficient post-processing of data mining results has yet to be studied. Future research includes integration of the Computational Theory of Perception with other rule extraction systems like C4.5 (Quinlan 1993) and Quest (Agrawal et al. 1996). Application of the same approach to non-relational data (e.g., time series databases and multi-media documents) is another important topic.

Acknowledgment

This work was partially supported by the USF Center for Software Testing under grant no. 2108-004-00.

References

1. R. Agrawal, M. Mehta, J. Shafer, and R. Srikant (1996). The Quest Data Mining System. Proc. of KDD-96, pages 244-249. AAAI Press.

2. W.-H. Au and K. C. C. Chan (1999). FARM: A Data Mining System for Discovering Fuzzy Association Rules. Proc. of IEEE International Fuzzy System Conference, pages 1217-1222. IEEE Press.

3. T. M. Cover (1991). Elements of Information Theory. Wiley.

4. U. Fayyad and K. Irani (1993). Multi-Interval Discretization of Continuous-Valued Attributes for Classification Learning. Proc. of the 13th International Joint Conference on Artificial Intelligence, pages 1022-1027. Morgan Kaufmann.

5. U. Fayyad, G. Piatetsky-Shapiro, and P. Smyth (1996a). From Data Mining to Knowledge Discovery: An Overview. In U. Fayyad, G. Piatetsky-Shapiro, P. Smyth, and R. Uthurusamy, Editors, Advances in Knowledge Discovery and Data Mining, , pages 1-30. AAAI/MIT Press.

6. H.F. Korth and A. Silberschatz (1991). Database System Concepts. McGraw-Hill, Inc.

7. M. Last and A. Kandel (1999). Automated Perceptions in Data Mining. Proc. of 1999 IEEE International Fuzzy Systems Conference, pages 190-197. IEEE Press.

8. M. Last, A. Schenker, and A. Kandel (1999). Applying Fuzzy Hypothesis Testing to Medical Data. Proc. of RSFDGrC'99, pages 221-229. Springer-Verlag.

9. O. Maimon, A. Kandel, and M. Last (1999). Information-Theoretic Fuzzy Approach to Knowledge Discovery in Databases. In R. Roy, T. Furuhashi and P.K. Chawdhry, editors, Advances in Soft Computing - Engineering Design and Manufacturing, , pages 315-326.

10. T.M. Mitchell (1997). Machine Learning. McGraw-Hill.

11. J.R. Quinlan (1986). Induction of Decision Trees. Machine Learning, 1 (1): 81-106.

12. J. R. Quinlan (1993). C4.5: Programs for Machine Learning. Morgan Kaufmann.

13. C.R. Rao and H. Toutenburg (1995). Linear Models: Least Squares and Alternatives. Springer-Verlag.

14. S. Shenoi (1993). Multilevel Database Security Using Information Clouding. Proc. of IEEE International Conference on Fuzzy Systems, pages 483-488. IEEE Press.

15. T. Slawinski, et. al. (1999). A Hybrid Evolutionary Search Concept for Data-based Generation of Relevant Fuzzy Rules in High Dimensional Spaces. Proc. of IEEE International Fuzzy System Conference, pages 1432-1437. IEEE Press.

16. R. Srikant and R. Agrawal (1996). Mining Quantitative Association Rules in Large Relational Tables. Proc. of ACM-SIGMOD 1996 Conference on Management of Data, pages 1-12.

17. L.-X. Wang and J.M. Mendel (1992). Generating Fuzzy Rules by Learning from Examples. IEEE Transactions on Systems, Man, and Cybernetics, 22 (6): 1414-1427.

18. L.-X. Wang (1997). A Course in Fuzzy Systems and Control. Prentice-Hall.

19. Y. Yuan, M.J. Shaw (1995). Induction of Fuzzy Decision Trees. Fuzzy Sets and Systems, 69 (0): 125-139.

20. L. A. Zadeh (1999). A New Direction in System Analysis: From Computation with Measurements to Computation with Perceptions. In N. Zhong, A. Skowron, S. Ohsuga, Editors, New Directions in Rough Sets, Data Mining, and Granular-Soft Computing , pages 10-11.

Mining Fuzzy Association Rules in a Database Containing Relational and Transactional Data

Keith C.C. Chan and Wai-Ho Au

Department of Computing, The Hong Kong Polytechnic University, Hung Hom, Kowloon, Hong Kong

Abstract. Many effective algorithms have been developed to mine association rules in relational and transactional data separately. In this paper, we present a technique for the mining of such rules in databases containing both types of data. This technique, which we call Fuzzy Miner, performs its tasks by the use of fuzzy logic, a set of transformation functions, and by residual analysis. With the transformation functions, new attributes and new item types can be derived for either relational or transactional data. They also make it possible for association rules relating the two types of data to be discovered, e.g., the buying patterns related to the demographics of a group of customers. With fuzzy logic, Fuzzy Miner is not only able to discover Boolean and quantitative but also fuzzy association rules. This makes the patterns discovered more easily understandable by human users and more resilient to noise and missing data values. With residual analysis, Fuzzy Minder does not require any user-supplied thresholds that are often hard to determine. The Fuzzy Miner also discovers relationship between fuzzy and quantitative values and allows quantitative values to be inferred by the rules. With these features, Fuzzy Miner can be applied to real-life databases containing relational and transactional data.

Keywords. Fuzzy data mining, fuzzy association rules, interestingness measure, relational and transactional databases, transformation, fuzzy data

1 Introduction

Given a database containing both transactional (such as records of purchase, electronic fund transfer or phone calls, etc.) and relational data (such as customer information and inventory records, etc.), the problem we are concerned with is to discover hidden associations within and between the two types of data. Many effective algorithms have been developed to mine association rules in either type of data separately (e.g. [1, 9, 13] on transaction and [14] on relational). How they can be used to handle both together is not obvious.

Given that many real-world database systems contain both transactional and relational data, it is important that hidden associations between them be discovered. For example, to discover useful rules such as "70% of the large transactions are made by high-income customers that live in New York City; 8% of all transaction records Figure such characteristics" in a database system that contains both relational data on customer background and transactional data on their purchases, we need an effective algorithm.

This algorithm should also be able to handle linguistic or fuzzy variables in the data as well as in the rules. This is because the ability to do so would allow some interesting patterns to be more easily discovered and expressed. For example, if crisp boundaries are defined for "large transactions" and "high-income" in the above rule, there is a possibility that it may not be interesting at all as the confidence and support measures is dependent to a large extent on the definitions of the boundaries. Despite its importance, many association rule-mining algorithms (e.g. [14]) were not developed to handle fuzzy data or fuzzy rules. They were used mainly to deal with qualitative and quantitative attributes. In particular, when dealing with quantitative attributes, their domains are usually divided up into equal-width or equal-frequency intervals. In most cases, the resulting intervals are not too meaningful and are hard to understand.

To mine association rules in both transactional and relational data on one hand and to deal with fuzzy data and fuzzy rules on the other, we present a data mining technique, called Fuzzy Miner, here. Fuzzy Miner employs *linguistic terms* to represent attributes and values and regularities and exceptions discovered. These linguistic terms can be defined as fuzzy sets so that, based on their membership functions, either qualitative or quantitative data, can be transformed by fuzzification. To deal with these fuzzified data so as to discover fuzzy rules, Fuzzy Miner utilizes the idea of *residual analysis* [2-5]. With it, Fuzzy Miner is able to reveal interesting *positive* and *negative* associations hidden in the database without the need for users' to supply some subjective thresholds. It is also able to discover fuzzy rules that relate two fuzzy attributes together. In other words, unlike many data mining algorithms (e.g. [1, 9, 13-14]) that only discover rules with consequent consisting only of qualitative or discretized crisp-boundary quantitative attributes, Fuzzy Miner is able to discover rules that allow quantitative values to be inferred.

The Fuzzy Miner has been used in different real applications. It has been found to be very effective. The details of the algorithm are given in the next two sections. In Section 4, we give an example of using Fuzzy Miner in a real application.

2 Data Transformation

To handle both transactional and relational data together, the Fuzzy Miner uses a set of transformation functions. These functions are introduced in this section. To handle fuzzy data and rules, Fuzzy Miner uses the concepts of fuzzy linguistic terms and a fuzzy inference technique. They are introduced in Sections 2.2 and 2.3, respectively.

2.1 The Transformation Functions

Let $A_{i1}, A_{i2}, \ldots, A_{in_i}$, $i = 1, 2, \ldots, I$, be the attributes of some real-world entities represented by the relational tables R_i, $i = 1, 2, \ldots, I$, respectively. Let the domain of A_{ik}, $k = 1, 2, \ldots, K_i$, be represented by $dom(A_{ik}) = \{a_{ik}^{(1)}, a_{ik}^{(2)}, \ldots, a_{ik}^{(m_{ik})}\}$, $i = 1, 2, \ldots, I$, $k = 1, 2, \ldots, K_I$, therefore, $R_i \subseteq dom(A_{i1}) \times dom(A_{i2}) \times \cdots \times dom(A_{iK_i})$. Let $\mathcal{A}_{R_i}$ denote the set of attributes in R_i, therefore, $\mathcal{A}_{R_i} = \{A_{i1}, A_{i2}, \ldots, A_{iK_i}\}$. Given R_i, we denote its primary key, which is composed of one or more attribute-value pairs and is associated with each n-tuple in a relation, as $\mathcal{K}_i \subseteq \{A_{i1}, A_{i2}, \ldots, A_{iK_i}\}$.

Given a set of transaction records, these records can be denoted as T_j, $j = 1, 2, \ldots, J$, where each T_j is characterized by a set of attributes denoted by $A_{j1}, A_{j2}, \ldots, A_{jL_j}$ and has a unique transaction identifier TID_j. In other words, $T_j \subseteq TID_j \times dom(A_{j1}) \times dom(A_{j2}) \times \cdots \times dom(A_{jL_j})$. In a database system that contains both relational and transactional data, one may identify some one-to-many relationships between the records in R_i, $i = 1, 2, \ldots, I$, and those in T_j, $j = 1, 2, \ldots, J$. For instance, a business transaction processing system may contain: (i) a set of relational tables containing the background information about the customers and (ii) a transactional database containing details (such as transaction date, time, and the amount purchased, etc.) of each transaction made by the customers. The relational data are related to the transactional data in some one-to-many relationship so that we can use $\mathcal{K}_i$, as a foreign key to provide reference to corresponding n-tuple in R_i, $i = 1, 2, \ldots, I$.

Given R_i and T_j, in order to be able to discover association rules relating the relational and transactional data and association rules involving attributes derived from those originally in the databases, we propose to define transformation functions, $f_1, f_2, \ldots, f_p$, on the attributes in R_i and T_j so that:

$$f_p : A_{p1} \times A_{p2} \times \cdots \times A_{pr_p} \rightarrow A'_p , p = 1, 2, \ldots , P$$

where $r_p \geq 1$

and $$A_{pu} \in \left(\bigcup_{i=1}^{I} \mathcal{A}_{R_i} \right) \cup \left(\bigcup_{j=1}^{J} \mathcal{A}_{T_j} \right), u = 1, 2, \ldots, r_p$$

Examples of these functions are *total*, *average*, or *count*, etc. Given these functions, we can construct a *transformed relation* R' that contains both original attributes in R_i and T_j and transformed attributes obtained by applying appropriate transformation functions. Let R' be composed of attributes $A'_1, A'_2, \ldots, A'_n$, that is, $R' \subseteq dom(A'_1) \times dom(A'_2) \times \cdots \times dom(A'_n)$ where A'_u, $u = 1, 2, \ldots, n$ can be any attribute in R_i, $i = 1, 2, \ldots, I$, or T_j, $j = 1, 2, \ldots, J$, or any transformed attribute. In other words, $A'_u \in \left(\bigcup_{i=1}^{I} \mathcal{A}_{R_i} \right) \cup \left(\bigcup_{j=1}^{J} \mathcal{A}_{T_j} \right) \cup \left(\bigcup_{p=1}^{P} f_p(A_{p1}, \ldots, A_{pr_p}) \right)$. Instead of performing data mining on the original R_i and T_j, we can now perform data mining on R'.

2.2 Linguistic Terms

Given the transformed relation, R', let us denote the set of attributes each record in R' contains be $\mathcal{I} = \{I_1, I_2, \ldots, I_n\}$, where I_v, $v = 1, 2, \ldots, n$ can be quantitative or categorical. For any record, $d \in R'$, $d[I_v]$ denotes the value i_v in d for attribute I_v. For any quantitative attribute, $I_v \in \mathcal{I}$, let $dom(I_v) = [l_v, u_v] \subseteq \Re$ denote the domain of the attribute Based on the fuzzy set theory, a set of linguistic terms can be defined over the domain of each quantitative attribute. Let us therefore denote the linguistic terms associated with some quantitative attribute, $I_v \in \mathcal{I}$ as $\mathcal{L}_{vr}$, $r = 1, 2, \ldots, s_v$ so that a corresponding fuzzy set, L_{vr}, can be defined for each $\mathcal{L}_{vr}$. The membership function of the fuzzy set is denoted as $\mu_{L_{vr}}$ and is defined as:

$$\mu_{L_{vr}} : dom(I_v) \rightarrow [0, 1]$$

The fuzzy sets L_{vr}, $r = 1, 2, \ldots, s_v$, are then defined as

$$L_{vr} = \begin{cases} \sum_{dom(I_v)} \dfrac{\mu_{L_{vr}}(i_v)}{i_v} & \text{if } I_v \text{ is discrete} \\ \int_{dom(I_v)} \dfrac{\mu_{L_{vr}}(i_v)}{i_v} & \text{if } I_v \text{ is continuous} \end{cases}$$

for all $i_v \in dom\ (I_v)$. The degree of membership of some value $i_v \in dom(I_v)$ with some linguistic term $\mathcal{L}_{vr}$ is given by $\mu_{L_{vr}}(i_v)$.

Note that $I_v \in \mathcal{I}$ can also be categorical and crisp. In such case, let $dom(I_v) = \{ i_{v1}, i_{v2}, ..., i_{vm_v} \}$ denote the domain of I_v. In order to handle categorical and quantitative attributes in a uniform manner, we can also define a set of linguistic terms, $\mathcal{L}_{vr}$, $r = 1, 2, \ldots, m_v$, for each categorical attribute, $I_v \in \mathcal{I}$, where $\mathcal{L}_{vr}$ is represented by a fuzzy set, L_{vr}, such that

$$L_{vr} = \frac{1}{i_{vr}}$$

Using the above technique, we can represent the original attributes, $\mathcal{I}$, using a set of linguistic terms, $\mathcal{L} = \{\mathcal{L}_{vr} \mid v = 1, 2, \ldots, n, r = 1, 2, \ldots, s_v\}$ where $s_v = m_v$ for categorical attributes. Since each linguistic term is represented by a fuzzy set, we have a set of fuzzy sets, $L = \{L_{vr} \mid v = 1, 2, \ldots, n, r = 1, 2, \ldots, s_v\}$. Given a record, $d \in R'$, and a linguistic term, $\mathcal{L}_{vr} \in \mathcal{L}$, which is, in turn, represented by a fuzzy set, $L_{vr} \in L$, the degree of membership of the values in d with respect to L_{vr} is given by $\mu_{L_{vr}}(d[I_v])$. In other words, d is characterized by the term $\mathcal{L}_{vr}$ to the degree $\mu_{L_{vr}}(d[I_v])$. If $\mu_{L_{vr}}(d[I_v]) = 1$, d is completely characterized by the term $\mathcal{L}_{vr}$. If $\mu_{L_{vr}}(d[I_v]) = 0$, d is not characterized by the term $\mathcal{L}_{vr}$ at all. If $0 < \mu_{L_{vr}}(d[I_v]) < 1$, d is partially characterized by the term $\mathcal{L}_{vr}$.

Realistically, d can also be characterized by more than one linguistic term. Let φ be a subset of integers such that $\varphi = \{v_1, v_2, \ldots, v_m\}$ where $v_1, v_2, \ldots, v_m \in \{1, 2, \ldots, n\}$, $v_1 \neq v_2 \neq \ldots \neq v_m$ and $|\varphi| = h \geq 1$. We further suppose that $\mathcal{I}_\varphi$ be a subset of $\mathcal{I}$ such that $\mathcal{I}_\varphi = \{I_v \mid v \in \varphi\}$. Given any $\mathcal{I}_\varphi$, it is associated with a set of linguistic terms, $\mathcal{L}_{\varphi r}$, $r = 1, 2, \ldots, s_\varphi$ where $s_\varphi = \prod_{v \in \varphi} s_v$. Each $\mathcal{L}_{\varphi r}$ is defined by a set of linguistic terms, $\mathcal{L}_{v_1 r_1}, \mathcal{L}_{v_2 r_2}, \ldots, \mathcal{L}_{v_m r_m} \in \mathcal{L}$. The degree, $\lambda_{\mathcal{L}_{\varphi r}}(d)$, to which d is characterized by the term $\mathcal{L}_{\varphi r}$ is defined as

$$\lambda_{\mathcal{L}_{\varphi r}}(d) = \min(\mu_{L_{v_1 r_1}}(d[I_{v_1}]), \mu_{L_{v_2 r_2}}(d[I_{v_2}]), \ldots, \mu_{L_{v_m r_m}}(d[I_{v_m}])$$

Based on the linguistic terms, we can apply Fuzzy Miner to discover fuzzy association rules in fuzzy data and present them to human users in a way that is much easier understood. Due to the use of fuzzy techniques blurring the boundaries of adjacent intervals of numeric qualities, Fuzzy Miner is resilient to such noise types as inaccuracies in physical measurements of real-life entities.

2.3 Handling Fuzzy Data

The transformed relation R' can be represented by a set of fuzzy data, $\mathcal{F}$, which is characterized by a set of linguistic attributes, $\mathcal{L} = \{\mathcal{L}_1, \mathcal{L}_2, \ldots, \mathcal{L}_n\}$. For any linguistic attribute, $\mathcal{L}_v \in \mathcal{L}$, the value of $\mathcal{L}_v$ in a record, $t \in \mathcal{F}$, is a set of ordered pairs such that

$$t[\mathcal{L}_v] = \{(\mathcal{L}_{v1}, \mu_{v1}), (\mathcal{L}_{v2}, \mu_{v2}), \ldots, (\mathcal{L}_{vs_v}, \mu_{vs_v})\}$$

where $\mathcal{L}_{lk}$ and μ_{lk} , $k \in \{1, 2, \ldots, s_v\}$, are a linguistic term and its degree of membership respectively.

For any record, $t \in \mathcal{F}$, let $o_{\mathcal{L}_{pq}\mathcal{L}_{\varphi k}}(t)$ be the degree to which t is characterized by the linguistic terms $\mathcal{L}_{pq}$ and $\mathcal{L}_{\varphi k}$, $p \notin \varphi$. $o_{\mathcal{L}_{pq}\mathcal{L}_{\varphi k}}(t)$ is defined as

$$o_{\mathcal{L}_{pq}\mathcal{L}_{\varphi k}}(t) = \min(\mu_{pq}, \mu_{\varphi k}) \tag{1}$$

We further suppose that $deg_{\mathcal{L}_{pq}\mathcal{L}_{\varphi k}}$ is the sum of degrees to which records in $\mathcal{F}$ characterized by the linguistic terms $\mathcal{L}_{pq}$ and $\mathcal{L}_{\varphi k}$. $deg_{\mathcal{L}_{pq}\mathcal{L}_{\varphi k}}$ is given by

$$deg_{\mathcal{L}_{pq}\mathcal{L}_{\varphi k}} = \sum_{t \in \mathcal{F}} o_{\mathcal{L}_{pq}\mathcal{L}_{\varphi k}}(t) \tag{2}$$

3 The Fuzzy Miner in Details

3.1 The Fuzzy Mining Algorithm

A fuzzy association rule describes an interesting relationship between two or more linguistic terms. It can be of different orders. A first-order fuzzy association rule can be defined to be a fuzzy association rule involving one linguistic term in its antecedent; a second-order rule can be defined to have two; and a third-order rule can be defined to have three linguistic terms, etc. Given these definitions, the algorithm that Fuzzy Miner adopts to discover fuzzy association rules is given in Fig. 1 below.

1) R_1 = {first-order fuzzy association rules};
2) **for**($m = 2$; $|R_{m-1}| \geq minrules$; $m++$) **do**
3) **begin**
4) C = {each conjunct in the antecedent of $r \mid r \in R_{m-1}$};
5) **forall** φ composed of m elements in C **do**
6) **begin**
7) **forall** $t \in \mathcal{T}$ **do**
8) **forall** $(\mathcal{L}_{pq}, \mu_{pq}) \in t[\mathcal{L}_p], (\mathcal{L}_{\varphi k}, \mu_{\varphi k}) \in t[\mathcal{L}_\varphi], p \notin \varphi$ **do**
9) $deg_{\mathcal{L}_{pq}\mathcal{L}_{jk}} += \min(\mu_{pq}, \mu_{\varphi k})$;
10) **forall** $(\mathcal{L}_{pq}, \mu_{pq}) \in t[\mathcal{L}_p], (\mathcal{L}_{\varphi k}, \mu_{\varphi k}) \in t[\mathcal{L}_\varphi], p \notin \varphi$ **do**
11) **if** $interesting(\mathcal{L}_{pq}, \mathcal{L}_{\varphi k})$ **then**
12) $R_m = R_m \cup rulegen(\mathcal{L}_{pq}, \mathcal{L}_{\varphi k})$;
13) **end**
14) **end**
15) $\mathcal{R} = \bigcup_m R_m$

Fig. 1. Algorithm Fuzzy Miner.

To discover interesting first-order rules, Fuzzy Miner makes use of an objective interestingness measure introduced in Section 3.2 below. After these rules are discovered, they are stored in R_1 (Fig. 1). Rules in R_1 are then used to generate second-order rules that are then stored in R_2. R_2 is then used to generate third-order rules that are stored in R_3 and so on for 4th and higher order. Fuzzy Miner iterates, using the A Priori algorithm as described in [1], until the number of rules in R_m is less than a user-specified threshold *minrules*.

The function, *interesting*($\mathcal{L}_{pq}$, $\mathcal{L}_{\varphi k}$), computes an objective measure to determine whether the association between $\mathcal{L}_{pq}$ and $\mathcal{L}_{\varphi k}$ is interesting. If *interesting*($\mathcal{L}_{pq}$, $\mathcal{L}_{\varphi k}$) returns true, a fuzzy association rule is then generated by the *rulegen* function. For each rule generated, this function also returns an uncertainty measure associated with the rule (see Section 3.3). All fuzzy association rules generated by *rulegen* are stored in $\mathcal{R}$ that will then be used later for inference or for the users to examine.

3.2 Discovering Interesting Associations in Fuzzy Data

In order to decide whether the association between a linguistic term, $\mathcal{L}_{\varphi k}$, and another linguistic term, L_{pq}, is interesting, we determine whether

$$\Pr(\mathcal{L}_{pq} \mid \mathcal{L}_{\varphi k}) = \frac{\text{sum of degrees to which objects characterized by } \mathcal{L}_{pq} \text{ and } \mathcal{L}_{\varphi k}}{\text{sum of degrees to which object characterized by } \mathcal{L}_{\varphi k}} \tag{3}$$

is significantly different from

$$\Pr(\mathcal{L}_{pq}) = \frac{\text{sum of degrees to which objects characterized by } \mathcal{L}_{pq}}{M} \tag{4}$$

where $M = \sum_{u=1}^{s_p} \sum_{i=1}^{s_\varphi} deg_{\mathcal{L}_{pu}\mathcal{L}_{\varphi i}}$. If this is the case, we consider the association between $L_{\varphi k}$ and L_{pq} interesting.

The significance of the difference can be objectively evaluated based on the idea of an *adjusted residual* defined as [2-5]:

$$d_{\mathcal{L}_{pq}\mathcal{L}_{\varphi k}} = \frac{z_{\mathcal{L}_{pq}\mathcal{L}_{\varphi k}}}{\sqrt{\gamma_{\mathcal{L}_{pq}\mathcal{L}_{\varphi k}}}} \tag{5}$$

where $z_{\mathcal{L}_{pq}\mathcal{L}_{\varphi k}}$ is the *standardized residual* [2-5] and is given by

$$z_{\mathcal{L}_{pq}\mathcal{L}_{\varphi k}} = \frac{deg_{\mathcal{L}_{pq}\mathcal{L}_{\varphi k}} - e_{\mathcal{L}_{pq}\mathcal{L}_{\varphi k}}}{\sqrt{e_{\mathcal{L}_{pq}\mathcal{L}_{\varphi k}}}} \tag{6}$$

where $e_{\mathcal{L}_{pq}\mathcal{L}_{\varphi k}}$ is the sum of degrees to which records are expected to be characterized by $\mathcal{L}_{pq}$ and $\mathcal{L}_{\varphi k}$. It is defined as

$$e_{\mathcal{L}_{pq}\mathcal{L}_{\varphi k}} = \frac{\sum_{i=1}^{s_\varphi} deg_{\mathcal{L}_{pq}\mathcal{L}_{\varphi i}} \sum_{i=1}^{s_p} deg_{\mathcal{L}_{pi}\mathcal{L}_{\varphi k}}}{M} \tag{7}$$

and $\gamma_{\mathcal{L}_{pq}\mathcal{L}_{\varphi k}}$ is the *maximum likelihood estimate* [2-5] of the variance of $z_{\mathcal{L}_{pq}\mathcal{L}_{\varphi k}}$ and is given by

$$\gamma_{\mathcal{L}_{pq}\mathcal{L}_{\varphi k}} = \left(1 - \frac{\sum_{i=1}^{s_\varphi} deg_{\mathcal{L}_{pq}\mathcal{L}_{\varphi i}}}{M}\right)\left(1 - \frac{\sum_{i=1}^{s_p} deg_{\mathcal{L}_{pi}\mathcal{L}_{\varphi k}}}{M}\right) \tag{8}$$

If $|d_{\mathcal{L}_{pq}\mathcal{L}_{\varphi k}}| > 1.96$ (the 95 percentiles of the normal distribution), we can conclude that the discrepancy between Pr ($\mathcal{L}_{pq} \mid \mathcal{L}_{\varphi k}$) and Pr ($\mathcal{L}_{pq}$) is significantly different and hence the association between $\mathcal{L}_{\varphi k}$ and $\mathcal{L}_{pq}$ is interesting. If $d_{\mathcal{L}_{pq}\mathcal{L}_{\varphi k}} > +1.96$, the presence of $\mathcal{L}_{\varphi k}$ implies the presence of $\mathcal{L}_{pq}$. In other words, it is more *likely* for a record having both $\mathcal{L}_{\varphi k}$ and $\mathcal{L}_{pq}$. We say that $\mathcal{L}_{\varphi k}$ is *positively* associated with $\mathcal{L}_{pq}$. If $d_{\mathcal{L}_{pq}\mathcal{L}_{\varphi k}} < -1.96$, the absence of $\mathcal{L}_{\varphi k}$ implies the presence of $\mathcal{L}_{pq}$. In other words, it is more *unlikely* for a record having $\mathcal{L}_{\varphi k}$ and $\mathcal{L}_{pq}$ at the same time. We say that $\mathcal{L}_{\varphi k}$ is *negatively* associated with $\mathcal{L}_{pq}$.

3.3 Uncertainty Representation

Given that a linguistic term $\mathcal{L}_{\varphi k}$ is positively or negatively associated with another linguistic term $\mathcal{L}_{pq}$, we can form the following fuzzy association rule.

$$\mathcal{L}_{\varphi k} \Rightarrow \mathcal{L}_{pq}\ [w_{\mathcal{L}_{pq}\mathcal{L}_{\varphi k}}; s_{\mathcal{L}_{pq}\mathcal{L}_{\varphi k}}; c_{\mathcal{L}_{pq}\mathcal{L}_{\varphi k}}]$$

where $s_{\mathcal{L}_{pq}\mathcal{L}_{\varphi k}} = \Pr(\mathcal{L}_{\varphi k} \cup \mathcal{L}_{pq})$ and $c_{L_{pq}L_{\varphi k}} = \Pr(L_{pq} \mid L_{\varphi k})$ is the support and confidence of the rule, respectively. As for $w_{\mathcal{L}_{pq}\mathcal{L}_{\varphi k}}$, it is a *weight of evidence* measure that is defined as follows.

Since the association between $\mathcal{L}_{\varphi k}$ and $\mathcal{L}_{pq}$ is interesting, there is some evidence for or against a record to be characterized by $\mathcal{L}_{pq}$, given it has $\mathcal{L}_{\varphi k}$. The weight of evidence measure is defined in terms of an information theoretic measure known as *mutual information*. Mutual information measures the change of uncertainty about the presence of $\mathcal{L}_{pq}$ in a record given that it has $\mathcal{L}_{\varphi k}$ is and in turn defined as

$$I(\mathcal{L}_{pq} : \mathcal{L}_{\varphi k}) = \log \frac{\Pr(\mathcal{L}_{pq} \mid \mathcal{L}_{\varphi k})}{\Pr(\mathcal{L}_{pq})} \tag{9}$$

Based on mutual information, the weight of evidence measure is defined in [3-8] as

$$\begin{aligned} w_{\mathcal{L}_{pq}\mathcal{L}_{\varphi k}} &= I(\mathcal{L}_{pq} : \mathcal{L}_{\varphi k}) - I\Big(\bigcup_{i \neq q} (\mathcal{L}_{pi} : \mathcal{L}_{\varphi k})\Big) \\ &= \log \frac{\Pr(\mathcal{L}_{\varphi k} \mid \mathcal{L}_{pq})}{\Pr(\mathcal{L}_{\varphi k} \mid \bigcup_{i \neq q} \mathcal{L}_{pi})} \end{aligned} \tag{10}$$

$w_{\mathcal{L}_{pq}\mathcal{L}_{\varphi k}}$ can be interpreted intuitively as a measure of the difference in the gain in information when a record with $\mathcal{L}_{\varphi k}$ characterized by $\mathcal{L}_{pq}$ and when characterized by $\mathcal{L}_{pi}$, $i \neq q$. The weight of evidence is positive if $\mathcal{L}_{\varphi k}$ is positively associated with $\mathcal{L}_{pq}$ whereas the weight of evidence is negative if $\mathcal{L}_{\varphi k}$ is negatively associated with $\mathcal{L}_{pq}$. The weight of evidence measure can be used to weigh the significance or importance of fuzzy association rules.

Given that $\mathcal{L}_{\varphi k}$ is defined by a set of linguistic terms, $\mathcal{L}_{v_1 r_1}, \mathcal{L}_{v_2 r_2}, \ldots, \mathcal{L}_{v_m r_m} \in \mathcal{L}$, we have a high-order fuzzy association rule as follows:

$$\mathcal{L}_{v_1 r_1} \wedge \mathcal{L}_{v_2 r_2} \wedge \ldots \wedge \mathcal{L}_{v_m r_m} \Rightarrow \mathcal{L}_{pq}[\, w_{\mathcal{L}_{pq}\mathcal{L}_{\varphi k}}; s_{\mathcal{L}_{pq}\mathcal{L}_{\varphi k}}; c_{\mathcal{L}_{pq}\mathcal{L}_{\varphi k}} \,]$$

where $v_1, v_2, \ldots, v_m \in \varphi$.

4 Mining Data in A Personal Communication System

4.1 The Relational and Transactional Data

The Fuzzy Miner has been successfully applied to several different real applications. In particular, it was used to mine a database of a personal communication system owned by a telecom company in Malaysia. The database contains both relational and transactional data. For the relational data, over 30,000 customer records that were stored in 200 relational tables each contains 20 to 250 attributes were used. For the transactional data, over one million telephone call records, collected over a two-month period, were selected. These call records are of different structures and are characterized by 17 to 24 different attributes depending on the origin and destination of the call (e.g. whether or not it is from a mobile phone to another mobile phone) and whether or not connection can be established, etc. Among the different types of data used for the data mining tasks, some were concerned about usage, some about the background of the customers, some about marketing and sales, etc. Table 1 shows some of the attributes used.

Table 1. Some of the attributes in the PCS database.

Attribute	Type	Description
TID	Code/ID	Transaction Identifier
CALL_NUM	Phone No.	Call No.
CUST_ID	Code/ID	Customer ID No.
S_DATE	Date	Date of the call starts
E_DATE	Date	Date of the call ends
START_TIME	Time	Time the call starts
END_TIME	Time	Time the call ends
BSC	Code/ID	BSC No.
BTS	Code/ID	BTS No. of BSC
CELL	Code/ID	Cell No.
CHANNEL	Code/ID	Channel No.
LOST	Categories/Types	Whether the call is lost
SUCCESS	Categories/Types	Whether the call is successful

(a) Some of the attributes, which are concerned with usage.

Table 1 (continued). Some of the attributes in the PCS database.

Attribute	Type	Description
CUST_ID	Code/ID	Customer ID No.
CUST_NAME	Name	Customer name
SEX	Categories/Types	Sex
M_STATUS	Categories/Types	Marital status
DATE_BIRTH	Date	Date of birth
NATIONALITY	Categories/Types	Nationality
TEL_NO	Phone No.	Tel. No.
ADDRESS	Address	Address
CO_NAME	Name	Company name
CO_TEL_NO	Phone No.	Company Tel. No.
CO_ADDRESS	Address	Company address
DATE_USE	Date	Date becoming customer
PRICE_PLAN	Categories/Types	Price Plan No.
ED_LEVEL	Categories/Types	Education level
SALARY	Quantity/Amount	Monthly salary
JOB_FCT	Categories/Types	Job function of customer
CO_BUSS	Categories/Types	Primary business of company
NO_OF_EMP	Quantity/Amount	No. of employees of company

(b) Some of the attributes that are concerned about the customers.

Attribute	Classification	Description
CUST_ID	Code/ID	Customer ID No.
APP_INF	Categories/Types	Influence of using the service
AP_FR	Categories/Types	The way the customer apply from

(c) Some of the attributes that are concerned with marketing and sales.

4.2 The Transformation

To discover such interesting rules as how the background of a customer affects his/her calling patterns, it should be noted that the direct application of data mining techniques to the universal relation of the PCS database will result in some interesting rules being neglected. For instance, the rule "customers whose job function is sales and the primary business of their companies is advertising / PR / marketing make more than 80 phone calls per day during the working days" cannot be discovered. In order to discover such rules, we applied different transformation functions to some of the data before the actual data mining tasks. Specifically, we created a number of new attributes and a new relation. The relation is constructed by summarizing the attributes related to usage and then joining the transformed usage table containing the attributes related to usage with the tables relating to customer background and marketing and sales. Consequently, there is a record for each customer in the transformed relation. This relation aims at discovering knowledge of how the background of customers affects their usage of phone services. An example of the rules discovered is "students joined price plan 1 make twice as many long-duration phone calls during Christmas holidays". Table 2 gives a list of some of the transformed attributes and relations. Fig. 2 and 3 gives two of the fuzzy attributes used in the data mining tasks. They are derived from two different quantitative attributes, time-of-call-origination and duration-of-call respectively.

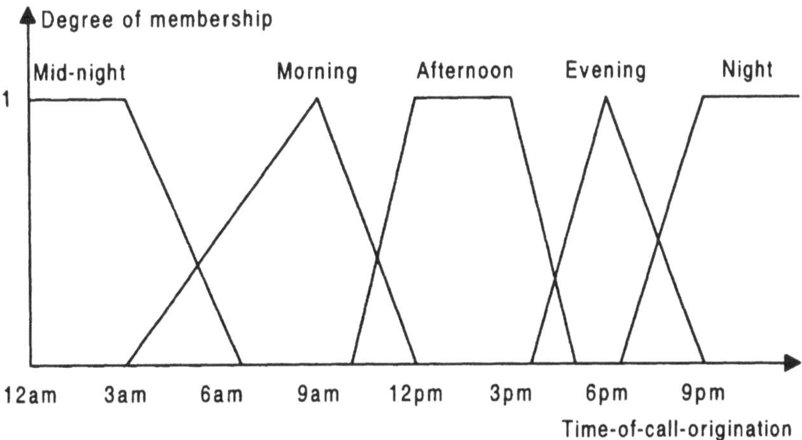

Fig. 2. Definition of linguistic terms for the attribute *Time-of-call-origination*.

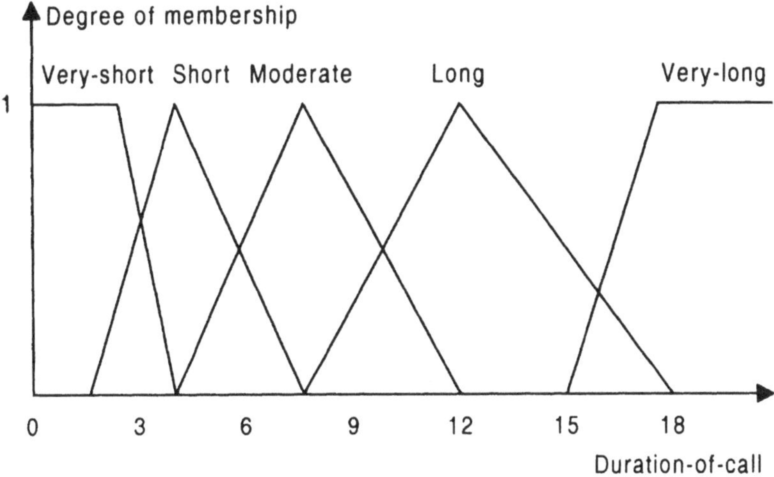

Fig. 3. Definition of linguistic terms for attribute *Duration-of-call*.

Table 2. The transformed attributes and relations

Attribute	Description
SEX	Sex
M_STATUS	Marital status
AGE	Age
DISTRICT	District
CO_DISTRICT	Company district
ED_LEVEL	Education level
SALARY	Monthly salary
JOB_FCT	Job function
CO_BUSS	Primary business of company
NO_OF_EMP	No. of employees of company
PRICE_PLAN	Price Plan No.
NUM_CALLS	Average no. of calls per day
DURATION	Average call duration
APP_INF	Influence of using the service
AP_FR	The way the customer apply from
N_CALL_P11	Average no. of calls in weekdays per day
N_CALL_P12	Average no. of calls in weekends per day
D_CALL_P11	Average call duration in weekdays
D_CALL_P12	Average call duration in weekends
N_CALL_P21	Average no. of calls in working days per day
N_CALL_P22	Average no. of calls in Christmas per day
N_CALL_P23	Average no. of calls in New Year per day
N_CALL_P24	Average no. of calls in Easter per day
N_CALL_P25	Average no. of calls in other public holidays per day
D_CALL_P21	Average call duration in working days
D_CALL_P22	Average call duration in Christmas
D_CALL_P23	Average call duration in New Year
D_CALL_P24	Average call duration in Easter
D_CALL_P25	Average call duration in other public holidays
N_CALL_TP11	Average no. of calls in morning per day
N_CALL_TP12	Average no. of calls in afternoon per day
N_CALL_TP13	Average no. of calls in evening per day
D_CALL_TP11	Average call duration in morning
D_CALL_TP12	Average call duration in afternoon
D_CALL_TP13	Average call duration in evening
N_CALL_TP21	Average no. of calls in busy hours per day
N_CALL_TP22	Average no of calls in normal hours per day
D_CALL_TP21	Average call duration in busy hours

Table 2. The transformed attributes and relations (continued).

Attribute	Description
D_CALL_TP22	Average call duration in normal hours
N_CALL_TP31	Average no. of calls in period with discounted charge per day
N_CALL_TP32	Average no. of calls in period with normal charge per day
D_CALL_TP31	Average call duration in period with discounted charge
D_CALL_TP32	Average call duration in period with normal charge

4.3 Evaluation of Effectiveness

After data transformation, Fuzzy Miner is applied to the PCS database that contains also the transformed data. The fuzzy association rules discovered from the PCS database are found to be very useful to senior management of the company for customer profiling and market segmentation. They have had some significant impact on their marketing efforts. To objectively evaluate the performance of the Fuzzy Miner, we have developed an evaluation scheme described in the following. The performance of Fuzzy Miner has been shown to be very satisfactory.

Using the fuzzy association rules discovered, Fuzzy Miner is able to predict the values of some of the attributes of records not in the original database. These predictions can be quantitative or categorical depending on the nature of the attributes being considered. Unlike typical predictive data mining techniques, which predict discrete non-overlapping class labels, Fuzzy Miner allows quantitative values to be inferred from fuzzy association rules.

Given a record, $t \in dom\ (I_1) \times \cdots \times dom\ (I_p) \times \cdots \times dom\ (I_n)$, let t be characterized by n attribute values, $\alpha_1, \ldots, \alpha_p, \ldots, \alpha_n$, where α_p is the value to be predicted. Let $\mathcal{L}_p$, $p = 1, 2, \ldots, s_p$, be the linguistic terms corresponding to the class attribute, I_p. We further let l_p be a linguistic term with domain $dom\,(l_p) = \{\mathcal{L}_{p1}, \mathcal{L}_{p2}, \ldots, \mathcal{L}_{ps_p}\}$.

The value of α_p is assigned according to the value of l_p. To predict the correct value of l_p, Fuzzy Miner searches the association rules with $\mathcal{L}_{pq} \in dom(l_p)$ as consequent. If some attribute value, say α_j, $j \neq p$, of t, is characterized by the linguistic term in the antecedent of a rule which implies $\mathcal{L}_{pq}$, it can be considered as providing some evidence for or against the value of l_p being assigned to $\mathcal{L}_{pq}$. By repeating this procedure, that is, by matching each attribute value of t against the rules, Fuzzy Miner can determine the value of l_p by computing the total weight of evidence measure.

Since each of the attributes of t may or may not provide evidence, and for those that do, they may support the assignment of different values, the different pieces of evidence are quantitatively measured and combined for comparison in order to find the most suitable value of l_p. For any combination of attribute values, α_φ, $p \notin \varphi$, of t, it is characterized by a linguistic term, $\mathcal{L}_{\varphi k}$, to a degree of compatibility, $\mu_{\mathcal{L}_{\varphi k}}(t)$, for each $k \in \{1, 2, \ldots, s_\varphi\}$. Given those rules implying the assignment of $\mathcal{L}_{pq}$, $\mathcal{L}_{\varphi k} \Rightarrow \mathcal{L}_{pq}\,[w_{\mathcal{L}_{pq}\mathcal{L}_{\varphi k}}; s_{\mathcal{L}_{pq}\mathcal{L}_{\varphi k}}; c_{\mathcal{L}_{pq}\mathcal{L}_{\varphi k}}]$, for all $k \in \zeta \subseteq \{1, 2, \ldots, s_\varphi\}$, the evidence provided by α_φ for or against such assignment is given by

$$w_{\mathcal{L}_{pq}\alpha_\varphi} = \sum_{k \in \zeta} w_{\mathcal{L}_{pq}\mathcal{L}_{\varphi k}} \cdot \mu_{\mathcal{L}_{\varphi k}}(t) \tag{11}$$

Suppose that, of the $n - 1$ attribute values excluding α_p, only some combinations of them, $\alpha_{[1]}, \ldots, \alpha_{[j]}, \ldots, \alpha_{[\beta]}$ with $\alpha_{[j]} = \{\alpha_i \mid i \in \{1, 2, \ldots, n\} - \{p\}\}$, are found to match one or more rules, then the overall weight of evidence for or against the value of l_p to be assigned to $\mathcal{L}_{pq}$ is given by

$$w_q = \sum_{j=1}^{\beta} w_{\mathcal{L}_{pq}\alpha_{[j]}} \tag{12}$$

In case that l_p is categorical, l_p is assigned to $\mathcal{L}_{pc}$ if

$$w_c > w_g,\ g = 1, 2, \ldots, s'_p \text{ and } g \neq c \tag{13}$$

where s'_p ($\leq s_p$) denotes the number of linguistic terms implied by the rules. α_p is therefore assigned to $i_{pc} \in dom\,(l_p)$.

If l_p is quantitative, a novel method is used to assign an appropriate value to α_p. Given the linguistic terms, $\mathcal{L}_{p1}, \mathcal{L}_{p2}, \ldots, \mathcal{L}_{ps_p}$, and their overall weights of evidence, $w_1, w_2, \ldots, w_{s_p}$, let $\mu'_{L_{pu}}(i_p)$ be the weighted degree of membership of $i_p \in dom\,(l_p)$ to the fuzzy set L_{pu}, $u \in \{1, 2, \ldots, s_p\}$. $\mu'_{L_{pu}}(i_p)$ is given by

$$\mu'_{L_{pu}}(i_p) = w_u \cdot \mu_{L_{pu}}(i_p) \tag{14}$$

where $i_p \in dom(I_p)$ and $u = 1, 2, \ldots, s_p$. The defuzzified value, $F^{-1}(\bigcup_{u=1}^{s_p} L_{pu})$, is then defined by

$$F^{-1}(\bigcup_{u=1}^{s_p} L_{pu}) = \frac{\int_{dom(I_p)} \mu'_{L_{p1} \cup L_{p2} \cup \cdots \cup L_{ps_p}}(i_p) \cdot i_p \, di_p}{\int_{dom(I_p)} \mu'_{L_{p1} \cup L_{p2} \cup \cdots \cup L_{ps_p}}(i_p) \, di_p} \tag{15}$$

where $\mu'_{X \cup Y}(i) = \max(\mu'_X(i), \mu'_Y(i))$ for any fuzzy sets X and Y. This defuzzified value, $F^{-1}(\bigcup_{u=1}^{s_p} L_{pu})$, provides an appropriate value for α_p.

For quantitative predictions, we use the *root-mean-squared error* as a performance measure. Given a set of testing records, $\mathcal{T}$, let n be number of records in $\mathcal{T}$. For any record, $r \in \mathcal{T}$, let $[\, l, u \,] \subset \Re$ denote the domain of the class attribute. We further let t_r be the target value of the class attribute in r and o_r be the predicted value given by Fuzzy Miner. The root - mean - squared error, *rms*, is defined as

$$rms = \sqrt{\frac{1}{n} \sum_{r \in \mathcal{T}} \left(\frac{t_r - l}{u - l} - \frac{o_r - l}{u - l} \right)^2} \tag{16}$$

5 Summary

In summary, we have introduced the Fuzzy Miner for the mining of fuzzy association rules in a database containing both transactional and relational data. Fuzzy Miner performs its tasks by first applying different types of transformation to the data in the database. The types of transformation include also fuzzification of some of the attributes. After transformation, data mining is then performed on the original and transformed data using the ideas of residual analysis. With these characteristics, Fuzzy Miner is able to discover fuzzy association rules that relate fuzzy transactional and relational data. Its ability to handle fuzzy data makes Fuzzy Miner more resilient to noise and its ability to handle linguistic terms in the rules makes them more easily understood. The use of an objective interestingness measure by Fuzzy Miner also makes it possible for it to avoid the use of some user-supplied thresholds, which are often difficult to determine. In addition to these, Fuzzy Miner is able to discover both positive and negative associations. It is able to differentiate between more relevant and important attribute values using a weight-of-evidence measure. Another unique feature about Fuzzy Miner is that it provides a way to allow quantitative values to be inferred from fuzzy association rules so that interesting associations between different quantitative values can be revealed without the need to perform discretization. Fuzzy Miner has been applied to in different real applications and the results were found to be very satisfactory.

References

[1] R. Agrawal, T. Imielinski, and A. Swami, "Mining Association Rules between Sets of Items in Large Databases," in *Proc. of the ACM SIGMOD Int'l Conf. on Management of Data*, Washington D. C., May 1993, pp. 207-216.

[2] W.-H. Au and K.C.C. Chan, "An Effective Algorithm for Discovering Fuzzy Rules in Relational Databases," in *Proc. of the 1998 IEEE Int'l Conf. on Fuzzy Systems*, Anchorage, Alaska, May 1998, pp. 1314-1319.

[3] W.-H. Au and K.C.C. Chan, "FARM: A Data Mining System for Discovering Fuzzy Association Rules," in *Proc. of the 1999 IEEE Int'l Conf. on Fuzzy Systems*, Seoul, Korea, Aug. 1999.

[4] K.C.C. Chan and W.-H. Au, "Mining Fuzzy Association Rules," in *Proc. of the 6th ACM Int'l Conf. on Information and Knowledge Management*, Las Vegas, Nevada, Nov. 1997, pp. 209-215.

[5] K.C.C. Chan and A.K.C. Wong, "APACS: A System for the Automatic Analysis and Classification of Conceptual Patterns," *Computational Intelligence*, vol. 6, pp. 119-131, 1990.

[6] M.-S. Chen, J. Han, and P.S. Yu, "Data Mining: An Overview from A Database Perspective," *IEEE Trans. on Knowledge and Data Engineering*, vol. 8, no. 6, pp. 866-883, Dec. 1996.

[7] V. Dhar and A. Tuzhilin, "Abstract-Driven Pattern Discovery in Databases," *IEEE Trans. Knowledge and Data Engineering*, vol. 5, no. 6, pp. 926-938, 1993.

[8] U.M. Fayyad, G. Piatetsky-Shapiro, P. Smyth, and R. Uthurusamy (Eds.), *Advances in Knowledge Discovery and Data Mining*, AAAI/MIT Press, 1996.

[9] J. Han and Y. Fu, "Discovery of Multiple-Level Association Rules from Large Databases," in *Proc. of the 21st VLDB Conf.*, Zurich, Switzerland, 1995, pp. 420-431.

[10] D.H. Lee and M.H. Kim, "Database Summarization Using Fuzzy ISA Hierarchies," *IEEE Trans. on Systems, Man, and Cybernetics – Part B: Cybernetics*, vol. 27, no. 4, pp. 671-680, Aug. 1997.

[11] W. Pedrycz, "Data Mining and Fuzzy Modeling," in *Proc. of 1996 Biennial Conf. of the North American Fuzzy Information Processing Society*, Berkeley, California, June 1996, pp. 263-267.

[12] G. Piatetsky-Shapiro and W.J. Frawley (Eds.), *Knowledge Discovery in Databases*, AAAI/MIT Press, 1991.

[13] R. Srikant and R. Agrawal, "Mining Generalized Association Rules," in *Proc. of the 21st VLDB Conf.*, Zurich, Switzerland, 1995, pp. 407-419.

[14] R. Srikant and R. Agrawal, "Mining Quantitative Association Rules in Large Relational Tables," in *Proc. of the ACM SIGMOD Int'l Conf. on Management of Data*, Monreal, Canada, June 1996, pp. 1-12.

[15] R.R. Yager, "On Linguistic Summaries of Data," in [12], pp. 347-363.

Fuzzy Linguistic Summaries via Association Rules

Janusz Kacprzyk and Sławomir Zadrożny

Systems Research Institute, Polish Academy of Sciences, 01-447 Warsaw, ul. Newelska 6, Poland. Email: {kacprzyk, zadrozny}@ibspan.waw.pl

Abstract. In this contribution, we discuss how a fuzzy querying interface can support the generation of linguistic database summaries - a special technique of data mining. Links between our approach to linguistic summaries and the well-known technique of association rules is shown. The generation of linguistic summaries is implemented by using the authors' FQUERY for Access package.

Keywords: fuzzy querying, linguistic terms, data mining, database summaries, association rules

1 Introduction

Modern database management systems (DBMS) provide efficient tools for transaction-oriented applications. Recently, more and more attention is paid to the development of database-related decision-making support tools. Large collections of data gathered either in "regular" databases, or in data warehouses call for some intelligent techniques to make a more efficient use of data. Approaches that are already well known include on-line analytical processing (OLAP) or data mining. The approach we advocate here refers to so-called *linguistic summaries of data*, as introduced by Yager [27] , exemplified by "*Most expensive real estate properties posses large land area*" (in case of a real estate database). Thus, briefly speaking summaries provide us with highly aggregated information on the data in question. The use of linguistic terms makes the summaries more *human consistent*, abstracting, at the same time, from unnecessarily detailed numerical presentation.

The point of departure here is our add-in to Microsoft Access DBMS that makes possible the use of flexible (fuzzy) queries, cf. Kacprzyk and Zadrożny [10-13,

16]. Such queries themselves offer some advantages for a decision maker in comparison to regular queries. Namely, the use of linguistic terms in queries provides for some form of information aggregation. Nevertheless, a further extension of the user interface towards data mining functionality seems to be worthwhile. Moreover, our design of a fuzzy querying interface inherently supports some features required for an efficient implementation of linguistic summaries due to Yager (see also Kacprzyk and Yager [7]). In our previous works (e.g., Kacprzyk, Yager and Zadrożny [8, 9]) we described a preliminary implementation of linguistic summaries within our FQUERY for Access package. So far, only a limited subset of possible types of summaries has been implemented. The most sophisticated form of the summary is computationally very difficult. Here we propose a way to implement its slightly simplified version using the concept of *association rules*.

The association rules were originally meant for binary data mining. A number of efficient algorithms have been devised to generate them. Moreover, the concept is easily extendable to more complex data, including real valued and scalar data as well as taxonomies of values. Our approach consists in adapting the rules discovery algorithm to linguistic terms so that we are able to set up either fuzzy querying or data mining on the same vocabulary of linguistic terms.

The organization of this paper is as follows. First we discuss the basics of our fuzzy querying concept and briefly describe the FQUERY for Access package. Then, we describe the linguistic summaries as proposed by Yager and introduce our classification of various types of summaries. Finally, we explain how linguistic summaries are implemented in the FQUERY for Access. We focus on the interrelations between linguistic summaries and association rules.

2 The Concept of Fuzzy Querying

The idea of fuzzy querying that we have adopted consists in a direct use of linguistic terms in queries. It is widely argued that for a human being natural language is a natural medium to form and express thoughts. Obviously, this also applies to a query that may be treated as a set of search criteria conceived by a user. Thus, a possibility to use elements of a natural language should make the querying of a database to be much more a comfortable experience for an average user. This is especially promising in case of a frequent use of a database by the same user. In such a situation a querying interface may learn more efficiently the dictionary of given user. It often happens that the same words mean something completely different for distinct humans. In case of one user and a rather limited universe of discourse, as defined by the subject of the database, one can expect a much more stable semantics of the user's dictionary.

Often the meaning of linguistic terms is vague. This implies that we have to adopt some special formal means to deal with them. Moreover, it would be unreasonable to require the answer for a vague query to be completely precise, adhering to the classical yes-no logic. Thus, instead of listing the crisp set of matching database rows, a fuzzy query against precise data yields a *fuzzy* set of such rows. Namely, each listed row is accompanied by its *matching degree* against the query.

In our approach, we employ fuzzy logic to represent the meaning of linguistic terms used in queries. The following types of linguistic terms are assumed:

- *numerical fuzzy values*, exemplified by *low* in "profitability is *low*",
- *scalar fuzzy values*, exemplified by *Central Europe* in "country is in *Central Europe*",
- *fuzzy relations*, exemplified by *much greater than* in "income is *much greater than* spending", and
- *linguistic quantifiers*, exemplified by *most* in "*most* conditions have to be met".

The first elements are straightforward while the fuzzy linguistic quantifiers are meant and handled as proposed by Zadeh [29, 30] in a calculus of linguistically quantified propositions.

Basically, the problem is to calculate the truth-value of a proposition like:

"Most elements of set X posses property S" (1)

that may be formally expressed as follows:

$$\underset{x \in X}{Q}\, S(x) \tag{2}$$

where Q denotes a fuzzy linguistic quantifier (e.g., "most"), $X = \{x_1, \ldots x_m\}$ is a universe of discourse, and $S(\cdot)$ is a property which is assumed fuzzy and its interpretation may be informally equated with a fuzzy set, i.e.:

$$\text{truth}\,(S(x_i)) = \mu_S(x_i)$$

In this calculus, propositions of the following type are also considered:

"Most elements of set X possessing property F posses also property S" (3)

that may be formally expressed as:

$$\underset{x \in X}{QF\,S}\,(x) \tag{4}$$

Property F is also here assumed fuzzy, and may be equated with a fuzzy set F, i.e.:

$$\text{truth}\,(F\,(x)\,) = \mu_F\,(x)$$

A linguistic quantifier is represented as a fuzzy set Q in [0, 1]. Informally, each number from this interval represents what fraction of the elements of the universe of discourse satisfies the proposition. Then, the membership function of a quantifier is defined so as to represent its semantics. For example, in case of "most", the higher the fraction the better, and this may be expressed by the membership function defined by (5) and sketched in Figure 1.

$$\mu_Q\,(y) = \begin{cases} 1 & \text{for } \ y \geq 0.8 \\ 2y - 0.6 & \text{for } \ 0.3 < y < 0.8 \\ 0 & \text{for } \ y \leq 0.3 \end{cases} \tag{5}$$

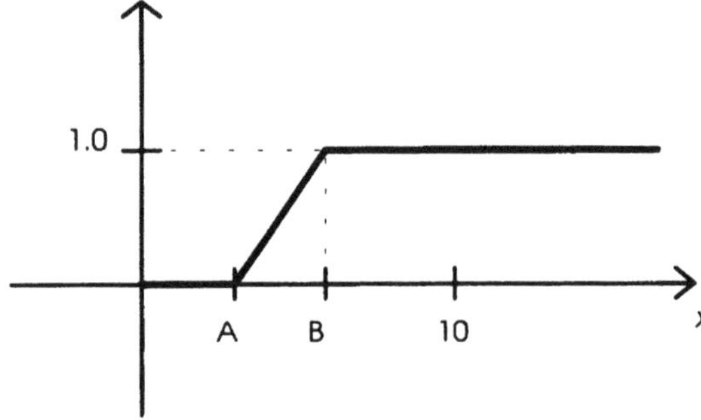

Figure 1. The membership function of the fuzzy linguistic quantifier "*most*"

In the context considered here, we are interested in monotonous quantifiers only exemplified by "most" and characterized by a monotonous membership function, μ_Q, assumed to be piece-wise linear, as in Figure 1.

The following formula is employed to determine the truth of proposition (2):

$$\text{truth}(QS(X)) = \mu_Q\left(\sum \text{Count}(S) / \sum \text{Count}(X)\right) = \mu_Q\left(\sum_{i=1}^{m} \mu_S(x_i) / m\right) \quad (6)$$

where m = card (X) and $\sum \text{Count}(A)$ refers to the cardinality of a fuzzy set A, given by:

$$\sum \text{Count}(A) = \sum_{x_i \in X} \mu_A(x_i)$$

In case of proposition (4) the following formula is employed:

$$\text{truth}(QFS(X)) = \mu_Q\left(\sum \text{Count}(S \cap F) \,/\, \sum \text{Count}(F)\right) =$$
$$= \mu_Q\left(\sum_{i=1}^{m} (\mu_S(x_i) \wedge \mu_F(x_i)) / \sum_{i=1}^{m} \mu_F(x_i)\right) \quad (7)$$

where, $\sum_{i=1}^{m} \mu_F(x_i) \neq 0$, and $\wedge$ is a t-norm (see, e.g. [26]).

For more information on fuzzy linguistic quantifiers in the context of database querying we refer the reader to the authors works, e.g., Kacprzyk and Zadrożny [10-15].

The above four elements are building blocks of fuzzy queries in our approach. All these linguistic terms, similarly to linguistic quantifiers, are represented as fuzzy sets. Scalar fuzzy values are for obvious reasons dedicated for specific attributes. For example, an imprecise term "*Central Europe*" is meaningful only in the context of attributes related to the country. Thus, "*Central Europe*" has to be defined as a fuzzy set in the (finite) space of all values of given attribute by, e.g., the following membership function:

1.0 / CzechRepublic + 1.0 / Hungary + 1.0 / Poland +

+ 1.0 / Slovakia + 0.8 / Austria + 0.6 / Ukraine + ...

On the other hand, in our approach *numerical fuzzy values* may be applicable for any numerical attribute, provided it is declared what is the range of values this attribute takes. These fuzzy values are defined as fuzzy sets on a universal interval [-10, +10] and are appropriately converted when used along with a given numerical attribute. This does not prevent the definitions of numerical fuzzy values specific for particular attributes.

Usually, a query consists of a number of simple conditions combined using the classical logical connectives AND and OR. In our approach, *linguistic quantifiers* provide for a more flexible aggregation scheme of simple conditions in queries. For example, instead of requiring that all simple conditions are to be met, using an appropriate linguistic quantifier one may indicate that *most* of them are to be met.

Before a linguistic term may be used in a query, it has to be defined and stored internally. The definition consists of a label of the term and a membership function of the associated fuzzy set. This feature, i.e. the maintenance of *dictionaries* of linguistic terms defined by users as well as predefined in the system, supports both fuzzy querying and data mining, to be discussed next.

This concludes a brief presentation of our concept of fuzzy querying. It has been implemented in our software, the FQUERY for Access package (cf. Kacprzyk and Zadrożny [10]). It is an add-in to Microsoft Access providing the user of this popular desktop database management system with fuzzy querying capabilities.

3 Data Mining through Linguistic Database Summaries

Data mining, also known as knowledge discovery in databases, deals with finding interesting patterns, dependencies, regularities etc. in bodies of data stored in databases. Yager [27] proposed to use linguistically quantified propositions to *summarize* the content of a database, i.e. to grasp characteristic features of analyzed data. Here we follow and extend this idea in the context of a fuzzy querying concept briefly presented in the previous section.

We start by restating the primary concepts of the calculus of linguistically quantified propositions in terms relevant for database summaries. Thus, (1) becomes:

"*Most rows match query S*" (8)

Similarly, (3) becomes:

"*Most rows meeting conditions F match query S*" (9)

The query is meant here as a collection of conditions on the values of attributes combined using some logical connectives (including linguistic quantifiers). These conditions may refer to various linguistic terms mentioned in the previous section. Effectively, a query S defines a fuzzy subset (fuzzy property) on the set of the rows, whereas the membership of them is determined by their matching degree with the query. Thus, (8) states that most of the rows posses a certain property defined by a query - possibly an interesting piece of knowledge about data. The more complex the query involved is, the less trivial the summary obtained. In large data sets it may relatively seldom happen that most of the rows satisfy a given non-trivial query. Then, a proposition of type (9) may be helpful. Namely, it states that a subset of rows satisfies conditions specified in a query. In the database terminology, F corresponds to a *filter* and (9) asserts that *most* rows passing through F match query S. Moreover, since the filter may be fuzzy, a row may pass through it to a degree from [0, 1]. As this is more general than (8), we will assume (9) as a basis for our further considerations.

In Yager's approach [27] the truth-value of a given linguistically quantified proposition of type (8) or (9) is a primary measure of quality of the obtained summary. Practically, such a basic quality indicator has to be supplemented with some measure of "interestingness" ("non-triviality", "unexpectedness", ...). In what follows, we will discuss different types of linguistic data summaries based on the general scheme given by (9). For other aspects, see Kacprzyk and Yager [7].

Thus, the generation of a linguistic summary consists in finding propositions of type (9) that have a high truth-value. Basically, a proposition sought consists of three elements: a fuzzy filter F (optional), a query S, and a linguistic quantifier Q. There are two limit cases, where we:

- do not assume anything about the form of any of these elements
- assume concrete forms of a fuzzy filter and query, and look only for a linguistic quantifier Q.

Obviously, in the first case the process of data summarization will be extremely time-consuming but may produce interesting results, not predictable by the user in any other way. In the second case the user somehow has to guess a good candidate formula for the summarization but the evaluation is fairly simple as it requires more or less only the same resources as the answering of a (fuzzy) query. Thus, the second case refers to the summarization known as *ad hoc queries*, extended with an automatic determination of a linguistic quantifier.

In-between these two extreme cases there are different types of summaries, with various assumptions on what is given and what is sought. In case of a linguistic quantifier the situation is simple: it may be given or sought. In case of a fuzzy filter F and a fuzzy query S, more possibilities exist. Basically, both F and S consist of simple conditions, each stating what *value* an *attribute* should take on, and connected using logical connectives. Here we assume that the query refers to the attributes from one, fixed table. Obviously, such a table may be prepared by joining several source tables before the summary is started. An automatic selection of tables to be considered by summaries seems to be very complicated. It would require some additional meta-data on data stored in a database and / or some user's intervention during the generation of a summary. Some useful meta-data comes from integrity constraints - typically identified during a relational database design and encoded within some system tables. Still, we assume here only one table of interest.

We will use the following notation to describe what is given or what is sought with respect to the fuzzy filter F and query S (below A stands for either F or S):

- A - all is given (or sought), i.e., attributes, values and the structure,
- A^{fc} - attributes and structure are given, but values are left out,
- A^{v} - denotes sought left out values referred to in the above notation, and
- A^{f} - only a set of attributes is given, the other elements are sought.

Using the above notation we may propose the following classification of the summaries:

Type	Given	Sought	Remarks
1	S	Q - sought	Simple summaries through ad-hoc queries
2	$S\ F$	Q - sought	Conditional summaries through ad-hoc queries
3	$Q\ S^{fc}$	S^{v}	Simple value oriented summaries
4	$Q\ S^{fc}\ F$	S^{v}	Conditional value oriented summaries
5	nothing	$S\ F\ Q$	General fuzzy rules

Thus, we distinguish five main types of data summarization. Type 1 may be easily produced by a simple extension of fuzzy querying as proposed and implemented in our FQUERY for Access package, see Section 6 for more details. Basically, the user has to construct a query - a candidate summary. Then, it has to be determined what is the fraction of the rows matching this query and what linguistic quantifier best denotes this fraction. The primary target of this type of summarization is certainly to propose such a query that a large proportion, e.g., *most*, of the rows satisfies it. On the other hand, it may be interesting to learn that only *few* rows satisfy some meaningful query. A Type 2 summary is a straight extension of Type 1 summaries by adding a fuzzy filter. As soon as a fuzzy querying engine deals with fuzzy filters, the computational complexity of this type of summaries is the same as for Type 1. For more on these types of summaries, see for instance [14], and [2] for a non-fuzzy approach.

The summaries of Type 3 require much more effort. A primary goal of this type of summary is to determine typical (exceptional) values of an attribute. In such a special case, query S consists of only one simple condition [built of the attribute whose typical (exceptional) value is sought], the ' = ' relational operator and a placeholder for the value sought. For example, using the following summary in a context of personal data:

Q = " *most* " and S = " age = ? " (" ? " denotes placeholder mentioned above)

we look for a typical value of the age of the employees.

Then, we try to find such a (possibly fuzzy) value that the query matches to a high degree Q of the rows. Depending on the category of the Q used as, e.g., *most* versus *few*, typical or exceptional values are sought, respectively. Some more considerations are required since in some cases all values may turn out to be exceptional and none to be typical. This type of summaries may be used with more complicated, regular queries but it may quickly become computationally infeasible (due to combinatorial explosion) and the interpretation of results becomes vague. A Type 4 summary may produce typical (exceptional) values for some, possibly fuzzy, subset of rows. From the computational point of view, the same remarks apply as for Type 1 versus Type 2 summaries.

A Type 5 summary represents the most general form considered here. In its full version it is to produce fuzzy rules describing dependencies between specific values of particular attributes. Here the use of the filter is essential, in contrast to the previous types where it was optional. The very meaning of a fuzzy rule obtained is that if a row meets the condition of a filter, then it also meets the condition of a query – this corresponds to a classical IF-THEN rule. For a general form of such a rule it is difficult to devise an effective and efficient generation algorithm. Full search may be acceptable only in case of restrictively limited sets of rule building blocks, i.e. attributes and their possible values. Here, some genetic algorithm based approaches are often employed [6]. In order to alleviate the computational complexity, additional assumptions may also be made. For example, some sets of relevant (interesting, promising, etc.) attributes for the query (S^f) and the filter (F^f) may be selected in advance. Some constraints may also be put on the structure of the query S and filter F (in terms of the number of logical connectives allowed). Another, important special case of Type 5 summaries refers to the situation where the query (S) is fixed and only the filter (F) and quantifier (Q) are sought, i.e. we look for causes of given data features. For example, we may set in a query that profitability of a venture is *high* and look for the characterization of ventures (rows) securing such a high profitability.

The summaries of Type 1 and 3 have been implemented as an extension to our FQUERY for Access - see Section 6 for more details.

In the next section we discuss in a more detailed way one more special case of Type 5 summary for which computationally efficient algorithms are known in the literature.

4 Association Rules and Fuzzy Summaries

The concept of data mining presented in the previous section features an attractive uniform theoretical background referring to the calculus of linguistically quantified propositions. This paves the way for a consistent use of linguistic terms in database summaries. Unfortunately, in the original Yager's version as well as in the previous section there are rather limited clues as to the devising of efficient algorithms generating summaries of large data sets. The simplest types of summaries are directly computationally tractable. Another general approach calls for the use of genetic algorithms [6]. Thus, in this section while looking for efficient algorithms we investigate the similarity of our Type 5 summaries to what is known in the literature as *association rules* [1].

Originally, the association rules were defined for binary valued attributes in the following form:

$$A_1 \wedge A_2 \wedge \ldots \wedge A_n \rightarrow A_{n+1} \tag{10}$$

Such an association rule states, that if in a database row all the attributes from the set $\{A_1, A_2, \ldots, A_n\}$ take on value 1, then also the attribute A_{n+1} is expected to take on value 1 (remember that all attributes are assumed to take on their values from the set $\{0, 1\}$).

A row in a database (table) is said to *support* a set of attributes $\{A_i\}_{i \in I}$ if all attributes from the set take on in this row value 1. There are two measures of the quality of an association rule used:

- the *support* of a rule (10) is the fraction of the number of rows supporting the set of attributes $\{A_i\}$, $i \in \{1,.., n + 1\}$ in a database (table), and
- the *confidence* of a rule in a database (table) is the fraction of the number of rows supporting the set of attributes $\{A_i\}$, $I \in \{1, ..., n + 1\}$ among all rows supporting the set of attributes $\{A_i\}$, $i \in \{1, ..., n\}$.

Thus, while the support determines a statistical significance of a rule, the confidence measures its strength in the database. Usually, we are interested in rules having values of the support measure above some minimal threshold and a high value of the confidence measure. This form of association rules was motivated by their early applications for a so-called customer's basket analysis.

A number of efficient algorithms for finding all association rules possessing a required support measure were devised, see e.g. [1, 18]. Due to that fact, the association rules have become a very popular tool for data mining. An original concept of the association rule essentially evolved over time but still the same algorithms are applicable. The extensions to the initial form of the association rule include:

- the right-hand side, like the left-hand side, may contain a conjunction of the attributes instead of just one attribute,
- many-valued scalar values and their hierarchies may be used in rules [22]
- numerical, real-valued attributes may be used in rules [23]
- some constraints may be imposed on combinations of attributes used in rules [24].

Let us verify how the concept of an association rule fits into our general format of summaries of Type 5 mentioned in the previous section.

The left-hand and right-hand sides correspond to the filter F and the query S, respectively. In our fuzzy querying framework of Section 3, a query may be composed of a set of simple conditions combined using the classical AND and OR logical connectives as well as linguistic quantifiers. Thus, the structure of the filter and the query available in case of association rules is rather limited but this simplicity secures the existence of efficient algorithms for the generation of rules.

The truth-value of the summary, defined by (7), corresponds to a confidence measure of a rule. Both definitions become identical when we assume a linguistic quantifier in (7) to be a so-called uniform quantifier characterized by the following membership function: $\mu(y) = y$, for each $y \in [0, 1]$.

Thus, in fact an association rule may be viewed as a special case of our Type 5 summary. The structure of the filter and the query is limited - only the conjunction of simple conditions is allowed - but the number of these conditions and the attributes involved are sought.

A fuzzy querying interface may offer practical ways to circumvent some problems the "classical" [1, 23, 24] search for the association rules faces. For example, when dealing with a numerical attribute, one has to partition its domain into a number of intervals. Then, treating each interval as an additional binary attribute, one can employ known algorithms for the generation of association rules. The question remains how to partition the domain. Srikant and Agrawal [23] advocate the partition into equal intervals but admit that in some cases this may fail. Miller and Yang [19] claim that cluster analysis should be used to determine a proper partition. In fact, they go even further by proposing an extension of the association rule concept in the following way. They suggest that it may be advantageous to group attributes provided the distance in corresponding multi-dimensional spaces may be defined in a meaningful way. Then, in a simple condition of a rule - instead of requiring that a numerical attribute lies in given interval - we may require that the values of a group of attributes lie in a cluster.

The use of numerical fuzzy values itself alleviates the problem of a proper partition of an attributes domain. The domain may be covered by a number of overlapping fuzzy values making the partitioning more flexible. Lee and Lee-Kwang [17] discuss the use of classical algorithms to produce association rules referring to fuzzy values. A fuzzy querying interface makes it even simpler as we have a dictionary of fuzzy values at hand, ready to be used in the rules. Moreover, these fuzzy values are familiar for the user as they were defined and tested by him or her in some fuzzy queries. Thus, the meaning of rules produced using such fuzzy values should be much more clear to the user. Context independence of numerical fuzzy values, mentioned in Section 3, is here of special importance as all these values may be used along with all attributes.

Data mining in the framework of a fuzzy querying interface has an additional benefit, since some software modules may be used for both tasks. The simplest summaries may be produced as a side effect of running a query - as it is briefly described in the next section.

5 Data Mining via FQUERY for Access

The concept of fuzzy querying presented in Section 2 has been implemented by the authors in the FQUERY for Access package. Thus, it extends the querying capabilities of Microsoft Access by making it possible to handle linguistic terms in the queries. This alone makes it an interesting tool for data mining. The simplest method of data mining through ad-hoc created queries becomes much more powerful by using linguistic terms. Nevertheless, the implementation of various types of summaries mentioned in Section 3 seems to be worthwhile. Fortunately, by the very design of FQUERY for Access, such an implementation is relatively straightforward.

We rely on dictionaries of linguistic terms maintained and extended by the users during subsequent sessions. The main feature supporting an easy generation of summaries is the adopted concept of context independent definitions of particular linguistic terms. Hence, looking for a summary we may employ any term in the context of any attribute. Thus, we have summary building blocks at hand and what is needed is an efficient procedure for their composition, compatible with the rest of the fuzzy querying system.

In case of Type 1 summaries, only the list of defined linguistic quantifiers is employed. The user provides a query S and what is sought is a linguistic quantifier describing in a best way the fraction of rows satisfying this query. Hence, we are looking for a fuzzy set in the space of linguistic quantifiers, such that:

$$\mu_{\Sigma}(Q) = \text{truth}\,(Q\,S(x)) = \mu_Q\Big(\sum_{i=1}^{m} \mu_S(x_i)/m\Big) \tag{11}$$

where $X = \{x_1, \ldots, x_m\}$ is the set of rows.

FQUERY for Access processes the query in the usual way additionally summing up the matching degrees for all rows. Thus, the sum in (11) is easily calculated. Then the results of the query, i.e. rows accompanied by a matching degree, are displayed in the usual form. In another window, the sought fuzzy set of linguistic quantifiers is shown, as it is shown in Figure 1. Currently, FQUERY for Access does not support fuzzy filters. As soon as this capability is added, also summaries of Type 2 will be available. Simply, when evaluating the filter for particular rows, another sum used in (7) will be calculated and the final results will be presented as in case of Type 1 summaries.

Type 3 summaries require more effort and a redesign of the query results display. Now, we are given a quantifier (currently the "most" quantifier is assumed) and the whole query but without some values. Thus, first of all, we have to extend the syntax of the query language introducing a *placeholder* for a fuzzy value. That is, the user may leave out some values in the query's conditions and ask the system to find a best fit for them. During the query processing this left out values are treated in the same way as regular numerical fuzzy values. However, the matching degree is calculated not just for one fuzzy value but also for all fuzzy values defined in the dictionary. The matching degrees of the whole query against the subsequent rows, calculated for different combination of fuzzy values are summed up. Finally, it is computed for particular combinations of fuzzy values how well the query is satisfied when a given combination is put into the query. Thus, we again receive as a result a fuzzy set but this time defined in the space of fuzzy values' vectors, as it is shown in Figure 2.

Obviously, such computations are extremely time-consuming and are practically feasible only for one placeholder in a query. On the other hand, the case of one placeholder, corresponding to the search for typical or exceptional values, seems to be most useful form of a Type 3 summary.

6 Mining Association Rules in FQUERY for Access

Our implementation of association rules is based on the Agrawal and Srikant's AprioriTid algorithm [1]. Originally, this algorithm was designed to mine binary data. Thus, some extensions mentioned in the previous section have to be implemented. Although the algorithm applied is very efficient, it still requires a lot of processing time and extensive storage of partial results. We do not follow the recommendations of the authors of AprioriTid in respect to data structures to be used during the mining. This is partly due to the specificity of fuzzy mining. The second reason is the assumed development environment, i.e. Microsoft Access that also makes some original recommendations less attractive. Many assumed solutions are aimed at limiting the search space of possible rules.

Basically, the original algorithm (for binary data) consists in finding *large itemsets*. An itemset, is a set of items (attributes), which may be interpreted as a logical formula comprising a conjunction of the member items. A record in the database is said to *support* an itemset if the corresponding conjunction "is true" for this record, i.e. all member items (attributes) take on value 1 in this record. An itemset containing k items is called a k-itemset. The algorithm starts with the evaluation of 1-itemsets. These itemsets, which are not supported by sufficient number of records, are deleted. Then, the 2-itemsets are evaluated. Thanks to the specific scheme (see [1]), not all combinations of pairs of items are taken into account. Generally, the evaluation of the k-itemsets is done in two steps. First, promising k-itemsets are generated from large (k-1)-itemsets. Then, all generated k-itemsets are evaluated against all records in the database. Finally, all k-itemsets (for each k) are a basis for the generation of rules. More precisely, for each large itemset, *LIT*, all possible proper subsets of items, *PREM*, are considered as a premise of a hypothetical rule - the rest of items constitute the consequence of such a rule. Notice that both the premise and the consequence of the rule are large itemsets. The rule is accepted if its *confidence*, calculated as the fraction of records supporting the whole large itemset *LIT* among the records supporting the premise *PREM*, is higher than a pre-specified *confidence threshold*. Observe that due to the definition of large itemsets, the former number of records is always less or equal to the latter one; hence, the confidence of a rule belongs to [0, 1].

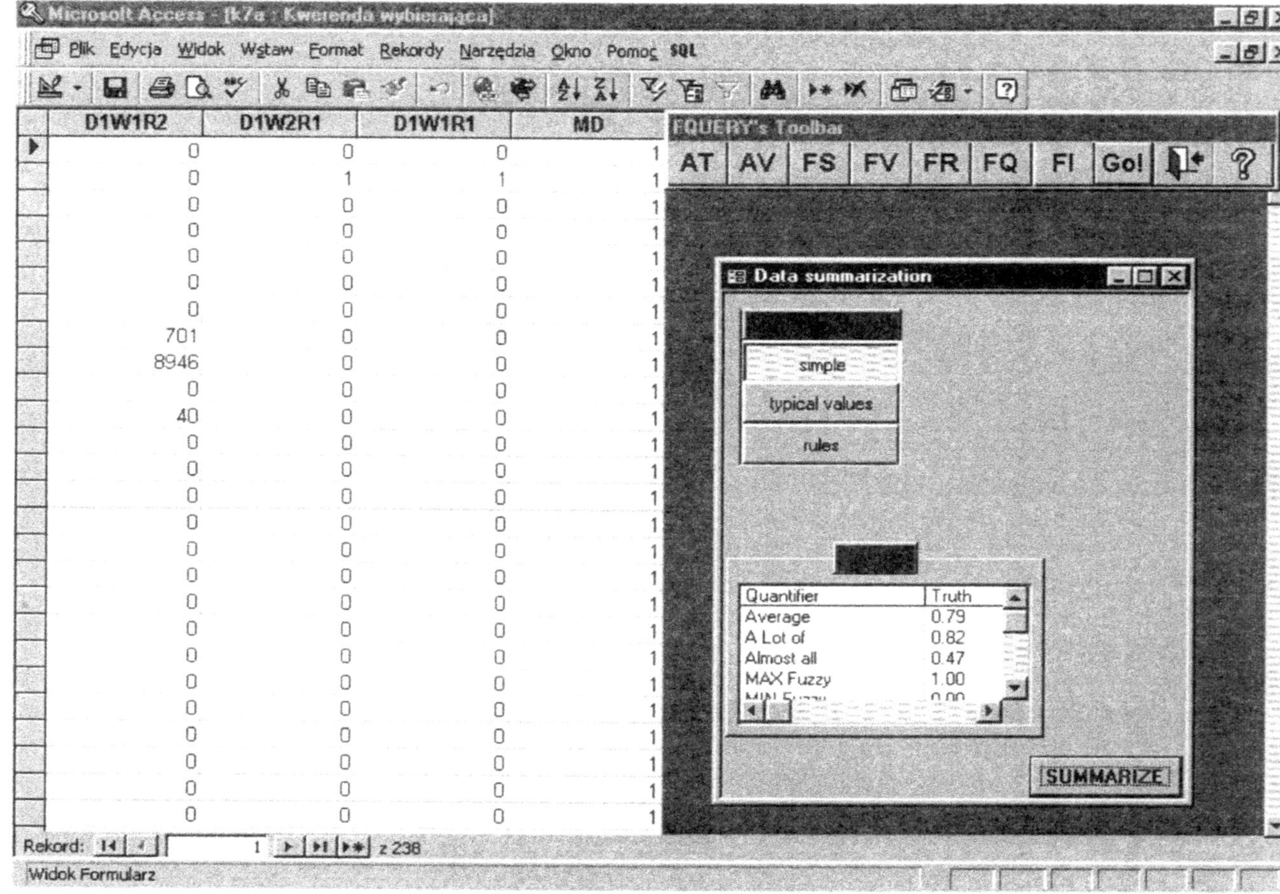

Figure 2. Results of a Type 1 summary

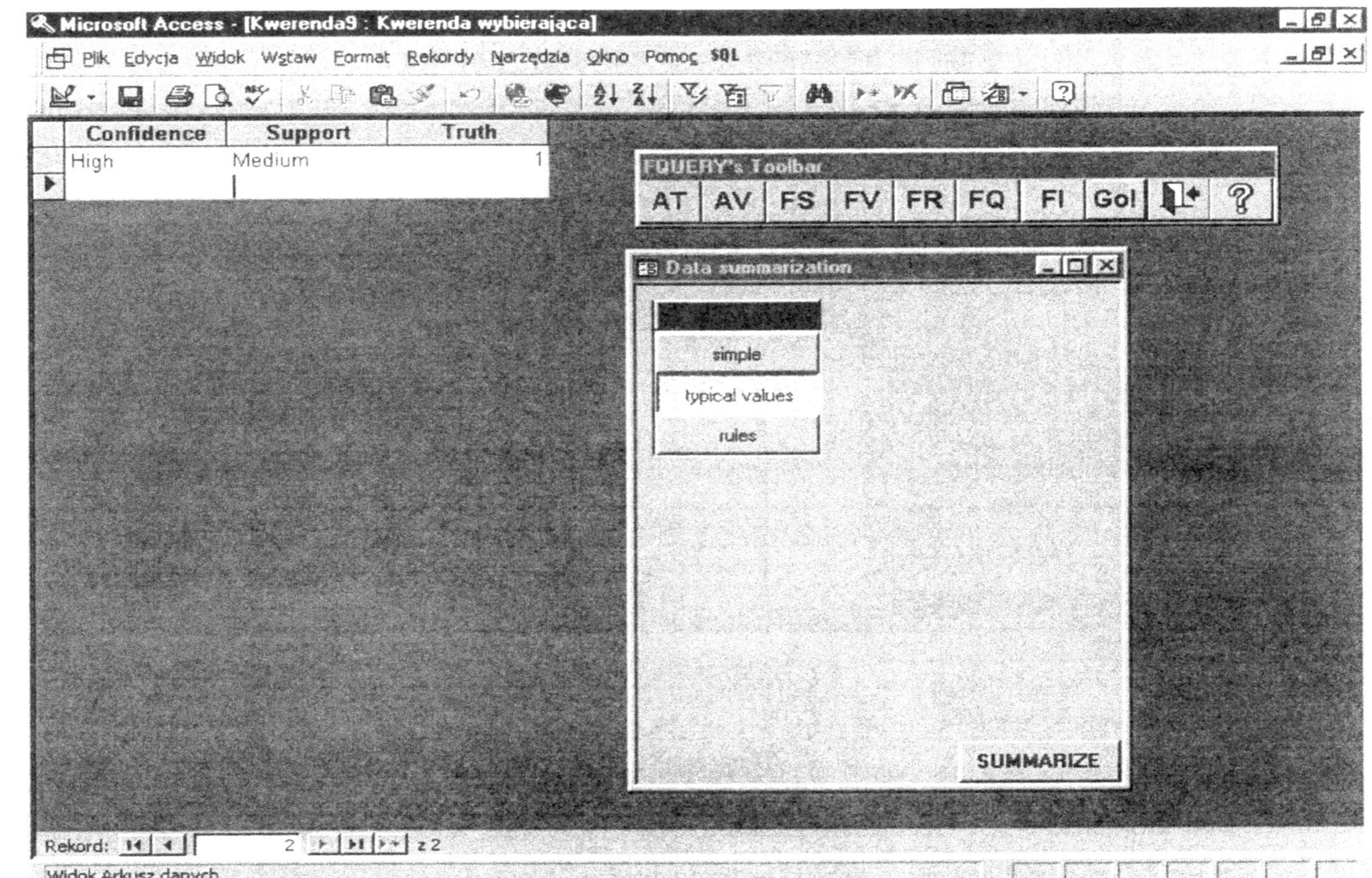

Figure 3. Results of a Type 3 summary

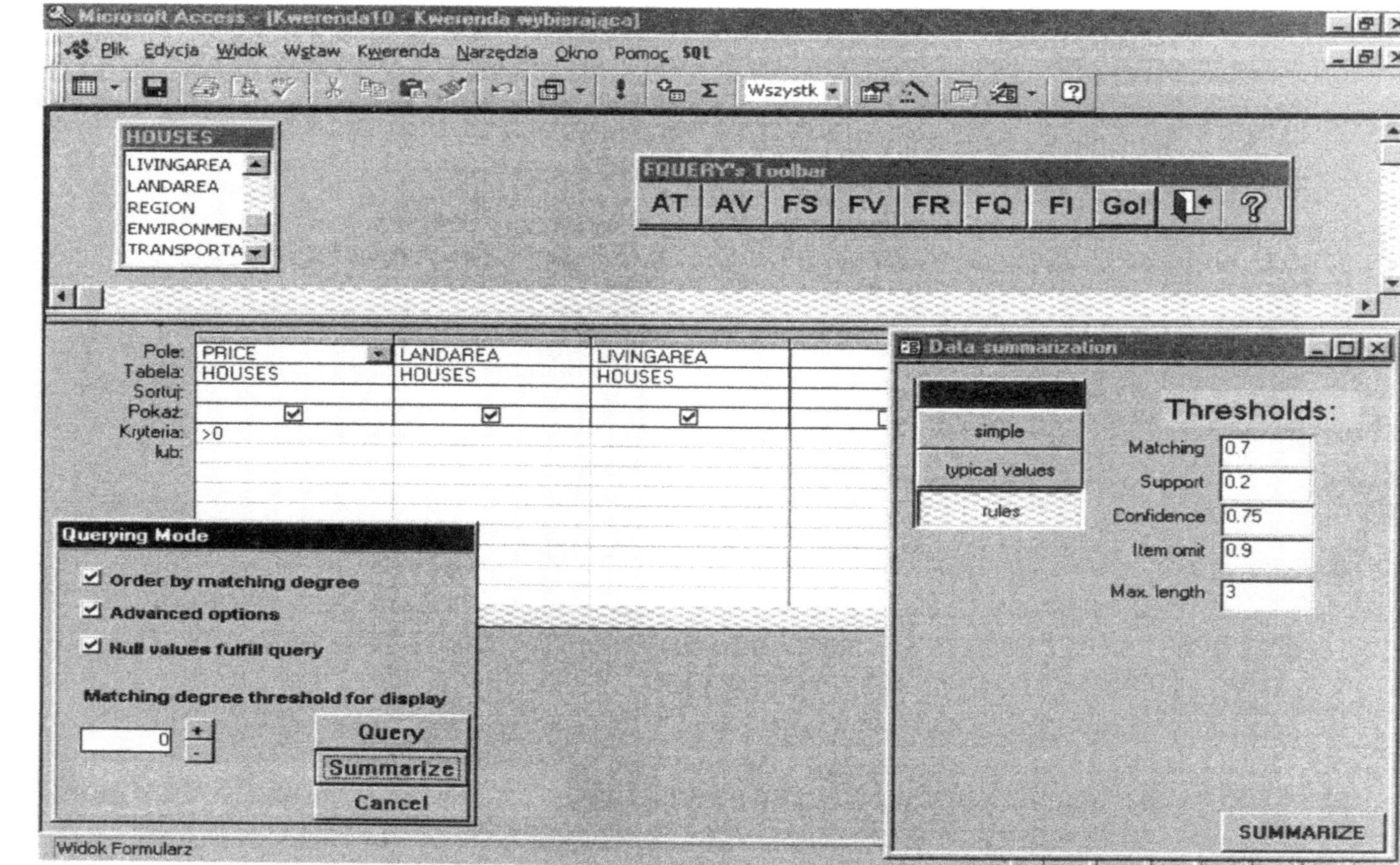

Figure 4. Elements of rule generation interface

Microsoft Access - [Kwerenda10 : Kwerenda wybierająca]

Body	Confidence	St
IF 'Price = High AND Living area = Low AND Bedrooms = Low AND Bathrooms = Low THEN Land area = Low	0.8271956	1
IF 'Price = High AND Land area = Low AND Bedrooms = Low AND Bathrooms = Low THEN Living area = Low	0.8683646	1
IF 'Price = High AND Land area = Low AND Living area = Low AND Bathrooms = Low THEN Bedrooms = Low	0.9512689	1
IF 'Price = High AND Land area = Low AND Living area = Low AND Bedrooms = Low THEN Bathrooms = Low	1	1
IF 'Price = High AND Living area = Low THEN Land area = Low AND Bedrooms = Low AND Bathrooms = Low	0.7801442	1
IF 'Price = High AND Living area = Low AND Bathrooms = Low THEN Land area = Low AND Bedrooms = Low	0.7801442	1
IF 'Price = High AND Living area = Low AND Bedrooms = Low THEN Land area = Low AND Bathrooms = Low	0.8271956	1
IF 'Price = High AND Land area = Low AND Bedrooms = Low THEN Living area = Low AND Bathrooms = Low	0.8683646	1
IF 'Price = High AND Land area = Low AND Living area = Low THEN Bedrooms = Low AND Bathrooms = Low	0.9512689	1
IF 'Price = High AND Living area = Low AND Bedrooms = Low THEN Land area = Low	0.8271956	1
IF 'Price = High AND Land area = Low AND Bedrooms = Low THEN Living area = Low	0.8683646	1
IF 'Price = High AND Land area = Low AND Living area = Low THEN Bedrooms = Low	0.9512689	1
IF 'Price = High AND Living area = Low THEN Land area = Low AND Bedrooms = Low	0.7801442	1
IF 'Price = High AND Living area = Low THEN Land area = Low AND Bedrooms = Low	0.7801442	1
IF 'Price = High AND Living area = Low AND Bathrooms = Low THEN Land area = Low	0.820109	1
IF 'Price = High AND Land area = Low AND Living area = Low THEN Bathrooms = Low	1	1
IF 'Price = High AND Living area = Low THEN Land area = Low AND Bathrooms = Low	0.820109	1
IF 'Price = High AND Living area = Low THEN Land area = Low AND Bathrooms = Low	0.820109	1
IF 'Land area = Low AND Bedrooms = Low AND Bathrooms = Low THEN Price = High	0.7647916	1
IF 'Price = High AND Bedrooms = Low AND Bathrooms = Low THEN Land area = Low	0.8094818	1
IF 'Price = High AND Land area = Low AND Bathrooms = Low THEN Bedrooms = Low	0.781801	1
IF 'Price = High AND Land area = Low AND Bedrooms = Low THEN Bathrooms = Low	1	1
IF 'Price = High AND Land area = Low THEN Bedrooms = Low AND Bathrooms = Low	0.7512387	1
IF 'Price = High AND Bedrooms = Low THEN Land area = Low AND Bathrooms = Low	0.8094818	1
IF 'Land area = Low AND Bedrooms = Low THEN Price = High AND Bathrooms = Low	0.7647916	1
IF 'Land area = Low AND Bedrooms = Low THEN Price = High AND Bathrooms = Low	0.7647916	1

Rekord: 17 z 77

Widok Arkusz danych

Figure 5. Examples of generated rules

In our implementation, we deal with real valued attributes. Thus, following previously mentioned approaches, for each such an attribute we introduce a number of artificial attributes (item), which may be treated as binary attributes. For example, the attribute PRICE may be replaced with the following artificial attributes: PRICEIsLow, PRICEIsMedium and PRICEIsHigh. The meaning of these attributes is obvious: a record supports, for example, PRICEIsLow if the value of the original attribute PRICE in this record falls into an interval identified as 'Low'. Instead of the intervals of values, employed in non-fuzzy approaches, we use fuzzy values (linguistic terms), see also [17]. The use of fuzzy values implies that a record supports a given artificial attribute to a degree from the interval [0, 1]. It is possible to use such a degree directly or to "defuzzify" it employing a threshold.

We will sketch the pilot implementation illustrating it on an example.

Step 1. Selection of the attributes and fuzzy values

In all but trivial cases, the use of all attributes for rules construction is not recommended. Thus, the user has to choose which attributes should be used during the mining. Moreover, these attributes should be accompanied with some meaningful description, which will be used in the rules presentation. In the current implementation, the user simply builds a query referring somehow to all attributes, which should be taken into account.

The same applies to the selection of fuzzy values.

Then, the user initiates the data summarization and the system automatically performs the rest of steps.

Step 2. Construction of the artificial attributes (items)

For each pair - one of selected attributes and fuzzy values - the system creates an artificial attribute (item), as it is described earlier. Thus, the number of selected fuzzy values determines the complexity of required computation in the same way as the number of attributes. An item may be treated as a fuzzy set in the domain of corresponding attribute. Each generated item constitutes the separate 1-itemset.

Step 3. Calculation of the support for 1-itemsets

This step requires a full search of the database. For each record, the membership degrees, *MD*, of the values of relevant attributes in fuzzy sets corresponding to items generated in Step 2 are calculated. Here, the fuzzy querying module is employed to calculate the membership degree, *MD*, sought. Only items for which the corresponding membership degree is greater than the *matching threshold* are considered as supported by given record. Thus, as a result of the database search we obtain for each item its *support*, i.e. the total number of records supporting it. The *fuzzy support* is also computed. While for the sum corresponding to the support each record contributes 0 or 1, for the fuzzy support, each record contributes the value of membership degree *MD*, unless it is below the matching threshold - then the record contributes 0.

Step 4. Pruning of the set of 1-itemsets

We omit all itemsets with the support lower than a *support threshold*. The reasons for that are twofold. First of all, only rules that may be checked against large enough subsets of records are interesting. Second, such a pruning makes it possible to limit the complexity of further calculations. Additionally, we also omit itemsets with the support higher than another threshold, *item omit threshold*. The reason is that items present in almost all records will contribute nothing interesting to the produced rules.

As a result, we obtain the large 1-itemsets.

Step 5. Construction of the new transaction table

The calculation of the support for 1-itemsets is rather expensive and grows for k-itemsets, $k > 1$. Thus, following the idea of Apriori Tid algorithm, we create special *transaction table* containing for each record all 1 - itemsets supported by this record to the degree higher than matching threshold. It saves the computation time, but at the expense of needed storage.

SET k = 2

Step 6. Generate k-itemsets

Basically, they are generated from large (k - 1)-itemsets as in original Apriori Tid algorithm. Briefly, pairs of large (k - 1)-itemsets of the form (we follow here the notation of (10)) $A_1 \wedge A_2 \wedge ... \wedge A_{k-1}$ and $B_1 \wedge B_2 \wedge ... \wedge B_{k-1}$, where $A_i = B_i$ for i = 1, ..., k-2 are sought. Then, the new k-itemset of the form $A_1 \wedge A_2 \wedge ... \wedge A_{k-1} \wedge B_{k-1}$ is generated. In the original algorithm, the rules generated this way are additionally tested and possibly eliminated before the evaluation done in Step 7. On the other hand, due to the approach adopted here, we add another k-itemset generation limitation, namely the items A_{k-1} and B_{k-1} have to correspond to different original attributes (remember that each item is based on the pair (attribute,fuzzy value) - see Step 2).

Step 7. Calculate support for all k - itemsets

The procedure is as in the Step 3, but this time the transaction table generated for $(k - 1)$ - itemsets is employed.

Step 8. Pruning of the set of k - itemsets (as in Step 4)

As the result we obtain the large k - itemsets.

IF the set of k-itemsets is empty, then GOTO Step 10

Step 9. Construction of the new transaction table

As in Step 5 but this time the transaction table is generated for k-itemsets

SET k = k + 1; GOTO Step 6

Step 10. Generate rules from large l-itemsets, $l = 1, ..., k - 1$

7 Concluding Remarks

By combining fuzzy querying with data mining techniques, we may produce interesting tools. The use of fuzzy (linguistic) terms makes the data mining results more human-consistent and comprehensible. Moreover, the building blocks of fuzzy queries - fuzzy values and linguistic quantifiers - are readily available for the inclusion into the summaries or association rules. A further research on adaptation and extension of efficient association rules generation algorithms for the case of linguistic setting may be very fruitful.

Further research comprises the implementation of fuzzy filters, association rules - in the spirit of [17], and some more advanced "interestingness" measures of the summaries. An appropriate combination of the functionality of querying and data mining within the same interface poses also a challenge from the software engineering point of view.

References

[1] Agrawal R. and Srikant R., "Fast algorithms for mining association rules", in: Proceedings of the 20th International Conference on Very Large Databases, Santiago, Chile, 1994.

[2] Anwar T.M., Beck H.W. and Navathe S.B., "Knowledge mining by imprecise querying: A classification based system", in: Proceedings of the International Conference on Data Engineering, Tampa, USA, 1992, 622-630.

[3] Bosc P. and J. Kacprzyk (eds.), *Fuzziness in Database Management Systems*. Physica-Verlag, Heidelberg, 1995.

[4] Bosc P. and O. Pivert, "Fuzzy querying in conventional databases". In: L.A. Zadeh and J. Kacprzyk (eds.): *Fuzzy Logic for the Management of Uncertainty*. Wiley, New York, 1992, 645-671.

[5] Bosc P., L. Lietard and O. Pivert, "Quantified statements and database fuzzy querying, in P. Bosc and J. Kacprzyk (eds.): *Fuzziness in Database Management Systems*. Physica-Verlag, Heidelberg, 1995, 275-308.

[6] George R. and R. Srikanth, "Data summarization using genetic algorithms and fuzzy logic", in: F. Herrera and J.L. Verdegay (eds.): *Genetic Algorithms and Soft Computing*. Physica-Verlag, Heidelberg and New York, 1996, 599 - 611.

[7] Kacprzyk J. and R.R. Yager (2000) "Linguistic summaries of data using fuzzy logic". International Journal of General Systems (in press)

[8] Kacprzyk J., R.R. Yager, and S. Zadrożny (2000) "Fuzzy linguistic summaries of databases for an efficient business data analysis and decision support". In W. Abramowicz and J. Żurada (Eds.) „Selected Aspects and New Trends in Knowledge Discovery for Business Information Systems. Kluwer, Boston (in press)

[9] Kacprzyk J., R.R. Yager, and S. Zadrożny (2000) "A fuzzy logic based approach to linguistic summaries of databases". International Journal of Applied Mathematics and Computer Science (in press)

[10] Kacprzyk J. and S. Zadrożny, "FQUERY for Access: fuzzy querying for a Windows-based DBMS", in: P. Bosc and J. Kacprzyk (eds.) *Fuzziness in Database Management Systems*, Physica-Verlag, Heidelberg, 1995, 415 - 433.

[11] Kacprzyk J. and S. Zadrożny, "Fuzzy queries in Microsoft Access v. 2.", in: D. Dubois, H. Prade and R.R. Yager (eds.): *Fuzzy Information Engineering - A Guided Tour of Applications*, Wiley, New York, 1997, 223 - 232.

[12] Kacprzyk J. and S. Zadrożny, "Implementation of OWA operators in fuzzy querying for Microsoft Access", in: R.R. Yager and J. Kacprzyk (eds.) *The Ordered Weighted Averaging Operators: Theory and Applications*, Kluwer, Boston 1997, 293 - 306.

[13] Kacprzyk J. and S. Zadrożny, "Flexible querying using fuzzy logic: An implementation for Microsoft Access", in: T. Andreasen, H. Christiansen and H.L. Larsen (eds.): *Flexible Query Answering Systems*, Kluwer, Boston, 1997, 247-275.

[14] Kacprzyk J. and S. Zadrożny, “Data mining via linguistic summaries of data: An interactive approach”, in T. Yamakawa and G. Matsumoto (eds.): *Methodologies for the Conception, Design and Application of Soft Computing* (Proceedings of IIZUKA’98), Iizuka, Japan, 1998, 668-671.

[15] Kacprzyk J. and S. Zadrożny, ”On sumarization of large datasets via a fuzzy-logic-based querying add-on to Microsoft Access”, in: Intelligent Information Systems VII (Malbork, Poland), IPI PAN, Warsaw, 1998, 249-258.

[16] Kacprzyk J. and Ziółkowski A., "Database queries with fuzzy linguistic quantifiers", *IEEE Transactions on Systems, Man and Cybernetics* SMC - 16, 1986, 474 - 479.

[17] Lee J.-H. and Lee-Kwang H., "An extension of association rules using fuzzy sets", in: Proceedings of the Seventh IFSA World Congress, 1997, Prague, Czech Republic. Vol. 1, 399-402.

[18] Mannila H., Toivonen H. and Verkamo A.I., "Efficient algorithms for discovering association rules", in: U.M. Fayyad and R. Uthurusamy (eds.) Proceedings of the AAAI Workshop on Knowledge Discovery in Databases, Seattle, USA, 1994, 181-192.

[19] Miller R.J. and Yang Y., "Association rules over interval data". in: Proceedings of the ACM SIGMOD International Conference on the Management of Data, Tucson, USA, 1997, 452-461.

[20] Petry F.E. *Fuzzy Databases: Principles and Applications*. Kluwer, Boston, 1996.

[21] Rasmussen D. and R.R. Yager (1997) Fuzzy query language for hypothesis evaluation, in Andreasen T., H. Christiansen and H. L. Larsen (eds.) *Flexible Query Answering Systems*. Kluwer, Boston/Dordrecht/London, 23-43.

[22] Srikant R. and Agrawal R., "Mining generalized association rules", in: Proceedings of the 21st International Conference on Very Large Databases", Zurich, Switzerland, 1995.

[23] Srikant R. and Agrawal R., "Mining quantitative association rules in large relational tables", in: Proceedings of the ACM-SIGMOD 1996 Conference on Management of Data, Montreal, Canada, 1996.

[24] Srikant R., Vu Q. and R. Agrawal, "Mining association rules with item constraints", in: Proceedings of the 3rd International Conference on Knowledge Discovery in Databases and Data Mining, Newport Beach, USA, 1997.

[25] Vila M.A., Cubero J.C., Medina J.M. and Pons O., "Logic and fuzzy relational databases: a new language and a new definition", in P. Bosc and J. Kacprzyk (eds.) *Fuzziness in Database Management Systems*. Physica-Verlag, Heidleberg, 1994, 114 - 138.

[26] Weber S., "A general concept of fuzzy connectives, negations and implications based on t-norms and t-conorms", *Fuzzy Sets and Systems* 11, 1983, 115-134.

[27] Yager R.R., "On linguistic summaries of data", in: G. Piatetsky-Shapiro and W.J. Frawley (eds.) *Knowledge Discovery in Databases*. AAAI Press/The MIT Press, Menlo Park, 1991, 347 - 363.

[28] Zemankova M. and J. Kacprzyk, "The roles of fuzzy logic and management of uncertainty in building intelligent information systems", *Journal of Intelligent Information Systems* 2, 1993, 311-317.

[29] Zadeh L.A., "A computational approach to fuzzy quantifiers in natural languages", *Computers and Maths. with Appls.* 9, 1983, 149 - 184.

[30] Zadeh L.A.,"A computational theory of dispositions", *International Journal of Intelligent Systems* 2, 1987, 39-64.

The Fuzzy-ROSA Method: A Statistically Motivated Fuzzy Approach for Data-Based Generation of Small Interpretable Rule Bases in High-Dimensional Search Spaces

T. Slawinski[1], A. Krone[1], P. Krause[1] and H. Kiendl[1]

Department of Control Engineering, University of Dortmund, 44221 Dortmund, Germany. E-mail: [Slawinski, Krone, ...]@esr.e-technik.uni-dortmund.de

Abstract. In the field of data mining, fuzzy approaches are predominantly applied, if interpretable results are desired. The applicability of different methods for data-based rule generation has been demonstrated impressively in numerous real-world tasks. However, there are still difficulties in generating small interpretable rule bases efficiently, especially for applications with many input variables. The Fuzzy-ROSA method presented here was developed to overcome these problems. With the aim of reducing the computational effort for rule generation, the basic concept of the Fuzzy-ROSA method is to test and rate individual rules according to their ability to describe a relevant aspect of the system under consideration, instead of evaluating and optimizing complete rule bases. The rule base generation process is divided into the following main steps: data pre-processing for search space structuring, rule search based on rule test and rating, on- and offline rule reduction and finally rule base analysis and optimization. With respect to the broad spectrum of applications, there are different methods available for each of these steps. An overview is given in the first part of this paper, with emphasis on the rule search and rule test and rating strategies, because they are essential for the efficiency of rule generation and model quality, respectively. In the second part of the paper, the performance of the Fuzzy-ROSA method is compared with other fuzzy modeling approaches by means of benchmark problems. Moreover, we consider real-world applications: the classification of automatic gearboxes by 149 characteristics, the prediction of the duration of insurance contracts and the parameter adaptation of a position controller in robotics. It turns out that the Fuzzy -ROSA method can deal with very large search spaces, with noisy and contradictory data and that it is possible to learn from examples with different performance or quality.

Keywords. Fuzzy modelling, data-based rule generation, rule test and rating, Fuzzy-ROSA method.

1 Introduction

Data Mining has started to receive significant attention during the last decade and a variety of applications in science and industry have already been published. The applications domains can basically be distinguished as classification or approximation tasks. In both cases, the goal of data mining is to find (unknown) structures or relations in the given input-output data of the system under consideration. Beside other methods, such as statistics or machine learning, new approaches, such as computational intelligence, have been established in some fields of application. Possible results of the data mining process are a grouping of the data in several classes and building a model of the considered system. Depending on the chosen method, the model obtained either simply describes the input-output behavior of the system or can in addition be interpretable, thus providing insight into the system. The main advantages of such an interpretable model are higher acceptance by experts and an increased ability to adapt the model by hand.

When interpretable models are desired, fuzzy modeling is frequently applied. The qualitative relations between the input and output variables of the system considered are described by if-then rules. This corresponds to the way human knowledge is usually presented. In process monitoring and process control, as well as in finance and trade, the strategies of human experts are often rule-based. Most of the early fuzzy systems were designed through knowledge extraction. However, for more complex systems or if no prior knowledge is available, such a design is very time consuming or perhaps impossible. In these cases, a data-based approach is more promising.

Common approaches for data-based fuzzy modeling are based on clustering algorithms, classical optimization methods, decision trees, neural networks (NN), and evolutionary algorithms (EA). Clustering algorithms have been established as methods for search space structuring and preliminary modeling. In a second step, the model quality is improved by an optimization, which for example is supplied by an EA or NN technique. In other approaches, the rules, the composition of the rule base, or both, are optimized by classical methods or EA. In order to exploit the high modeling quality of NN, in recent research NN structures are proposed, that can be converted into fuzzy rule bases.

The applicability of data-based fuzzy modeling methods depends mainly on two factors. First, the resulting model is accepted better if the applied method allows the generation of small and transparent rule bases. Second, the computing time must be acceptable even if many linguistic variables and values are considered. In the literature, only a few examples with five to ten input variables are found and more complex examples are rarely published. Few of the proposed fuzzy modeling methods can be applied to very complex problems, due to the exponential increase in computing time. Additionally, if the rule base is optimized as a whole, by simply minimizing the modeling error, it cannot be guaranteed that each individual rule of the rule base obtained is reasonable, i.e., locally relevant.

The Fuzzy-ROSA[1] method (FRM) has been developed to overcome these problems [1]. The basic concept of the FRM is to add to the rule base only those fuzzy rules that pass a statistical relevance test (Section 2.1). Consequently, each accepted fuzzy rule describes a relevant aspect of the system under consideration (Section 2.2). This reduces the problem of finding a good rule base to the problem of finding individual relevant rules. Further, since each rule with high relevance is supposed to express an important aspect of the system, such a rule is meaningful by itself. Therefore, the obtained rule base is more transparent and comprehensible.

The handling of complex applications requires a suitable structure of the rules. In this context it is favorable that the FRM can also handle generalizing (incomplete) rules. These rules need not to consider all the linguistic input variables provided and therefore the length of the premises may differ (Section 2.2.1). If a single rule is composed of fewer expressions than the total number of input variables, the rule covers several linguistic input situations. In particular, for large search spaces with a large number of input variables, such rule bases turn out to be much smaller than rule bases consisting of complete rules only.

Moreover, an efficient complete rule search, which aims at finding all relevant rules, has been designed (Section 2.3). It is based on the notion that the amount of available data is always limited, so that certain parts of the input space do not include any data sets and consequently need not to be considered. In addition, in order to handle very high-dimensional search spaces where a complete rule search fails, a hybrid evolutionary search concept has been developed (Section 2.4).

It should be noted that the FRM approach does not attempt to generate the optimal model (which in general cannot be obtained in polynomial time and therefore is impractical for the majority of applications), but at finding a satisfactory model in acceptable time. The applicability of the FRM has been demonstrated by solving various benchmark problems (Section 3.1) and by several successful real-world applications (Section 3.2).

2 The Fuzzy-ROSA Method (FRM)

A survey of the rule base generation process and the strategy elements of the FRM is given in Section 2.1. This provides the necessary information for the solutions of the applications described in Section 3. The additional sections are addressed to

---

[1] **R**ule-**O**riented **S**tatistical **A**nalysis

those who are interested in a more detailed explanation of the essential parts of the FRM. Starting with a formal description of the rule structure, the rule test and rating strategies are motivated, presented and compared in Section 2.2. The efficiency of the complete rule search, presented in Section 2.3, is based on exploiting the structure of the search space. A sophisticated hybrid evolutionary search concept, an approach for rule generation in high-dimensional search spaces, is briefly introduced in Section 2.4.

2.1 Rule Base Generation Process

The rule base generation process of the FRM is divided into five main steps. There are alternative strategies available for each step, so that the method can be adapted to different application requirements (e.g., for modeling, classification, approximation or prediction) and problem sizes (e.g., numbers of variables, linguistic values and data sets).

2.1.1 Project Definition

An essential prerequisite for high quality and efficiency of data-based methods is appropriate feature generation and feature selection. The quality of the resulting model depends on the choice of input variables (features) used. Furthermore, the complexity of the corresponding search space can be reduced if only relevant and non-redundant features are used for rule generation. Such a feature generation and selection process can be based on statistical methods (e.g., correlation analysis), on NN methods or on fuzzy-based methods [2].

Prior to rule generation, the membership functions for the linguistic values of the input and output variables of the system considered must be defined. This can be done as a knowledge-based process by an expert, if corresponding domain knowledge is available. Otherwise it can be done either heuristically or by a data-based process. Common heuristic approaches suggest the choice of an equidistant partition or careful provision of evenly distributed data with regard to the membership functions. In data-based approaches cluster algorithms are usually used to define membership functions [3, 4]. In order to enforce the interpretability of the generated rules, triangular or trapezoidal membership functions are predominantly used in the FRM in the form of a fuzzy information system[2].

The size of the search space can be restricted by a maximum allowed combination depth c_{max}, i.e., the maximum number of linguistic expressions in the premise. Usually we start with a preliminary model with a low combination depth to become familiar with the problem being considered. If satisfactory settings for the project definition are found, a search with a higher maximum combination depth can be started, to improve the results.

---

[2] The sum of the membership degrees is one at each point.

For modeling time series or for considering time-varying variables of a dynamic process, a maximum time depth t_{max} can be chosen in the FRM. Then the modeling is based, not only on the linguistic values of the actual data set, but also on the linguistic values of the data sets corresponding to t_{max} preceding time steps. Within the FRM, time depth is treated as an additional linguistic variable, e.g., *"temperature two time steps ago"*. Therefore, time depth is not explicitly considered in the following. However, we found that it is sometimes more profitable to consider the time dependency by aggregated features, as for example, the trend or the derivative of an input variable.

2.1.2 Rule Search

The basic task of the rule search is to set up potential rules (hypotheses) and apply a statistical relevance test to the hypotheses. Only hypotheses that pass this test are accepted as relevant fuzzy rules. As a result of the test, each rule is given a rating index, which can be interpreted as a certainty factor. The rule base is generated by iteratively collecting relevant rules. To meet different modeling goals, three different rule test and rating strategies have been developed (Section 2.2).

Depending on the size of the search space, a complete search, an evolutionary search, or a combination of both is applied. The complete search, which is described in Section 2.3, guarantees that all relevant rules are found. We found that a complete search can usually be applied successfully for a maximum combination depth of up to four. For higher combination depths, we usually apply the hybrid evolutionary search concept (Section 2.4).

2.1.3 Restrictions

The FRM allows us to introduce the following restrictions, in order to prohibit the generation of undesired or infeasible rules. To preserve maximum flexibility, these restrictions can be activated optionally.

Combination Restriction: The default is that the combinations of linguistic expressions that refer to the same linguistic variables are prohibited, because a premise of the type *if "temperature is high" and "temperature is low"* is usually not desired. A deactivation of this restriction, in the case of a fuzzy information system, is only useful for the purpose of analysis. In that case, rules might be generated that combine two neighboring membership functions in the premise. This means that decisive data sets are in the fuzzy range of both membership functions.

Minimal Data Support: The "trustworthiness" of a rule depends strongly on the number of supporting data sets. In the FRM the data support of a given premise is defined by the sum over the degrees of membership for each data set (see Eq. 8). This restriction allows us to define a minimal data support. The default value of the minimal data support is chosen as one.

Complement Restriction: In the FRM each linguistic expression can be used in a negated form to formulate premises of the type *if "temperature is not high"*. This restriction is activated as the default, because few of the common fuzzy tools can process negated statements. In the following, negated statements in the premise are not considered.

Only Positive Rules: As described in [5], conventional fuzzy systems can process only positive rules that express recommendations. This is a serious drawback of conventional fuzzy systems. In many applications, both positive experience, in the form of recommendations, and also negative experience, in the form of warnings and prohibitions to avoid undesirable operating situations, are important. Negative rules can be processed – together with positive rules – by the two-way fuzzy system based on hyperinference introduced by Kiendl [5,6]. An essential advantage of the FRM is that as a result of the rule test, it extracts both positive and negative rules from the data (Section 2.2). If a fuzzy tool that cannot process negative rules is used, this restriction should be activated. Furthermore, if the hybrid evolutionary search concept is applied, positive rules should be searched separately, because otherwise the population is usually dominated by negative rules.

It must be pointed out, that especially in high-dimensional search spaces, the combination/complement restriction and minimal data support can lead to a drastic reduction of the number of rules that need to be tested (Section 2.3).

2.1.4 Rule Reduction

The rule generation process considers only the quality (relevance) of the individual rules and not that of the complete rule base. Consequently, there is still potential for optimization. In order to create small transparent rule bases or to improve the model quality, subsequent rule reduction steps can be applied. There are two main types of reduction strategies [7].

Online reduction aims at preventing redundant rules. It is applied if a new rule is found and added to the rule base. Rules are considered as redundant in the rule base if the latter already contains a more general rule with a higher rating index and the same conclusion.

The methods for offline reduction are developed to meet different requirements. On the one hand, it is of interest to reduce the number of rules in order to create small and transparent rule bases. On the other hand it is possible to improve the modeling error. The following offline reduction strategies are available:

Situation-Based Conflict Reduction (SitCR): Situation-based conflict reduction deletes rules that do not belong in any complete linguistic input situation (Section 2.2.1) to the best rules (rules with the highest rating indices). This reduction strategy guarantees that the resulting rule base covers as many linguistic input situations after applying the reduction as it did before. Therefore, if the original rule base covers all possible linguistic input situations, the reduced rule base will also do so. Situation-based conflict reduction requires computing time that is proportional to the number of complete input situations (Eq. 11 with $c = V$). Therefore, situation-based conflict reduction can only be applied to smaller problems.

Structure-Based Conflict Reduction (StrCR): To handle more complex problems, we have developed structure-based conflict reduction. This strategy removes rules that do not belong to the best rules (rules with the highest rating indices) in any generalizing input situation (structure) with a maximum combination depth $c_{\max}$. It also maintains the completeness of a rule base; however, this approach may remove fewer rules than situation-based conflict reduction.

Data-Based Conflict Reduction (DCR): In contrast to situation-based conflict reduction, this method is not based on analyzing input situations but data points supporting multiple rules. Rules that are mainly based on data points that also support better rules are removed. Therefore, the rule test is applied again to each rule of the rule base, beginning with the best. The difference to the relevance test of the rule search is that the data points can only support a restricted number of rules and then they are removed from the learning data. The disadvantage of this method is that it can not be guaranteed that the number of covered input situations is preserved. On the other hand, the great advantage is that this rule reduction method has always a practicable computing time, i.e. a small fraction of the computing time of the rule search. Additionally, the amount of reduction is usually higher than in case of situation-based conflict reduction.

Optimizing Conflict Reduction (OCR): This strategy aims at increasing the quality of the model by removing contradictory rules. Starting with the given rule base, certain combinations of rules are tested with respect to their input/output behavior, in order to find the rule base with the best model quality. For this complex optimization problem we have developed a special genetic algorithm (GA) [8]. The main advantage of this approach in comparison to other approaches in the literature is that in our approach the GA needs only to optimize a rule base of relevant rules and not the set of all possible rules.

2.1.5 Analysis and Optimization

The final step of the rule generation process is analysis and optimization. The analysis of the rule base allows us to rate the modeling process as well as the obtained model quality and provides feedback that can be used to modify the problem formulation. Finally, the input/output behavior of the resulting fuzzy system can be optimized by tuning the remaining free parameters, such as the output membership functions [9].

2.2 Rule Test and Rating Strategies

The result of the rule generation process of the FRM depends on the quality (relevance) of the individual rules. The quality of a model, on the other hand, must be rated based on the modeling objective. Different rule tests and rating strategies have been developed to meet different requirements, such as the following.

Relevance: The relevance index (Section 2.2.2) attempts to find rules that describe a "causal" dependency between the input situation in the premise and the linguistic output value.

Correctness: The normalized hit rate (Section 2.2.3) attempts to find rules that recommend the "correct" linguistic output value in a given input situation with high probability.

Approximation Quality: The mean value-based test (Section 2.2.4) attempts to find rules that recommend the mean value of an output variable in a given input situation.

These partly contradictory requirements usually cannot be fulfilled simultaneously. Priorities must therefore be imposed. This is illustrated by the following example.

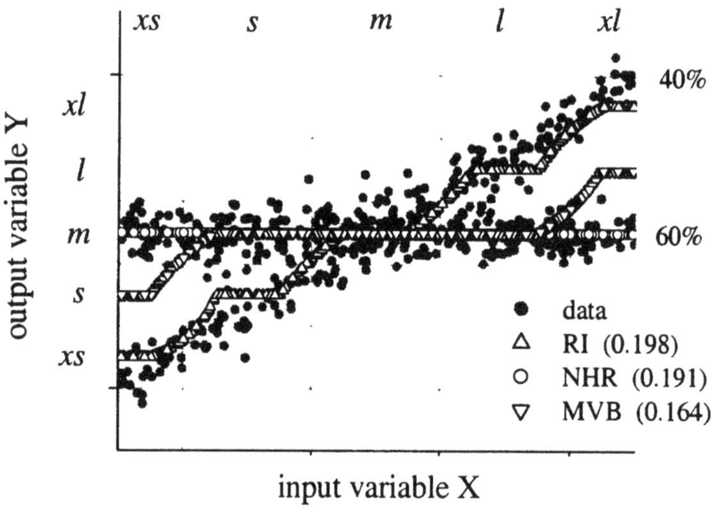

Fig. 2.1. Modeling of a contradictory dependency between the input variable X and the output variable Y, by using different test and rating strategies: relevance index (RI), normalized hit rate (NHR) and the mean value-based test (MVB). The corresponding mean square error of the strategies is indicated in brackets.

A contradictory dependency between input variable X and output variable Y is obtained by the superposition of two linear dependencies. For the data generation, 500 data sets were generated randomly with additional Gaussian noise (Fig. 2.1).

The linear dependencies are supported by 60% and 40% of the data, respectively. Five linguistic values (*xs* = extra small, *s* = small, *m* = medium, *l* = large, *xl* = extra large) are provided for the input and output variables. Fig. 2.1 shows the corresponding partitions.

Considering the premise *if* " *X* = *xl* ", we cannot determine *a priori*, which of the conclusions " *Y* = *m* " and " *Y* = *xl* " models the data better. The answer depends on the modeling objective.

- Consider, for example, a classification task, such as the quality control of automatic gearboxes (Section 3.2.1). The priority is to reject all defective gearboxes with an unusual sound during operation, for example, if they are too loud. In this case, an appropriate rule is if " X = xl " then "loudness = extra large". This rule rejects all gearboxes for which the premise if " X = xl " is fulfilled. In order to guarantee that no faulty gearboxes are delivered, a classification error of 60% must be accepted.
- Now we consider the task to find decision rules for stock changes, which is important in the domain of finance and trade. A possible dependency could be modeled by a rule in the form of if "economic growth = xl" then "stock goes up = ...". In reality, due to unknown or stochastic influences, considering Fig. 2.1, the stock is going up extra large and medium in 40% and 60% of cases, respectively. In this case, a good prediction might be to take the mean value, i.e., if "economic growth = xl" then "stock goes up = large". However, it must be pointed out, that the recommended linguistic value "stock goes up = large" is not supported by any data point. Consequently, this approach should not usually be applied to classification task. The results are probably unreasonable, especially for nominal output values (classes).
- In classification tasks with nominal output values (classes), the modeling objective may be to have a low error rate. In this case, we are interested in rules that recommend the correct output value (class). For example, consider the problem of classifying the sex ("m = male" and "xl = female") of a car owner by the horsepower of his/her car. In this case, an appropriate rule might be if "horse power = xl" then "owner = m (male)". In contrast to the preceding task, here the mean value is unreasonable. In this constructed example, all data sets with a linguistic output value not equal to m (male) or xl (female) must be neglected.

The above discussion may illustrate that with more input variables and generalizing rules, we mostly need to experimentally investigate which rule test and rating strategy supply the best results. One approach in this direction is to use preliminary models with a low combination depth for this investigation. In the following, based on a formal description of the provided rule structure, we describe the different rule test and rating strategies in detail.

2.2.1 Structure of the Rules and Data Sets

The fuzzy rules generated by the FRM are of the Mamdani type [5]

$$\textit{if } P \textit{ then } C \textit{ with } \quad P = e_1 \wedge \cdots \wedge e_c \quad \textit{and} \quad C = e_Y \ . \tag{1}$$

The premise P consists of a conjunction[3] of c linguistic expressions e referring to the input variables X and the conclusion C is a linguistic expression e_Y referring to the output variable Y. The number of linguistic expressions c is called the combination depth. A linguistic expression e is defined by $(X_i = s_{ij})$, where X_i denotes the i-th input variable and s_{ij} the j-th linguistic value for this variable. The S_i linguistic values (sets) s_{ij} are defined by membership functions $\mu_{i,j}(x_i)$, where x_i denotes a real (crisp) input value of the variable X_i. A linguistic output expression is defined analogously. In the FRM the number of linguistic expressions in the premise can be restricted by the maximum combination depth $c_{\max}$, which is usually chosen to be smaller than the number V of input variables. The premise of a rule can also be interpreted as a linguistic input situation. If $c = c_{\max} = V$, i.e., each linguistic variable is considered, we speak of a complete input situation and rule, respectively. Otherwise, if $c < c_{\max}$, we speak of an incomplete or generalizing input situation and rule, respectively. In the following, the n-th data set is defined by the tuple $d_n = (x_{n,1}, \ldots, x_{n,V}, y_n)$ and D is the total number of data sets.

2.2.2 Relevance Index (RI) and Relevant Hit Rate (RHR)

According to this rule test and rating strategy, a rule is relevant if the constrained probability $p(C \mid P)$ of its conclusion C for a given premise P exceeds the unconstrained probability $p(C)$, where these probabilities are estimated based on the given data sets [10,11]. The unconstrained probability $p(C)$ of the conclusion $C = (Y = s_{Yj})$, for a given linguistic output value s_{Yj}, is estimated by

$$\hat{p}(C) = \frac{\sum_{n=1}^{D} \mu_{Y,j}(y_n)}{D} \ . \tag{2}$$

The constrained probability $p(C \mid P)$ is estimated by

$$\hat{p}(C \mid P) = \frac{\sum_{n=1}^{D} \mu_{Y,j}(y_n) \wedge \left(\bigwedge_{k=1}^{c} \mu_{i_k,j_k}(x_{n,i_k}) \right)}{\sum_{n=1}^{D} \bigwedge_{k=1}^{c} \mu_{i_k,j_k}(x_{n,i_k})} \ , \tag{3}$$

where $\mu_{i_k j_k}(x_{n,i_k})$ denotes the membership degree of the k-th linguistic expression in the given premise P for the data set n. In order to consider the statistical credibility of a rule, the confidence intervals $[I_L, I_U]$ are calculated

---

[3] In the FRM, the logical AND is realized by the product [10].

with respect to a given confidence level α and used instead of the estimated probabilities. The unconstrained probability $\hat{p}(C)$ is replaced by the upper bound $I_U(C)$ and the constrained probability $\hat{p}(C \mid P)$ is replaced by the lower bound $I_L(C \mid P)$. A hypothesis *if P then C* is accepted as a positive rule, if $I_L(C \mid P) > I_U(C)$ holds. If $I_L(C) > I_U(C \mid P)$, the hypothesis induces a negative rule. Otherwise, the hypothesis is rejected. The accepted rules can be rated by the relevance index

$$J_{RI} = \begin{cases} \dfrac{I_L(C \mid P) - I_U(C)}{1 - \hat{p}(C)} & \text{for positive rules} \\ \dfrac{I_L(C) - I_U(C \mid P)}{\hat{p}(C)} & \text{for negative rules} \end{cases} \tag{4}$$

Here, the distance between the decision boundaries of the two confidence intervals is normalized by its theoretical maximum value. By this rating, rules with a large difference between the constrained and the unconstrained probability receive a high rating index. Another rating strategy, called the relevant hit rate (RHR) considers the estimated probability of the occurrence of the output value $C = s_{Y_j}$ if the premise is met. We set

$$J_{RHR} = \begin{cases} \hat{p}(C \mid P) & \text{for positive rules} \\ 1 - \hat{p}(C \mid P) & \text{for negative rules} \end{cases} \tag{5}$$

2.2.3 Normalized and Confident Hit Rate (NHR/CHR)

The rule test and rating according to the normalized hit rate (NHR) is independent of the unconstrained probability of the conclusion part. NHR tests whether the estimated constrained probability $\hat{p}(C \mid P)$ is higher than a given threshold θ. A common choice is $\theta = 0.5$. In this case, a positive rule is accepted if the conclusion is more likely to be true than false. An accepted rule is rated by mapping its constrained probability to the interval [0, 1].

$$J_{NHR} = \begin{cases} \dfrac{\hat{p}(C \mid P) - \theta}{1 - \theta} & \text{if } \hat{p}(C \mid P) > \theta \quad \text{for positive rules} \\ \dfrac{\theta' - \hat{p}(C \mid P)}{\theta'} & \text{if } \hat{p}(C \mid P) < \theta' \quad \text{for negative rules} \end{cases} \tag{6}$$

The threshold θ' for negative rules can be adjusted separately, in order to avoid a too large number of negative rules. If $\theta = \theta' = 0.5$ is chosen, nearly each rule that does not pass the test for positive rules is taken as a negative rule.

The NHR does not consider statistical credibility and is especially useful with small data sets. If a sufficient number of data sets is available, either the restriction on minimal data support mentioned above should be activated or the confident hit rate (CHR) might be applied: For this, the estimated probabilities in Eq. 6 are replaced by the upper and lower confidence interval bounds, respectively. We thus obtain

$$J_{CHR} = \begin{cases} \dfrac{I_L(C|P)-\theta}{1-\theta} & \text{if } I_L(C|P) > \theta \quad \text{for positive rules} \\ \dfrac{\theta' - I_U(C|P)}{\theta'} & \text{if } I_U(C|P) < \theta' \quad \text{for negative rules} \end{cases} \tag{7}$$

2.2.4 Mean Value-Based Index (MVB)

In the case that the data for the output variables is very noisy or strongly disturbed, so the above tests might have difficulties in finding appropriate rules. In this case, the mean of the output value in a given input situation may be of interest. The t-test is a test strategy on hypotheses that refer to means [11]. For the t-test, the constrained mean value $\bar{y}_P$ of the output value y for a given premise P is calculated by

$$\bar{y}_P = \frac{\sum_{n=1}^{D} y_n \cdot \bigwedge_{k=1}^{c} \mu_{i_k, j_k}(x_{n,i_k})}{N_P} \quad \text{with} \quad N_P = \sum_{n-1}^{D} \bigwedge_{k=1}^{c} \mu_{i_k, j_k}(x_{n,i_k}) \ , \tag{8}$$

and tested. Essentially, the t-test investigates whether the constrained mean value $\bar{y}_P$ is significantly different from the unconstrained mean $\bar{y}$ of all output values. For a given confidence level α, a rule is accepted if

$$\left| \frac{\bar{y}_P - \bar{y}}{s_P / \sqrt{N_P}} \right| > t(N_P, \alpha) \quad \text{with} \quad s_P = \sqrt{\frac{\sum_n (y_n - \bar{y}_P)^2 \cdot \bigwedge_{k=1}^{c} \mu_{i_k, j_k}(x_{n,i_k})}{N_P - 1}} \tag{9}$$

holds. Here, s_P is the estimated constrained standard deviation and $t(N_P,\alpha)$ is the critical value[4] to reject the hypothesis at the confidence level α. The rating index of an accepted rule is supposed to increase as the constrained standard deviation s_P becomes smaller in comparison to the unconstrained standard deviation s. This leads to the index

$$J_{MVB} = e^{-s_P/s} \qquad \text{for positive rules} \ . \tag{10}$$

The conclusion part is chosen as s_{Y_j}, so that $\mu_{Y,j}(\bar{y}_P) \rightarrow \max$. It should be noted that this test does not find rules that recommend the unconstrained mean value $\bar{y}$. We overcome this drawback by choosing $\bar{y}$ as the default value when no rule is activated.

---

[4] The critical value can be calculated based on approximations or taken from a table of t-distributions.

2.3 Efficiency of the Complete Rule Search

The complete search method, presented in this section, is especially designed for efficient rule generation in high-dimensional search spaces [12]. As logical conjunctions of output variables are not supported by the FRM, the complexity arises predominantly from the number of input variables and their linguistic values. Therefore, in the following, the influence of the output variables is neglected and only the premises are considered.

On the one hand, the number of feasible premises increases exponentially with the number of input variables. On the other hand, the number of available data sets is strictly limited in most applications. In this case, the number of data sets per premise decreases drastically if the combination depth is increased. By exceeding a certain combination depth, a large number of the premises are no longer supported by any data point and when combined with any conclusion will not pass the rule tests described above. If further linguistic expressions are added to such a premise in order to generate a more special premise, the derived premise is also not supported by the data. Thus, it needs no longer to be considered in the generation process. The tree-oriented search algorithm, presented in Section 2.3.1, takes advantage of this fact.

In order to obtain a more precise impression of the search space being considered, in Section 2.3.2 the number of possible premises is compared to the number of premises that need to be tested on average for a simple example.

2.3.1 Tree-Oriented Complete Search

In the tree-oriented complete search (TOCS), all possible premises are set up and tested with respect to all linguistic output values. The TOCS concept is based on the linguistic expressions (see Section 2.2.1). Therefore, the latter are numbered serially: $\tilde{e}_1 = (X_1 = s_{11})$, $\tilde{e}_2 = (X_1 = s_{12})$, ..., $\tilde{e}_E = (X_V = s_{VS_V})$, where the total number of linguistic expressions is denoted by $E = \sum_{\iota=1}^{V} S_\iota$. Starting from the first linguistic expression $\tilde{e}_1$ all the more special premises are generated as diagrammed in Fig. 2.2.

Consider now the n-th linguistic expression $\tilde{e}_n$. For the combination depth $c = 1$ the premise is given by "*if* $\tilde{e}_n$ *then* ...". Based on this premise, rules are set up by combining $\tilde{e}_n$ with all linguistic output values as conclusions. The chosen test and rating strategy are applied, and each rule found relevant is added to the rule base.

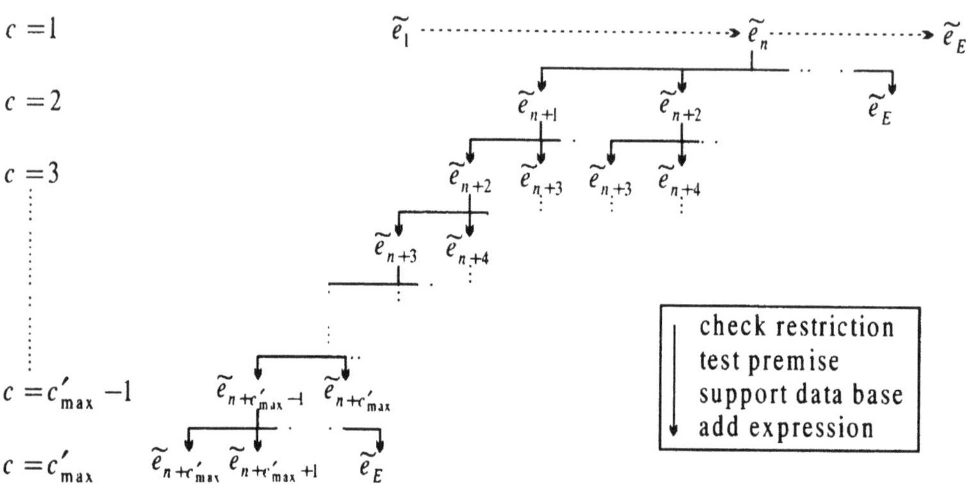

Fig. 2.2. The tree-oriented complete search (TOCS). Starting from a given premise, the necessary specialization (generation) steps are indicated in the box. First the restrictions are checked. If the premise is restricted, the branch need not to be considered any more. Then the premise is tested. A result of the test are the supporting data sets, which are taken as a data base in the next specialization step. Finally, a new term is added to the premise.

Then a new linguistic expression $\tilde{e}_{n+1}$ is added to the premise, until the maximum combination depth $c'_{\max}$ is reached. In order to avoid infeasible premises, the maximum combination depth $c'_{\max} \leq c_{\max}$ has to be defined, so that the index i of an added expression $\tilde{e}_i$ does not exceed E. If the TOCS is applied in this way, all possible rules are set up and tested. By activating combination restriction and minimal data support, the TOCS can be speeded up drastically as follows.

- A rule is unreasonable in the sense of combination restriction, if two linguistic expressions refer to the same linguistic variable. If this occurs at a certain point, the premise remains restricted, even if it is specialized. Consequently, this branch need not to be considered further.
- Rules with a high combination depth are more likely to be not supported by any data sets. Therefore, if a rule is not supported, no more specialized rule with additional linguistic expressions based on that rule can be found relevant. This means that if such a point is reached in a branch of the TOCS, the branch need not to be followed further. The computational savings are estimated in (Section 2.3.2).
- Following one branch, a decreasing number of supporting data sets need to be considered. Therefore, the calculation of Eq. 2, Eq. 3 and Eq. 8 can be implemented very efficiently by considering only the supporting database.

It should be noted that it is also possible to design a tree-oriented search in which rules restricted by the combination restriction are not set up. On the other hand, the TOCS presented here is more flexible and the computational effort to check the restrictions can be neglected in comparison to rule test and rating.

2.3.2 Search Space Structure

In this section, the size of the search space, i.e., the total number of possible premises, is specified by combinatorial calculations. As mentioned above, the number of data sets is usually limited. Taking this into account, the maximum number of premises that can be supported by the available data sets is calculated. Finally, an estimation is made of the number of hypotheses that must be tested on average for a simple synthetic example.

For simplification the following considerations are made (a more general view can be found in [13]):

- the combination and complement restrictions are activated (compare Section 2.1.3),
- each linguistic variable has the same number of linguistic values (sets) S, and
- the influence of the output variable is neglected.

In the following, the number of input variables is V. Due to the activated restrictions, each input variable can arise in only one linguistic expression in the premise of the rule. Based on this fact, the number of possible premises P_c^{pos} for a certain combination depth c can be calculated as follows

$$P_c^{pos} = \binom{V}{c} \cdot S^c \ . \tag{11}$$

The number of possible combinations for the given input variables is calculated by the first factor in Eq. 11 and the second factor considers the influence of the different linguistic values of the input variables. The total number of possible premises P_{tot}^{pos} is the result of a summation over all combination depths

$$P_{tot}^{pos}(c_{\max}) = \sum_{c=1}^{c_{\max}} P_c^{pos} \quad , \quad with \quad c_{\max} \le V \ . \tag{12}$$

To compare the total number of possible premises P_{tot}^{pos} with the estimated total number $P_{tot}^{\sup}$ of premises that can be supported by the given data sets, the following assumptions are made:

- the partition of the linguistic values is defined as hard, i.e., not overlapping,

- the number of data sets is D, and
- the distribution of the data sets is presumed to be the worst case, i.e., the maximum possible number of premises is supported.

The maximum number of premises P_c^{max} of a given combination depth c that can be supported by a single data set is calculated as

$$P_c^{max} = \binom{V}{c}. \tag{13}$$

In comparison to Eq. 11, the number of linguistic values has no influence, because only one linguistic value of each variable is supported by a data set, due to the hard partition. The maximum number of supported premises P_c^{sup} of the given combination depth and the total number P_{tot}^{sup} is given by

$$P_c^{sup} = \min\{\, D \cdot P_c^{max}, P_c^{pos} \,\} \;\; and \;\; P_{tot}^{sup} = \sum_{c=1}^{c_{max}} P_c^{sup}, \tag{14}$$

where the number of supported premises P_c^{sup} is limited to the maximum number of possible premises P_c^{pos}. As shown in Fig. 2.3, for a given combination depth c' the number of supported hypotheses $P_{c'}^{sup}$ is smaller than the number of possible premises $P_{c'}^{pos}$. Applying the tree-oriented search concept presented in Section 2.3.1, some of the premises need not to be specialized and consequently not all premises of the following combination depth are generated. The number of premises $P_{c=c'+1}^{save}$ not tested is difficult to determine, because it depends on the order in which the premises are generated. Therefore, P_c^{save} and the number of generated premises P_c^{gen} are estimated by calculating the average number of premises not tested

$$\overline{P}_c^{save} = \frac{P_{c-1}^{pos} - P_{c-1}^{sup}}{P_{c-1}^{pos}} \cdot P_c^{pos} \;\; and \;\; \overline{P}_c^{gen} = P_c^{pos} - \overline{P}_c^{save}, \; with \; 1 < c' < c$$

$$. \tag{15}$$

Consequently, the total number of premises P_{tot}^{gen} that must be generated can be estimated by

$$\overline{P}_{tot}^{gen}(c_{max}) = P_{tot}^{pos}(c_{max}) - \overline{P}_{tot}^{save} \quad , \; with \;\; \overline{P}_{tot}^{save} = \sum_{c=c'+1}^{c_{max}} \overline{P}_c^{save} . \tag{16}$$

The total number of possible premises P_{tot}^{pos} is calculated using Eq. 12 and $\overline{P}_{tot}^{save}$ denotes the estimated total number of premises not tested.

The numbers of possible, supported, saved and generated premises are illustrated in Fig. 2.3 and Fig. 2.4 for the following example: number of input variables

$V = 20$, number of linguistic values per input variable $S = 5$ and number of data sets $D = 10000$.

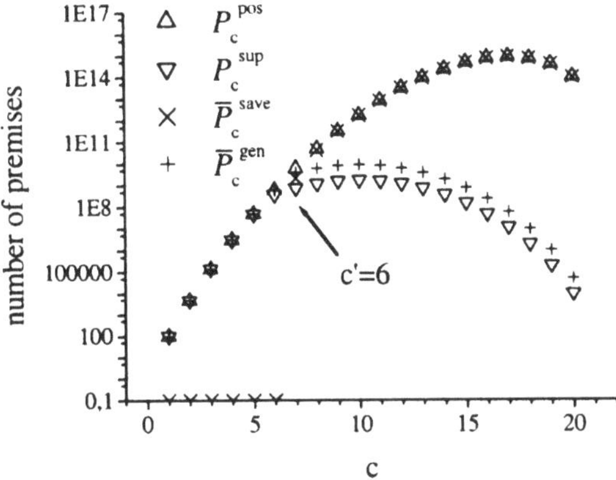

Fig. 2.3. Number of possible, supported, saved and generated premises as functions of the combination depth.

Considering Fig. 2.3 , after the critical combination depth c' is exceeded, it can be seen that the number of tested premises P_c^{gen} decreases in a similar manner as the number of supported premises $P_c^{\sup}$ with increasing combination depth c. Due to this fact, the increase of the total number of generated premises $\overline{P}_{tot}{}^{gen}$ is dramatically smaller than the increase of the total number of possible premises $P_{tot}{}^{pos}$ (Fig. 2.4).

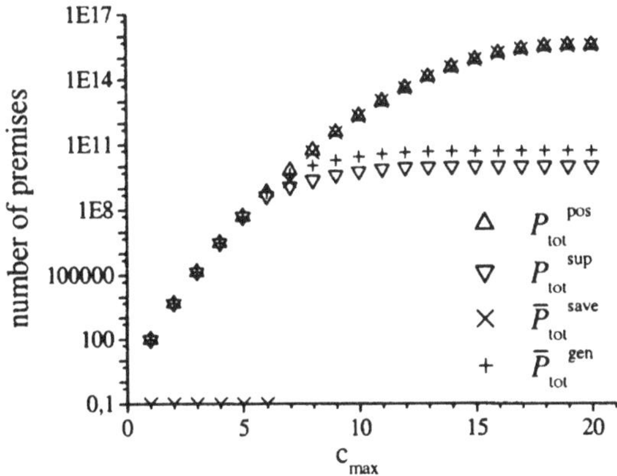

Fig. 2.4. Total number of possible, supported, saved and generated premises as functions of the maximum combination depth.

2.4 Hybrid Evolutionary Search Concept

In the literature, we find three main application areas of evolutionary algorithms in the field of fuzzy modeling: optimization of membership functions, optimization (generation) of rules and simultaneous optimization of both. In the case of rule base optimization (generation), most evolutionary algorithms use a fixed rule base structure of complete rules, where one individual in the evolving population represents a whole rule base (Pittsburgh style). The Pittsburgh style is often not practicable for more than three or four variables and more complex applications are rarely published.

In contrast, in our approach, which is depicted in Fig. 2.5, each individual represents a single fuzzy rule (Michigan style). While the evolutionary algorithm is searching for the "best" rule, many good rules are generated. The basic concept is to collect these good (relevant) rules during the course of evolution. In comparison to other approaches that also take single rules as individuals, our concept is based on one population and a single evolution process. Since the FRM makes use of generalizing (incomplete) rules, it was necessary to develop a sophisticated genetic representation and extended genetic operators [14].

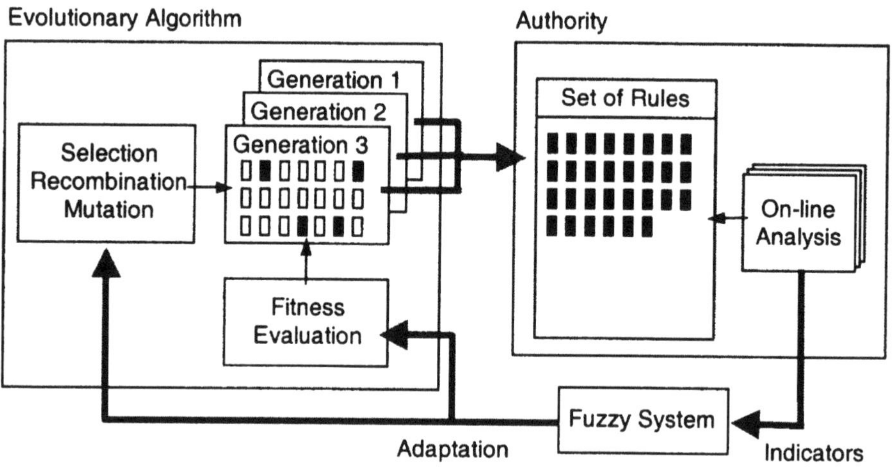

Fig. 2.5. Hybrid evolutionary search concept

As described above, the fitness evaluation of individuals is based solely on the relevance of single rules. Thus, the overall quality of the rule base collected at the current generation does not influence the evolutionary search process directly. In some situations, this might lead to a rule base consisting of a few rules of high relevance, but poor overall performance. Consequently, additional measures have been introduced in order to avoid premature stagnation and to keep the algorithm exploring the search space. This has been achieved by dynamically adapting some of the strategy variables depending on the performance of the current rule base collected during the course of evolution. The implementation is based on a hybrid fuzzy evolutionary approach, described in [14], where a fuzzy system is used to adapt the strategy parameters of the evolutionary algorithm.

3 Applications

The usefulness of the concept of the FRM presented above is shown in this section. Based on the benchmark problems described in Section 3.1, the performance of the FRM is demonstrated. Finally, several successful applications of the FRM to real-world tasks are presented briefly in Section 3.2.

3.1 Benchmark Problems

In the following, we briefly describe solutions for benchmark problems obtained with the FRM. Due to space limitations, we do not compare our results with other approaches in detail; the corresponding literature is cited instead. The complexity of each problem is specified by the number of linguistic variables V, the total number of linguistic values E, and the number of data sets D.

iris ($V=4$, $E=20$, $D=150$): A simple classification problem[5] for iris flowers. The task is to distinguish the flowers, based on four characteristics in three classes. Our results are in the range of other approaches, e.g. presented in [15].

mackey ($V=4$, $E=16$, $D=1000$): The task for the Mackey-Glass time series is to predict the next value based on recent values. Our approach is described in [13] and compared to other approaches [16-18].

wine ($V=13$, $E=65$, $D=178$): A classification problem based on data[5] sets that result from chemical analyses of wine grown in the same region in Italy, but derived from three different cultivators. The analysis determines the quantities of 13 constituents found in each of the three types of wines. In comparison to our results presented here, the approaches described in [19] are using all data sets for learning. If we apply the same strategy as for the improved results in Table 3.2 based on all data sets, we get results in the same range as the approaches mentioned above ($e_{learn}=1.4\%$, $N_{rule}=27$ and $t_{gen}<20$ min).

kin32nm ($V=32, E=224$, $D=8192$): The kin datasets are a family of datasets from the Delve[6] repository. The tasks associated with these datasets consist of predicting the distance of the end-effector of an eight-link all-revolute

---

[5] UCI Repository of Machine Learning Databases
http://*www.ics.uci.edu/~mlearn/MLRepository.html*

[6] Data for Evaluating Learning in Valid Experiments
http://www.cs.utoronto.ca/~delve/data/datasets.html.

robot arm from a target, given the eight angular positions of the joints. Our approach is described in [9] and compared to other approaches.

sat ($V = 36$, $E = 272$, $D = 4435$): The original Landsat data[5] is from NASA and contains the intensities of four spectral bands for 82 x 100 pixels. The task is to classify the soil represented by each pixel. Our approach is described in [8] and compared to other approaches.

gene ($V = 60$, $E = 240$, $D = 4175$): This benchmark problem comes from the field of molecular biology and deals with splice junctions[5]. The task is to recognize if, in the middle of a sequence of DNA with 60 nucleotides, there is an intron-exon boundary, an exon-intron boundary, or neither. Our approach is described in [13] and compared to other approaches [20-22].

In order to provide a fair comparison, two modeling approaches are performed for each problem.

- First, a complete rule search with a maximum combination depth $c_{max} = 2$ is applied. Furthermore, all rules with a rating index J smaller than a minimum rating index J_{min} are removed from the rule base. J_{min} is chosen by considering the modeling error and the covering rate on the learning data sets. In order to demonstrate that acceptable results can be obtained by this simple approach, no further strategy elements are applied here.
- Second, complete rule generation with a higher combination depth $c_{max} > 2$ is applied, depending on the benchmark problem. If necessary, additional rules are generated by the evolutionary search (HESC). In a subsequent step, the obtained rule base is optimized.

In both cases, the combination/complement restrictions are activated, only positive rules are used, and the minimal data support is equal to one. The results[7] on validation data[8], are presented in Table 3.1. Considering the first simple approach, it can be seen that satisfactory solutions are obtained in very short computing times.

If the combination depth is increased and additional FRM strategy elements are applied, the quality of the resulting model can be further improved. Simultaneously, for some of the applications the number of rules decreases drastically. Altogether, the benchmarks illustrate that the FRM is an efficient

---

[7] Obtained on a Pentium 200 MHZ (MMX), 128 MB RAM, Winrosa 2.0 software tool *http://esr.e-technik.uni-dortmund.de/winrosa/winrosa.htm.*

[8] For all benchmark problems we divided the data sets randomly in two halves. Both halves are taken as learning data sets and the other halve is used for validation respectively (cross validation). Only the error on validation data for the improved results of kin32nm, sat and gene are obtained as described in [8, 9].

approach for the generation of small rule bases even in high-dimensional search spaces. Furthermore, we found that the quality of our results is in the upper range of results reported for other approaches, especially if interpretable results are desired [8, 9, 13].

Table 3.1. Results for the different benchmark problems with a maximum combination depth $c_{\max} = 2$, where e_{vali} denotes the mean error (in percent for classification tasks and the absolute mean error for modeling tasks) on validation data, N_{rules} the mean number of rules, t_{gen} the average time for the rule base generation process and J the chosen rating method with threshold for the index. The applied strategy elements are also indicated.

	e_{vali}	N_{rule}	t_{gen}	J
iris	4.7%	7	<1 sec	$J_{RI} > 0.0$
mackey	0.056	130	<1 sec	$J_{RHR} > 0.2$
kin32nm	0.327	1544	<6 min	$J_{RI} > 0.0$
wine	21.9%	55	<1 sec	$J_{CHR} > 0.1$
sat	17.7%	5363	<13 min	$J_{RI} > 0.5$
gene	8.3%	958	<2 min	$J_{RI} > 0.2$

Table 3.2. Improved results for the different benchmark problems, where $c_{\max}$ denotes the maximum combination depth. The additional applied FRM strategy elements are also indicated.

	e_{vali}	N_{rule}	t_{gen}	$c_{\max}$	strategy elements
iris	4.7%	5	<1 min	4	TOCS+OCR
mackey	0.025	78	<1 min	4	TOCS+OCR
kin32nm	0.329	74	<30 min	1	TOCS+OCR
wine	11.8%	29	<10 min	13	TOCS+OCR
sat	11.0%	200	<2 h	2	TOCS+DCR+OCR
gene	5.8%	221	<3 h	6	TOCS+HESC+OCR

3.2 Real-World Applications

In this section it is shown that the FRM can meet the requirements of real-world applications. Due to space limitations, only three applications in the domains of *classification in quality control*, *prediction of contract durations* and *controller adaptation in robotics* are described here. They are chosen as examples of fuzzy modeling in high-dimensional search spaces and learning from noisy and contradictory data. Additional interesting applications of the FRM, not presented here, are:

- stock exchange market analysis for the Greek market index [23]
- access to the creditworthiness of enterprises [24]
- L-dopa dosing in Parkinson's disease pharmacotherapy [25]
- design of a fuzzy controller for an alkoxylation process by fuzzy modeling human control strategies [26] and
- electrical load prediction for a power control system [27].

3.2.1 Classification of Automatic Gearboxes in Quality Control

In quality control, different parameters are inspected during a test to detect material faults, production faults, assembly faults, or unusual sounds during operation. In our application, automatic gearboxes produced by an automobile manufacturer are tested acoustically by human specialists. With 149 acoustic input characteristics, the design of a fuzzy classifier is a very complex problem (10^{17} possible rules with maximum combination depth of six).

As described in [28, 2], data-based generation of a fuzzy classifier is possible using the FRM based on 1060 data sets (1000 *"o.k."* and 60 *"not o.k."*). Five equidistant membership functions were chosen heuristically for each characteristic. After a 20-hr hybrid evolutionary search and subsequent rule reduction, the resulting rule base (with less than 100 rules and a maximum combination depth of six) achieved a 100% correct classification on the learning data. In order to test the system's capability of generalizing classification results, learning was repeated on 90% of the data set. The remaining 10% were taken as test data. The classification error was 8% (5% for *"ok"* and 30% for *"not ok"*).

3.2.2 Prediction of the Duration of Insurance Contracts

Insurance companies are interested in contracts with long durations to avoid high administration costs. Therefore, statistical methods are used to analyze the dependency of contract durations on client profiles. Contract duration is the time between the start of the contract and the date of cancellation. Here, the profile of a client is characterized by the following seven socio-demographic characteristics: *social status*, *profession*, *sex*, *age*, *type of first contract*, *place of residence* and *state of residence*. Data-based rule generation of a fuzzy system to predict contract duration is a transparent approach, as the premise of a fuzzy rule can be interpreted as a profile of a client. The premise is a fuzzy conjunction of the socio-demographic characteristics. Initial results are presented in [28]. In a 24-hr hybrid evolutionary search, a rule base of 2297 rules with a certain minimal rating index was generated and used directly without any subsequent reduction for prediction. The comparisons[9] in Fig. 3.1 between real and predicted contract durations lead to the conclusion that in principle it is possible to learn fuzzy rules for typical client profiles. We are at present designing a fuzzy classifier.

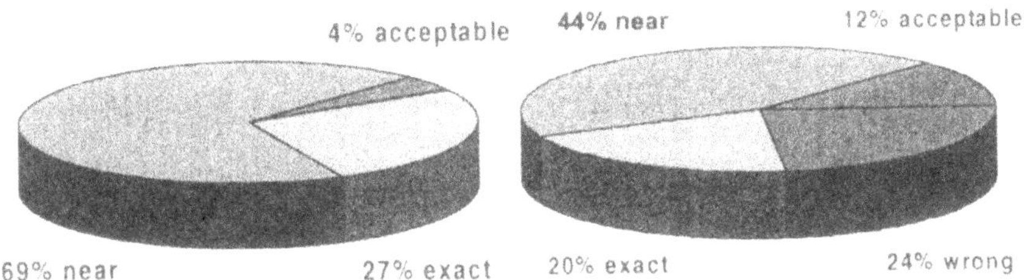

Fig. 3.1. Prediction for 4761 (26%) of 18399 learning data sets (left chart); prediction for 251 (31%) of 808 validation data sets (right chart).

3.2.3 Controller Adaptation in Robotics

For continuous path motions of a six-axis robot arm in Cartesian space, a high accuracy is required in particular applications. In [29] it was shown that the parameters of the axis controller could be adapted according to the operating point, by learning from good and poor control strategies. In order to obtain learning data sets for different operating points, the robot arm was moved along several selected Cartesian path trajectories with 27 parameter settings. Along these ten paths, the most influential variables were recorded while controller parameters were kept constant.

As the FRM can find a statistically relevant compromise in contradictory data, it will do the same when observation data from different control strategies and control performances are used. However, this will lead to the problem that bad controller outputs in the observation data are integrated in the compromise and different control strategies are mixed in an uncontrolled way. The following concept was proposed in order to overcome the disadvantages caused by the contradictions in the data. The observation data sets were rated with regard to the achieved control performance. A linear or nonlinear function transforms the values of this performance index to a rating factor. The rating factors are used to achieve rated degrees of matching of the conclusions. These are finally used to generate positive and negative rules. Consequently, all aspects of control performance are integrated in finding the most relevant and performance-oriented

[9] If the prediction error is larger than four years, the result is called **wrong**; if it is between two and four years, it is called **acceptable;** and if it is between four months and two years, it is called **near**. An **exact** prediction means the error is less than four months.

rules. The result is a set of relevant fuzzy rules, which for particular situations recommend those control parameters that lead to good control performance and warn against those control parameters that lead to poor control performance. By using this rule base for the fuzzy adaptation of the control parameters, the dynamic control error of the axis could be considerably improved [28].

4 Summary

In this paper, a complete survey of the concept of the Fuzzy-ROSA method (FRM) is given and the available strategy elements for the necessary steps of the rule generation process are presented. In particular, the different rule test and rating strategies are formally described and their dependence on the modeling objective is discussed. The efficiency of the tree-oriented complete rule search (TOCS) presented here is analyzed by considering the search space structure. Additionally, a hybrid evolutionary search concept is introduced for fuzzy modeling in high-dimensional search spaces.

The performance of the FRM is demonstrated by benchmark problems. It is shown that the FRM is an efficient approach for the data-based generation of small transparent rule bases, especially in high-dimensional search spaces. Furthermore, the modeling results of the FRM are located in the upper range of modeling quality compared to other approaches. We show that the FRM can meet the requirements of real-world tasks, using several applications with many input variables or noisy and contradictory data.

Acknowledgment

This research was sponsored by the "*Deutsche Forschungsgemeinschaft (DFG)*", as part of the Collaborative Research Center "*Computational Intelligence*" (531) of the University of Dortmund.

Some of the references and demonstration software can be **downloaded** from: *http://esr.e-technik.uni-dortmund.de/winrosa/winrosa.htm.*

References

[1] Krone, A., Kiendl H.: Automatic generation of positive and negative rules for two way fuzzy controllers. In *Proc. of EUFIT'94*, p. 438-442, Aachen, Germany, 1994.

[2] Praczyk, J., Kiendl, H., Slawinski, T.: Finding relevant process characteristics with a method for data-based complexity reduction. In *Proc. of 6th Fuzzy–Days, Int'l Conference on Computational Intelligence*, p. 548-555, Springer Verlag, Germany, 1999.

[3] Bezdek, J. C.: Pattern recognition with fuzzy objective function algorithms. Plenum Press USA, New York, USA, 1981.

[4] Krone, A., Slawinski, T.: Data-based extraction of unidimensional fuzzy sets for rule generation. In *Proc. of the 7th IEEE Int'l Conf. on Fuzzy Systems, FUZZ-IEEE'1998*, Vol. 2, p. 1032-1037, Alaska, USA, 1998.

[5] Kiendl, H.: Decision analysis by advanced fuzzy systems. In *Computing with Words in Information/Intelligent Systems 2 (Applications)*, p. 223-242, Physica-Verlag, Heidelberg, Germany, 1999.

[6] Kiendl, H.: Verfahren zur Erzeugung von Stellgrößen am Ausgang eines Fuzzy-Reglers und Fuzzy-Regler hierfür. Patent DE 43 08 083, 1994. Kiendl, H.: System of controlling or monitoring processes or industrial plants employing dual-line fuzzy unit. U. S. Patent Number 5,826,251, 1998.

[7] Krone, A.: Advanced rule reduction concepts for optimizing efficiency of knowledge extraction. In *Proc. of EUFIT'96*, p. 919-923, Aachen, Germany, 1996.

[8] Krone, A., Krause, P., Slawinski, T.: A new rule reduction method for finding interpretable and small rule bases in high dimensional search spaces. To appear in *Proc. of the 9th IEEE Int'l Conf. on Fuzzy Systems, FUZZ-IEEE'2000*, Texas, USA, 2000.

[9] Krause, P., Krone, A., Slawinski, T.: Fuzzy system identification by generating and evolutionary optimizing fuzzy rule bases consisting of relevant fuzzy rules. In *Computational Intelligence,* CI-84/00, ISSN1433-3325, Collaborative Research Center 531, University of Dortmund, Germany, 2000.

[10] Krone, A., Taeger, H.: Relevance test for fuzzy rules. In *Computational Intelligence,* CI-40/98, ISSN1433-3325, Collaborative Research Center 531, University of Dortmund, Germany, 1998.

[11] Jessen, H., Slawinski, T.: Test and rating strategies for data-based rule generation. In *Computational Intelligence,* CI-39/98, ISSN1433-3325, Collaborative Research Center 531, University of Dortmund, Germany, 1998.

[12] Slawinski, T., Krone, A., Krause, P.: Efficient design of a complete rule search in sparsely populated spaces. In: *Computational Intelligence, CI-77/99*, Collaborative Research Center 531, University of Dortmund, Germany, 1999.

[13] Krone, A., Slawinski, T., Krause, P.: Search space structuring as a key to cope with different problem sizes in the field of fuzzy modelling. To appear in *World Automation Congress, WAC'2000*, Hawaii, USA, 2000.

[14] Slawinski, T., Krone, A., Hammel, U., Wiesmann, D., Krause, P.: A hybrid evolutionary search concept for data-based generation of relevant fuzzy rules in high dimensional spaces. In *Proc. of 8th IEEE Int'l Conf. on Fuzzy Systems, FUZZ-IEEE '99*, p. 1432-1437, Seoul, South Korea, 1999.

[15] Holve, R.: Investigation of automatic rule generation for hierarchical fuzzy systems. In *Proc. of the 7th IEEE Int'l Conf. on Fuzzy Systems, FUZZ-IEEE'1998*, Vol.2, p. 1032-1037, Alaska, USA, 1998.

[16] Chen, C.-L., Hsu, S.-H., Hsieh, C.-T., Lin, W.-K.: Generating crisp-type fuzzy models from operating data. In *Proc. of the 7th IEEE Int'l. Conf. on Fuzzy Systems, FUZZ-IEEE'98*, Vol. 1, p. 686-691, Alaska, USA, 1998.

[17] Nauck, D., Kruse, R.: A neuro-fuzzy approach to obtain interpretable fuzzy systems for function approximation. In *Proc. of the 7th IEEE Int'l. Conf. on Fuzzy Systems, FUZZ-IEEE'98* Vol. 2., p. 1106-1111 Alaska, USA, 1998.

[18] Cho, K.B., Wang, B.H.: Radial basis function based adaptive fuzzy system and their applications to system identification and prediction. In *Fuzzy Sets and Systems* 83 (1996), p. 325-339, 1996.

[19] Corcoran, A. L., Sandip, S., Using real-valued genetic algorithms to evolve rule sets for classifications. In *Proc. of the 1st IEEE Int'l. Conf. on Evolutionary Computing, ICEC'94*, Vol. 1, p. 120-124, Orlando, USA, 1998.

[20] Michie, D., Spiegelhalter, D.J., Taylor, C. C.: Machine learning, neural and statistical classification. Hemel Hempstead, UK: Ellis Horwood, 1994.

[21] Prechelt, L.: PROBEN 1 – A set of neural network benchmark problems and benchmarking rules / Faculty of Computer Science, University of Karlsruhe, Germany, 1994.

[22] Brameier, M., Banzhaf, W.: A comparison of genetic programming and neural networks in medical data analysis. In *Computational Intelligence*, CI-43/98, ISSN1433-3325, Collaborative Research Center 531, University of Dortmund, Germany, 1998.

[23] Thomaidis, N., Dounias, G., Tselentis, G.: Stock exchange market analysis using DataEngine and Winrosa. In *Proc. of EUFIT'99*, Aachen, Germany, 1999.

[24] Blochwitz, S., Eigermann, J.: Creation and application of fuzzy rules to access the creditworthiness of enterprises. In *Proc. of EUFIT'99*, Aachen, Germany, p. 188, 1999.

[25] Honczarenko, K., Jardzioch, A., Piegat, A., Honczarenko, J.: Application of soft computing method to Parkinson's disease therapy, In *Proc. of EUFIT'99*, p. 205, Aachen, Germany, 1999.

[26] Krone, A., Frenk, C., Russak, O.: Design of a fuzzy controller for an alkoxylation process using the ROSA method for automatic rule generation. In *Proc. of EUFIT'95*, p. 760-764, Aachen, Germany, 1995.

[27] Jessen, H.: A mean–value based test and rating strategy for automatic fuzzy rule generation and application to load prediction. In *Proc. of the International Conference on Computational Intelligence for Modelling Control and Automation (CIMCA'99)*, Wien, Austria, 1999.

[28] Slawinski, T., Praczyk, J., Schwane, U., Krone, A., Kiendl, H.: Data-based generation of fuzzy rules for classification, prediction and control with the Fuzzy-ROSA method. In *European Control Conference, ECC'99*, Summaries Volume p. 573, Karlsruhe, Germany, 1999.

[29] Krone, A., Schwane, U.: Generating fuzzy rules from contradictory data of different control strategies and control performances. In *Proc. of the 5th IEEE Int'l Conf. on Fuzzy Systems, FUZZ-IEEE'1996*, pages 492-497, New Orleans, USA, 1996.

Discovering Knowledge from Fuzzy Concept Lattice

Sadok Ben Yahia [1], **Ali Jaoua** [2]

[1] Faculty of Sciences of Tunis, Computer Science Department, Campus Universitaire, 1060 Tunis, Tunisia. E-mail: sadok.benyahia@fst.rnu.tn

[2] King Fahd University for Petroleum and Minerals, Information and Computer Science Department, Dhahran 31261, Saudi Arabia.
E-mail: ajaoua@ccse.kfupm.edu.sa

Abstract. Since its inception, association rule mining has become one of the core data mining tasks, and has attracted tremendous interest among researchers and practitioners. Many efficient algorithms have been proposed in the literature, e.g., Apriori, Partition, DIC, for mining association rules in the context of market-basket analysis. They are all based on apriori methods, i.e., pruning the itemset lattice, and requires multiple database accesses. However, research so far has mainly focused on mining over binary data, i.e., either an item is present in a transaction or not. Little attention was paid to mining over data where the quantity of items is considered. In this paper, we propose to address the problem of mining fuzzy association rules, by considering the quantity of items in the transactions. After the fuzzification of the transaction database, we apply a new efficient algorithm, called FARD (Fuzzy Association Rule Discovery), for mining fuzzy association rules. FARD is based on the pruning of the fuzzy concept lattice, and can be applied equally to classical or fuzzy databases, by scanning the database only once.

Keywords. Data mining, Fuzzy sets, Association rules, Fuzzy concept lattice.

1 Introduction

With large volumes of routine business data stored in databases, business organizations are increasingly turning to the extraction of useful information from databases. Such high-level inferences may provide information on customer buying patterns, shelving criteria in a supermarket, stock trends, etc. Data mining is an emerging research area, whose goal is to extract significant patterns or interesting rules from such large databases [1].

Data mining is in fact a broad area, which combines research in machine learning, statistics, and databases. It can be broadly classified into three main categories [2]:

Classification - finding rules that partition the database into disjoint classes; *Sequences* - extracting commonly occurring sequences in temporal data; and *Associations* - find the set of most commonly occurring groupings of items. In this paper, we will concentrate on data mining for association rules.

The problem of mining association rules over basket data was introduced in [3]. Basket data usually consists of a record per customer with a transaction date, along with items bought by the customer. Because the amount of these transactions data is very large, an efficient algorithm or technique needs to be devised for discovering useful knowledge (or rules) embedded in the transaction data. An example of an association rule over such a database could be that *80%* of the customers that bought bread and milk, also bought eggs. The data mining task for association rules can be broken into two steps. The first step consists of finding all the sets of items, called *itemsets* that occur in the database with a certain user-specified frequency, called the *minimum support* (*minSup*). Such itemsets are called large itemsets. An itemset of k items is called a k-itemset. A k-subset is a k-length subset of an itemset. The second step consists of generating all implication rules among the large itemsets found in the first step. The general structure of most algorithms for mining association rules is that during the initial pass over the database the support for all single items (1-itemsets) is counted. The large 1-itemsets are used to generate candidate 2-itemsets. The database is scanned again to obtain occurrence counts for the candidates, and the large 2-itemsets are selected for the next pass. This process is repeated, for $k = 3, 4, \ldots$, until no more large k-itemsets can be found.

Related Works: Several algorithms for mining association rules have been proposed in the literature [3, 5, 14, 17, 19, 22, 24]. Almost all the algorithms use the *downward closure* property of itemset support to prune the itemset lattice - the property that all subsets of a large itemset must themselves be large. Thus, only the large k-itemsets are used to construct *candidate* or *potential large* $(k + 1)$-itemsets. A pass over the database is made at each level to find the large itemsets. The algorithms differ to the extent that they prune the search space using efficient candidate generation procedures. The first algorithm *AIS* [3] generates candidates on-the-fly. All frequent itemsets from the previous transaction that are contained in the new transaction are extended with other items in that transaction. This results in to many unnecessary candidates. The *Apriori* algorithm [5], which uses a better candidate generation procedure, was shown to be superior to earlier approaches [3, 14]. The *DHP* algorithm [19] collects approximate support of candidates in the previous access for further pruning. However, this optimization may be detrimental to performance [4]. All these algorithms make multiple accesses over the database, once for each iteration k. The *Partition* algorithm [22] minimizes *I / O* by scanning the database only twice. It partitions the database into small chunks, which can be handled in memory. In the first access, it generates the set of all potentially large itemsets (any itemset locally large in a partition), and in the second access, their global support is obtained. Another way to minimize the

I/O overhead is to work with only a small sample of the database. An analysis of the effectiveness of sampling for association mining was presented in [29], and [24] presents an algorithm that finds all rules using sampling. The recently proposed *DIC* algorithm [7] dynamically counts candidates of varying length as the database scan progresses, and thus is able to reduce the number of scans. Approaches using only general-purpose DBMS systems and relational algebra operations have been studied [13, 14], but these do not compare favorably with the specialized approaches. A number of parallel algorithms have also been proposed [4, 8, 12, 20, 28]. Other extensions of association rules include mining for rules in the presence of a taxonomy on items [6]. There has also been work in finding large sequences of itemsets over temporal data [6, 16 , 18, 23].

Limitations: The main limitation of almost all the proposed algorithms is that they make repeated accesses over the disk-resident database, incurring high I/O overheads. Moreover, all the noticeable algorithms for mining basket data are applicable to only binary data, i.e., either an item is present or it is not in a transaction. The quantity bought of an item is not token into consideration (i.e., is not stored in the database transactions). For example, we store the fact that a customer has bought *5* dozen eggs, equivalently to another customer who has bought only *two* eggs. However, we feel that the item quantity may play an important role in giving more meaning to association rules, and to the manager, more valuable and precise information about the customer buying patterns. Indeed, a rule such as "*80%* of the customers that bought at least *8* pieces of bread and *9* bottles of milk, also bought *4* dozen eggs" is richer in information than the classical rule "*80%* of the customers that bought bread and milk, also bought eggs".

In this paper, we propose an algorithm for mining association rules over data where the quantity of items is considered. Given a transaction database, we assume that the quantity of each item bought is stored. We propose to transform this transaction database into a fuzzy relation, on which we apply a new algorithm, called *FARD* (Fuzzy Association Rule Discovery), for mining fuzzy association rules. The algorithm FARD is fundamentally different from the existing ones, since it is based on the pruning of the fuzzy concept lattice. Indeed, in addition to being a technique for classifying and defining concepts from data, the fuzzy concept lattice may be exploited to discover dependencies among objects and their properties. The process may be undertaken in two different ways, depending on the peculiarities of the database and the needs of the users: (i.) scan the whole lattice, or part of it, in order to generate a set of rules that can be used later in a knowledge-based system, (ii.) browse to check if a given rule holds, not by generating the whole set of rules, but rather by looking for a node with some specific description. The motivation behind this second usage is users want to confirm a hypothesis or invalidate a claim based on the analysis of the input data [10].

In order to be efficient, FARD performs only one scan over the database and can also be applied equally well on crisp and fuzzy databases. In order to handle the user-defined constraints, e.g., minimal support and minimal confidence, we present an extension of FARD, called *FCARD* (Fuzzy user-Constrained Association Rule Discovery), is also presented.

The rest of the paper is organized as follows. In the next section, we introduce the fuzzy concepts based on the *fuzzy Galois connection*. Some useful properties of fuzzy Galois connection used in FARD are defined and proved. In section *3*, the FARD algorithm is presented. An extension of the FARD algorithm, taking into consideration some user-defined constraints, is also presented in this section. Finally, section *4* concludes this paper.

2 Fuzzy concepts

2.1 Basic definitions

In this section, we start by presenting some classical notions of fuzzy sets [27]. Then, we introduce the notions of fuzzy data mining context, fuzzy Galois connection, fuzzy concepts, and fuzzy Galois lattice.

2.1.1 Fuzzy Sets

Let U be a classical set of objects, called the universe of discourse. An element of U is denoted by lowercase letters.

Definition 1 *A fuzzy set F in a universe of discourse U is characterized by a membership function $\mu_F(u)$: $U \rightarrow [0, 1]$, where $\mu_F(u)$ denotes the degree of membership of u in the fuzzy set F. Hence, the fuzzy set F is denoted by the following (when U is a countable set of elements): $F = \{ \mu_F(u_1)^{u1}, \mu_F(u_1)^{u2}, \ldots, \mu_F(u_n)^{un} \}$.*

Example 1 *If $U = \{a, b, c\}$, then $X = \{a^{0.5}, b^{0.1}, c^{0.9}\}$ is an example of a fuzzy set. The degrees of membership of a,b and c in X are, respectively, 0.5 , 0.1 and 0.9. The fuzzy values 0.5, 0.1 and 0.9 determine the strength of membership of a particular element. Here, c with a membership degree of 0.9 has a strong membership in X.*

Crisp sets can be defined as special cases of fuzzy sets with the membership degrees restricted to the set *{0, 1}*.

Example 2 *If $U = \{a, b, c\}$, then $Y = \{a, b\}$ is an example of a crisp set. Y can also be written as a fuzzy set with membership degrees restricted to the values 0 and 1. Thus $Y = \{ a^1, b^1, c^0 \}$ is another way of expressing the set Y.*

Basic Set-Theoretic operations on Fuzzy Sets: The fundamental set-theoretic operations on fuzzy sets, which are of concern to us, are inclusion, union, intersection, and Cartesian product.

- **Inclusion**: A fuzzy set A is said to be included in another fuzzy set B if : $\forall x \in U\ \mu_A(x) \leq \mu_B(x)$.
- **Intersection:** The membership function $\mu_C(x)$of the intersection $C = A \cap B$ is defined by $\mu_C(x) = \min \{\mu_A(x), \mu_B(x)\}$.
- **Union:** The membership function $\mu_D(x)$ of the union $D = A \cup B$ is defined by $\mu_D(x) = \max \{\mu_A(x), \mu_B(x)\}$.
- **Cartesian Product**: The cartesian product $R = A \times B$ is defined by $R= \{x , y) \mid min (\mu_A(x), \mu_B(y)), \forall x \in A, y \in B\}$.

Example 3 *Consider $A = \{a^1, b^0\}$ and $B = \{p^{0.1}, q^{0.9}\}$. The Cartesian product of A and B is: $R = \{(a, p)^{0.1}, (b, p)^0, (a, q)^{0.9}, (b, q)^0\}$. R is a fuzzy binary relation.*

Definition 2 *Let R be a fuzzy binary relation, I a fuzzy set and $a^\alpha \in I$. We define $support(a^\alpha) = \{ \beta \mid (x, a)^\beta \in R \text{ and } \alpha < \beta \leq 1\}$.*

Example 4 *Let the fuzzy binary relation $R = \{(a, p)^{0.1}, (a, p)^{0.3}, (b, p)^{0.9}, (a, q)^{0.8}, (b, q)^0\}$. Then, the support $(p^{0.1}) = \{0.3, 0.9\}$.*

Fuzzy data mining context: A fuzzy data mining context is a triple $\boldsymbol{D} = (\boldsymbol{O}, \boldsymbol{I}, \boldsymbol{R})$ describing a finite set $\boldsymbol{O}$ of objects, a fuzzy finite set $\boldsymbol{I}$ of database items and a fuzzy binary relation $\boldsymbol{R}$ (i.e., $R \subseteq \boldsymbol{O} \times \boldsymbol{I}$). Each couple $(o, i)^\alpha \in \boldsymbol{R}$, means that the object $o \in \boldsymbol{O}$, has the item $i \in \boldsymbol{I}$, at least with a degree α.

Fuzzy Galois connection [15]: Let $\boldsymbol{D} = (\boldsymbol{O}, \boldsymbol{I}, \boldsymbol{R})$ be a fuzzy data mining context. For $O \subseteq \boldsymbol{O}$ and $I \subseteq \boldsymbol{I}$, we define:

$f(O): P(O) \rightarrow P(I)$: $\quad f(O) = \{d^\alpha \mid \forall g, g \in O, \alpha = min\ \mu_R(g, d)\}$

$h(O): P(I) \rightarrow P(O)$: $\quad h(I) = \{ g \mid \forall d, d \in I, \mu_R(g, d) \geq \mu_I(d)\}$

We can remark that $O \times f(O)$ is the biggest relation of the form $O \times X \subseteq R$, and that $h(I) \times I$ is the biggest relation of the form $X \times I \subseteq R$. In other words, f computes the maximal range for a domain O, and h computes the maximal domain for a range I.

The operators $h \circ f$ in $\boldsymbol{O}$ and $f \circ h$ in $\boldsymbol{I}$ [1] are called fuzzy Galois connection operators [15].

---

[1] $h \circ f(O) = h(f(O))$ and $f \circ h(I) = f(h(I))$

Proposition 1 *Given the fuzzy Galois connection (f, h), then the following properties hold for all $O, O_i, O_j \in \boldsymbol{O}$ and $I, I_i, I_j \in \boldsymbol{I}$.*

(A1) $O_i \subseteq O_j \Rightarrow f(O_i) \supseteq f(O_j)$	**(B1)** $I_i \subseteq I_j \Rightarrow h(I_i) \supseteq h(I_j)$
(A2) $O \subseteq h \circ f(O)$	**(B2)** $I \subseteq f \circ h(I)$
(A3) $f(O) = f \circ h \circ f(O)$	**(B3)** $h(I) = h \circ f \circ h(I)$
(A4) $O_i \subseteq O_j \Rightarrow h \circ f(O_i) \subseteq h \circ f(O_j)$	**(B4)** $I_i \subseteq I_j \Rightarrow f \circ h(I_i) \subseteq f \circ h(I_j)$
(A5) $h \circ f(h \circ f(O_i)) = h \circ f(O_i)$	**(B5)** $f \circ h(f \circ h(I_i)) = f \circ h(I_i)$

(AB6) $O \subseteq f(I) \Leftrightarrow I \subseteq h(O)$

Proof.

- *For (A1), we have* $f(O_i) = \{d^{\alpha_i} \mid \forall g,\ g \in O,\ \alpha_I = \min \mu_R(g, d)\}$, *and* $f(O_j) = \{d^{\alpha_J} \mid \forall g,\ g \in O,\ \alpha_j = \min \mu_R(g, d)\}$. *If* $O_i \subseteq O_j \Rightarrow \alpha_i \geq \alpha_j$. *Hence,* $f(O_i) \supseteq f(O_j)$. *This proves (A1).*

- *For (B1), if* $I_i \subseteq I_j \Rightarrow \forall d \in I_i,\ \mu_{I\,i}(d) \geq \mu_{I\,j}(d)$

$$h(I_i) = \{g_i \mid \forall d,\ d \in I_i,\ \mu_R(g, d) \geq \mu_{I\,i}(d)\}$$

$$h(I_j) = \{g_j \mid \forall d,\ d \in I_j,\ \mu_R(g, d) \geq \mu_{I\,j}(d)\}$$

If $g_j \in h(I_j) \Rightarrow \mu_R(g_j, d) \geq \mu_{I\,J}(d) \geq \mu_{I\,I}(d) \Rightarrow g_j \in h(I_i)$. *Hence,* $h(I_i) \supseteq h(I_j)$ *and this proves (B1).*

- *For (A2),* $f(O) = \{d^{\alpha} \mid \forall g,\ g \in O,\ \alpha = \min \mu_R(g, d)\}$

$H \circ f(O) = \{g \mid \forall d,\ d \in f(O), \Rightarrow \mu_R(g, d) \geq \min \mu_R(g, d)\}$

Obviously, if $g \in O \Rightarrow g \in h \circ f(O) \Rightarrow O \in h \circ f(O)$. *This proves (A2).*

- *For (B2), similarly, let* $d \in \boldsymbol{I}$ *with* $\mu_I(d)$. *Then,*

$$h(I) = \{g \mid \forall d,\ d \in I,\ \mu_R(g, d) \geq \mu_I(d)\}$$

$$f \circ h(I) = \{d^{\alpha} \mid \forall g,\ g \in h(I),\ \alpha = \min \mu_R(g, d)\}$$

$\alpha \geq \mu_I(d) \Rightarrow I \subseteq f \circ h(I)$. This proves (B2).

- *For (A3), with* $I = f(O)$ *by (A2)*

$$\Rightarrow f(O \subseteq f \circ h \circ f(O) \qquad (1)$$

and from $O \subseteq h \circ f(O)$ *by (A1)*

$$\Rightarrow f(O) \supseteq f \circ h \circ f(O) \qquad (2)$$

(1) and (2) $\Rightarrow f(O) = f \circ h \circ f(O)$. *(B3) can be proved similarly.*

- *For (A4),* $O_i \subseteq O_j \Rightarrow f(O_i) \supseteq f(O_j) \Rightarrow h \circ f(O_i) \subseteq h \circ f(O_j)$. *Similarly, for (B4),* $I_i \subseteq I_j \Rightarrow h(I_i) \supseteq h(I_j) \Rightarrow f \circ h(I_i) \subseteq f \circ h(I_j)$.
- For (A5). From (A3), we have $f \circ h(f(O_i)) = f(O_i) \Rightarrow h \circ f(h \circ f(O_i)) = h \circ f(O_i)$. *Similarly for (B5), from (B3), we have* $h \circ f(h(I_i)) = h(I_i) \Rightarrow h(f \circ h(I_i)) = h(I_i) \Rightarrow f \circ h(f \circ h(I_i)) = f \circ h(I_i)$.
- *For (AB6).* $O \subseteq f(I)$ *by (A1)* $\Rightarrow h(O) \supseteq f \circ h(I)$ *and by (B2)* $\Rightarrow h(O) \supseteq I$. *This proves that* $O \subseteq f(I) \Rightarrow I \subseteq h(O)$. *The other direction follows symmetrically.*

Proposition 2 Let $I_1, I_2 \in \boldsymbol{I}$, then $h(I_1 \cup I_2) = h(I_1) \cap h(I_2)$.

Proof.

Let $I_3 = I_1 \cup I_2$. *Then,*

$h(I_3) = \{g \mid \forall d, d \in I_3, \Rightarrow \mu_R(g, d) \geq \mu_{I3}(d)\}$

$= h(I_3) = \{g \mid \forall d, d \in I_3, \Rightarrow \mu_R(g, d) \geq \mu_{I1 \cup I2}(d)\}$

$= h(I_3) = \{g \mid \forall d, d \in I_3, \Rightarrow \mu_R(g, d) \geq max(\mu_{I1}(d), \mu_{I2}(d))\}$

$= h(I_3) = \{g \mid \forall d, d \in I_3, \Rightarrow \mu_R(g, d) \geq \mu_{I1}(d) \text{ and } \mu_R(g, d) \geq \mu_{I2}(d))\}$

$= h(I_3) = \{g \mid \forall d, d \in I_3, \Rightarrow \mu_R(g, d) \geq \mu_{I1}(d)\} \text{ and } \{g \mid \forall d, d \in I_3, \Rightarrow \mu_R(g, d) \geq$

$\mu_{I2}(d))\} = h(I_1) \cap h(I_2)$.

Proposition 3 $f \circ h(I_1 \cup I_2) = f \circ h(f \circ h(I_1) \cup f \circ h(I_2))$

Proof. *It can be proved as the classical case in [21].*

Fuzzy concept Let $C \subseteq \boldsymbol{I}$ be a set of items. C is called a *fuzzy concept*, if and only if it is equal to its *closure*, i.e., $f \circ h(C) = (C)$. $h(C)$ the *domain* of C. Hence, $f \circ h(C)$ is the minimal fuzzy concept containing *C.*

Fuzzy concept lattice: Let *C* be the set of fuzzy concepts derived from D using the fuzzy Galois connection. In [15], we have proved that the pair $L_c = (C, <<)$ is a complete fuzzy lattice called the fuzzy concept lattice or fuzzy Galois lattice, in which the following properties hold.

1. A partial order on the fuzzy Galois lattice elements, such that for every fuzzy concept $c_1, c_2 \in L_c$, $c_1 << c_2$ if $c_1 \subseteq c_2$. There is a dual relationship between the concepts c_i and their domains h (c_i) in the fuzzy Galois lattice, $c_1 \subseteq c_2 \Leftrightarrow h(c_2) \subseteq h(c_1))$, and therefore $c_1 << c_2 \Leftrightarrow h(c_2) \subseteq h(c_1)$.
2. All subsets of L_c have one greatest common element, the *Join* element, and one smallest common element, the *Meet* element, i.e., for all $S \subseteq L_c$:

   Join (S) = $f \circ h(\cup_{c \in S} c)$ Meet (S) = $\cap_{c \in S} c$

The partial order is used to generate a graph in the following way: there is an edge from c_1 to c_2 if $c_1 << c_2$, and there is no other element c_3, such that $c_1 << c_3 << c_2$. In that case, we say that c_1 is covered by c_2. The graph is usually called a *Hasse diagram* and the precedent covering relation means that c_1 is the parent of c_2 [9]. The Hasse diagram of a lattice represents a generalization/specialization relationship between the concepts. Besides its role as an effective tool for symbolic data analysis and knowledge acquisition [11, 25], the lattice of concepts can be exploited to discover dependencies among the objects and the items [10].

3 The FARD algorithm

The FARD algorithm is based on the incremental discovery of fuzzy concepts (FCs). Indeed, the use of the fuzzy concept lattice, which is a sub-lattice of the subset lattice, can improve the efficiency of association rule discovery by reducing the search space. Hence, we reduce both the number of database scans and the CPU overhead incurred by the generation of fuzzy itemsets. In fact, the size of fuzzy itemset lattice is exponential in the size of the set of items, i.e., $||L_s|| = 2^{||I||}$. Although in the worst case, the fuzzy concept lattice may grow exponentially, the growth is linear with respect to $||D||$, when there exists an upper bound K on the object size $||O||$. Then, the size of the fuzzy concept lattice is $||L_C|| \leq 2^{k} ||D||$ [10].

The FARD algorithm generates all fuzzy association rules in two successive steps:

1. Discovering all FCs,
2. For each fuzzy concept c discovered in the first step, generate all fuzzy association rules r, that can be derived from c.

Remark 1: *The first step is the most computationally intensive part of the algorithm. In fact, once all the required information to process Step 2 is collected (i.e., all the FCs and their domains), there is no need to access the database again. Step 2 can be performed in a straightforward manner in main memory.*

3.1 Discovering fuzzy concepts

The pseudo-code for discovering fuzzy concepts is given in algorithm *1*. The notation and parameters used in this algorithm are summarized in table *1*. We suppose that items are sorted in a lexicographic order. In each iteration, the algorithm constructs a set of candidate fuzzy concepts (CFC), and prunes this set, thus yielding a set of non-redundant fuzzy concepts. Finally, using this set, it computes the set of fuzzy generators that will be used during next iteration.

CFCk	Set of candidate *k*-fuzzy itemsets (potential fuzzy *itemsets).* Each element of this set has three fields: i) gen: *the generator* ii) *dom: the domain and iii) clos: the closure(i.e.,* $f \circ h$ *(gen)).*
FCk	Set of *k*-fuzzy itemsets. Each element of this set has *three fields:* i) gen: *the generator* ii) *dom: the domain and iii) clos: the closure (i.e.,* $f \circ h$ *(gen))*

Table 1. Notations

	B	C	E	M
O_1	*5*	*1000*	*7*	*5*
O_2	*6*	*700*	*10*	*5*
O_3	*10*	*700*	*10*	*1*
O_4	*10*	*900*	*9*	*1*

Table 2a. The transaction database D

⇒

	B	C	E	M
O_1	*0.5*	*1*	*0.7*	*0.5*
O_2	*0.6*	*0.7*	*1*	*0.5*
O_3	*1*	*0.7*	*1*	*0.1*
O_4	*1*	*0.9*	*0.9*	*0.1*

Table 2b. Fuzzy transaction database D

Discovering FCS

Input: D

Output $FC = \cup_i FC_i$

Begin

CFC_1 = {1-fuzzy itemsets}

For ($I = 1$; $CFC_i.gen \neq \varnothing$; $I++$) **do begin**

$CFC_i.clos = \varnothing$

$CFC_i.dom = \varnothing$

FC_i = Gen_concepts (CFC_i)

CFC_{i+1} = Gen_next (FC_i)

End

End.

Algorithm 1 : FCS Discovering

For example, let us consider the transaction database D, given in table *2a*. It is possible to fuzzify this transaction database by normalizing each item quantity as in table *2b*. Initially, $CFC_1 = \{A_i^{\beta}\}$, where $\beta = support(A_i)$, $A_i \in I$. For example, given the fuzzy transaction database D, then $CFC_1 = \{B^{0.5}, B^{0.6}, B^{1}, C^{0.7}, C^{0.9}, C^{1}, E^{0.7}, E^{0.9}, E^{1}, M^{0.1}, M^{0.5}\}$. Each iteration is composed of two phases:

1. The function Gen_concept (described in subsection 3.1.1), is applied to each fuzzy generator in CFC_i, determining its domain and its closure.
2. The set of the generators used in the next iteration, i.e., CFC_{i+1}, is computed by applying the function Gen_next (described in subsection 3.1.2) to FC_i.

The algorithm terminates when there are no more fuzzy generators to process, i.e., CFC_i, is empty.

3.1.1 The Gen_concepts function

The function Gen_concepts computes, for all $c \in CFC_i$, the domain and the closure of c. The pseudo-code of Gen_concepts function is given below.

Function Gen_concepts

Input: CFC_i

Output: FC_i

Begin

$FC_i = \varnothing$

Forall $c \in CFC_i$ **do begin**

$FC_i . gen = c$

$c. dom = h(c)$

$c. clos = f \circ h(c)$

If $h(c) \notin FC_i$ **then** \\ c is a non redundant fuzzy concept

$FC_i = FC_i \cup \{c\}$

End

End.

Function: Gen_concepts.

The set CFC_i is pruned using proposition 4, in order to avoid redundant generators.

Proposition 4 *Let I_1 and I_2 two distinct i-fuzzy itemsets, such that $f \circ h(I_1) = f \circ h(I_2)$. Then, it is useless to use I_2 as new potential $(I + 1)$ - fuzzy itemsets generator.*

Proof .

Let $I \in CFC_i$, we have $f \circ h\ (I \cup I_1) = f \circ h\ (f \circ h\ (I) \cup f \circ h\ (I_1))$. Since, $f \circ h(I_1) = f \circ h(I_2)$, then $f \circ h\ (f \circ h\ (I) \cup f \circ h\ (I_1)) = f \circ h\ (f \circ h\ (I) \cup f \circ h\ (I_2))$ $= f \circ h\ (I \cup I_2)$.

For example, suppose that the set FC_1 contains the *1*-fuzzy itemset generators $A^{0.8}$, B^{1}, $E^{0.7}$, with respective closures $\{A^{0.8}C^{1}\}$, $\{B^{1}E^{0.7}\}$, $\{B^{1}E^{0.7}\}$. The function Gen_next, instead of blindly generating $A^{0.8}B^{1}$, $A^{0.8}E^{0.7}$, $B^{1}E^{0.7}$ as potential 2-fuzzy itemsets as in Apriori-Gen [5], will remove $E^{0.7}$ from FC_1, since $f \circ h\ (B^{1}) = f \circ h\ (E^{0.7})$. Indeed, composing $A^{0.8}$ with B^{1} is the same as composing $A^{0.8}$ with $E^{0.7}$. Hence, using $E^{0.7}$ as a generator will be a source of redundancy.

3.1.2 Gen_next function

The function Gen_next takes as argument the set of fuzzy concepts FC_i and computes the set CFC_{i+1} containing all $(i + 1)$-fuzzy itemsets, which will be used as fuzzy generators, during the next iteration.

Gen_next works as follows. We apply the combinatorial phase of Apriori-Gen to the set FC_i. In fact, two distinct fuzzy generators of size i in FC_i, with the same first $(i - 1)$-fuzzy items are joined, producing a new potential fuzzy generator of size $(i + 1)$. The pseudo-code of the new potential generators is given below.

Insert into $CFC_{i+1}.gen$

Select $p.item_1, p.item_2, \ldots, p.item_i, q.item_i$

From $FC_i.gen\ p$, $FC_i.gen\ q$

Where $p \neq q$, $p.item_1 = q.item_1$, $p.item_2 = q.item_2$, ...,

$p.\ item_{i-1} = q.item_{i-1}$, $p.item_i < q.item_i$

Then a filter based on proposition 5 is applied. In fact, for each potential fuzzy generator g in CFC_{i+1}, we test if the closure of one of its i-subsets s_a, or the closure of a superset of s_a in FC_i, is a superset of g. In that case, g is removed from CFC_{i+1}.

Proposition 5 *Let I be a fuzzy generator i - itemset and $S = \{s_1, \ldots, s_j\}$ a set of (i-1) - subsets of I, where $\cup_{s \in S}\, s = I$. If $\exists\, s_a \in S$ and X is a superset of s_a, and if $I \subseteq f \circ h\ (X)$ and $h\ (I) \subseteq h\ (X)$, then $f \circ h\ (I) = f \circ h\ (X)$.*

Proof.

$$I \subseteq f \circ h\ (X) \Rightarrow f \circ h\ (I) \subseteq f \circ h\ (f \circ h\ (X)) \Rightarrow f \circ h\ (I) \subseteq f \circ h\ (X) \quad (3)$$

$$H\ (I) \subseteq h\ (X) \Rightarrow f \circ h\ (I) \supseteq f \circ h\ (X) \quad (4)$$

Hence, from (3) and (4), we have $f \circ h\ (I) = f \circ h\ (X)$.

The pseudo code of the filter is given below.

Forall $g \in CFC_{i+1}.gen$ **do begin**

S_g = i – subset (FC_i.gen, p)

// All i - subsets of g and their supersets that are existing generators in FC_i

Forall $s \in S_g$ **do begin**

If $g \subseteq s.clos$ *and* $h(g) \subseteq h(s)$ **then**

Delete g from $CFC_{i+1}.gen$

End

End

For example, let $FC_1 = \{A^{0.8}, B^{1}, D^{0.8}, D^{0.9}\}$, with respective closures $\{A^{0.8}C^{1}\}$, $\{B^{1}E^{1}\}$, $\{D^{0.8}\}$, $\{A^{1}C^{1}D^{0.9}\}$. The function Apriori-Gen will generate $A^{0.8}B^{1}$, $A^{0.8}D^{0.8}$, $A^{0.8}D^{0.9}$, $B^{1}D^{0.8}$, $B^{1}D^{0.9}$ as new fuzzy potential generators. However, the filter will remove $A^{0.8}D^{0.8}$ and $A^{0.8}D^{0.9}$, since they are included in $f \circ h\ (D^{0.9})$, which implies that computing their closures is redundant.

Example 5 *Let us consider the fuzzy transaction database D , given in table 2b. Then, figure 1 shows the execution of FARD fuzzy concepts discovery on the transaction database D.* $CFC_1 = \{B^{0.5}, B^{0.6}, B^{1}, C^{0.7}, C^{0.9}, C^{1}, E^{0.7}, E^{0.9}, E^{1}, M^{0.1}, M^{0.5}\}$. *The function Gen_concept computes for each fuzzy generator g of* CFC_1 *its domain and its closure.* FC_1 *is obtained from* CFC_1, *once all fuzzy generators having redundant closures have been removed. Thus,* $C^{0.7}, E^{0.7}, M^{0.1}$ *have been removed from* FC_1, *since their respective closures are equal to* $f \circ h$ $(B^{0.5})$. *Also,* $E^{0.9}$ *has been removed since its closure is equal to* $f \circ h\ (C^{0.6})$. CFC_2 *is obtained by applying Gen_next to* FC_1. *The fuzzy generators* $B^{0.5}, C^{0.9}$ *of* FC_1 *do not produce the fuzzy generator* $B^{0.5}C^{0.9}$, *since* $B^{0.5}C^{0.9} \subseteq f \circ h\ (C^{0.9})$. *Calling Gen_concepts with* CFC_2 *gives the domain and the closure of each fuzzy generator g of* CFC_2. *After the pruning of* CFC_2, *the algorithm terminates, since* CFC_3 *is empty as no fuzzy generators in* FC_2 *have the same first 2-itemset. The fuzzy concept lattice is depicted in figure 2, where the fuzzy concepts are labeled from FC0 to FC9, such that FC0 is the smallest fuzzy concept and is equal to* $\{B^{1}, C^{1}, E^{1}, M^{1}\}$ *with an associated domain equal to* $\varnothing$.

3.2 Discovering knowledge from fuzzy concept lattices

In this subsection, we present an algorithm for discovering fuzzy association rules from a fuzzy concept lattice. We begin, by formally presenting the fuzzy association rules. Let $I = \{A_1^{\alpha 1}, A_2^{\alpha 2}, \ldots, A_p^{\alpha p}, A_q^{\alpha q}, \ldots, A_n^{\alpha n}\}$ be a n-fuzzy itemset. A fuzzy association rule is an implication of the form $r\colon I_1 \Rightarrow I_2$, where

$I_1, I_2 \subseteq I$ and $I_1 = \{A_1^{\alpha 1}, A_2^{\alpha 2}, \ldots, A_p^{\alpha p}\}$ and $I_2 = \{A_q^{\alpha q}, \ldots, A_n^{\alpha n}\}$. I_1 and I_2 are called, respectively, the *premise part* and *conclusion part* of the fuzzy rule *r*. The value α_i, $i = 1, \ldots, n$, is called *local weight* of the item A_i. This value indicates the relative degree of importance of each item contributing to the conclusion of the rule, and plays an important role in many real world problems [26]. For example, in medical diagnostic systems, it is common to assign a local weight to each symptom in order to show the relative importance (weight) of each symptom leading to the conclusion (a disease).

Note that classical (or crisp) association rules can be defined as a special case of fuzzy association rules. Indeed, when $I = \{A_1^{\alpha 1}, A_2^{\alpha 2}, A_n^{\alpha n}\}$ and $\alpha_I = 1, I = 1, \ldots, n$, then a fuzzy association rule is equivalent to a classical one.

The algorithm, for which the pseudo-code is given in algorithm 2, works as follows. For each non empty node $N \in L_c$ in ascending $\|N\|$, we generate all rules with one fuzzy item conclusion. Then, starting with the set of one fuzzy item conclusions found in this step, we apply the function Apriori-gen in order to generate the set of two fuzzy items conclusions. Next, the fuzzy rules with two fuzzy item conclusion are generated. The same process is applied to generate conclusions with three fuzzy items, and so on until conclusions with $(n - 1)$-fuzzy items have been generated.

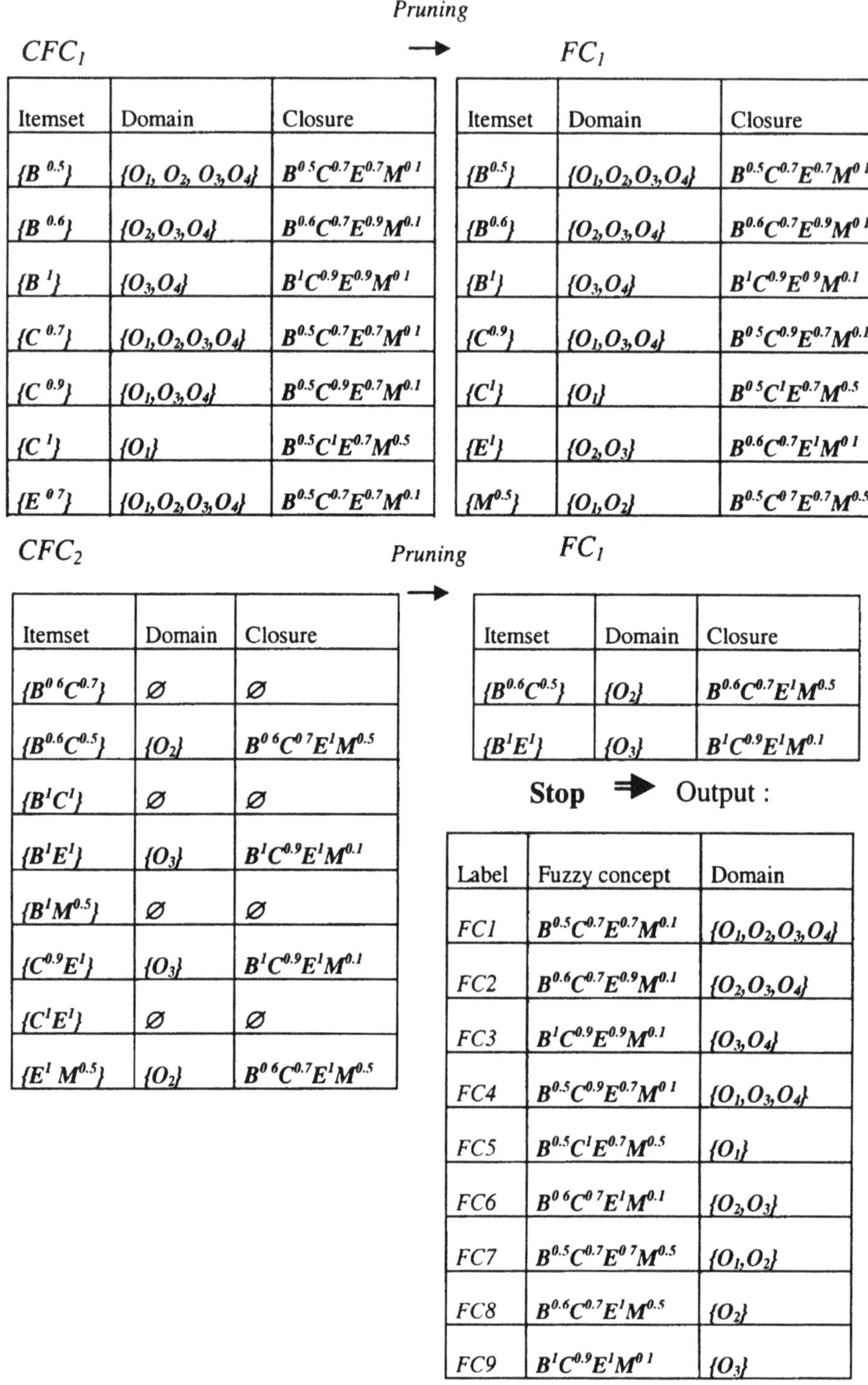

CFC_1 —Pruning→ FC_1

Itemset	Domain	Closure
$\{B^{0.5}\}$	$\{O_1, O_2, O_3, O_4\}$	$B^{0.5}C^{0.7}E^{0.7}M^{0.1}$
$\{B^{0.6}\}$	$\{O_2, O_3, O_4\}$	$B^{0.6}C^{0.7}E^{0.9}M^{0.1}$
$\{B^{1}\}$	$\{O_3, O_4\}$	$B^{1}C^{0.9}E^{0.9}M^{0.1}$
$\{C^{0.7}\}$	$\{O_1, O_2, O_3, O_4\}$	$B^{0.5}C^{0.7}E^{0.7}M^{0.1}$
$\{C^{0.9}\}$	$\{O_1, O_3, O_4\}$	$B^{0.5}C^{0.9}E^{0.7}M^{0.1}$
$\{C^{1}\}$	$\{O_1\}$	$B^{0.5}C^{1}E^{0.7}M^{0.5}$
$\{E^{0.7}\}$	$\{O_1, O_2, O_3, O_4\}$	$B^{0.5}C^{0.7}E^{0.7}M^{0.1}$

Itemset	Domain	Closure
$\{B^{0.5}\}$	$\{O_1, O_2, O_3, O_4\}$	$B^{0.5}C^{0.7}E^{0.7}M^{0.1}$
$\{B^{0.6}\}$	$\{O_2, O_3, O_4\}$	$B^{0.6}C^{0.7}E^{0.9}M^{0.1}$
$\{B^{1}\}$	$\{O_3, O_4\}$	$B^{1}C^{0.9}E^{0.9}M^{0.1}$
$\{C^{0.9}\}$	$\{O_1, O_3, O_4\}$	$B^{0.5}C^{0.9}E^{0.7}M^{0.1}$
$\{C^{1}\}$	$\{O_1\}$	$B^{0.5}C^{1}E^{0.7}M^{0.5}$
$\{E^{1}\}$	$\{O_2, O_3\}$	$B^{0.6}C^{0.7}E^{1}M^{0.1}$
$\{M^{0.5}\}$	$\{O_1, O_2\}$	$B^{0.5}C^{0.7}E^{0.7}M^{0.5}$

CFC_2 —Pruning→ FC_1

Itemset	Domain	Closure
$\{B^{0.6}C^{0.7}\}$	∅	∅
$\{B^{0.6}C^{0.5}\}$	$\{O_2\}$	$B^{0.6}C^{0.7}E^{1}M^{0.5}$
$\{B^{1}C^{1}\}$	∅	∅
$\{B^{1}E^{1}\}$	$\{O_3\}$	$B^{1}C^{0.9}E^{1}M^{0.1}$
$\{B^{1}M^{0.5}\}$	∅	∅
$\{C^{0.9}E^{1}\}$	$\{O_3\}$	$B^{1}C^{0.9}E^{1}M^{0.1}$
$\{C^{1}E^{1}\}$	∅	∅
$\{E^{1}M^{0.5}\}$	$\{O_2\}$	$B^{0.6}C^{0.7}E^{1}M^{0.5}$

Itemset	Domain	Closure
$\{B^{0.6}C^{0.5}\}$	$\{O_2\}$	$B^{0.6}C^{0.7}E^{1}M^{0.5}$
$\{B^{1}E^{1}\}$	$\{O_3\}$	$B^{1}C^{0.9}E^{1}M^{0.1}$

Stop ⇒ Output :

Label	Fuzzy concept	Domain
FC1	$B^{0.5}C^{0.7}E^{0.7}M^{0.1}$	$\{O_1, O_2, O_3, O_4\}$
FC2	$B^{0.6}C^{0.7}E^{0.9}M^{0.1}$	$\{O_2, O_3, O_4\}$
FC3	$B^{1}C^{0.9}E^{0.9}M^{0.1}$	$\{O_3, O_4\}$
FC4	$B^{0.5}C^{0.9}E^{0.7}M^{0.1}$	$\{O_1, O_3, O_4\}$
FC5	$B^{0.5}C^{1}E^{0.7}M^{0.5}$	$\{O_1\}$
FC6	$B^{0.6}C^{0.7}E^{1}M^{0.1}$	$\{O_2, O_3\}$
FC7	$B^{0.5}C^{0.7}E^{0.7}M^{0.5}$	$\{O_1, O_2\}$
FC8	$B^{0.6}C^{0.7}E^{1}M^{0.5}$	$\{O_2\}$
FC9	$B^{1}C^{0.9}E^{1}M^{0.1}$	$\{O_3\}$

Figure 1. Fuzzy concepts discovery

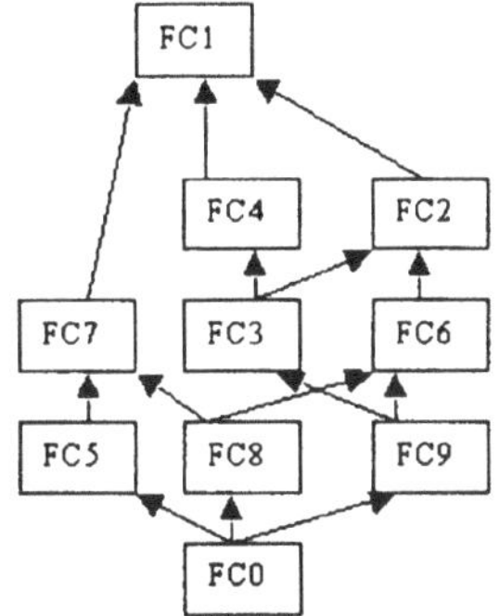

Figure 2. Fuzzy concepts lattice

Node	1-item conclusion	2-item conclusion	3-item conclusion
FC1	$C^{0.7}E^{0.7}M^{0.1} \Rightarrow B^{0.5}$	$E^{0.7}M^{0.1} \Rightarrow B^{0.5}C^{0.7}$	$M^{0.1} \Rightarrow B^{0.5}C^{0.7}E^{0.7}$
	$B^{0.5}E^{0.7}M^{0.1} \Rightarrow C^{0.7}$	$C^{0.7}M^{0.1} \Rightarrow B^{0.5}E^{0.7}$	$E^{0.7} \Rightarrow B^{0.5}C^{0.7}M^{0.1}$
	$B^{0.5}C^{0.7}M^{0.1} \Rightarrow E^{0.7}$	$C^{0.7}E^{0.7} \Rightarrow B^{0.5}M^{0.1}$	$C^{0.7} \Rightarrow B^{0.5}E^{0.7}M^{0.1}$
	$B^{0.5}C^{0.7}E^{0.7} \Rightarrow M^{0.1}$	$B^{0.5}M^{0.1} \Rightarrow C^{0.7}E^{0.7}$	$B^{0.5} \Rightarrow C^{0.7}E^{0.7}M^{0.1}$
		$B^{0.5}E^{0.7} \Rightarrow C^{0.7}M^{0.1}$	
		$B^{0.5}C^{0.7} \Rightarrow E^{0.7}M^{0.1}$	
FC2	$C^{0.7}E^{0.9}M^{0.1} \Rightarrow B^{0.6}$	$E^{0.9}M^{0.1} \Rightarrow B^{0.6}C^{0.7}$	$E^{0.9} \Rightarrow B^{0.6}C^{0.7}M^{0.1}$
	$B^{0.6}C^{0.7}M^{0.1} \Rightarrow E^{0.9}$	$C^{0.7}E^{0.9} \Rightarrow B^{0.6}M^{0.1}$	$B^{0.6} \Rightarrow C^{0.7}E^{0.9}M^{0.1}$
		$B^{0.6}E^{0.9} \Rightarrow C^{0.7}M^{0.1}$	
		$B^{0.6}C^{0.7} \Rightarrow E^{0.9}M^{0.1}$	
FC3	$C^{0.9}E^{0.9}M^{0.1} \Rightarrow B^{1}$	$E^{0.9}M^{0.1} \Rightarrow B^{1}C^{0.9}$	$B^{1}E^{0.9}M^{0.1} \Rightarrow C^{0.9}$
	$B^{1}E^{0.9}M^{0.1} \Rightarrow C^{0.9}$	$C^{0.9}M^{0.1} \Rightarrow B^{1}E^{0.9}$	$B^{1} \Rightarrow C^{0.9}E^{0.9}M^{0.1}$
		$C^{0.9}E^{0.9} \Rightarrow B^{1}M^{0.1}$	
		$B^{1}M^{0.1} \Rightarrow C^{0.9}E^{0.9}$	
		$B^{1}E^{0.9} \Rightarrow C^{0.9}M^{0.1}$	
		$B^{1}C^{0.9} \Rightarrow E^{0.9}M^{0.1}$	
FC3	...	. ..	...
FC4	...	..	...

Figure 3. Fuzzy association rule generation

Generating fuzzy association rules

Input: Fuzzy concept lattice

Output : FRS: Fuzzy Rules Set

Begin

Forall $N \in L_c$ in ascending $||N|| \setminus N \neq \varnothing$ **do begin**

H_1 = fuzzy *1*-itemsets that are subsets of N

Forall $h_1 \in H_1$ **do begin**

r.premise = $(N - h_1)$

r.conclusion = h_1

IF $(N - h_1) \notin FRS$ **and** $h_1 \notin FRS$ **then**

FRS = $FRS \cup r$

Call GenRules (N, H_1)

End

End.

Procedure GenRules (N: k - itemsets, H_m: set of m - item conclusion

If $(k > m + 1)$ **then do begin**

H_{m+1} = Apriori - Gen (H_m)

Forall $h_{m+1} \in H_{m+1}$ **do begin**

r.premise= $(N - h_{m+1})$

r.conclusion = h_{m+1}

If $(N - h_{m+1}) \notin$ FRS **and** $h_{m+1} \notin$ FRS **then**

$FVRS = FVRS \cup r$

End

Call GenRules (N, H_{m+1})

End

End.

Algorithm 2. Fuzzy association rules generation

Example 6 *Figure 3 shows the process of fuzzy association rule generation, using the fuzzy concepts given in figure 1.*

3.3 Integrating user constraints

In this section, we address the problem of discovering all fuzzy association rules under specified user constraints. These user constraints are of three types:

1. Selected items, with a minimal degree, to appear in the discovered fuzzy association rules,
2. Minimal support of the discovered fuzzy concepts,
3. Minimal confidence of the discovered fuzzy association rules.

Hence, in the sequel, we propose an algorithm, called *FCARD* (Fuzzy user-Constrained Association Rules Discovery), for generating all fuzzy association rules in three successive steps, as described below.

Algorithm FCARD

Input: D, $S = \{A_1^{\alpha 1}, A_2^{\alpha 2}, \ldots, A_m^{\alpha m}\}$, *minSup* and *minConf*.

Output: *IFRS* (Interesting Fuzzy Rules Set)

Begin

1. Discover all large fuzzy concepts (*LFCs*), i.e., discover all fuzzy concepts *C* with support greater than or equal to *minSup*, where $support\ (C) = \|\ h\ (C)\ \|\ /\ \|O\|$,
2. Derive all large fuzzy itemsets from the discovered LFCs. This step consists of extracting all $(i - 1)$-fuzzy itemsets from all LFCs of size *i*. Indeed, we prove later that these $(i - 1)$-fuzzy itemsets are also large,
3. For each large fuzzy itemset I derived in the second step, generate all *interesting* fuzzy association rules $r: I_1 \Rightarrow (I - I_1)$, where $I_1 \subseteq I$, that is can be derived from *I*. By interesting, we mean confidence (r)$\geq$ *minConf*, where $confidence\ (r) = \|\ h\ (I)\ \|\ /\ \|\ h\ (I_1)\ \|$.

End.

As inputs, the FCARD algorithm takes the transaction database *D*, the fuzzy set $S = \{A_1^{\alpha 1}, A_2^{\alpha 2}, \ldots, A_m^{\alpha m}\}$, *minSup* and *minConf*. The fuzzy set ***S*** constitutes a set of item-constraints on the discovered LFCs, and therefore on the fuzzy association rules. For example, if $S = \{A^{0.8}, B^{1}, C^{0.7}\}$, then the user wishes to discover all the fuzzy association rules (resp. LFCs), with respect to *minSup* and *minConf*, such that the items *A, B, C* appear in these rules (resp. LFCs) with a degree equal to or greater than *0.8, 1, 0.7*, respectively. Note that in the classical case, introduced by Agrawal et al [3], the set *S* is equal to $\{A_1^1, A_2^1, \ldots, A_m^1\}$. This fact explains why all the items appearing in classical association rules have a degree equal to *1*.

The FCARD algorithm is based on the two properties proved in the following proposition.

Proposition 6

1. *All subsets of a LFC are large,*
2. *All supersets of an infrequent fuzzy concept are infrequent.*

Proof.

1. *If C is LFC, then* $\forall I \subseteq C$, *I is large fuzzy itemset(i.e., support* $(I) \geq minSup$). *In fact,* $I \subseteq C \Rightarrow h(I) \supseteq h(C) \Rightarrow minSup \leq \| h(C)\| \leq \| h(I)\|$. *Hence, support* $(I) \geq minSup$ *and I is large.*
2. *Let* I_1, I_2 *be two fuzzy concepts, where* $I_1 \subseteq I_2$, *and* I_1 *is infrequent (i.e., support* $(I_1) < minSup$). *We have to prove that* I_2 *is infrequent. In fact,* $I_1 \subseteq I_2 \Rightarrow h(I_2) \subseteq h(I_1) \Rightarrow \| h(I_2)\| \leq \| h(I_1)\| \Rightarrow support(I_2) \leq support(I_1) < minSup$. *Hence,* I_2 *is infrequent.*

In what follows, we will concentrate on the second step of the FCARD algorithm. The other steps remain practically unchanged from those described in FARD algorithm. The minimal changes consist of the pruning the infrequent fuzzy concepts and the uninteresting fuzzy association rules in the first and the third step, respectively.

3.3.1 Deriving large fuzzy itemsets

Given the LFCs discovered in the first step, we derive the large fuzzy itemsets, i.e., for each *LFC* C of size i, we derive all its $(i - 1)$ - subsets. Based on proposition *6a*, all these fuzzy itemsets are also large. Note that the supports of these $(i - 1)$ - subsets of *C* need not to be stored, since they are determined using the following proposition.

Proposition 7 *Let C be a LFC and a fuzzy itemset* $I \subseteq C$. *If* $f \circ h(I) = C$, *then support* $(I) =$ *support* (C).

Proof.

We have $f \circ h(I) = C \Rightarrow h(f \circ h(I) = h(C) \Rightarrow h \circ f(h(I)) = h(C) \Rightarrow \| h \circ f(h(I))\| = \| h(C)\| \Rightarrow$ *(by B3)* $\| h(I))\| = \| h(C)\| \Rightarrow$ *support* $(I) =$ *support* (C).

Hence, based on proposition *7*, the supports of all $(i - 1)$ - subsets of a LFC *C* of size *i* are equal to the support of *C*, except the case when this $(i - 1)$ - subset is a LFC and has its own support. For example, let the resulting set of step *1*, *LFC* = $\{A^{0.8} B^{1} C^{0.7}, A^{0.8} B^{1}\}$, with respective supports *2* and *3*. Then, deriving large fuzzy itemsets from $A^{0.8} B^{1} C^{0.7}$, yields $A^{0.8} B^{1}$, $A^{0.8} C^{0.7}$ and $B^{1} C^{0.7}$ with respective supports *3*, *2* and 2.

The pseudo-code for deriving large fuzzy itemsets is given in algorithm *3*. The set of large fuzzy concepts $LFC = \cup_i LFC_i$ represents the input to this algorithm. As output, the set of large fuzzy itemsets $LFI = \cup_k LFI_k$ is determined.

The algorithm works as follows. First, we put each large fuzzy concept c from LFC in the set $LFI_{\|c\|}$ corresponding to the size of c and determining the size k of the largest LFC. Then, the sets LFI_i are constructed starting from LFI_k to LFI_l. Each iteration consists in completing the LFI_{i-1} using the fuzzy items in LFI_i. In fact, for all i-fuzzy itemset c in LFI_i, we generate all $(i - 1)$-subsets of c. All these subsets that are not existing in LFI_{i-1} are added to LFI_{i-1}, with a support value equal to support (c). The algorithm terminates when LFI_2 is completely treated.

Deriving large fuzzy itemsets

Input: $LFC = \cup_i LFC_i$

Output: $LFI = \cup_k LFI_k$

Begin

Forall large fuzzy concept $c \in LFC$ **do begin**

$LFI_{\|c\|} = LFI_{\|c\|} \cup c$

If ($k < \|c\|$) **then** $k = \|c\|$)

End

For ($i = k; i > 1; i$--) **do begin**

Forall $I \in LFI_i$ **do begin**

Forall $(i - 1)$ - fuzzy subsets s of I **do begin**

If ($s \notin LFI_{i-1}$) **then begin**

$s.supp = I.supp$

$LFI_{i-1} = LFI_{i-1} \cup s$

End

End

End

End

End.

Algorithm 3. Large fuzzy items derivation

3.3.2 Illustrative example

Let us consider the transaction database D, given in table $2b$. Then, we give, in what follows, the execution of FCARD fuzzy association rule discovery for a minimum support of 2 (*50%*), a minimal confidence of *0.75* and the set $S = \{B^{0.6}, C^{0.9}, E^{1}, M^{0.5}\}$ on the transaction database D.

1. **LFC discovery**: $CLFC_1 = \{B^{0.6}, B^{1}, C^{0.9}, C^{1}, E^{1}, M^{0.5}\}$. The function gen_concepts computes the support and the closure of each fuzzy generator, g of $CLFC_1$. LFC_1 is obtained by pruning the set $CLFC_1$. First, with respect to S, we remove all A^{α} from $f \circ h(A^{\alpha})$ such that $\alpha < \mu_S(A)$, e.g., $C^{0.7}$, $M^{0.1}$ have been deleted from $f \circ h(B^{0.6})$, since the required degrees in S for the fuzzy items C, M are respectively, *0.9, 0.5*. Second, all infrequent fuzzy generators, with respect to *minSup*, are removed (e.g., C^{1}) from $CLFC_1$. $CLFC_2$ is obtained by applying Gen_next to LFC_1. As we can see in figure 4, $CLFC_2 = \{B^{0.6}M^{0.5}, B^{1}E^{1}, B^{1}M^{0.5}, C^{0.9}E^{1}, C^{0.9}M^{0.5}, E^{1}M^{0.5}\}$. $\{B^{0.6}, C^{0.9}\}$, $\{B^{0.6}, E^{1}\}$ and $\{B^{1}, C^{0.9}\}$ in LFC_1 do not produce, respectively, the fuzzy generators $B^{0.6}C^{0.9}$, $B^{0.6}E^{1}$, $B^{1}C^{0.9}$, since $B^{0.6}C^{0.9} \subseteq f \circ h(B^{1})$, $B^{0.6}E^{1} \subseteq f \circ h(E^{1})$, $B^{1}C^{0.9} \subseteq f \circ h(B^{1})$, and by proposition 5 computing their closures is redundant. The function Gen_concepts computes the support and, eventually, the closure of each fuzzy generator g of $CLFC_2$. After the pruning of $CLFC_2$, we find that LFC_2 is empty and the discovery process of LFCs terminates.

2. **Generating large fuzzy itemsets** : First, the set of LFCs is split in n sets, where n is the size of the largest fuzzy concept, as depicted in figure 5. Second, we complete the set LFI_1 by deriving the fuzzy itemsets $B^{0.6}$, $E^{0.9}$, from $B^{0.6}E^{0.9}$, and B^{1} and E^{1}, respectively, from $B^{1}C^{0.9}$ and $B^{0.6}E^{1}$.

3. **Generating interesting fuzzy association rules**: Given the set of large fuzzy itemsets, we generate all the interesting fuzzy association rules with respect to *minConf*, as given in figure 6. Note that the fuzzy association rules $C^{0.9} \Rightarrow B^{1}$ and $B^{0.6} \Rightarrow E^{1}$ were not generated since their confidence is equal to *0.66* which is less than *minConf*.

4. Conclusion

Data mining is an emerging research area, whose goal is to extract significant rules from large databases. Many efficient algorithms have been proposed in the literature, e.g., Apriori, Partition, DIC, for mining association rules in the context of market-basket analysis. They are all based on the Apriori mining method, i.e., pruning the itemset lattice, and need multiple database accesses. In this paper, we have proposed a new efficient algorithm, called FARD, for mining fuzzy association rules. FARD is based on the pruning of the fuzzy concepts lattice, performs only one scan on the database, and can be applied equally to classical or fuzzy databases. In order to consider user-defined constraints, e.g., *minSup* and *minConf*, we have proposed an extension of the algorithm FARD.

Acknowledgements

We thank particularly Dr. Yahya Slimani and Samir Elloumi for their help and useful comments.

Scan D →

$CLFC_1$

Itemset	Support	Closure
$\{B^{0.6}\}$	3	$B^{0.6}E^{0.9}$
$\{B^{1}\}$	2	$B^{1}C^{0.9}$
$\{C^{0.9}\}$	3	$C^{0.9}$
$\{C^{1}\}$	1	!!!!
$\{E^{1}\}$	2	$B^{0.6}E^{1}$
$\{M^{0.5}\}$	2	$M^{0.5}$

Pruning →

LFC_1

Itemset	Support	Closure
$\{B^{0.6}\}$	3	$B^{0.6}E^{0.9}$
$\{B^{1}\}$	2	$B^{1}C^{0.9}$
$\{C^{0.9}\}$	3	$C^{0.9}$
$\{E^{1}\}$	2	$B^{0.6}E^{1}$
$\{M^{0.5}\}$	2	$M^{0.5}$

$CLFC_2$

Itemset	Domain	Closure
$\{B^{0.6}M^{0.5}\}$	1	!!!
$\{B^{1}E^{1}\}$	1	!!!
$\{B^{1}M^{0.5}\}$	1	!!!
$\{C^{0.9}E^{1}\}$	1	!!!
$\{C^{0.9}M^{0.5}\}$	1	!!!
$\{E^{1}M^{0.5}\}$	1	!!!

Stop ⇒ Output

Label	Fuzzy concept	Support
FC1	$B^{0.6}E^{0.9}$	3
FC2	$B^{1}C^{0.9}$	2
FC3	$C^{0.9}$	3
FC4	$B^{0.6}E^{1}$	2
FC5	$M^{0.5}$	2

Figure 4. Large fuzzy concepts Discovery

Fuzzy concept	Support
$B^{0.6}E^{0.9}$	3
$B^{1}C^{0.9}$	2
$C^{0.9}$	3
$B^{0.6}E^{1}$	2
$M^{0.5}$	2

Splitting LFCs →

LFI_2

Itemset	Support
$B^{0.6}E^{0.9}$	3
$B^{1}C^{0.9}$	2
$B^{0.6}E^{1}$	2

LFI_1

Itemset	Support
$C^{0.9}$	3
$M^{0.5}$	2

LFI_2

Itemset	Support
$B^{0.6}E^{0.9}$	3
$B^{1}C^{0.9}$	2
$B^{0.6}E^{1}$	2

Deriving large fuzzy itemsets →

LFI_1

Itemset	Support
$C^{0.9}$	3
$M^{0.5}$	2
$B^{0.6}$	3
$E^{0.9}$	3
B^{1}	2
E^{1}	2

Figure 5. Large fuzzy itemsets Derivation

Itemset	Support
$B^{0.6}E^{0.9}$	3
$B^{1}C^{0.9}$	2
$B^{0.6}E^{1}$	2

→

Fuzzy rule	Confidence
$B^{0.6} \Rightarrow E^{0.9}$	$3/3 = 1$
$E^{0.9} \Rightarrow B^{0.6}$	$3/3 = 1$
$B^{1} \Rightarrow C^{0.9}$	$2/2 = 1$

Figure 6. Interesting Association Rules Generation itemsets Derivation

References

[1] P. Adriaans and D. Zantinge. *Data mining*. Addion-Wesley Longman, 1997.

[2] R. Agrawal, T. Imielinski, and A.Swami. Database mining: a performance perspective. *IEEE Transactions on Knowledge and Data Engineering*, 5(6):914-925, 1993.

[3] R. Agrawal, T. Imielinski, and A. Swami. Mining Association Rules between sets of items in large Databases. *ACM SIGMOD Records*, pages 207-216, 1993.

[4] R. Agrawal and J. Shafer. Parallel mining of association rules. *IEEE Trans. on Knowledge and Data Engg* , 8(6):962-969, 1996.

[5] R. Agrawal and R. Skirant. Fast algorithms for mining association rules. In *Proceedings of the 20th Intl. Conference on Very Large Databases*, pages 478-499, June 1994.

[6] R. Agrawal and R. Skirant. Mining sequential patterns. In *Proceedings of International Conference on Data Engineering*, 1995.

[7] S. Brin, R. Motawni, and J. D. Ullman. Dynamic itemset counting and implication rules for market basket data. In *Proceedings of the ACM SIGMOD Intl. Conference on Management of Data*, pages 255-264, May 1997.

[8] D. Cheung, V. Ng, A. Fu, and Y. Fu. Efficient mining of association rules in distributed databases. *IEEE Trans. on Knowledge and Data Eng.*, 8(6):911-922, 1996.

[9] B. Ganter and R. Wille. *Formal Concept Analysis*. Springer-Verlag, Heidelberg, 1999.

[10] R. Godin and R. Missaoui. An incremental concept formation approach for learning from databases. *Theoretical Computer Science*, (133):387-419, 1994.

[11] R. Godin, R. Missaoui, and A. April. Experimental comparision of Galois lattice browsing with conventional information retrievel methods. *Internat. J. Man-Machine studies*, (38):747-767, 1993.

[12] E.-H. Han, G. Karypis, and V. Kumar. Scalable parallel data mining for association rules. In *Proceedings of ACM SGMOD Conference Management of Data*, pages 277-288, May 1997.

[13] M. Holsheimer, M.Kersten, H. Manilla, and H. Toinoven. A perspective on databases and data mining. In *Proceedings of 1st Intl. Conf. Knowledge Discovery and Data Mining*, August 1995.

[14] M. Houtsma and A. Swami. Set-oriented mining of association rules in relational datbases. In *Proceedings of 11th Intl. Conf. on Data Engineering*, 1995.

[15] A. Jaoua, F. Alvi, S. Elloumi, and S. Ben Yahia. Galois connection in fuzzy binary relations: applications for discovering association rules and decision

making. In *Proceedings of the 5th Intl. Conference RELMICS'2000*, pages 141-149, Canada , 10-14 January 2000.

[16] H. Manilla and H. Toinoven. Discovering generalized episodes using minimal occurences. In *Proceedings of 2nd Intl. Conf. knowledge discovery and Data mining*, 1996.

[17] H. Manilla, H. Toinoven, and I. Verkamo. Efficient algorithms for discovering association rules. In *AAAI Worshop on Knowledge Discovery in Databases*, pages 181-192, July 1994.

[18] H. Manilla, H. Toinoven, and I. Verkamo. Discovering frequent episodes in sequences. In *Proceedings of 1st Intl. Conf. Knowledge Discovery and Data Mining*, 1995.

[19] J. Park, M. Chen, and P. Yu. An effective hash based algorithm for mining association rules. In *Proceedings of the ACM SIGMOD Intl. Conference on Management of Data*, pages 175-186, May 1995.

[20] J. Park, M. Chen, and P. Yu. Efficient parallel data mining for association rules. In *Proceedings of the ACM Intl. Conf. Information and Knowledge* Management, pages 31-36, November 1995.

[21] N. Pasquier, Y. Bastide, R. Touil, and L. Lakhal. Pruning closed itemset lattices for association rules. In *Proceedings of the 14th Intl. Conference BDA*, Hammamet, Tunisia, pages 177-196, December 1998.

[22] A. Savarese, E. Omiecinski, and S. Navathe. An efficient algorithm for mining association rules in large databases. In *Proceedings of the 21th VLDB Conference*, pages 432-444, September 1995.

[23] R. Skirant and R. Agrawal. Mining sequential patterns: Generalizations and performance improvements. In *Proceedings of Intl Conf. Extending Database Technology*, March 1996.

[24] H. Toinoven. Sampling large databases for association rules. In *Proceedings of 22nd Intl. VLDB Conf.*, pages 134-145, September 1996.

[25] R. Wille. *Knowledge acquisition by methods of formal concept analysis.* Nova Science, New York, 1989.

[26] D. Yeung and E. Tsang. Weighted fuzzy production rules. *Fuzzy Sets and Systems*, 88:299-313, 1997.

[27] L. Zadeh. Fuzzy sets. *Information and Control*, (69):338-353, June 1965.

[28] M.Zaki, M. Ogihara, S. Pathasarathy, and W. Li. Parallel data mining for association rules on shared-memory processors. In *Proc. Supercomputing'96 IEEE Computer Soc., Los Alamitos*, 1996.

[29] M. Zaki, S. Pathasarathy, M. Ogihara, and W. Li. Evaluation of sampling for data mining for association rules. In *Proceedings of 7th Workshop Research Issues in Data Eng.*, April 1997.

Mining of Labeled Incomplete Data Using Fast Dimension Partitioning

Bill C.H. Chang* **& Saman K. Halgamuge**

Mechatronics Research Group, Department of Mechanical and Manufacturing Engineering, The University of Melbourne, Victoria 3010, Australia

Abstract. Two Dimensional Partitioning Techniques are proposed in this paper for fast mining of labeled data with missing values. The first Dimensional Partitioning Technique (DPT1) generates a classifier model by the use of Single Attribute Partitioning Method and neural network training. Single Attribute Partitioning Technique partitions a single input dimension at a time using proportional analysis. The second Dimensional Partitioning Technique (DPT2), on the other hand, partitions the best performing attributes simultaneously. The best performing attributes are found by the use of Single Attribute Partitioning Method. DPT2 utilizes Cross Attribute Partitioning Method which can identify correlation across attributes. DPT1 has the advantage of fast mining while DPT2 has the advantage of associative rule identification. Both DPT1 and DPT2 have shown good results on various classification problems, in particular on applications with missing input data.

Keywords. Classification, dimension partitioning, radial basis function network.

1 Introduction

Supervised data mining, or mining of labeled data, can generally be categorized into three types: class boundary identification (or class discrimination), clustering, and dimensional partitioning. Gradient descent [1] methods, which belong to the first type, identify the class boundaries by training a neural network using gradient descent algorithms. Clustering methods such as Learning Vector Quantization (LVQ) [2], Fuzzy C-Means [3] and Fuzzy Min-Max Neural Networks [4] identifies clusters of data with similar features by finding cluster centers and their

---

* This work is partially supported by Advanced Engineering Centre for Manufacturing, Melbourne, Australia

effective regions. These cluster centers and their effective regions are optimized to generate a satisfactory classifier. Dimensional Partitioning methods such as Adaptive Resonance Theory (ART) networks [5], on the other hand, partition the input dimension space into regions and then classify data.

Dimensional Partitioning Technique I (DPT1) and Dimensional Partitioning Technique II (DPT2) are proposed in this paper. DPT1 is a modification of a heuristic dimensional partitioning method proposed in [6]. DPT1 attempts to partition one input dimension at a time, whereas DPT2 partitions multiple input dimensions simultaneously. Both techniques perform proportional analysis to identify class boundaries. In experimental tests, it is found that the classifiers generated from the proposed techniques are as good - or even better - in performance, and faster than other supervised data mining techniques. The advantages and disadvantages of both DPT1 and DPT2 are also discussed.

The rest of this chapter is organized in the following manner. In Section 2 and Section 3, two new algorithms, Dimensional Partitioning Technique I (DPT1) and Dimensional Partitioning Technique II (DPT2) are described. The comparison of these two techniques and their relative advantages and disadvantages are presented in Section 4. In Section 5, labeled data sets with missing values are examined with the proposed algorithm. The results are discussed and compared to that of published results.

2 Dimensional Partitioning Technique I

This technique attempts to partition the data set using a single attribute at a time. The partitioned model is represented by fuzzy rules with Radial Basis Function membership functions. For data sets with multiple input attributes, the partitioned models generated for each attribute are combined to form a classifier model. By using Radial Basis functions, a neural network equivalent fuzzy classifier [7] can be implemented to further improve the performance of the classifier model. Figure 2.1 shows the main steps of DPT1.

2.1 Single Attribute Partitioning Method

The input dimension can be quickly divided into regions of different classes by the use of proportional analysis. The algorithm involves three steps: Segmentation, Proportional Calculation, and Identification.

2.1.1 Segmentation

An input space is divided into segments of equal length. The number of segments to be introduced is dependant on the complexity of the data being investigated.

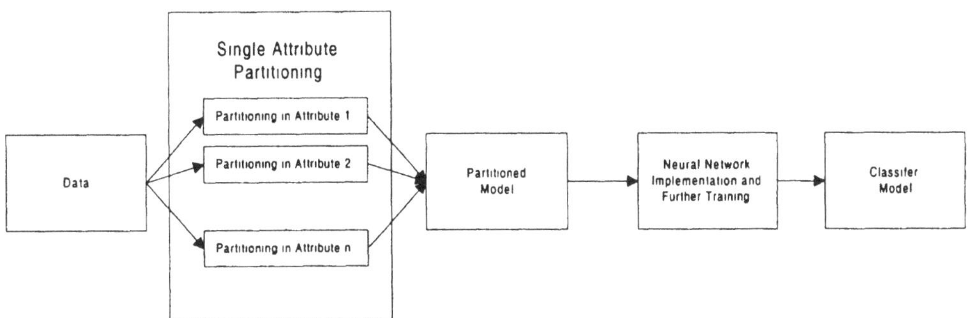

Figure 2.1. Overview of Dimensional Partitioning Technique I.

The number of classes in a data set should equal the minimum number of segments used. For example, a data set with three classes should have at least three segments in each of its dimensions. More segments enable a finer resolution of the partitioned spaces, however, generalization of a classifier model may be lost if too many segments are introduced. Experiment results indicate that the maximum number of segments should equal to three times the number of minimum segment. Figure 2.2(b) shows an example where the input dimension 'Attribute 1' is divided into three equal segments.

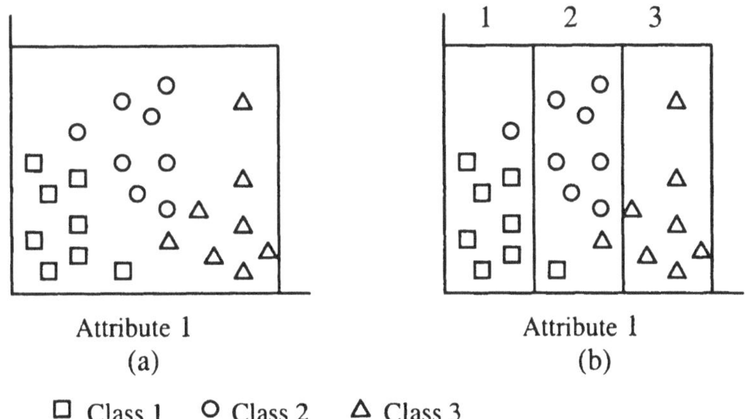

Figure 2.2. Division of attribute 1 into three segments.

2.1.2 Proportional Calculation

In each segment, the proportion of data belonging to each class is calculated. In the example shown in Figure 2.2, the results of the proportional calculation using conditional probabilities, P (segment i / class j), can be summarized as in Table 2.1.

	Class 1	Class 2	Class 3
Segment 1	87.5 %	11.1 %	0.0 %
Segment 2	12.5 %	77.8 %	0.0 %
Segment 3	0.0 %	11.1 %	100 %

Table 2.1. Summary of proportional calculation.

2.1.3 Identification

Segments can be classified after Proportional Calculation. A segment can be classified as class ' x ' if the proportion of data belonging to ' x ' is greater than a threshold value *maj* (majority). The variable *maj* can be optimized so the partitioned model can give the best classification performance. The optimal *maj* value can be generally found within two or three iterations.

In the above example, if a *maj* value of 75% is used, the following partitions are generated:

- If an input data vector is within Segment 1 of Attribute 1, then it belongs to class 1.
- If an input data vector is within Segment 2 of Attribute 1, then it belongs to class 2.
- If an input data vector is within Segment 3 of Attribute 1, then it belongs to class 3.

These partitions can be represented by fuzzy rules. The degree to which a data point belongs to a segment can be represented by a radial basis function membership function where the membership function value at the center of segment is one (Figure 2.3). This partitioned model consists of three fuzzy rules, or three prototypes. The rule with highest strength after evaluation is activated.

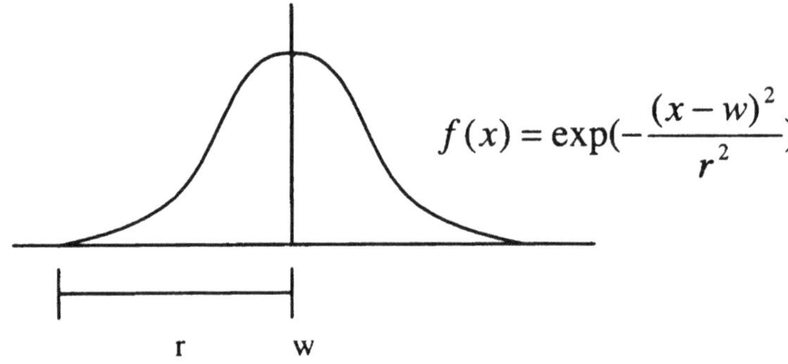

Figure 2.3. Radial Basis Function.

The above Partitioned Model can successfully classify 87.5% of data. On the other hand, if a *maj* value of 80% is used, following partitions are generated:

- If an input data vector is within Segment 1 of Attribute 1, then it belongs to class 1.

- If an input data vector is within Segment 3 of Attribute 1, then it belongs to class 3.

This partitioned model can only successfully classify 56% of the data. The performance of the partitions generated can vary considerably depending on the value of *maj*; however, the optimal *maj* value can be easily found by trial and error.

2.2 Classifier Model Generation

Once every input dimension has been partitioned, a classifier model can be generated to classify the relevant data. Rules for each input dimension are combined using the 'AND' operator. For example, consider the partitioning result shown in Table 2.2:

	Class 1	Class 2	Class 3
Attribute 1	Segment 1	Segment 2	Segment 3
Attribute 2		Segment 1	Segment 2
Attribute 3	Segment 2		

Table 2.2. Example of partitioning results.

With the above three partitioned models, the following classifier model is generated:

- The data belongs to Class 1 if:

  A data vector is in Segment 1 of Attribute 1 AND in Segment 2 of Attribute 3.
- The data belongs to Class 2 if:

  A data vector is in Segment 2 of Attribute 1 AND in Segment 1 of Attribute 2.
- And the data belongs to Class 3 if:

  A data vector is in Segment 3 of Attribute 1 AND in Segment 2 of Attribute 2.

The fuzzy 'AND' operator uses the algebraic product.

2.2.1 Rule Pruning

When the inclusion of a partitioned model (model for a single attribute) does not improve the classifier model's performance, the partitioned model should not be used. This can happen when too many segments are introduced in an input dimension with overlapping data vectors. Consider the example in Figure 2.4.

By using Segmentation and Proportional Calculation as discussed in section 2.1.2 and 2.1.3, no segment can be classified in Figure 2.4 (a), whereas for Figure 2.4 (b), segment 1 is classified as Class 1 and segment 6 is classified as Class 3.

Since the rules for all the input dimensions are combined using 'AND' (multiplication) operator, the inclusion of rules generated in this attribute would actually decrease the overall performance of the final classifier model. Also, by examining the distribution of the data in Figure 2.4, it is straight forward that no partitions should be generated along the "Attribute 1" input dimension.

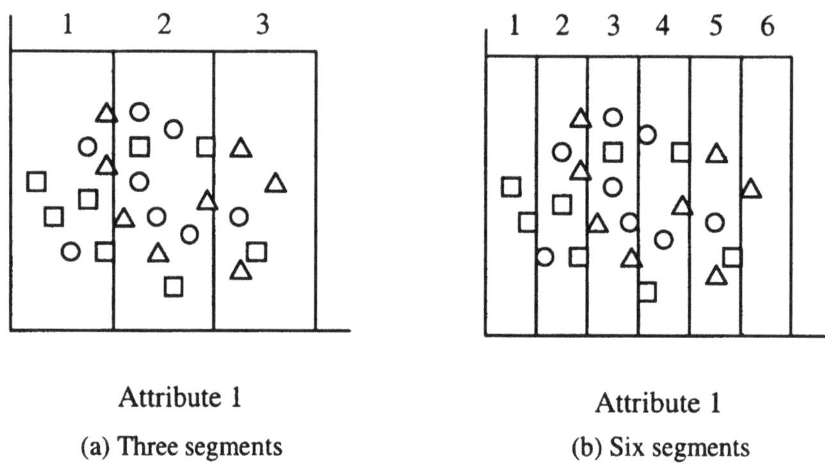

Figure 2.4. Effect of number of segmentation and rule pruning.

Also, when a subset of available attributes can clearly classify the data of one particular class, the remaining attributes are no longer required. The following two rules are used to prune unnecessary rules:

- When the classification performance for all data points is below a threshold value, P_L, the partitions generated in that class are discarded.
- When the classification performance for one particular class is above a threshold value, P_H, the partitions generated for that particular class in other attributes are discarded.

2.3 Neural Network Implementation

The classification performance of a classifier model generated from the Single Attribute Partitioning technique can be further improved with a neural network implementation. One drawback of the partitioning technique is that the number of segments introduced at the Segmentation stage can influence its classification performance. By mapping the partitioned result generated from the Dimensional Partitioning technique into a neural network structure, the classification performance can be further improved.

2.3.1 Neural Network Structure

A fuzzy classifier equivalent radial basis function network structure [7] is shown is Figure 2.5. There are three layers in this structure, with one input layer, one output layer, and one rule inference layer. All rule nodes have radial basis functions, and the value of an output neuron is the maximum of values of all rule neurons connecting to it. The number of input dimensions and classes should match the number of input neurons and output neurons, and the number of rule nodes in the network should match the number of prototypes generated from the Single Attribute Partitioning method. The value of *w* and *r* in the radial basis function (Equation 1) should match the center and range of the classified segment, respectively.

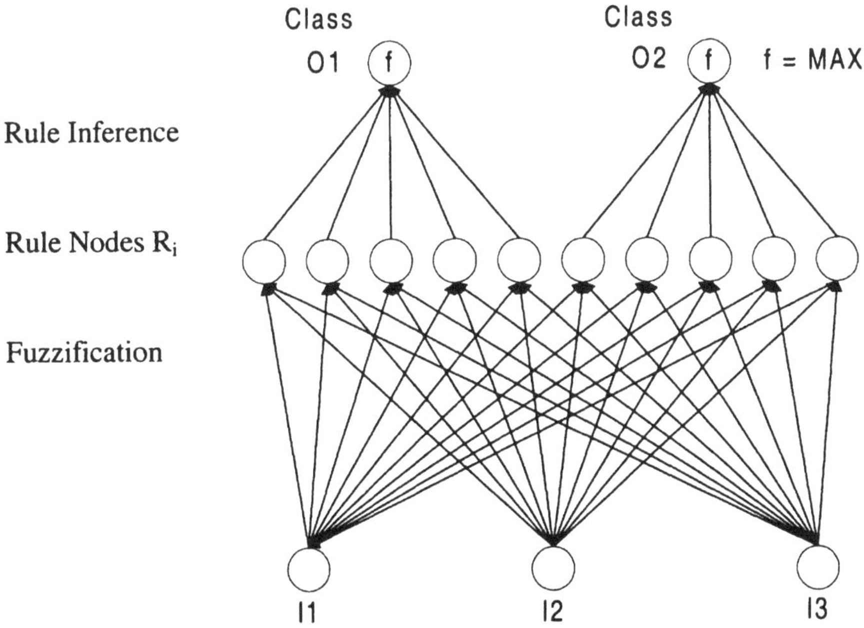

Figure 2.5. Fuzzy Classifier Equivalent Neural Network.

2.3.2 Heuristic Training Algorithm for RBF classifier

To preserve the speed and performance of Dimensional Partitioning technique, a heuristic training scheme is developed. With this scheme, only one training epoch is required, and the performance of a trained classifier should be at least equal to that of an untrained classifier model. This algorithm attempts to move the partition boundaries to achieve an improvement in the classification performance. Consider the example in Figure 2.6:

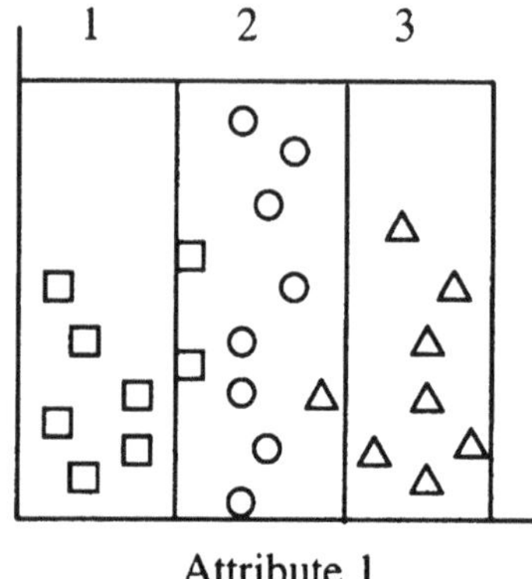

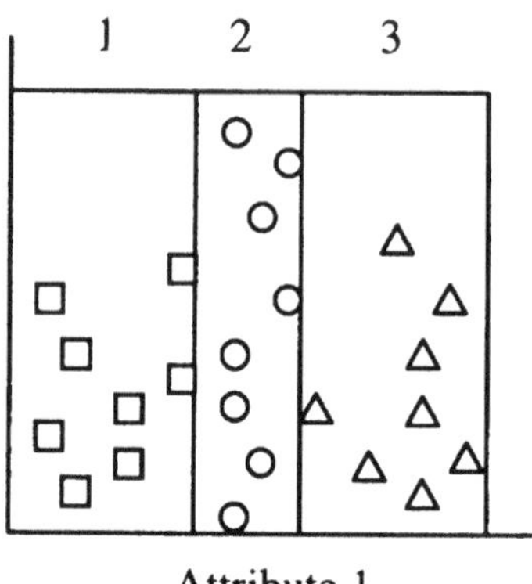

Figure 2.6. Improving a classifier model by neural network training.

The classification performance of the model in Figure 2.6 (a) is improved by shifting the two boundaries towards the center to isolate the data points within the same class. As a result, the new classifier model in Figure 2.6 (b) has a classification performance of 100%. However, it is sometimes not desirable to isolate all the data points having the same class in one partitioned region. Figure 2.7 shows a situation where the isolation of data points within the same class is not preferred.

In the situation in Figure 2.7, the classification performance would be decreased if the 'include all data points' strategy is adopted. The classifier performance would be better without excluding the two wrongly classified points in Figure 2.7 (a). The performance of a classifier model can be improved by including the adjacent misclassified data in Figure 2.6. On the other hand, the performance is decreased if the adjacent data points are included in Figure 2.7. Therefore, a training scheme which allows a partition boundary to move within a specified range is developed:

Heuristic Training Scheme

1. Present an input vector I to the network.
2. Expand the partition boundaries within the expansion boundary value R by adjusting values of w and r in the radial basis function.
3. Present the next input vector and repeat step 2 until all vectors are presented.

In this scheme, only the data points within a specified radius R from the initial w value are used to modify the partition boundaries. For $R = 0$, partition boundaries are not allowed to move and no change is observed. The optimal value of R depends on the data distribution. The empirical value for R is around 1.5 times the initial r value.

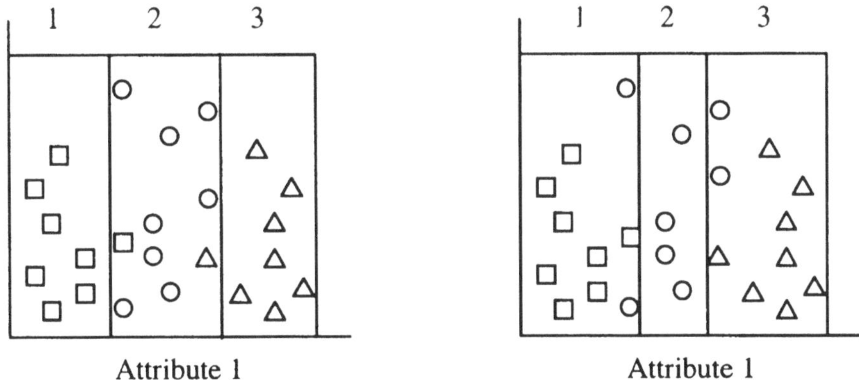

Figure 2.7. Situation where moving the partitioned boundary would decrease the classification performance.

3 Dimensional Partitioning Technique II

In more complicated data sets, the proposed Single Attribute Partitioning Method may not give satisfactory results. Consider the two classification situations in Figure 3.1. By using Single Attribute Partitioning Method, with an initial number of three equal segments (see Figure 3.3(a)) and a *maj* value of 75%, the partitioned model shown in Table 3.1 is obtained for data in Figure 3.1(a):

	Class 1	Class 2	All Data
Attribute 1	Segment 1	Segment 3	
Attribute 2	Segment 3	Segment 1	
Classification Performance	12.5%	25%	18.8%

Table 3.1. Classifier Model generated for data in Figure 3.1(a) using Single Attribute Partitioning Method.

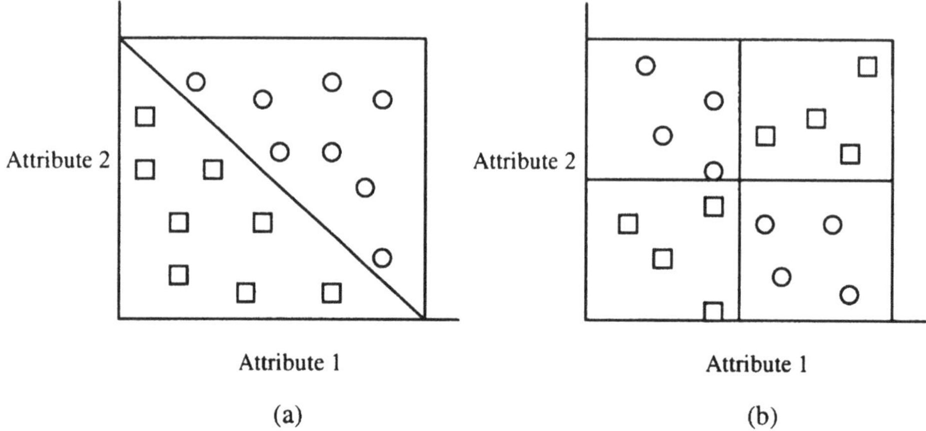

Figure 3.1. Situations where Single Attribute Partitioning Method does not provide a satisfactory result.

Using 4 segments in Attribute 1 and 6 segments in attribute 2 (see Figure 3.3(b)) to classify data in Figure 3.1(b), the result shown in Table 3.2 is obtained :

	Class 1	Class 2	All Data
Attribute 1	Segment 1		
Attribute 2			
Classification Performance	12.5%	0.0%	6.2%

Table 3.2. Classifier Model generated for data in Figure 3.1(b) using Single Attribute Partitioning Method.

Single Attribute Partitioning Method fails to give a satisfactory classifier model in these two situations because it does not have the ability to identify associative rules [8].

To successfully classify the above data distributions, the correlation between attributes must be identified. A Cross Attribute Partitioning Method is proposed in the following section which has capability to identify associative rules. The main steps of DPT2 are shown in Figure 3.2.

The Single Attribute Partitioning Method identifies the 'good performing' attributes and uses them in the Cross Attribute Partitioning Analysis. Instead of generating a classifier model with the partitioned models, the classification performance of each partitioned model is ranked from the best to the worst. The top two performing attributes are used in Cross Attribute Partitioning Method (described below) to classify a data set. Two attributes are required because the Cross Attribute Partitioning Method requires at least two input dimensions. If the performance is not satisfactory, the next ranked attribute is added to the analysis. This algorithm allows the optimal number required attributes to be found.

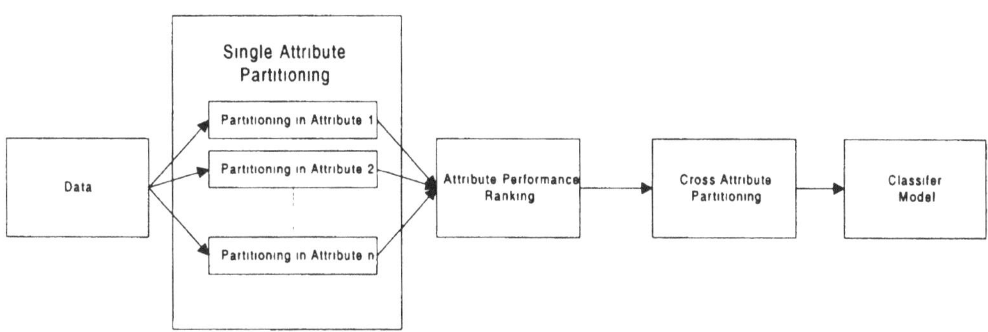

Figure 3.2. Overview of Dimensional Partitioning Technique II.

3.1 Cross Attribute Partitioning Method

When correlation exists between two or more attributes, it is difficult to partition the input space one dimension at a time. This method attempts to partition data points by considering all input dimensions once. This is more computationally intensive than the Single Attribute Partitioning Method and hence, it is preferable to use the minimum number of attributes required. The algorithm of Cross Attribute Partitioning Method is as follows:

1. Introduce equal number of segments k1, k2, ..., kn, in Attribute 'A1, A2, ..., An', where n = number of attributes.
2. Given the data is in segment '$x1_1$' of Attribute 'A1', and in segment '$x2_1$' of Attribute 'A2', ..., and segment 'xn_1' of Attribute 'An', classify the region using the Proportional Analysis and Identification technique described in Section 2.1.2 and 2.1.3.
3. Analyze the next region, segment '$x1_1$' of Attribute 'A1', segment '$x2_1$' of Attribute 'A2', ..., and segment 'xn_2' of Attribute 'An'.
4. Continue Step 3 until all regions are analyzed, i.e. segment '$x1_{k1}$' of Attribute 'A1', segment '$x2_{k2}$' of Attribute A2, ..., and segment 'xn_{kn}' of Attribute 'An'.

To demonstrate this method, the examples shown in Figure 3.1 are used. With the same number of introduced segments for DPT1, the input space is divided into 'regions' as shown in Figure 3.3.

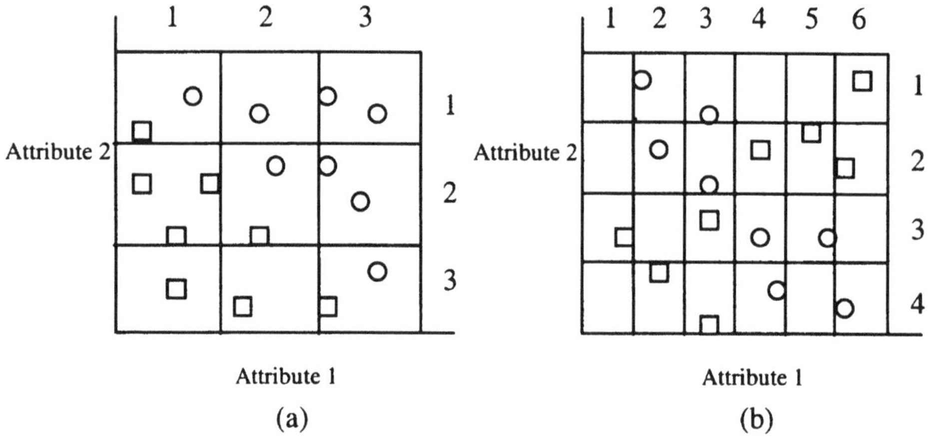

Figure 3.3. Generated Regions using Cross Attribute Partitioning Method.

Prototypes	Regions	Class
1	Attribute 1- Segment 1, and Attribute 2- Segment 2 & 3	1
2	Attribute 1- Segment 2, and Attribute 2- Segment 3	1
3	Attribute 1- Segment 2, and Attribute 2- Segment 1	2
4	Attribute 1- Segment 3, and Attribute 2- Segment 1 & 2	2

Table 3.3. Classifier Model generated for data in Figure 3.1(a) using Cross Attribute Partitioning Technique.

Table 3.3 shows the classifier model for the problem in Figure 3.1(a) generated using Cross Attribute Partitioning Technique. This partition can classify 10 out of 16 data points, or 62.5%, an improvement of 43.7% from the Single Attribute Partitioning method. If more segments are introduced, a classification performance of 100% can be obtained. The number of prototypes is now 4 compared to 2 previously:

- If an input vector is in Segment 1 of Attribute 1 AND (Region 2 or Region 3) of Attribute 2, then it belongs to class 1.
- If an input vector is in Segment 2 of Attribute 1 AND Segment 3 of Attribute 2, then it belongs to class 1.
- If an input vector is in Segment 2 of Attribute 1 AND Segment 1 of Attribute 2, then it belongs to class 2.
- If an input vector is in Segment 3 of Attribute 1 AND (Segment 1 or Segment 2) of Attribute 2, then it belongs to class 2.

For the problem in Figure 3.1(b), the model in Table 3.4 is generated with a classification performance of 100%.

Prototypes	Regions	Class
1	Attribute 1- Segment 1 and Attribute 2- Segment 3	1
2	Attribute 1- Segment 2 and Attribute 2- Segment 4	1
3	Attribute 1- Segment 3 and Attribute 2- Segment 3 & 4	1
4	Attribute 1- Segment 4 and Attribute 2- Segment 2	1
5	Attribute 1- Segment 5 and Attribute 2- Segment 2	1
6	Attribute 1- Segment 6 and Attribute 2- Segment 1 & 2	1
7	Attribute 1- Segment 1 and Attribute 2- Segment 1 & 2	2
8	Attribute 1- Segment 2 and Attribute 2- Segment 1 & 2	2
9	Attribute 1- Segment 3 and Attribute 2- Segment 1 & 2	2
10	Attribute 1- Segment 4 and Attribute 2- Segment 3 & 4	2
11	Attribute 1- Segment 5 and Attribute 2- Segment 3	2
12	Attribute 1- Segment 6 and Attribute 2- Segment 4	2

Table 3.4. Classifier Model generated for data in Figure 3.1(b) using Cross Attribute Partitioning Technique.

4 Results on Benchmarks and Discussion

In the following, two well-known classification problems, Iris and Monk's Problems, are used to illustrate the two classification techniques.

4.1 Iris Database

4.1.1 DPT1

The Iris data [9-10] is one of the most widely used examples for testing the effectiveness of a classifier. It has four attributes, Sepal length, Sepal width, Petal length and Petal width and three classes, Iris-setosa, Iris-versicolor and Iris-virginica. The version of Iris data used is the same as the one shown in [11]. Plots of the Iris data set are shown in Figure 4.1.

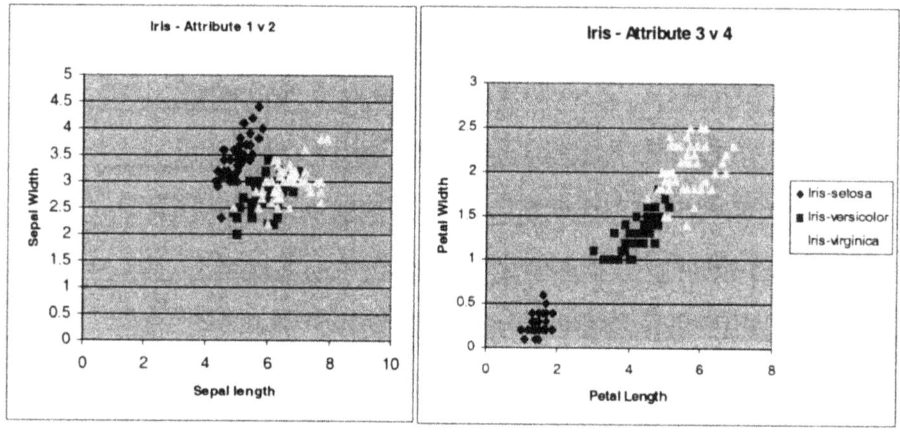

Figure 4.1. Iris Data.

Using the Single Attribute Partitioning Method with eight initial segments for each input dimension, and with a *maj* value of 80%, the result shown in Table 4.1 is obtained.

	Setosa (C1)	Versicolor (C2)	Virginica (C3)
A1 – Sepal length	4.3 → 4.8		7.5 → 7.9

A2 – Sepal width	3.5 → 4.4		
A3 – Petal length	1.0 → 2.5	3.2 → 4.7	5.4 → 6.9
A4 – Petal width	0.1 → 0.7	0.7 → 1.6	1.9 → 2.5

Table 4.1. Generated Iris classifier model using Single Attribute Partitioning Method.

A radial basis function (Equation 1) is used to represent the membership function in each classified segment, with the center of the segment located at the center of the radial basis function.In each of the input dimensions (attributes), the classification performance of rules is calculated and summarized in Table 4.2. Partitioned Model 1 is generated from Attribute A1, Partitioned Model A2 is generated from Attribute A2, and so on.

	% Correct Classification			
	All Data	C1 Data	C2 Data	C3 Data
Partitioned Model 1 (PM1)	58.7	100 (45.7)	0	76 (34.5)
Partitioned Model 2 (PM2)	33.3	100 (66.6)	0	0
Partitioned Model 3 (PM3)	93.3	100 (0)	100 (16.7)	80(0)
Partitioned Model 4 (PM4)	96.0	100 (0)	96 (7.69)	92(4.17)
PM3+PM4	96.0	100 (0)	100 (10.7)	88(0)
PM1 + PM2 + PM3 + PM4	68.0	76 (0)	100 (49)	28(0)

Table 4.2. Classification performance of Partition Models generated in each Iris attribute. The number inside of bracket indicates the percentage of noise.

PM3 + PM4 implies that the classifier model is generated by combining both PM3 and PM4. From the result, both Partitioned Model 4 and PM3 + PM4 give a classification performance of 96%. Since fewer rules are desirable, only PM4 is selected and the classifier model generated is:

- If its Petal width is between 0.1 and 0.7 cm, then it is Iris-setosa.
- If its Petal width is between 0.7 and 1.6 cm, then it is Iris-versicolor.
- If its Petal width is between 1.9 and 2.5 cm, then it is Iris-virginica.

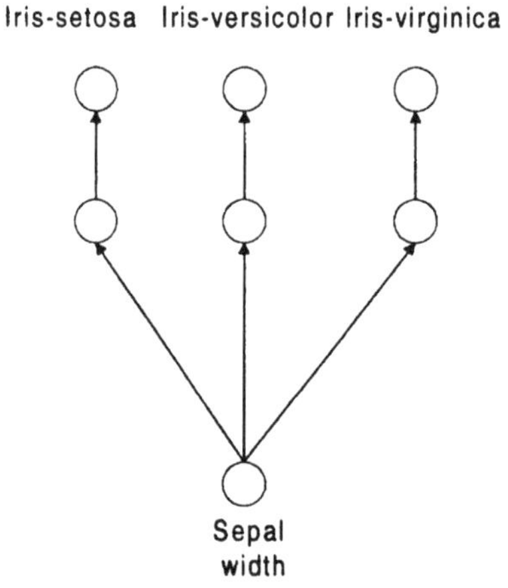

Figure 4.2. **Mapping the Iris classifier model onto RBFN neural network.**

Figure 4.2 represents the mapping of partitioned model PM4 into a RBFN neural network. Only three rule nodes are required since three prototypes are generated. By using the training scheme described in Section 2.2, the classification performance of the trained classifier improves to 97.3%. The expansion boundary value *R*, here is chosen as 1.5 times the value of initial *r* value. The improved classifier shown in Table 4.3 is obtained.

	All Data	Iris-setosa	Iris-versicolor	Iris-virginica
A4 – Petal width		$0.1 \rightarrow 0.7$ $(0.1 \rightarrow 0.7)$	$0.7 \rightarrow 1.6$ $(0.7 \rightarrow 1.6)$	$1.5 \rightarrow 2.5$ $(1.9 \rightarrow 2.5)$
Classification Performance	97.3% (96%)	100% (100%)	96% (96%)	96% (92%)

Table 4.3. Improved Partitioning results for Iris data. Values inside brackets are segment boundaries and classification performances before training.

4.1.2 DPT2

Single Attribute Partitioning Method is used to obtain the ranking of attributes in effectiveness of classifying the data. From Table 4.4, the best performing attributes are A3 and A4, and in the Cross Attribute Partitioning Method, only they are used as the input dimensions.

	% Correct Classification			
	All Data	C1 Data	C2 Data	C3 Data
A1 – Sepal length	58.7	100	0	76
A2 – Sepal width	33.3	100	0	0
A3 – Petal length	93.3	100	100	80
A4 – Petal width	96.0	100	96	92

Table 4.4. Top two ranked Attribute in Classification performance.

Using the Cross Attribute Partitioning Method, the following result is obtained:

- If the Petal length between 1 and 2.48 cm AND the Petal width is between 0.1 and 0.7 cm, then it is Iris-setosa.
- If the Petal length is between 2.48 and 5.43 cm AND the Petal width is between 0.7 and 1.9 cm, then it is Iris-versicolor.
- If the Petal length is between 3.95 and 6.9 cm AND the Petal width is between 1.3 and 2.5, then it is Iris-virginica.

The classification performance of this classifier on the Iris test data is 97.3% with 3 prototypes.

4.1.3 Comparison with other classification techniques

Using a two-fold cross validation scheme, average classification rate of 96.7% and 97.3% were achieved using DPT1 and DPT2 techniques respectively. Table 4.5 summarizes the results for various RBFN classification techniques [12]. It shows the advantages of the proposed techniques which give a good classification performance with a fewer generated prototypes.

	RCE	MRCE	GRCE	DPT1	DPT2
Number of prototypes	13	6	5	3	3
Classification performance	85.5%	92.1%	97.3%	96.7%	97.3%

Table 4.5. Number of generated prototypes and classification performance for RBFN variations (RCE = Restricted Coulomb Energy [13], MRCE = Modified RCE [14], GRCE = Generalized RCE [7], DPT1 = Dimensional Partitioning Technique I, DPT2 = Dimensional Partitioning Technique II).

4.2 Monk's Problems Database

Monk's Problem [9] is another widely used database for comparisons of classifiers' performance. There are three Monk's problems, Monk-1, Monk-2, and Monk-3. Each has its own training and testing data sets. It has two classes, Class 0 and Class 1, and six attributes, A1 to A6. All six attributes have discrete integer values. The aim of the classifier model is to determine the underlying rules within each of the problem:

- Monk-1: Class 1 when (A1 = A2) or (A5 = 1).
- Monk-2: Class 1 when exactly two of {A1 = 1, A2 = 1, A3 = 1, A4 = 1, A5 = 1, A6 = 1} are true.
- Monk-3: Class 1 when (A5 = 3 and A4 = 1) or (A5 ≠ 4 and A2 ≠ 3).

Monk-3 has 5% of noise added to its training set. Following is the possible values of a data in each attribute:

- A1: 1, 2, 3
- A2: 1, 2, 3
- A3: 1, 2
- A4: 1, 2, 3
- A5: 1, 2, 3, 4
- A6: 1, 2

4.2.1 DPT1

Since the data set only has discrete integer values in a small range, segments are introduced in a way that each possible value in an attribute is in a different segment. Hence, in attribute A1, A2 and A4, three equal segments are introduced. Two segments are introduced in A3 and A6 and four segments are introduced in attribute A5. The partitioned models' performance for Monk-1 is shown in Table 4.6 and 4.7. Likewise, PM1 is generated from attribute A1 and PM2 is generated from attribute A2 and so on.

Attribute	Class 0	Class 1
A1	1	2,3
A2	1	2,3
A3	2	1
A4	2,3	1
A5	2,3,4	1
A6	2	1

Table 4.6. Monk-1 partitioned models using *maj* = 50

Table 4.6 and 4.7 shows the partitioned result in each attribute and their respective classification performances. Notice that the value of majority, *maj*, used for classifying a segment is 50%. This is due to the fact that the correlation between attributes is high and must be identified to classify this data set satisfactorily. The best classification performance using this technique is only 73.4% using attribute A5.

	% Correct Classification		
	All Data	Class 0	Class 1
PM1	63.7	50 (33.1)	77.4 (39.2)
PM2	54	32.3 (42.9)	75.8 (47.2)
PM3	54	51.6 (45.8)	56.5 (46.2)
PM4	58.1	74.2 (43.9)	41.9 (38.1)
PM5	73.4	100 (34.7)	46.8 (0)
PM6	51.6	56.5 (48.5)	46.8 (48.2)
PM1 + PM2 + PM3 + PM4 + PM5 + PM6	70.2	85.5 (34.6)	54.8 (20.9)

Table 4.7. Monk-1 Classification performance of Partitioned Models. The number inside of bracket indicates the percentage of noise.

4.2.2 DPT2

Since all the attributes do not give a satisfactory result using the Single Attribute Partitioning Method, all six attributes are used as input dimensions in Cross Attribute Partitioning Method. The result is shown in Table 4.8.

	AQ17-DCI	AQ15-GA	Backpropagation + weight decay	DPT2
Monk-1	100%	100%	100%	100%
Monk-2	100%	86.8%	100%	100%
Monk-3	94.2%	100%	97.3%	96.3%

Table 4.8. Classification performance of generated classifier and its comparisons with other techniques AQ17-DCI [9] and AQ15-GA [9].

Backpropagation with weight decay method is the best performing algorithm on this problem so far [9]. The proposed method DPT2 can nearly match its classification performance.

4.3 Comparison of DPT1 and DPT2

The two proposed techniques, DPT1 and DPT2 both have their advantages and disadvantages. DPT1 is easy to use and fast. However, it cannot successfully generate a classifier model for data with correlation between attributes. On the other hand, the DPT2 is more time consuming, but it has the capability to classify data with correlation between attributes.

In the Iris application, both DPT1 and DPT2 give the same classification performance, and hence it is not necessary to use the DPT2. On the other hand, in the Monk's Problems application, only DPT2 can generate a satisfactory classifier model. Therefore, when applying the proposed techniques to classification problems, and without knowing any existing correlation between attributes, DPT1 should be used first. If it fails to generate a classifier model with good classification performance, DPT2 is then applied.

5 Application to Data with Missing Values

The proposed DPT1 and DPT2 are also suitable for generating classifiers for data with missing values. Missing values are simply ignored during the proportional calculation in its input dimension. For example, a data set containing 2 data vectors with 2 inputs and 2 classes is illustrated in Table 5.1.

Data Vector	Input 1	Input 2	Class
1	?	2.5	1
2	0.8	?	2

Table 5.1. Example of data set with missing values.

In this example, the following classifier model is generated ignoring the "missing values":

- If its value of Attribute 2 is 2.5, then it is class 1.
- If its value of Attribute 1 is 0.8, then it is class 2.

After a classifier model is generated, when evaluating a data with a missing value in attribute 'Ax', that missing value is treated as being within each of the classified segments in attribute 'Ax'. This can be interpreted as the data point being a "don't care".

In the following, the Wisconsin Breast Cancer Database and Hepatitis Database are used to demonstrate the effectiveness of the proposed DPT1 on data with missing values. It showed that this simple and fast technique can perform as well or even better than other techniques. DPT2 were also used but the results showed DPT1 is superior in classification performance in both cases.

5.1 Wisconsin Breast Cancer Database

The 1992 version of breast cancer database obtained from the University of Wisconsin Hospitals, Madison is used [9][15]. This database contains 699 data vectors, 9 attributes, and 2 classes, with 16 data vectors containing a single missing attribute value. The 9 attributes are: Clump Thickness, Uniformity of Cell Size, Uniformity of Cell Shape, Marginal Adhesion, Single Epithelial Cell Size, Bare Nuclei, Bland Chromatin, Normal Nucleoli and Mitoses. The range of values for each of the attribute is between 1 and 10, and each data vector has one of two possible classes: benign or malignant.

Data set is separated randomly into ten pairs of training and testing sets. Each training set contains 629 data vectors and each testing set containing the remaining 70 data vectors. A ten-fold cross validation scheme is adopted to test the capability of the proposed dimensional partitioning technique.

5.1.1 Single Attribute Partitioning

Table 5.2 summarizes the partitioned result obtained from one of the training data set. In this application, four equal segments are introduced in the Segmentation stage, and a majority value, *maj*, of 80% is used in the Identification stage.

	Benign	Malignant
Clump Thickness	$1 \rightarrow 4$	$7 \rightarrow 10$
Uniformity of Cell Size	$1 \rightarrow 2.5$	$4 \rightarrow 10$
Uniformity of Cell Shape	$1 \rightarrow 2.5$	$4 \rightarrow 10$
Marginal Adhesion	$1 \rightarrow 2.5$	$4 \rightarrow 10$
Single Epithelial Cell Size	$1 \rightarrow 2.5$	$4 \rightarrow 10$
Bare Nuclei	$1 \rightarrow 2.5$	$5.5 \rightarrow 10$
Bland Chromatin	$1 \rightarrow 2.5$	$4 \rightarrow 10$
Normal Nucleoli	$1 \rightarrow 2.5$	$4 \rightarrow 10$
Mitoses		$4 \rightarrow 10$

Table 5.2. Summary of partitioning results using dimensional partitioning technique.

The mean value of classification performance on the ten testing data is 96.4% with two generated prototypes.

5.1.2 Neural Network Implementation

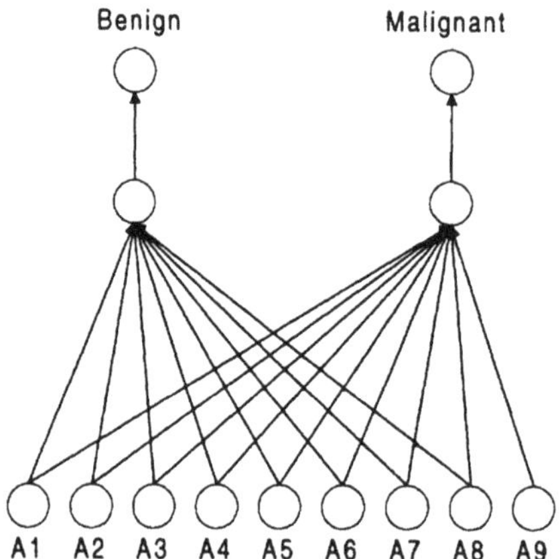

Figure 5.1. Mapping the Breast Cancer partitioned result into a RBFN neural network.

Figure 5.1 is the configuration of an equivalent RBFN neural network. Notice that A9 (Mitoses) is not connected to the 'Benign' class since this attribute does not have a partitioned segment for Class 'Benign'. After the training process, the classification performance improved slightly to 96.6%. The expansion value R used is 1.5 times the initial r value. The highest reported accuracy in [9] however is 94%.

5.2 Hepatitis Database

Hepatitis Database [9] has 19 attributes and 2 classes, Die and Live. There are 155 data vectors in this database and there is a total of 167 missing values. Class "Die" has 32 data vectors and class "Live" has 123 data vectors. The distribution of missing values in each of the attributes is as follows:

A1. Age	0	A11. Spiders	5
A2. Sex	0	A12. Ascites	5
A3. Steroid	1	A13. Varices	5
A4. Antivirals	0	A14. Bilirubin	6
A5. Fatigue	1	A15. Alk Phosphate	29
A6. Malaise	1	A16. Sgot	4
A7. Anorexia	1	A17. Albumin	16

A8. Liver Big	10	A18. Protime	67
A9. Liver Firm	11	A19. Histology	0
A10. Spleen Palpable	5		

5.2.1 Results

The classification performance of the partitioned model generated in each of the attribute is shown in Table 5.3. Notice that this database does not have equal numbers of data vectors in each of the classes (20.9% for class DIE and 79.5% for class LIVE). Thus, it is important that we choose the right partitioned models. The highlighted partitioned models cannot classify class DIE and partitioned models PM6, PM10, PM12 and PM13 cannot classify class LIVE. Therefore, they are not considered for the generation of the classifier model.

	% Correct Classification		
Partitioned Models	All Data	C1 (Die)	C2 (Live)
PM1	78.2	16	94.3
PM2	79.5	0	100
PM3	79.5	0	100
PM4	79.5	0	100
PM5	79.5	0	100
PM6	20.5	100	0
PM7	79.5	0	100
PM8	79.5	0	100
PM9	79.5	0	100
PM10	20.5	100	0
PM11	79.5	0	100
PM12	20.5	100	0
PM13	20.5	100	0
PM14	77.3	48	84.9

PM15	79.5	0	100
PM16	80.3	4	100
PM17	63.8	40	92.5
PM18	50.5	37.7	53.8
PM19	79.5	0	100

Table 5.3. Classification Performance of Partitioned Models.

The combination of PM1, PM14, PM17, and PM18 gave an overall classification performance of 83.2%. The performance of this classifier is compared to the published result in Table 5.4.

Classifier Model	Classification Performance
Statistical Method [9]	80%
Assistance-86 [9]	83%
DPT1	83.2%

Table 5.4. Comparison of classification performance on Hepatitis Database.

6 Conclusion and Future Work

It is observed that DPT1 performs well for data with missing values. However, in applications where associative rules are important, DPT2 is superior. The experimental results show that the proposed techniques can perform as good as other techniques or even better.

Noise in each partitioned model was included in the relevant tables. By reducing the percentage of noise data in each partitioned region, a better classification performance may be obtained. Future work should also include the investigation of methods to reduce the level of noise data in each partitioned region.

The value of *R*, the expansion ratio for training, and *maj*, the majority value for proportional calculation are to be further analyzed. The effect of rule pruning needs to be investigated, and also, the radial basis function neural network implementation can be modified to become a more flexible multiple shape basis function network proposed in [7][12].

References

[1] Y. Chauvin and D. E. Rumelhart, "*Back Propagation: Theory, Architectures, and Applications,*" Lawrence Erlbaum Associates, Hillsdale, N.J., 1995.

[2] T. Kohonen, "Statistical Pattern Recognition with Neural Networks: Benchmark Studies", *Proceedings of the Second Annual IEEE International Conference on Neural Networks*, vol. 1.

[3] Lam YC, Cheung KF, "Fuzzy topological map algorithms. A comprehensive comparison with Kohonen feature map and fuzzy C-mean algorithms," *Proceedings of 1997 IEEE International Symposium on Circuits and Systems. Circuits and Systems in the Information Age. ISCAS '97 (Cat. No.97CH35987). IEEE. Part vol.1, 1997, pp.505-8 vol.1. New York, NY, USA.*

[4] P. K. Simpson, "Fuzzy Min-Max Neural Networks – Part 2: Clustering", *IEEE Transactions on Fuzzy Systems,* vol. 1, no. 1, pp.32-45, February 1996.

[5] S. Grossberg, "Adaptive Pattern Classification and Universal Recoding: I. Parallel Development and Coding of Neural Feature Detectors", *Biological Cybernetics,* vol. 23, pp.121-134, 1976.

[6] S. K. Halgamuge, A. Brichard, and M. Glesner, "Comparison of a Heuristic Method with Genetic Algorithm for Generation of Compact Rule Base Classifiers", *In ACM Symposium on Applied Computing,* Nashville, USA, February 1995. ISBN: 089791-658-1.

[7] S. K. Halgamuge, "Self Evolving Neural Networks for Rule Based Data Processing," *IEEE Transactions on Signal Processing*, November 1997.

[8] R. Agrawal, et al, "*Fast Discovery of Association Rules*", Advances in Knowledge Discovery and Data Mining, chapter 12, MIT Press, 1996.

[9] Blake, C.L. & Merz, C.J. (1998). UCI Repository of machine learning databases [http://www.ics.uci.edu/~mlearn/MLRepository.html]. Irvine, CA: University of California, Department of Information and Computer Science.

[10] R. A. Fisher, "The use of multiple measurements in taxonomic problems," *Ann. Eugen.*, vol 7, no. 2, pp. 179-188, 1936.

[11] J. C. Bezdek, et al, "Will the *Real* Iris Data Please Stand Up?," *IEEE Transactions on Fuzzy Systems*, vol 7, no. 3, pp. 368-369.

[12] A. Jayasuria and S. K. Halgamuge, "An Enhanced Clustering Method for Multiple Shape Function Networks", *In IEEE International Joint Conference on Neural Networks,* Alaska, USA, May 1998.

[13] Hudak MJ, "RCE classifiers: theory and practice," *Cybernetics & Systems, vol.23, no.5, Sept.-Oct. 1992, pp.483-515. USA.*

[14] S. K. Halgamuge, W. Pöchmüller, and M. Glesner, "An Alternative Approach for Generation of Membership Functions and Fuzzy Rules Based

on Radial and Cubic Function Networks," *International Journal of Approximate Reasoning*, vol.12, no. ¾, pp. 279-298, April/May 1995, Elsevier.

[15] William H. Wolberg and O.L. Mangasarian: "Multisurface method of pattern separation for medical diagnosis applied to breast cytology", Proceedings of the National Academy of Sciences, U.S.A., Volume 87, December 1990, pp 9193-9196.

Mining a Growing Feature Map by Data Skeleton Modelling

D. Alahakoon*, S. K. Halgamuge and B. Srinivasan***

* School of Computer Science and Software Engineering, Monash University,

** Department of Mechanical and Manufacturing Engineering, University of Melbourne, Australia.

Abstract. The Growing Self Organising Map (GSOM) has been presented as an extended version of the Self Organising Map (SOM) which has significant advantages for knowledge discovery applications. In this article, we present a further extension to the GSOM in which the cluster identification process can be automated. The self-generating ability of the GSOM is used to identify the paths along which the GSOM grew, and these paths are used to develop a skeleton of the data set. Such a skeleton is then used as a base for separating the clusters in the data

Keywords. Self-organising maps, data mining, knowledge discovery, database segmentation, cluster analysis, clustering, vector quantisation, topological maps.

1 Introduction

A novel self-generating neural network algorithm called the Growing Self Organising Map (GSOM) has been described in [1-4]. Some experimental results were also discussed to highlight the difference between SOM and the GSOM, and also the advantages of the GSOM provided by its flexible structure. It was demonstrated that the GSOM grew nodes and spread out, while it self-organised to generate a structure that better represents the input data. The resulting feature maps were of different shapes and sizes, and it was seen that the shapes of the maps resulted from the inherent clustering present in the data. Therefore, the GSOM clusters were easier to visually identify compared to the SOM clusters, by observing the directions of growth.

In many current commercial and other applications, the clusters formed by feature maps are identified visually. Since the SOM is said to form a topology-preserving mapping of the input data, it is possible to visually identify the clusters and some relationships among them by studying the proximity of, or the distance between the clusters. Although the accuracy of such visualization is not very high, it has proved sufficient for many applications especially in industry as a database segmentation tool [5-6]. The GSOM highlights clusters by branching out in different directions, thus making it easier to identify clusters.

Visually identifying the clusters can have certain limitations, such as:

- It has been shown in [15] that the SOM does not provide complete topology preservation. Therefore, it is not possible to accurately translate the inter-cluster distances to a measure of their similarity (or difference). Therefore, visualization may not provide an accurate picture of the actual clusters in the data. This would occur in a data set with a large number of clusters with a skewed distribution, and will result in erroneous allocation of data points into clusters due to the inaccurate identification of cluster boundaries.
- In certain instances, it is useful to automate the cluster identification process. Since clusters in a data set are dependant on the distribution of data, it would be difficult to completely automate the process unless parameters such as the number of clusters and the size of a cluster are pre-defined. A useful partial automation can be implemented whereby the system will provide the analyst with a number of clustering options. For example, the system can provide the analyst with a list of distances between groupings in data, and let the analyst decide the optimal clustering for a given situation. Having to visually identify the clusters will be a hindrance in automating such a process.

In this paper, a method for automating the cluster identification process is proposed. This method takes into consideration the shape of the GSOM, as well as the visual separation between data, to identify the clusters. The advantages of this method are the identification of more accurate clusters, minimization of the erroneous allocation of data into clusters and the automation of the cluster identification process.

Section 2 of this paper presents a summary of the GSOM concept and the algorithm. In section 3, the usefulness of automated cluster identification for data mining is highlighted. The methods that can be employed are discussed and limitations are identified. Section 4 presents a description of the proposed method and the proposed algorithm. Some artificial and real data sets are used to demonstrate the method experimentally in section 5. Section 6 presents the conclusion for the paper.

2 The Growing Self Organising Map

2.1 The Concept of the GSOM

The GSOM can be considered as a novel neural network model, based on the concept of self-organization as implemented in the Self Organising Map (SOM) [9-11]. The SOM is usually a two dimensional grid of nodes with initial weight values randomly selected from the input data range, and the process called self organization orders, and then adjusts the weights to represent the input data. In the GSOM, the nodes are generated as the data is input. New nodes are created if and only if the nodes already present in the network are insufficient to represent the data. Therefore, the GSOM finally arrives at a map (network) that is a better representation of the input data, as well as having fewer redundant nodes than SOM. The main justification for the GSOM would therefore be that, instead of attempting to force a set of data into a two dimensional grid, the GSOM has the flexibility to spread out and thus arrive at a more representative shape and size for the data set.

Instead of initially starting with the complete network as the SOM, the GSOM starts small. It then generates new nodes where required, using a heuristic to identify such need. Therefore, the network designer need not determine a suitable network size and structure at the beginning. By providing a value called the spread factor (SF) at the start, the user (data analyst) has the ability to control the spread of the GSOM. The spread factor is used to calculate a value called the growth threshold (GT), which is then used as a threshold for initiating new node generation.

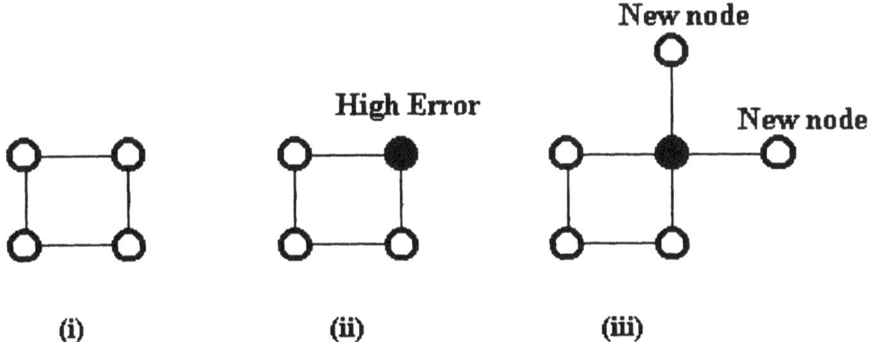

Figure1. New node generation in the GSOM

As shown in figure 1, the GSOM starts with an initial four nodes, the weight values of which are randomly initialized. This initial structure is selected since it is the most appropriate as a starting point for implementing a two-dimensional rectangular lattice structure. The justification for such a selection is provided in section 2.2.

Once the network is initialized, input is presented to the network. For each input the node with the weight vector closest to the input (measured by the Euclidean distance) is judged the winner, and neighboring weights are *nudged* (adjusted) closer to the input value by a learning rate factor. This process is similar to the SOM, but the neighborhood of the winner in the GSOM is much smaller. Each time a node is selected as the winner, the difference between the input vector and the weight vector is calculated and accumulated in the respective node as an *error* value. The network keeps track of the highest such error value and periodically compares this value with the growth threshold (GT). When the error value of a node exceeds the GT, it is selected as a branch point. This process continues until all inputs have been presented. When the number of inputs is small (small set of data), the same input set is repeatedly presented several times, until the frequency of new node generation drops below a specified threshold.

After the above described node generation phase, the same input data is presented to the network, which is *fully developed* at this time. On this occasion, the weight adjustment of winner and its neighbors continue without the node generation. At the beginning of this phase, the initial learning rate adjustment value is reduced from the value used in the node generation phase, and also the neighborhood for weight adjustment is restricted to the winner's immediate neighbors. The purpose of this phase is to smooth out any node weights which has not yet settled into their respective neighborhoods, and can be compared to the *convergence phase* in the SOM [12]. This process is continued until convergence (error ≈ 0) is achieved.

2.2 The GSOM Algorithm

The process is started by generating the initial network of four nodes. The user provides the values of the initial learning rate adaptation, spread factor and the number of instances (records) in the input data set.

1. Initialization Phase

(a) Initialize the weight vectors of the starting nodes in the initial map to random numbers between 0 and 1.

(b) Calculate the growth threshold (GT) for a given data set according to the spread factor (SF) using the formula

$$GT = -D \times \ln(SF) \tag{1}$$

where D is the dimensionality of the data set.

2. Growing Phase

(a) Present an input to the network.

(b) Determine the node with the weight vector that is closest to the input vector, using Euclidean distance measure (similar to the SOM). In other words, find q' such that $|v - w_{q'}| \leq |v - w_q| \; \forall q = 1 \ldots N$ where v, w are the input and weight vectors respectively, q is the position vector for nodes in the map and N is the number of existing nodes in the map.

(c) A weight vector adaptation occurs only in the neighborhood of the winner and the winner itself. The neighborhood is a set of nodes which are topographically close in the network up to a certain geometric distance. In the GSOM, the neighborhood for weight adaptation is smaller than in the SOM (localized weight adaptation). The amount of adaptation, also known as the learning rate, is reduced exponentially in subsequent iterations so that the weight values will converge to the input data distribution. Within the neighborhood, weights which are closer to the winner are adapted more than those further away. This will eventually result in similar inputs being clustered (or assigned to neighboring nodes) in the map. The weight adaptation can be described by:

$$w_j(k+1) = \begin{cases} w_j(k), j \notin N_{k+1} \\ w_j(k) + LR(k) \times (x_k - w_j(k)) \in N_{k+1} \end{cases} \tag{2}$$

where the learning rate LR(k), $k \in N$ is a sequence of positive parameters converging to 0 as $k \rightarrow \infty$. W_j (k), w_j (k + 1) are the weight vectors of the node j, before and after the $(k + 1)^{th}$ iteration, and N_{k+1} is the neighborhood of the winning neuron at $(k + 1)^{th}$ iteration. The rate of decay for LR (k) in the GSOM depends on the number of nodes in the network at time k.

(d) Adjust the error value of the winner (error value is the difference between the input vector and the weight vector) as:

$$E_i^{new} = E_i^{old} + \sum_{i=1}^{D} \sqrt{(x_i - w_i)^2} \tag{3}$$

where E_i is the error of node i, D is the dimension of the data and x_i and w_i are the input and weight vectors to node i respectively.

(e) When $E_i \geq GT$ (where E_i is the total error of node i and GT is the growth threshold), grow nodes if i is a boundary node, else distribute the error of the winner to its neighbors if it is a non-boundary node.

(f) Initialize the new node weight vectors to match the neighboring node weights.

(g) Reset the learning rate (LR) to its initial value.

(h) Repeat steps (a) ...(g) until all inputs have been presented and the frequency of node growth is reduced to below a given threshold.

3. Smoothing Phase

(a) Reduce the learning rate and choose a small starting neighborhood. In experiments with the GSOM, the initial learning rate was reduced by half in the smoothing phase, and the starting neighborhood was fixed as the immediate four neighboring nodes.

(b) Present an input to the network.

(c) Find the winner and adapt the weights of winner and neighboring nodes with the reduced parameters.

We can say that the SOM attempts to self-organize by weight adaptation, while the GSOM adapts its weights and architecture to represent the input data. In the GSOM, a node has a weight vector and two dimensional coordinates to identify its position in the net, while in the SOM the weight vector is also used as the position vector.

3 Methods for Cluster Identification from Feature Maps

In this section, we provide the basis and justification for the automated cluster identification method in the GSOM. We first introduce the SOM as a vector quantisation algorithm and then present the possible methods of identifying clusters from such a feature map. The difficulties faced by an analyst in identifying clusters from a traditional SOM are highlighted and the advantages of the GSOM in this regard are discussed.

3.1 Self Organising Maps and Vector Quantisation

Vector quantisation is a technique that exploits the underlying structure of input vectors for the purpose of data compression or bandwidth compression [8]. This method supposes that the input data are given in the form of a set of data vectors x (t), t = 1, 2, 3, ..., t is an index for the data vectors. In vector quantisation, an input data space is divided into a number of distinct regions and a *reconstruction (reproduction) vector* is defined for each region. This pre-supposes that a finite set W of reference vectors has been defined, such that a good approximate vector $w_s \in W$ can be found for each input data vector x (t). The set of such reconstruction vectors is called a *vector quantiser* for the given input data. When the quantiser is presented with a new input vector, the region in which the vector lies is first determined by identifying the reference vector w_s with the minimum difference $\delta = |x(t) - w_s|$. From then on x (t) is represented by the reconstruction (reference) vector w_s. The collection of possible reconstruction vectors is called the *codebook* of the quantiser.

A vector quantiser with this kind of minimum encoding distortion is called *a Voronoi quantiser*, since the *Voronoi cells* about a set of points in an input space correspond to a partition of that input space according to *the nearest neighbor rule* using the Euclidean metric. Figure 2 shows an input space divided into four Voronoi cells with the respective Voronoi vectors. Each Voronoi cell contains those points of the input space that are the closest to the Voronoi vector among the totality of such points.

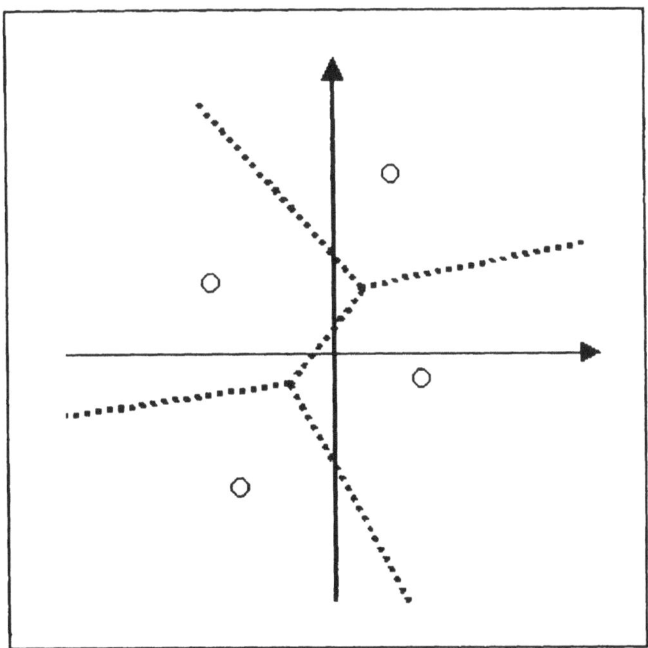

Figure 2. Four Voronoi regions

The Self Organising Feature Map (SOM), represented by the set of weight vectors

$\{w_j \mid j = 1, 2, ...N\}$, provides a good approximation to the input data space [8], [7]. We can interpret the basic aim of the SOM algorithm is to be storing (representing) a large set of input vectors by finding a smaller set of reference vectors, so as to provide a *good* approximation to the input space. The basis of this idea is the *vector quantisation theory* as described above, and SOM can be used as a method of dimensionality reduction or data compression. Therefore, the SOM algorithm can be said to provide an approximate method for unsupervised learning of the Voronoi vectors. The weight vectors in the feature map are the approximate Voronoi vectors of the data set.

3.2 Identifying Clusters from Feature Maps

As described in the previous section, the SOM provides a vector quantisation of a set of input data by assigning a reference vector for each value in the input space. The mapping of input data to the reference vectors has been called a non-linear projection of the probability density function of the high dimensional input data space on to a two dimensional display [12]. With this projection, the SOM achieves a dimensionality reduction by preserving the *topological relationships* existing in the high dimensional data in the two dimensional map. This topology preservation has been described as a mapping of the features in the input data and as such, these maps have been called *feature maps* [12]. We can thus identify the main advantages of the feature maps as :

(1) With the vector quantisation effect, the map provides a set of reference vectors which can be used as a codebook for data compression.

(2) The map will also result in producing a two dimensional topology preserving map of a higher dimensional input space, thus making it possible to visually identify similar groupings in the data.

Therefore, the feature map provides the data analyst with a set of two dimensional feature vectors that represent a more complex multi-dimensional data set. The analyst can then concentrate on identifying any patterns of interest in this codebook using one or more of several existing techniques.

The focus of this article is the GSOM, which is a neural network developed using an unsupervised learning technique. The advantage of unsupervised learning is that it is possible to obtain an unbiased segmentation of the data set without the need of any external guidance. Therefore, we will now consider some existing techniques which can be used on the feature map to identify clusters. We will then use these techniques as the basis of justifying a novel method of cluster identification, which has been developed mainly for the needs of the data mining analyst using the GSOM as a mining tool.

3.2.1 K-means Algorithm

Also called the moving center method, this algorithm was first introduced by McQueen in 1967, and also as ISODATA by Ball and Hall in 1967 [13]. The steps of the algorithm are as follows :

(1) Select K seed points from the data. The value K, which is the number of clusters expected from the data set has, to be decided by the analyst using prior knowledge and experience. In some instances, the analyst may even decide that the data needs to be segmented into K groups for the requirements of a particular application.

(2) Consider each seed point as a cluster with one element and assign each record in the data set to the cluster *nearest* to it. A distance metric such as the Euclidean

distance is used for identifying the distance of each record from the initial K seed points.

(3) Calculate the centroid of the K clusters using the assigned data records. The centroid is calculated as the average positions of all the records assigned to a cluster on each of the dimensions. i.e. if a data record can be denoted as $X = (x_1, x_2, ..., x_n)$,

$$Cluster_{i,\,centroid} = (\sum_{i-1}^{D} x_{i,1}, \sum_{i=1}^{D} x_{i,2}, \ldots \sum_{i=1}^{D} x_{i,n}) \tag{4}$$

where D is the dimension of the data.

(4) Re-assign each of the data records to the cluster centroid nearest to it, and recalculate the cluster centroids.

(5) Continue the process of re-assigning records and calculating centroids until the cluster boundaries stop changing.

There are several approaches when applying the K-means method to a feature map.

(1) Consider all the nodes (reference vectors are represented by the nodes) which have been assigned with at least N input vectors (records) and define these nodes as seed points. The value N will have to be decided by the analyst. The other nodes are then assigned to the clusters according to the above algorithm.

(2) Pre-define the number of seed points using external knowledge, or according to the needs of the application, and randomly assign nodes from the map as the seed points. The rest of the nodes are then assigned to clusters according to the algorithm described above. There can also be other methods of selecting the K nodes from the feature map as initial seed points.

3.2.2 Agglomeration Methods

In the K-means method the analyst has to start with a fixed number of clusters and gather data records around these points. Another approach to clustering, is agglomeration. In these methods, the analyst will start with each point in the data set as a separate cluster and gradually merge clusters until all points have been gathered into one cluster. At the initial stages of the process, the clusters are very small and very pure, with the members of the clusters being very closely *related*. Toward the end of the process, the clusters become very large and less well defined. With this method, the analyst can preserve the entire history of the cluster merging process, and has the advantage of being able to select the most appropriate level of clustering for the application. The main disadvantage of the method is that given a very large data set, it would be almost impossible to start with the entire data set as separate clusters.

With a feature map, all the nodes with at least one input assigned to it can be considered as an initial cluster. The *nearby nodes* can then be merged together until the analyst is satisfied, or a threshold value can be used to terminate the cluster merging. Therefore the data compression capability of the feature map will become very useful when using an agglomeration method on a large set of data, since this will cut down the number of clusters to be processed.

3.2.3 Divisive Methods

Divisive methods are similar to agglomeration methods, but use a top down cluster breaking approach instead of the bottom up cluster merging method used in the agglomeration method. The advantage of this method is that the whole data set is considered as one cluster at the beginning. Hence, it is not necessary to keep track of a large number of separate clusters as in the initial stages of the agglomeration method. A distance metric for calculating the distance between clusters will have to be defined. The points of cluster separation will then be identified by defining a threshold of separation. Such a threshold will depend on the requirements of the application.

3.3 Difficulties in Automating the Cluster Selection Process in Traditional SOMs

In most applications, the GSOM is used as a visualization method. Once the map is generated, the clusters are identified visually. Visually identified clusters have certain limitations as identified in section 1, but have proven to be sufficient for applications with a high level of human involvement, and where high accuracy is not required.

When automating cluster identification in the SOM, any of the above described methods can be used. With the K-means method, the analyst will need to identify the initial seed points and then the nodes with inputs assigned to them will need to be considered as separate data points for the process. The main limitation with this method is the large number of distance calculations that have to be carried out during the processing. The SOM is normally implemented as a two dimensional grid with each internal node having four or six immediate neighbor nodes (four in the GSOM). Therefore, each node will have four connections with other neighbors that have to be processed to determine the closest seed point. Since this is an iterative process that repeats until a satisfactory set of clusters are achieved, it can be time consuming in case of large maps. A large amount of information about the neighbors of each node will also have to be stored throughout the process.

With the Agglomeration method, each node is considered a separate cluster at the beginning. For each node, the neighboring node distances have to be measured, and the nodes with the smallest separation will be merged together as one cluster. This process will also result in a large amount of processing for large SOMs. The processing becomes complex since some nodes may not have immediate neighboring active nodes. In such situations, a search algorithm will have to consider the next level of neighbors and the distances from these neighbors, will have to be calculated.

When considering the divisive method for clustering a SOM, all the used nodes are considered as one cluster at the beginning. The distance calculations with neighbors will have to be made to identify the largest distance, where the *break* is to be made. This method again has the same limitations as the K-means method. Considering the SOM as a two dimensional grid as mentioned above, a node will not be separated from the grid by just eliminating one connection. Therefore, the same node may have to be processed several times for such separation. This will also need a large amount of information stored for processing.

4 Automating the Cluster Selection Process from the GSOM

4.1 The Method and its Advantages

Some methods that can be used for selecting clusters from feature maps were described in the previous section. The main limitations of these methods were also identified and discussed. In this section, we propose a novel method for cluster identification which attempts to take advantage of the extended features of the GSOM.

The cluster identification process is carried out after the GSOM has been fully generated, i.e. after the growing and smoothing phases described in section 2. Therefore, the cluster identification process that we propose can be considered as an optional utility available to the data analyst using the GSOM. As such, the analyst can use visualization to identify the clusters same as with the SOM, or else use the new method. Another option would be to complement the visualization technique with the automated cluster separation method. This process is designed so that a high user involvement can be accommodated. Since the main focus in developing the GSOM was data mining applications, it is essential that the data analyst has the freedom to select the *level* of clustering that is required. We use the term *level* as a way of referring to the threshold for cluster separation considered. A high threshold is considered a low level of clustering, where only the most significant clusters are separated. A low threshold will result in a finer clustering, where even the not so obvious sub clusters are separated.

The new cluster identification method is recommended for the data mining analyst in the following situations.

(1) When it is difficult to visually identify the clusters due to unclear cluster boundaries.

(2) When the analyst needs to confirm the visually identifiable boundaries with an automated method.

(3) When the analyst is not confidant of a suitable level of clustering, it is possible to break the map into clusters, starting from the largest distance and progressing to the next largest. Thus, the data set is considered as one cluster at the beginning and gradually broken into segments, providing the analyst with a progressive visualization of the clustering.

Before describing the method, we will define some terms that are required for understanding the process.

4.1.1 Definition: Path of Spread

The GSOM is generated incrementally from an initial network with four nodes. Therefore, the node growth will be initiated from the initial nodes and spread outwards. A path of spread (POS) is obtained by joining the nodes generated in a certain *direction* in the chronological order of their generation. Therefore, all POS will have their origin at one of the four starting nodes.

4.1.2 Definition: Hit Points

When the GSOM is calibrated using some test data, some of the nodes will be mapped (assigned) inputs. There will also be a number of nodes which are not assigned such *hits*. The nodes which obtain a mapping from an input test data set are called the hit-points.

4.1.3 Definition: Data Skeleton

Once all the POS are identified, it will be seen that some hit-points do not occur on the POS. These points are then linked to the *closest* points in a POS. Every POS joined to the initial four nodes, and the additional hit-points, will result in the data skeleton for a given set of data.

4.1.4 Definition: Path Segments and Junctions

When external hit-points are connected to the POS, if the point on the POS which is linked is not a hit-point, it will become a junction. The distance (Euclidean difference in weight vector value) between two consecutive hit-points, junctions or a hit-point/junction combination is called a path segment.

The proposed method considers the *paths of spread* of the network starting from the initial square grid of four nodes. Since the GSOM spreads out by new node generation, it is proposed that the paths of spread define the structure of the data set by following the *paths* along which the GSOM is generated.

A path of spread is identified by joining one of the four starting nodes with the nodes which *grew* new neighbors. Such joining is performed in the *direction* of growth or spread. Therefore, all paths of spread begin at one of the four initial nodes and spread away from the initial network.

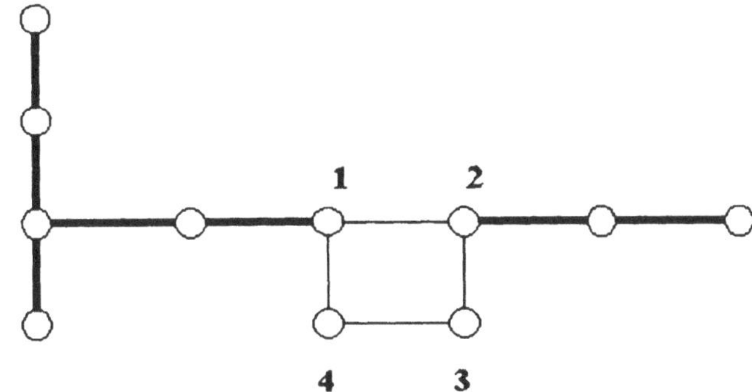

Figure 3. Path of spread plotted on the GSOM

As described in the definitions, once the POS are drawn there will be *some hit-points* that are not part of the POS i.e., which are not mapped to a node making up the POS. Since these nodes have to be included in the clusters, we join these nodes to the POS as shown in Figure 3. The POS joined by all the remaining hit points was defined as the data skeleton. A data skeleton is shown in Figure 4 where the external hit-point connections to the POS are shown by the broken lines. We propose that the data skeleton diagram represents the input data distribution in a skeletal form. The data skeleton thus generated is used to identify and separate the clusters by a progressive elimination of path segments as described below.

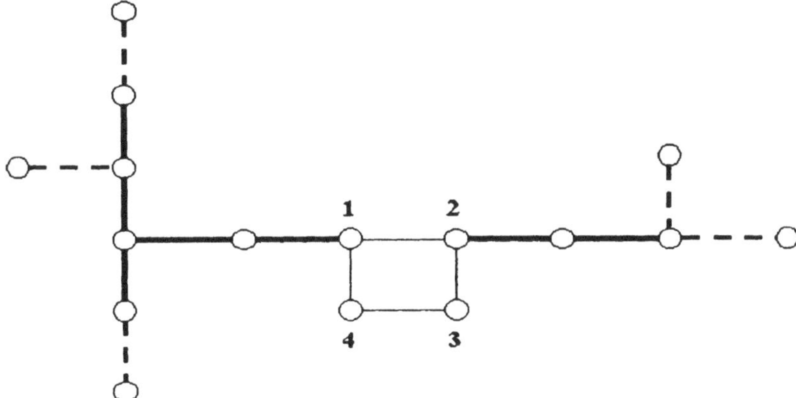

Figure 4. Data skeleton

4.2 Justification for Data Skeleton Building

It was described in section 3 that the feature map generated by the SOM can be considered as a Voronoi quantiser with the individual nodes (represented by their weight vectors) becoming the set of code book vectors representing the input data space. The GSOM is considered an extended version of the SOM which is incrementally built. Therefore, once the GSOM is fully built it can also be described as a Voronoi quantiser for the data. In the previous section, we used the incremental growth of the GSOM to identify the paths of spread (POS), which were then used to build the *skeleton* of the input data. Since the POS creation process made use of the order of the node creation, we need to identify the sequence in which regions are generated to interpret the POS. Therefore an incremental method of Voronoi diagram construction described by Okabe et. al [14] is used to analyze the POS identification from the GSOM.

4.2.1 Incremental Method of Voronoi Diagram Construction

This method starts with a simple Voronoi diagram for a few points (called generators) and modifies the diagram by adding other generators one by one. For $l = 1, 2, ..., n$, let V_l denote the Voronoi diagram for the first l generators $P_1, P_2, ... P_l$. The method has to convert V_{l-1} to V_l for each l. Figures 5, 6 and 7 shows the incremental addition of generators. Figure 5 shows the Voronoi diagram V_{l-1}. Figure 6 shows the addition of generator p_l to V_{l-1} such that it will become V_l. First, we need to find the generator p_i whose Voronoi region contains p_l, and draw the perpendicular bisector between p_l and p_i. The bisector crosses the boundary of $V(p_i)$ at two points; let the points be w_1 and w_2 such that p_l is on the left of the directed line Segment w_1w_2. The line segment w_1w_2 divides the Voronoi polygon $V(p_i)$ into two portions, the one on the left belonging to the Voronoi polygon of p_l. Thus, we get a Voronoi edge on the boundary of the Voronoi polygon of p_l.

Starting with the edge w_1w_2, the boundary of the Voronoi polygon of p_l is grown by the following procedure, which is called the *boundary growing procedure*. The bisector between p_i and p_l crosses the boundary of $V(p_i)$ at w_2, entering the adjacent Voronoi polygon, say $V(p_j)$. So the perpendicular bisector of p_l and p_j is drawn next. This identifies the point at which the bisector crosses the boundary of $V(p_j)$; this point is shown as w_3 in the diagram. The rest of the new region as shown in Figure 6 is calculated in a similar fashion. Figure 7 shows the final Voronoi diagram V_l.

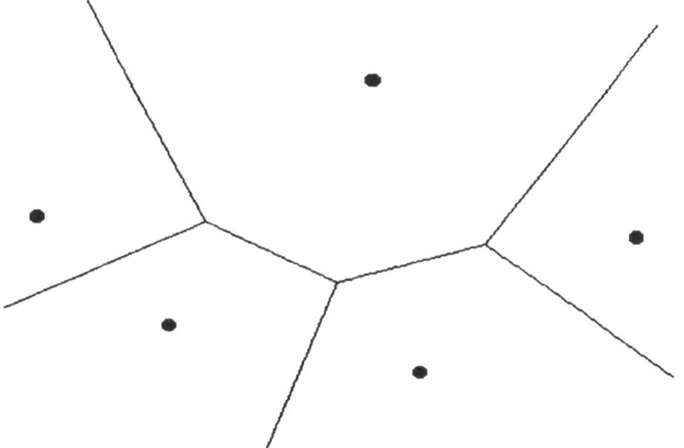

Figure 5. V_{l-1} - Initial Voronoi regions

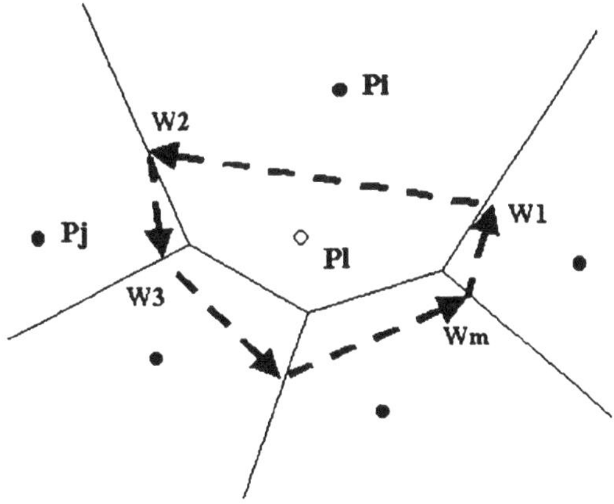

Figure 6. Incremental generation of Voronoi regions

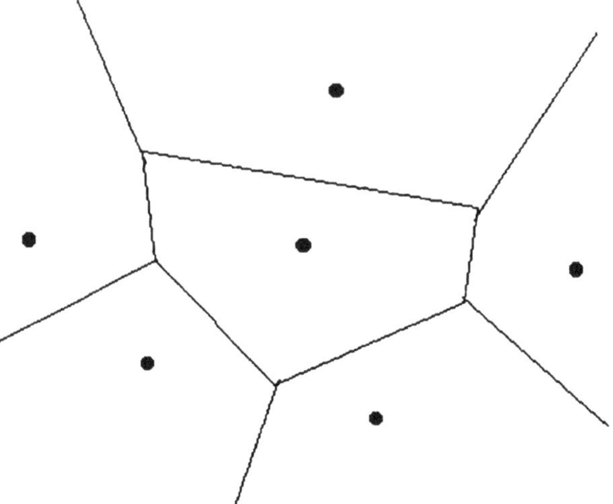

Figure 7. V_l Voronoi diagram with the newly added region

Now we present the new node generation from the GSOM as follows:

When a new node is grown, the parent node becomes a non-boundary node, and therefore we apply the boundary growing procedure above. In Figure 6, we consider point p_l as the parent node and p_i as the newly generated node. Therefore, a new finite Voronoi region is assigned to parent p_l since it has now become a non-boundary node. The child p_i represents an infinite region since it is in the boundary of the network.

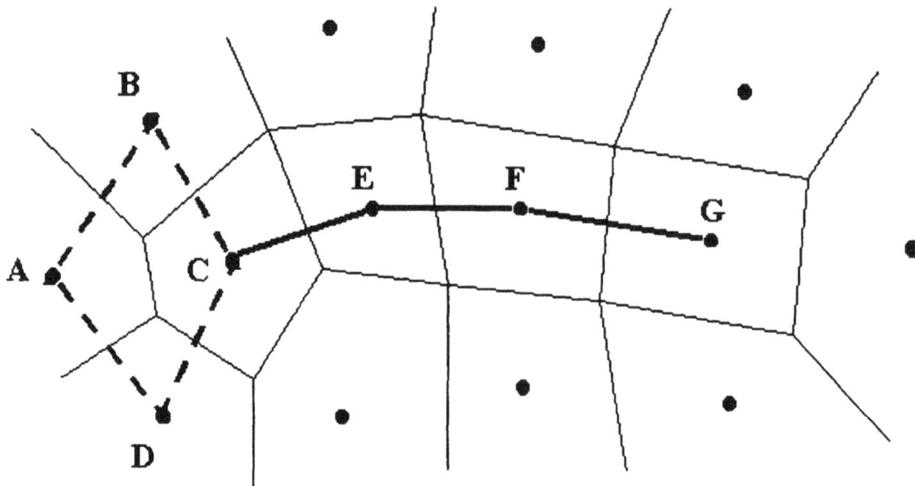

Figure 8. Path of spread plotted on the Voronoi regions

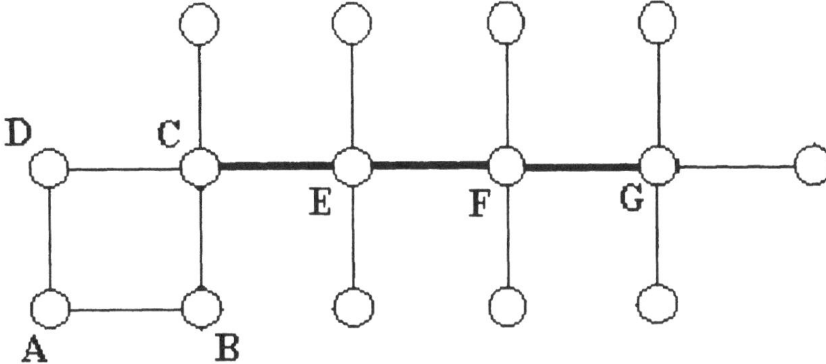

Figure 9. The GSOM represented by the Voronoi diagram in Figure 8

Figure 8 shows the Voronoi regions for a GSOM which has spread out in one direction. The GSOM represented by the Voronoi diagram is shown in Figure 9. In Figure 8, points A, B, C and D represent the initial four regions and E, F and G have been identified as the path of spread from point C. The POS was marked according to the chronological order of node growth in a particular direction, i.e. from E to G. Therefore we are justified in describing the points E, F and G as representing a set of regions that were generated one after the other in incremental region generating method as described above. Thus, points E, F and G can be called a chronological sequence of points generated to represent a region in the input space. Since these points represents the nodes in a feature map, their order of generation describes the direction of map growth. Therefore, we call the line joining points E, F and G as a path of spread (POS) of the feature map shown in Figure 9.

Once the feature map is generated, the hit-points are identified by calibrating the map with a set of test data. Since the path of spread describes the incremental spread of the feature map, it is possible for some parts of the POS to not be hit-points, depending on the input data distribution. These unused nodes in the paths can be called *stepping stone nodes,* since they have been generated solely for the purpose of reaching a hit-point or points further away, which are needed to represent a region or regions of the input distribution. Once the map is completely generated and used nodes have been identified, it will also be seen that some of the used nodes do not lie on the POS. These points represent regions which are neighboring regions of the POS, but have not spread out further as separate sub-paths. Since these points have *attracted* inputs, we have to consider that they represent some part of the input space as codebook vectors. Therefore, we have to take these points into consideration when selecting the clusters. These points are joined to the *nearest position* of the POS, and considered as *branches* off the POS. As defined above, the positions on the POS which are joined to such external hit-points are called junctions.

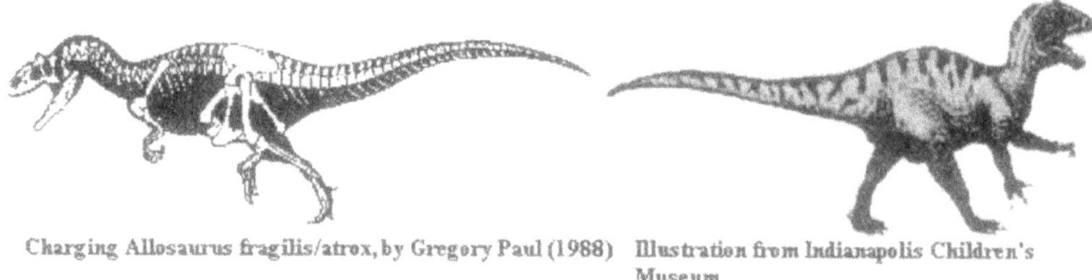

Figure 10. Creating a dinosaur from its skeleton

All the POS connected together by the initial four nodes, plus the sub branches, are called the skeleton of the input data space. As described in section 3.1, each point (node represented by a reference vector), can be considered a codebook vector which represents the input data values *around that region*. Since the POS is identified by effectively linking the codebook vectors of different regions of the input space we propose that the data skeleton produces a similar representation as a two dimensional projection of a skeleton of an animal. As shown in Figure 10, the two dimensional projection of a skeleton represents the real animal. Therefore, we propose that the data skeleton provides a method of visualizing the structure of an unknown set of data, taking into consideration the codebook vectors and the paths joining them. We suggest that this idea is similar to a dinosaur expert constructing the shape of a dinosaur Figure 10 (right) from its skeleton as shown in Figure 10 (left). Therefore, we propose that the structure of the input space can be visualized with the data skeleton built using the POS from the GSOM. The skeleton can then be used to automate the cluster identification process as described in the next section.

4.3 Cluster Separation from the Data Skeleton

The main purpose of generating feature maps is to identify the clusters in a set of input data. In current usage, cluster identification from feature maps is mainly done using visualization, and feature maps are being called a visualization tool. We identified the limitations of depending solely on visualization as a cluster identification method and presented three methods, K-means, divisive and agglomerative clustering as alternative methods.

The main limitation of the K-means method is that the number of clusters K has to be pre-defined. The main advantage of using the SOM or the GSOM for data mining is the unbiased nature of their unsupervised clusters. Therefore forcing a pre-defined number of clusters results in a loss of the independence of the feature map. This will also result in a reduction of GSOMs value as a data mining tool. The divisive and agglomerative methods do not have this limitation of pre-defining the clusters. Therefore, the data analyst has the option of selecting the level of clustering required according to the needs of the application. In the agglomerative method, the analyst can *watch* the clusters merging until the appropriate level of clustering is achieved. Similarly in the divisive method, the analyst can decide when to stop the clusters breaking apart. As described in section 3.2, the main limitation of these methods is the very large number of connections that have to be considered to identify the proper clusters.

Therefore, we propose a method which can be called a hybrid between all three techniques, which is built using the data skeleton from a GSOM. Once the data skeleton is built, the path segments have to be identified. The *distances* of the path segments are calculated as the difference between the weight values of the respective junction/hit-point nodes. The path segment distances are ordered and the system will begin removing the path segments starting from the largest segment. This process will continue until the analyst decides that there are a sufficient or appropriate number of clusters.

Since the method uses the data skeleton, it has to consider a smaller number of connections than with the agglomerative and divisive methods. This will result in faster processing and quicker separation of clusters, since in most cases only a single path has to be broken to separate the different parts of the skeleton. The method is demonstrated with artificial and real data sets in section 5.

4.4 Algorithm for Skeleton Building and Cluster Identification

The algorithm for data skeleton building and cluster separation is given below. The algorithm assumes that there is a fully generated GSOM to be used for this purpose.

(1) Skeleton modelling phase:

(a) Plot the *node numbers* for each node of the GSOM. The node numbers (1, ...N) are assigned to the nodes as they are generated. The initial four nodes have the numbers 1...4. The node numbers represent the chronological order of node generation in the GSOM.

(b) Join the four initial nodes to represent the *base* of the skeleton.

(c) Identify the nodes which initiated new node generation, and link such parent nodes to the respective child nodes. This linking process is carried out in the chronological order of node generation. The node numbers of nodes, which initiate growth are stored for this purpose during the growing phase of GSOM creation.

The linking process is depicted with Figures 11. Figure 11(a) shows the list of node numbers which initiated new node growth. Figures 11(b), (c) and (d) show the process of node linking according to the order specified by the list in 11(a). Therefore, the process can be described as a simulation of the GSOM generation.

(d) Identify the paths of spread (POS) from the links generated in (b).

(e) Plot the hit-points on the GSOM.

(f) Complete the data skeleton by joining the used nodes not on the POS, to the respective POS as sub-branches.

(g) Identify the junctions on the POS.

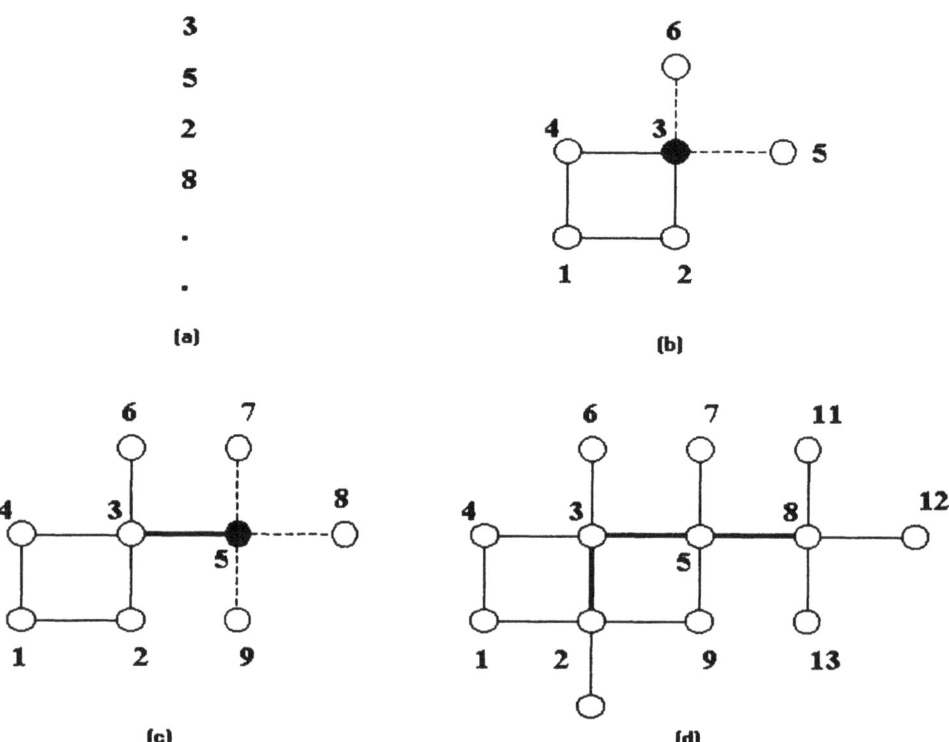

Figure 11. Identifying the POS and building the data skeleton

(2) Cluster separation phase

(a) Identify the path segments by using the POS, hit-points and the junctions.

(b) Calculate the distance between all neighboring junctions on the skeleton. The Euclidean metric is used as the distance measure:

$$D_{AB} = \sum_{i=1}^{D} (w_{i,A} - w_{i,B})^2 \tag{5}$$

where A, B are two neighboring hit-points/junctions and the line joining A, B is called the path segment AB.

(c) Delete path segments starting from the largest value:

find $D_{\{max\}} = D_{X,Y}$ such that

$$D_{X,Y} \geq [D_{i,j} \mid \forall i, j] \tag{6}$$

where X,Y, i, j are node numbers. Delete segment XY.

(d) Repeat (3) until the data analyst is satisfied with the separation of clusters in the GSOM.

The above algorithm results in a separation of the clusters using the data skeleton, such that the data analyst can observe the separation. We believe that this visualization of the clusters provides a better opportunity for the analyst to decide on the ideal *level* of clustering for the application.

5 Demonstration of Skeleton Modelling and Cluster Separation

In this section, we use several data sets to demonstrate the skeleton building and cluster separation processes. The first two experiments demonstrate the process using artificial data sets generated for the purpose of describing the different spreads of GSOMs. These input data sets are selected from the two dimensional space between the coordinates (0, 0), (0, 1), (1, 1), (1, 0). The third experiment uses a more realistic data set of 28 animals to describe the same process.

5.1 Experiment with Two Clusters

In this experiment we use a set of data selected from the two dimensional region as shown in Figure 12. The input data are selected as two clusters from the top right and bottom left corners of the region. Each cluster consists of 25 input points which are uniformly distributed inside the cluster.

5.1.1 Skeleton Building

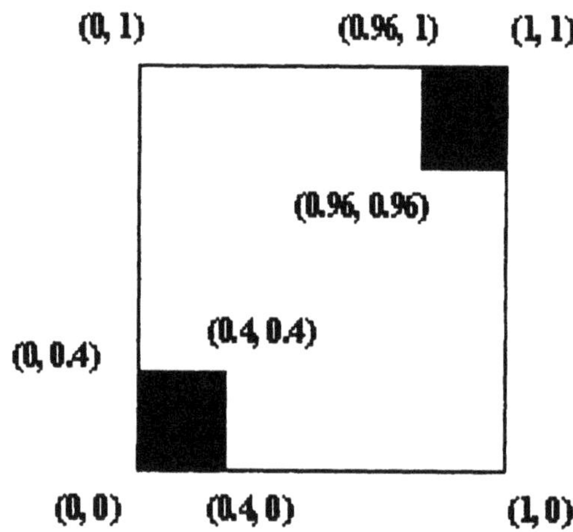

Figure 12. The input data set (for two clusters)

Figure 13 shows the GSOM generated on this data with a SF of 0.25. The nodes in color shows the nodes that were mapped with inputs when calibrated with the same data. It could be seen that the two clusters are shown separately in the GSOM and could be easily visually identified. The purpose of using this simple data set is to demonstrate the cluster separation method, in such a way that the effect of the method could be easily seen.

Figure 14 is the data skeleton for the two cluster data set. The broken lines in the middle of the figure shows the initial (starting) GSOM. The thicker lines show the paths of spread (POS) spreading outwards from the initial four node GSOM. The thin lines are the connections from the nodes outside the POS, which complete the skeleton. The hit nodes are shown colored in gray and the nodes colored in black are the junctions. Path segments are given identification numbers for future reference.

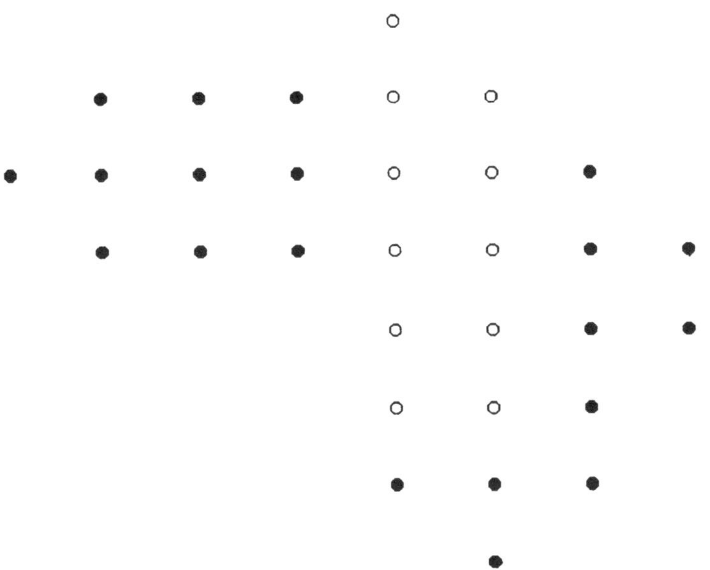

Figure 13. The GSOM with the *hit points* in black and shaded circles

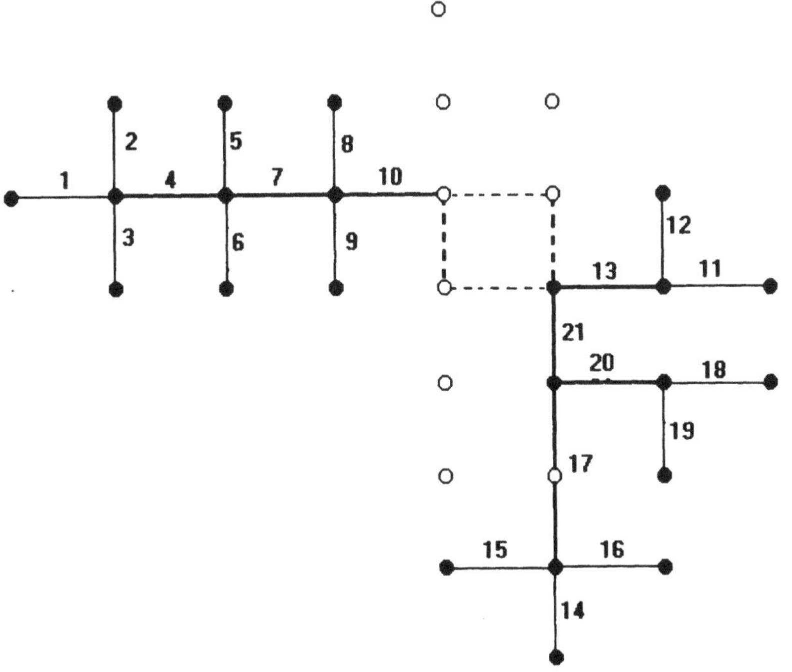

Figure 14. Data skeleton for the two cluster data set

5.1.2 Cluster Separation

Segment No.	Segment distance	Difference
10	1.06945733	
13	0.0935717	1.11E-05
17	0.03946001	0.05411169
20	0.03246394	0.00699607
21	0.01611298	0.01635096
19	0.00010408	0.0160089
8	0.0000797	0.00002438
12	7.88E-05	9E-07
4	0.0000701	8.7^{E}-06
5	0.00006642	3.68E-06
1	0.00006617	2.5^{E}-07
9	0.0000593	0.00000687
3	0.00005393	0.00000537
6	0.00005378	1.5^{E}-07
7	0.00005365	1.3^{E}-07
14	4.84E-05	0.00000523
2	0.00004514	0.00000328
16	3.33E-05	0.00001182
11	1.77E-05	0.00001559
15	0.00001322	0.00000451
18	1.11E-05	0.00000217

Table 1. Path segments of two cluster data sets

Once the data skeleton has been built, the distances for the path segments are calculated. Table 1 shows the distances calculated for the path segments of the two cluster data set. The third column provides the value $D_s - D_{s+1}$, where D_s and

D_{s+1} are the distances of two adjacent path segments. This value is provided for comparison by the analyst to identify significant variations in such differences. The distance values in table 1 are ordered in descending order for the ease of identifying the significant separations.

It can be seen from table 1 that segment 10 contains a large distance value compared to the rest of the values. When identified with Figure 14 it is seen that segment 10 *joins* the two clusters. The Path Segments will now be removed, starting with the largest. For this data set, it is obvious that segment 10 separates two clusters. Figure 15 shows the data skeleton with segment 10 removed. It can be seen that the two clusters have been separated. By observing the table values, further removal can be stopped since no significant separations appear in the rest of the data points.

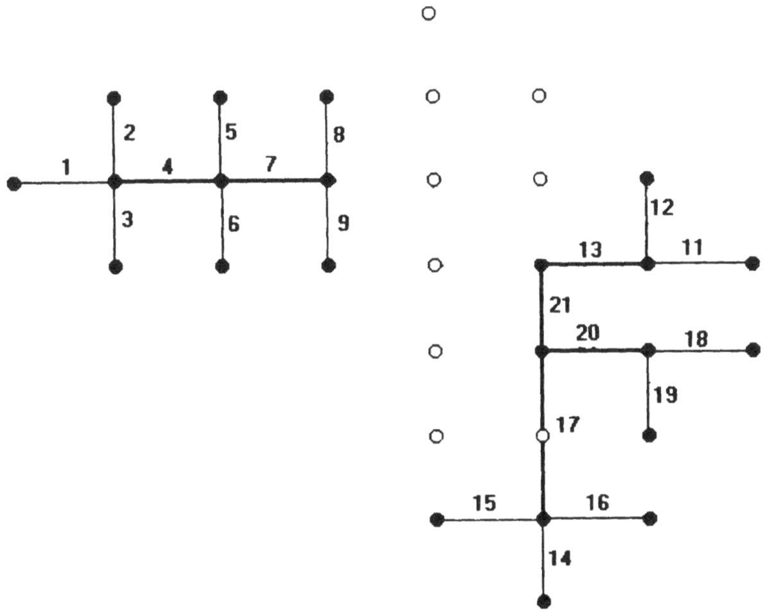

Figure 15. Clusters separated by removing segment 10

5.2 Experiment with Four Clusters

In this experiment, four clusters are selected from the same data set as above. The clusters selected are shown in Figure 16. The experiments carried out are similar to the two cluster method, but demonstrate the spread out of the POS's and the skeleton with a higher number of clusters. These two experiments also attempt to show the representation of the data set by the skeleton. This demonstrates our claim that the data skeleton provides an initial idea of the structure of the input data set.

Figure 17 shows the GSOM generated with a SF of 0.05 for the four cluster data set. In Figure 17, the hit nodes are shown by shading similar to the two cluster experiment. It can be seen that the GSOM has separated the four clusters and it is possible to easily visualize the cluster separation. Now we build the data skeletons, and use the automated cluster separation method to separate these clusters. Figure 18 is the data skeleton for the four clusters with the same symbols as in the two cluster experiment.

5.2.1 Data Skeleton Modelling

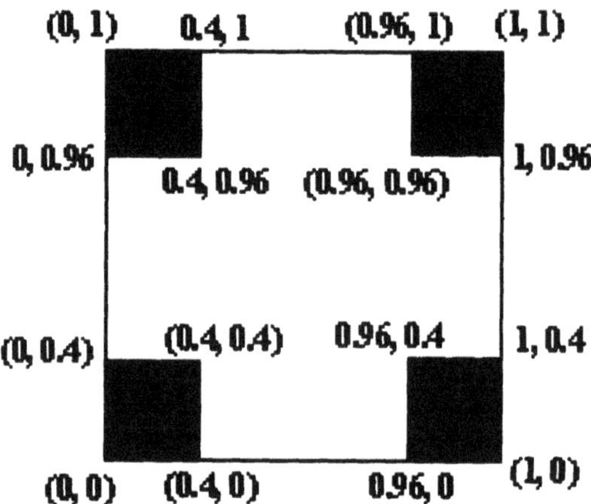

Figure 16. The input data set for four clusters

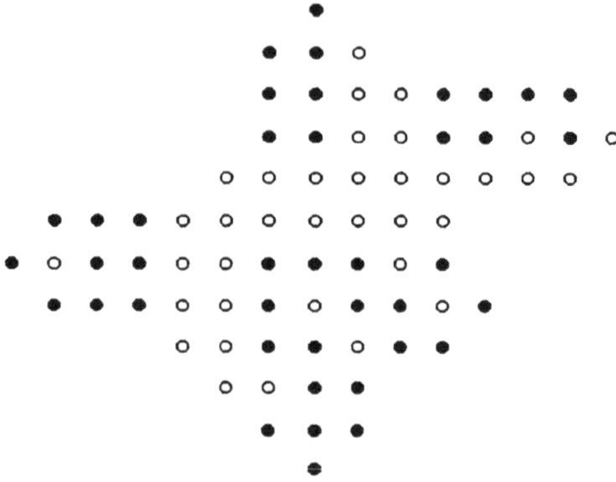

Figure 17. The GSOM for four clusters with the hit nodes shaded

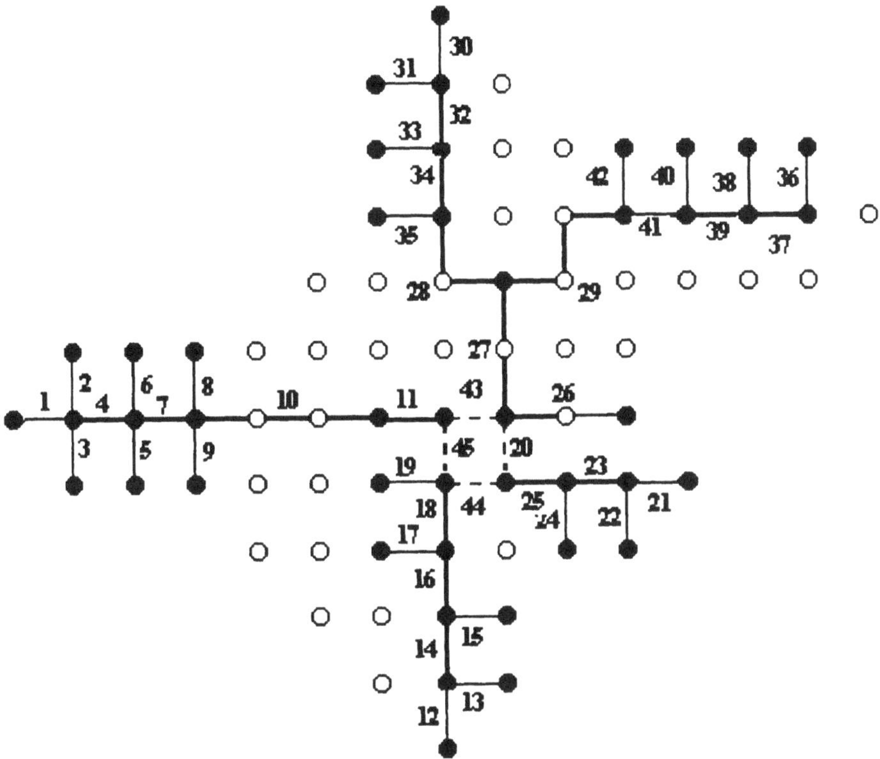

Figure 18. Data skeleton for four clusters

5.2.2 Cluster Separation

Segment No.	Segment Difference	Difference
10	0.86493025	
28	0.59618458	0.26874567
27	0.35666577	0.23951881
29	0.21922388	0.13744189

Table 2. Path segments for the four cluster data

Segment No.	Segment difference	Difference
34	0.00146005	0.21776383
35	0.00078201	0.00067804
11	0.00036194	0.00042007
.	.	.
.	.	.
.	.	.
.	.	.
7	0	7.8049E-133

Table 2. Path segments for the four cluster data (continued)

Table 2 shows the path segments from the four cluster skeleton. It can be seen that the segments 10, 27, 28, 29 are significantly larger than the rest. Figure 19 shows the skeleton with these segments removed. It can be seen that the four clusters have been separated.

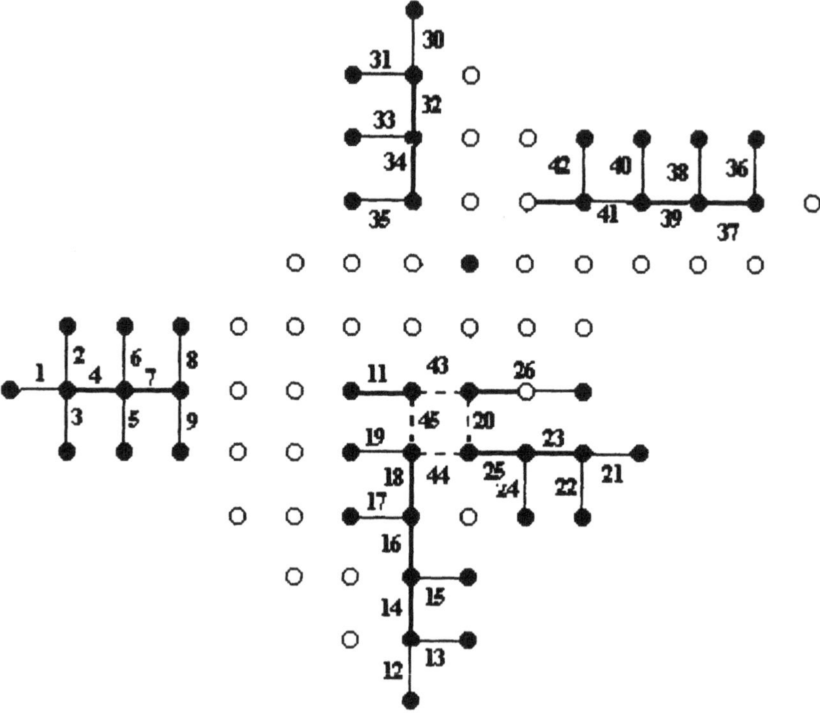

Figure 19. Four clusters separated

5.3 Application of the Method to a Real Data Set

We use a subset of an animal data set given in [16] is used to demonstrate the skeleton building and cluster separation process. 28 of original 100 animals were selected and the criteria for selection were as follows.

(1) Generally well known and familiar animals.

(2) Belongs to four main groups.

(3) Some sub-groupings exist inside the main groups.

The data consist of 18 attributes, of which the name and the type were not considered for training the GSOM. Most of the balance 16 attributes are binary (has hair, feeds milk, venomous etc.) other than the number of legs. The initial GSOM generated with the data is shown in Figure 20. It can be seen that the GSOM has spread out mainly in four directions which correspond to the four *types* of animals.

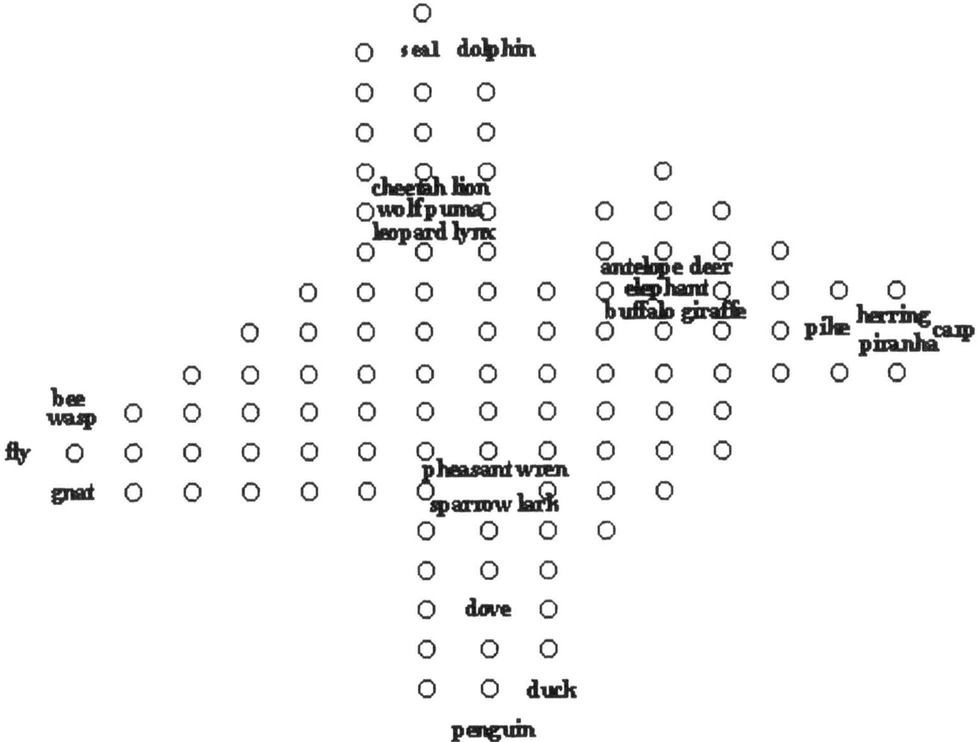

Figure 20. The GSOM for the 28 animals, with SF = 0.25

5.3.1 Skeleton Building

Figure 21 shows the data skeleton mapped on to the GSOM and the POS's spreading outwards from the initial square map. The symbols are the same as the previous two experiments. It can be seen from the skeleton that the main groups have spread out in different *directions* in the map. In fact, we can see that the GSOM has been generated by spreading out in these directions. It is interesting to see that the non-meat eating mammals have been mapped on a different POS from the meat eaters, but it can also be seen that both POS's *move* in the same direction. It can also be identified that the sub-groups inside the main groups have been mapped to the same POS in most cases.

Table 3 shows the distances for the path segments identified in the Figure 21. The data analyst can now remove segments starting from the top of the table until he is satisfied with the clusters (which will depend on the application at hand). It can be seen that segment 18 has a large distance compared to the others. This can be interpreted as the fish being considered as the most different cluster (group) from the other animals. The insect are separated next by removing segment 4. Segments 13 can be removed next and this separates the four main groups.

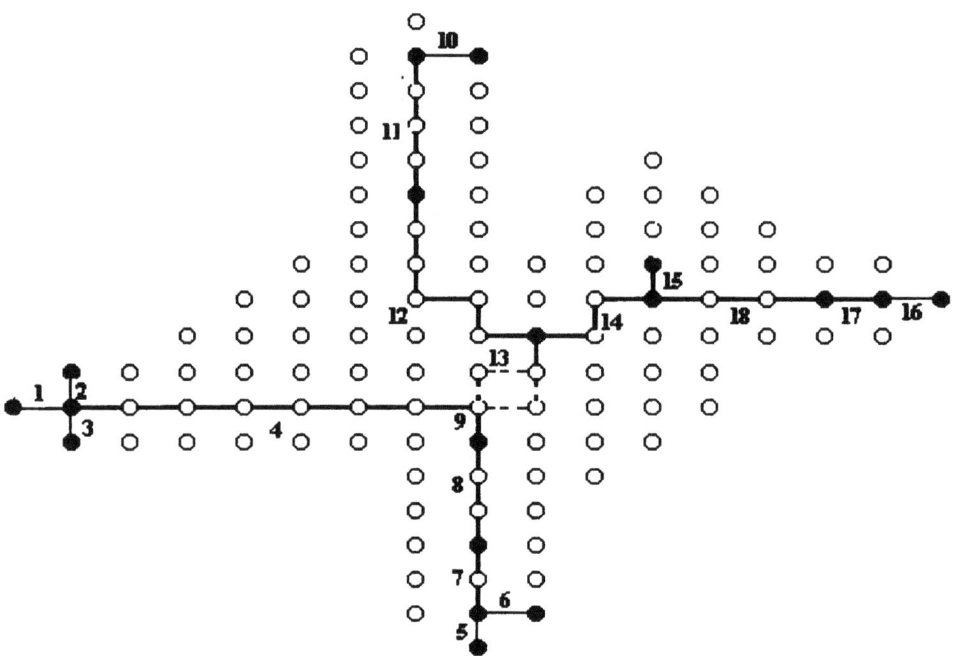

Figure 21. Data skeleton for the animal data

5.3.2 Cluster Separation

Segment	Segment distance	Difference
18	7.43525391	
4	4.31007765	3.12517626
13	3.76652902	0.54354863
11	2.76706805	0.99946097
7	1.56629396	1.20077409
12	1.32260106	0.2436929
8	0.7473245	0.57527656
14	0.49138419	0.25594031
5	0.27485321	0.21653098
3	0.19083773	0.08401548
10	0.15102813	0.0398096
16	0.14247555	0.00855258
2	0.12936505	0.0131105
6	0.12936505	0.04370601
17	0.12936505	0.01011911
1	0.12936505	0.04456131
9	3.45E-06	0.03097517
15	0.00000001	0.00000344

Table 3. Path segments for animal data set

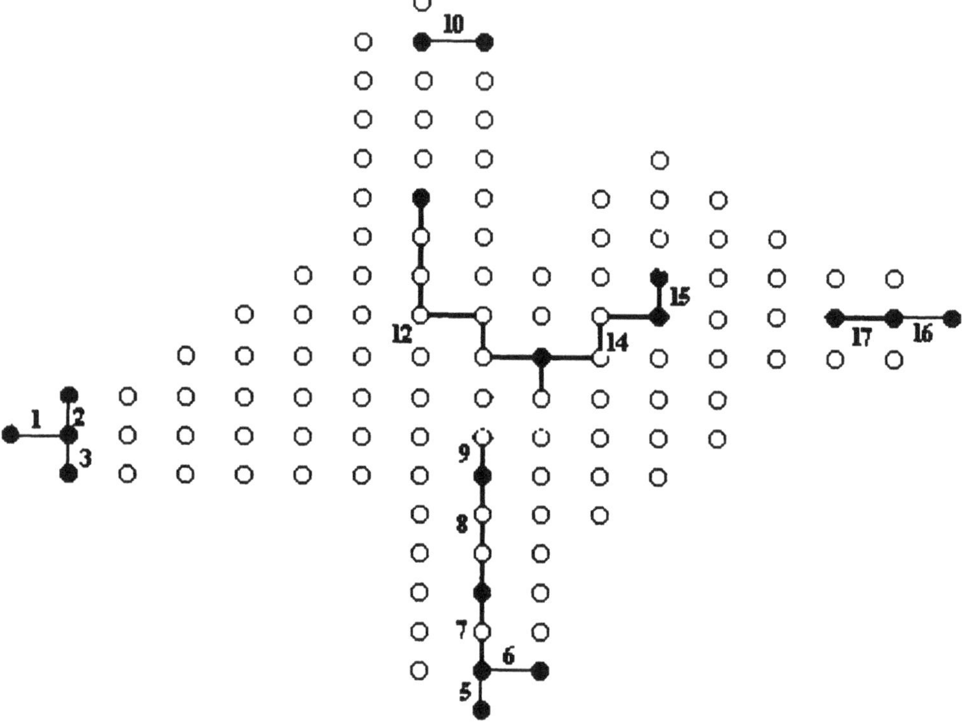

Figure 22. Clusters separated in the animal data

Now further segment removing will separate the subclusters inside the main clusters. Figure 22 shows the main groups separated in the animal data set. It can be seen from these experiments that the segment removing method separates the clusters and provides the analyst with a lot of independence in selecting (or deciding) the level of clustering.

6 Conclusions

In this article, a novel method of cluster identification from the GSOM was described. The motivation for developing this method is to enhance the traditional usage of feature maps from just visualization tools for data mining to more automated method of cluster identification. Since this method made use of the *growing* nature of the GSOM to build the data skeleton, we can also present this method as a *value added* over traditional SOM's.

The other advantages of this method are:

(1) The capability of the data analyst to be highly involved in the cluster separation even though the process is automated. The analyst can decide when to stop the path segment removal depending on the level of clustering required. On the other hand, the analyst can let the segment removing process run from start to end, which will provide a useful incremental picture of the level of clustering present in the data.

(2) It has been proved that the SOM does not provide complete topology preservation. Therefore, the visual separation of clusters may give a wrong impression about the actual *difference* in the groups. With the GSOM method the actual differences in weights are also considered, which combined with the visual separation provide better understanding of the clusters.

(3) The data skeleton provides the foundation for building a conceptual model for the input data set. Such a model can then be used for mining of rules and monitoring for changes.

Therefore, we can conclude that this article described a method of building a structure called the data skeleton and also a way of automated cluster identification using a GSOM. These methods enhance the suitability of the GSOM as a data mining tool compared to the SOM, which is currently used mainly as a visualization technique.

References

[1] Alahakoon L. D. and Halgamuge S. K. Knowledge Discovery with Supervised and Unsupervised Self Evolving Neural Networks. *In Proceedings of the International Conference on Information-Intelligent Systems*, pages 907-910, 1998.

[2] Alahakoon L.D., Halgamuge S. K. and Srinivasan B. A Self Growing Cluster Development Approach to Data Mining. *In Proceedings of the IEEE Conference on Systems Man and Cybernetics*, pages 2901-2906,1998.

[3] Alahakoon L.D., Halgamuge S. K. and Srinivasan B. A Structure Adapting Feature Map for Optimal Cluster Representation, *In Proceedings of the International Conference on Neural Information Processing*, pages 809-812, 1998.

[4] Alahakoon L.D., Halgamuge S. K. and Srinivasan B. Dynamic Self Organising Maps with Controlled Growth for Knowledge Discovery, *IEEE Transactions on Neural Networks, Special issue on Knowledge Discovery and Data Mining*, to be published in 2000.

[5] Bigus J. P. *Data Mining with Neural Networks*, McGraw Hill, 1996.

[6] Deboeck G. *Visual Explorations in Finance*, Springer Verlag, 1998.

[7] Hassoun M. *Fundamentals of Neural Networks*, Massachusetts Institute of technology, 1995.

[8] Haykin S. *Neural Networks : A Comprehensive Foundation*, Prentice Hall, 1994.

[9] Kohonen T. Analysis of Simple Self Organising Process, *Biological Cybernetics*, 44:139-140, 1982.

[10] Kohonen T. Self Organised Formation of Topological Correct Feature Maps, *Biological Cybernetics*, 43:59-69, 1982.

[11] Kohonen T. *Self Organization and Associative Memory*, Springer Verlag, 1989.

[12] Kohonen T. *Self Organising Maps, Springer Verlag*, 1995.

[13] Mirkin B. *Mathematical Classification and Clustering*, Kluwer Academic publishers, 1996.

[14] Okabe A., Boots B. and Sugihara K. *Spatial Tessellations, Concepts and Applications of Voronoi Diagrams*, John Wiley and Sons, 1992.

[15] Ritter H., Martinetz T. M. and Schulten K. *Neural Computation and Self Organising Maps*, Addison Wesley, 1992.

[16] Blake C., Keogh E. and Merz C. J. *UCI Repository of machine learning databases*, University of California, Irvine, Dept. of Information and Computer Sciences.

Soft Regression – A Data Mining Tool

E. Shnaider[1] and M. Schneider[2]

[1]School of Business, Netanya Academic College, Netanya, Israel.

[2]Department of Electrical Engineering – Systems, Tel Aviv University, Tel Aviv 69978, Israel.

Abstract. This chapter describes a method for knowledge discovery. First, we will describe the general approach to knowledge discovery, its characteristics and components. Then we will describe our method. Finally we will provide an example from the area of "economic modeling" to illustrate the use of soft regression in knowledge discovery.

Keywords: Soft regression, Fuzzy Logic, Pattern Matching, Significance Test.

1 Introduction

In the past few years, we have seen a tremendous growth of information available via all sorts of electronic media [1]. This explosive growth, together with the need to know, understand and take advantage of the information, created the need to develop tools that will enable us to reach the relevant information, analyze it and will produce reports that will be useful for any professional. The information is available, mainly, through 3 different formats: text, graphics and tables. In this chapter, we will describe a *data mining* tool that discovers knowledge from tables (or databases).

1.1 Knowledge Discovery and Data Mining

Knowledge discovery is the most desirable end product of computing. To be able to extract knowledge from data is a task that many researchers are trying to accomplish and when successful it is a good demonstration of intelligent computing. The goal of data mining is to develop tools that search a large database and discover significant patterns. Knowledge discovery is defined as [2]:

Knowledge discovery is the non trivial process of identifying valid, novel, potentially useful, and ultimately understandable patterns in data.

There are two major goals in data mining: *prediction* and *description*. Prediction is the task of finding unknown values from known data. Description focuses on the interpretation of data. In order to perform either of these tasks, we can use one or more of the following methods:

1. Classification learns a function that maps a data set into several predefined classes [3].
2. Regression learns a function that maps a data set into a prediction variable [4].
3. Clustering is a descriptive method to identify features of a given data [5].
4. Summarization is a method to compact data based on some criteria [6, 7].
5. Dependency modeling consists of finding a model that describes significant dependencies between variables [8, 9].
6. Deviation detection focuses on detecting changes in data [10].

In this chapter, we will present a method that in some cases can replace the classical regression algorithm. This method, denoted *soft regression*, uses fuzzy logic to find correlations among a set of numerical variables (vectors). A description of the method is provided in Section 2.

1.2 The Knowledge Discovery Process

The knowledge discovery process is iterative and interactive, involving many different steps with help from the user:

1. Developing an understanding of the application domain, and the relative prior knowledge and goals of the end-user. This is a general requirement. We need to define our goal very precisely, the environment in which the knowledge discovery process will take place, and some potential data mining tools we may use to discover the new knowledge.
2. Creating a target data set, focusing on the data over which discovery is to be performed. After defining the goal, we need to find the data that we "think" can help us to discover the new knowledge. The process of creating the target set involves either extracting the necessary variables from some database and creating a new data base (which is a subset of the original database), or deleting irrelevant variables from the existing database.
3. Data cleaning and preprocessing, removal of noisy information, and clustering the relevant information. As we will see later, the database can

be noisy and therefore may generate erroneous results. We can clean the data either by changing the data (if we know what values should be placed in the variables) or by removing the data altogether.

4. Data reduction and projection involves finding the useful features that represent the data, based on the user's specifications. After the data set is chosen, we may discover that some of the variables are redundant, and some of the variables (that first seemed irrelevant) are missing. Therefore, this phase focuses on reducing the number of variables and creating a data set that is clean and relevant to the domain of the goal.

5. Choosing the data mining task involves selecting which method to use for knowledge discovery. There are many different methods to perform mining. Each method has a different approach, with different weaknesses and strengths. We need to choose one method, and if necessary even more. This will ensure that the discovery process will lead to the best possible results.

6. Choosing the data mining algorithms: within the method selected, the most appropriate algorithm(s) are chosen. It is reasonable to expect that there is more than one way (more than one algorithm) to perform the data mining process based on any given method. After choosing a method, we need to choose the best algorithm (or in practical terms, choosing the appropriate software and the appropriate sub-components of that software) to perform the mining process.

7. Searching for patterns of interest in the particular representational form. After some knowledge or patterns have been discovered, we need to represent the result in a format that can be used for interpretation.

8. Interpreting the discovered patterns. This basically has to do with creating rules that describe the patterns when the goal is description, or creating additional data in cases where we try to predict new patterns.

9. Creating the final report. Here we create the report that describes the goal, process and the discovered knowledge.

The process described above can be depicted in Figure 1:

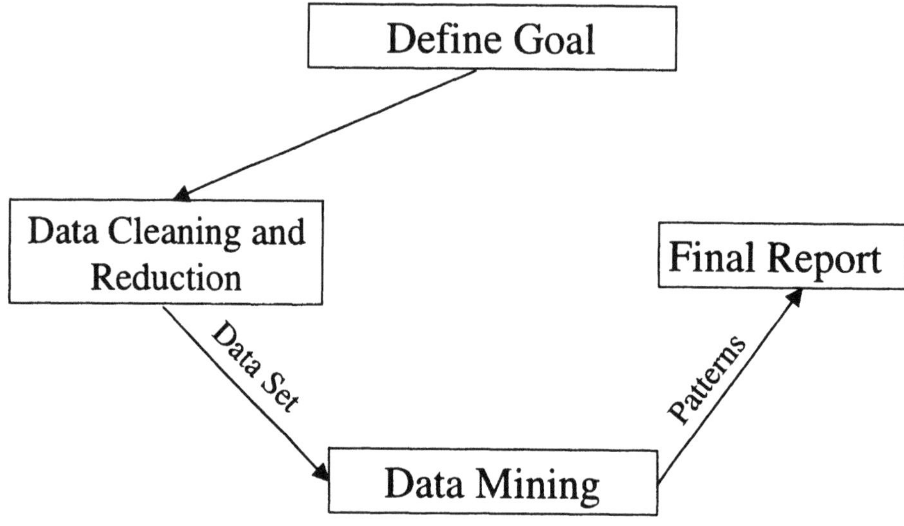

Figure 1. The knowledge discovery process

2 Soft Regression

This section describes a method to perform soft regression. Soft regression utilizes numerical variables as fuzzy sets. This way it can compare not only pairs of vectors, but also the behavior of one variable (vector) relative to a group of explanatory variables (vectors), similarly to the modeling performed with the help of econometric (regression) methods. In those cases, where the number of explanatory variables exceeds one, the method computes the relative importance of each of the explanatory variables. Also, we describe a method to compute the confidence level of results.

2.1. Introduction

This study presents a computerized method which uses fuzzy techniques to achieve greater flexibility, greater accuracy and generate more information in comparison to econometric modeling based on (statistical) regression techniques. In particular, the fuzzy method can potentially be more successful than conventional regression methods, especially under circumstances that severely violate the fundamental conditions required for the reliable use of conventional methods.

The basis for developing the soft regression method was established in [12], where an attempt was made to utilize numerical data to construct Fuzzy Cognitive Maps (FCMs) [11]. The method developed in [12] treats each variable as a fuzzy set of n elements (measurements). A measure for the degree of similarity in the behavior of numerical vectors (closeness of vectors) was developed, as well as a method to determine whether the vectors (variables) are directly or inversely related. However, the FCM method developed in [12] was only capable of showing closeness (relations) between *pairs* of numerical vectors. The complex Fuzzy Cognitive Maps showing degrees of relations between pairs of variables also show that variables often interrelate with several other variables. Therefore, in [13] a method was developed to model relations of a given variable (numerical vector) with a combination of several variables. In other words, it is of great importance to find out how several variables (which will be denoted as explanatory variables) together explain (relate to) the variable we are trying to model (which will be denoted as the dependent variable). In addition to the degree to which the behavior of the dependent variable is explained by the combination of all the explanatory variables, it is also of great importance to find the relative importance of each explanatory variables in "explaining " the behavior of the dependent variable. One should notice that we are using similar terms to those used in traditional regression modeling, where it is also possible to model the behavior of dependent variable with the help of several explanatory variables (which in the traditional regression methodology must be independent of each other). Traditional regression analysis also measures to what degree the behavior of the dependent variable is explained by the combined group of explanatory variables, and what is the contribution of each individual explanatory variable. However, the traditional regression methods require a very restrictive and rigid set of requirements, which often cannot be satisfied in the process of economic/business modeling, and often lead to the failure of such models. Therefore, the method developed in [13] actually represents the fuzzy equivalent of the traditional regression modeling tools. However, in order to be fully compatible with the conventional regression method, it was necessary to introduce significance tests: tests that will indicate which explanatory variables display a significant relation with the dependent variable and thus belong to the model, vs. insignificant variables that should be removed from the model. A method to measure the significance level in soft regression is described in Section 2.6.

2.2. Numerical Vectors as Fuzzy Sets

A numerical vector is a vector that consists of n elements (measurements). Each variable, for which there are n measurements, can be viewed as a numerical vector of n elements. Therefore, the relations among numerical vectors represent relations among corresponding variables. We can treat numerical vectors as fuzzy sets of n elements. The conversion of numerical vectors to fuzzy sets requires their projection into equivalent vector of the corresponding grades of membership (between 0 and 1). We use the following approach in converting a numerical vector into a fuzzy set:

Let V be a numerical vector where v represents one measurement (element) of the vector. Then we use the following method to convert such a numerical vector into a fuzzy set:

1. Find a maximum value in V, and assign $\mu = 1$ to it, that is:

$$Max(v) \Rightarrow \mu_v(v) = 1 \qquad (1)$$

2. Find a minimum value in V, and assign $\mu = 0$ to it, that is:

$$Min(v) \Rightarrow \mu_v(v) = 0 \qquad (2)$$

3. Project all other *i* vector elements (v_i) into the interval [0, 1] proportionally to normalize numeric variables. That is:

$$\mu_v(v_i) = \frac{v_i - Min(v)}{Max(v) - Min(v)} \qquad (3)$$

where $\mu_v(v_i)$ is a membership grade of a measurement.

2.3. Determining Direct vs. Inverse Relations

Following the transformation of numerical vectors into fuzzy sets, each element of the vector v_i is represented by some grade of membership $\mu(v_i)$. Let V_1 and V_2 be two numerical vectors, and let $\mu_1(v_i)$ and $\mu_2(v_i)$ be the grades of membership of the element *i* in vectors V_1 and V_2 respectively.

Definition 1: *Vectors V_1 and V_2 are directly (positively) related if $\mu_1(v_i)$ is similar to $\mu_2(v_i)$ for all or most of the corresponding elements of the two vectors.*

In other words, for elements in V_1 where $\mu_1(v_i)$ are close to 1, the equivalent elements of V_2 also have their grades of membership $\mu_2(v_i)$ close to 1. Similarly, when elements in V_1 have grades of membership $\mu_1(v_i)$ close to 0, the corresponding elements in V_2 also have grades of membership $\mu_2(v_i)$ close to 0. When elements of V_1 have grades of membership around 0.5, the corresponding elements in V_2 also have their grades of membership around 0.5, etc.

Definition 2: *Vectors V_1 and V_2 are inversely (negatively) related if $\mu_1(v_i)$ is similar to $(1 - \mu_2(v_i))$ for all or most of the corresponding elements of the two vectors.*

Namely, for elements in V_1 where $\mu_1(v_i)$ are close to 1, the corresponding elements of V_2 have their grades of membership $\mu_2(v_i)$ close to 0. Similarly, when elements in V_1 have grades of membership $\mu_1(v_i)$ close to 0, the corresponding elements in V_2 have grades of membership $\mu_2(v_i)$ close to 1. When elements of V_1 have grades of membership around 0.25, the corresponding elements in V_2 have their grades of membership around 0.75. However, when elements of V_1 have grades of membership around 0.5, the corresponding elements in V_2 also have their grades of membership around 0.5 (which is similar to the case of direct relation).

2.4. Computing Similarity of Relations Between Two Vectors

The similarity between two variables is based on the concept of distance between vectors [11]. The implementation of this concept in our system requires a different computation for vectors that are directly related, and vectors that are inversely related. If vectors V_1 and V_2 are directly related, then the closest relation possible between them is when for each i (i = 1, ..., n), $\mu_1(v_i) = \mu_2(v_i)$. Let d_i be the distance between the corresponding elements of V_1 and V_2 such that

$$d_i = |\mu_1(v_i) - \mu_2(v_i)| \tag{4}$$

and let AD be the average distance (hamming distance) between the vectors V_1 and V_2. Then utilizing Equation (4):

$$AD = \frac{\sum_{i=1}^{n} d_i}{n} \tag{5}$$

Once the average distance between the two variables is computed, the closeness, or similarity between the two vectors (denoted as S) is computed using the following equation:

$$S = 1 - AD \tag{6}$$

For perfectly identical sets, where for each element $\mu_1(v_i) = \mu_2(v_i)$, the average distance between the vectors (AD) is (using Equation (5)):

$$AD = \frac{\sum_{i=1}^{n} d_i}{n} = 0$$

and the similarity between the two vectors is equal to (utilizing Equation (6)):

$$S = 1 - AD = 1 - 0 = 1$$

which indicates perfect similarity.

The greatest degree of dissimilarity is possible only in the case of binary sets. That is: for every element in V_1 where $\mu_1(v_i) = 1$, the corresponding element in V_2 has the grade of membership of 0 and vice versa. In this case, the average distance between the vectors (AD) using Equation (5) is:

$$AD = \frac{\sum_{i=1}^{n} d_i}{n} = \frac{n}{n} = 1$$

and thus, using Equation (6):

$$S = 1 - AD = 1 - 1 = 0$$

which indicates the extreme degree of dissimilarity.

In the case of fuzzy sets, where most of the elements have grades of membership between 0 and 1, no perfect similarity or perfect dissimilarity is expected, but similarity to some degree is a reasonable outcome.

The method for computing distance (similarity) for inversely related vectors is in principle very similar to that of the directly related vectors, with the exception that the distance between the corresponding elements of the inversely related vectors V_1 and V_2 is:

$$id_i = |\mu_1(v_i) - (1 - \mu_2(v_i))| \tag{7}$$

where id_i is the distance (inverse) between the corresponding elements of inversely related vectors. Then utilizing Equation (7):

$$AD = \frac{\sum_{i=1}^{n} id_i}{n} \tag{8}$$

Once the average distance between the two vectors is computed, the inverse similarity between the two vectors (denoted as S) is computed using the following equation:

$$S = 1 - AD \tag{9}$$

The inversely related numerical vectors are perfectly related to each other if for each element, $\mu_1(v_i) = 1 - \mu_2(v_i)$. Then the average distance between the vectors (based on Equation (8)) is:

$$AD = \frac{\sum_{i=1}^{n} id_i}{n} = \frac{0}{n} = 0$$

and the similarity between the two vectors is (using Equation (9)):

$$S = 1 - AD = 1 - 0 = 1$$

which indicates perfect inverse similarity.

The greatest degree of inverse dissimilarity is possible only in the case of binary sets (as in the case of direct relation), such that for every i ($i = 1, \ldots, n$), the corresponding elements of the two vectors have the same grade of membership (either 1 or 0). In this case:

For the case where $\mu_1(v_i) = 1$ and $\mu_2(v_i) = 1$, for every i ($i = 1, \ldots, n$)

$$id_i = |\mu_1(v_i) - (1 - \mu_2(v_i))| = |1 - (1 - 1)| = 1$$

For the case where $\mu_1(v_i) = 0$ and $\mu_2(v_i) = 0$, for every i ($i = 1, \ldots, n$)

$$id_i = |\mu_1(v_i) - (1 - \mu_2(v_i))| = |0 - (1 - 0)| = 1$$

Thus,

$$AD = \frac{\sum_{i=1}^{n} id_i}{n} = \frac{n}{n} = 1$$

and

$$S = 1 - AD = 1 - 1 = 0$$

which indicates perfect inverse dissimilarity between the two vectors.

However, when studying relations between numerical vectors represented as fuzzy sets, neither perfect similarity nor perfect dissimilarity is expected. The most likely representation of the relations between vectors is in terms of similarity to some degree. The similarity between vectors (S) represents a difference between 1 (which represents perfect similarity) and the average difference between the grades of membership of all the corresponding elements of the two vectors (which represents the dissimilarity between the vectors). In other words, the measure of similarity is derived by subtracting the average dissimilarity between the vectors from the measure of perfect similarity. The measure of dissimilarity here differs from the term *statistical error of regression analysis* (which is the average difference between the values of the vector elements and the corresponding computed values on the regression line). For each pair of vectors the system computes similarity twice: once based on direct relation and then based on the inverse relation. The higher degree of similarity determines the type of relation (direct vs. inverse) and the degree of similarity.

2.5 Relation of One Vector with Several Explanatory Variables

The difficulty of econometric modeling based on traditional regression methods has been, in addition to the near - impossibility of determining a precise model specification, the near impossibility of having all explanatory variables independent of one another. The inability to satisfy these conditions has often led to distorted models and a high probability of failure.

In SOFT REGRESSION, the model relating the explanatory variables with the dependent variable is based on the following concept:

Let V_j be a set of numerical vectors, where V_1 represents the dependent variable and V_j (j = 2, ..., *m*) represents an explanatory variable. Let v_i (i = 1, ..., n) be an observation in a vector (a member of the fuzzy set represented by that vector). Then for every v_i (i = 1, ..., n), the distance (similarity) between the dependent variable and the combined group of all explanatory variables (j = 2, ..., m) is:

$$d_{MIN_i} = MIN\ (|V_{1_i} - V_{J_i}|) \qquad \text{for } i = 1, ..., n \tag{10}$$

Here m is the number of variables, n is the number of elements in V, and i is the ith element in vector V (i = 1, ..., n). The combined (average) distance between the dependent variable, and the combined group of explanatory variables is :

$$AD_{comb} = \frac{\sum_{i=1}^{n} d_{MIN_i}}{n} \tag{11}$$

AD represents an average distance between elements in V_1 and the corresponding elements from the set of explanatory variables, which are the closest to the elements in V_1, for all *n* elements of the vectors. Thus the similarity between the behavior of V_1 and the combined group of vectors V_j ($J = 2, \ldots, m$), is:

$$S_{COMB} = 1 - AD_{COMB} \tag{12}$$

The relative importance of each explanatory variable in "explaining" the behavior of the dependent variable is determined as follows:

For every element of the numerical vectors representing explanatory variables, it is possible to construct a vector V_{CL}, so that every element *i* in V_{CL} is equal to:

$$V_{CL_i} = V_{J_i} \qquad \text{For } i = 1, \ldots, n \tag{13}$$

where $V_{J_{(i)}}$ is one of the i th elements from (m - 1) explanatory variables such that

$$d_{MIN_i} = | V_{1_i} - V_{J_i} | \tag{14}$$

The numerical vector V_{CL} consists of *n* elements, where the i th element of V_{CL} is selected from the set of i th of V_j, j = (1, ..., m). V_{Cl_i} is the closest element in this set to the i th element of the dependent variable. Therefore, the meaning of V_{CL} is as follows: it is the vector artificially constructed from the elements of explanatory variables, with each element being the closest to the corresponding element of the dependent variable. Once the vector V_{CL} is constructed, the relative contribution of each explanatory variable is reflected by the distance of that variable to V_{CL} (or in other words, the similarity of each explanatory variable to V_{CL}), where the similarity between the vectors is computed in the manner described in Section 2.4:

For every explanatory variable V_J (j = 2, ..., m):

$$d_{CL_{J_i}} = V_{CL_i} - V_{J_i} \qquad i = 1, \ldots, n \tag{15}$$

The distance of each explanatory variable V_J from the vector V_{CL} is:

$$AD_{CL_J} = \frac{\sum_{i=1}^{n} d_{CL_{J_i}}}{n} \tag{16}$$

The similarity (closeness) of each explanatory variable V_J to V_{CL} (which represents the contribution of explanatory variable V_J to explaining the behavior of the dependant variable) is then computed as:

$$S_J = 1 - AD_{CL_J} \tag{17}$$

The relative weight of each explanatory variable in explaining the behavior of the dependant variable is computed as follows:

$$RELIMP_J = \frac{S_J}{\sum_{k=2}^{m} S_k} \quad \text{for } j = 2, ..., m \tag{18}$$

2.6 Confidence Level

SOFT REGRESSION is basically a modeling tool that parallels traditional regression. It is a modeling tool that can be used for the same purpose as present tools based on regression methods. However, SOFT REGRESSION (as demonstrated above), in contrast to the regression methods, does not require restrictive conditions for its application. Of course, the interpretation of results in SOFT REGRESSION must reflect the lack of restrictive conditions. Thus, the results of a traditional regression model must be interpreted as a complete model including all the significant explanatory variables, their precise functional representation, and structural form. The users must assume they know all those factors even if they do not. On the other hand, the interpretation of SOFT REGRESSION results is more intuitive; it shows the relation of a dependent variable to one or several explanatory variables without any claim that the resulting model is a complete model. It is up to the user to experiment with various variables, until reaching conclusion that the resulting model is complete enough to be usable. However, any incomplete (and therefore misspecified) model based on regression methods is expected to generate distorted results, while the results based on SOFT REGRESSION are expected to be reliable even when the model is incomplete (since precise specification is not required). The results of SOFT REGRESSION maintain their consistency as additional explanatory variables are added or as some explanatory variables are removed from the model (which is not the case when utilizing traditional regression methods).

However, in order for SOFT REGRESSION to be a complete modeling tool (similarly to the traditional regression methods), it is necessary to define a method for determining the significance level (confidence level) of the results. In other words, in addition to finding similarity between (among) numerical vectors, it is also important to determine the degree of confidence in the results. Since SOFT REGRESSION is based on fuzzy logic, it is desirable that a method for determining the confidence level will be based on heuristic reasoning rather than statistical approach.

Let us assume that A, B, C, D and E are numerical vectors representing variables in the model. Assume that A is a dependent variable, and denote S1 to be a similarity measure between vectors A and B (as described in section 4). It is logical to expect that a successful modeling tool will maintain consistency between S1 and the measure of similarity between A and B within a more complex model where B is just one of several explanatory variables (B, C, D and E).

In order to compare SOFT REGRESSION to previously published results, our study of confidence levels was based on the same data that was utilized in [12-14]. The idea was to develop a heuristic method for measuring the confidence level, by observing the behavior of a large body of results. The procedure was to observe large number of relations S_l between the variables and to determine (based on expert knowledge and common sense) in what cases and for what values of S_l the results seem reliable. It was decided to use twenty economic/demographic variables, and to compare each one of those variables to all others and to observe the relations S_l. The study compares the value of each S_l vs. the evaluation of the relevancy/correctness of results (the relation between pairs of numerical vectors that each S_l represents). A total of 190 comparisons were made and evaluated[10], including comparisons of variables that are logically unrelated.

In order to observe differences in the behavior of relations between numerical vectors S_l, these relations were divided arbitrarily into the following six groups:

$0.85 \leq S_l \leq 1.00$

$0.80 \leq S_l < 0.85$

$0.77 \leq S_l < 0.80$

$0.74 \leq S_l < 0.77$

$0.70 \leq S_l < 0.74$

$0.65 \leq S_l < 0.70$

---

[10]The first variable (numerical vector) was compared against 19 others, then the second against remaining 18, etc.

All the cases below $S_l = 0.65$ were ignored as too unreliable. As explained in detail in sections 2.3 and 2.4, the methodology for calculating relations S consists of two separate computations. One is based upon the assumption that the relation between the two vectors is direct, and the other is based upon the assumption that the relation between the two vectors is inverse. Let us assume that, based on the assumption of a direct relation, the computed measure of similarity (S) between the two vectors is D1, and that based on the assumption of inverse relation, the computed measure of similarity between the same two vectors is D2. The two computed measures of similarity (D1 and D2) are then compared (in absolute terms) and the larger of the two is selected to represent the relation (similarity) S between the two vectors.

It is reasonable to expect that as the difference between |D1| and |D2| is greater, our confidence in our choice between them is greater. On the other hand, if |D1| and |D2| are almost of the same value, our confidence in the correctness of our decision to choose between them must be correspondingly low. It is, of course, impossible to have both |D1| and |D2| close to 1. If one of them is close to 1, the other must be low and therefore the difference between |D1| and |D2| (as well as the ratio of the bigger D to smaller D) will be correspondingly large. As logically expected (when observing the behavior of |D1| and |D2| in the 190 comparisons between the variables), the following pattern became noticeable immediately: when one of the computations (either |D1| or |D2|) is close to 1, then the other is correspondingly low and closer to 0.5. On the other hand, as the higher of the two results (either |D1| or |D2|) is lower, so the difference and the ratio between the two values displays the pattern of becoming smaller and smaller.

Let us denote:

$$DIFF = \| D_1 | - | D_2 \| \tag{19}$$

and

$$RATIO = \frac{\max(|D_1|, |D_2|)}{\min(|D_1|, |D_2|)} \tag{20}$$

The first step in the direction of establishing confidence levels in SOFT REGRESSION is to observe the relations among S_l , $DIFF_l$, and $RATIO_l$. The results are summarized in Table 1, and they clearly indicate some fundamental patterns.

Range of S	Range of DIF	Range of RATIO
0.850 - up	0.36 – 0.68	1.74 – 4.19
0.800 – 0.849	0.30 – 0.62	1.57 – 4.02
0.770 – 0.799	0.24 – 0.48	1.46 – 2.54
0.740 – 0.769	0.21 – 0.43	1.38 – 2.37
0.700 – 0.739	0.15 – 0.37	1.27 – 2.12
0.650 – 0.699	0.05 – 0.28	1.08 – 1.74

Table 1. Pattern of Behavior of DIFF and RATIO

The content of Table 1 clearly indicates that there is a general pattern of decline in DIFF and RATIO as the measure of similarity S declines. As was indicated above, such results could be logically expected.

The next step consists of evaluating in more detail each one of the six ranges of S from Table 1 in order to observe the patterns of the results. At this stage, it is necessary to conduct an heuristic evaluation of the relations between the variables, based on expert knowledge and common sense. When conducting such non-computerized, heuristic evaluation of relations between pairs of variables (numerical vectors), it is possible (using natural language) to categorize these relations in the following way:

1. Strong and expected relation: the relation and its direction (direct or inverse) are definite and unambiguous.
2. Indirect relation: the relation might exist, but it is not direct. The sign (direct or inverse) can be correct, if in fact the indirect influence (relation) actually exists.
3. No relation expected: it is difficult in this case to determine whether any relation, even indirect, exists. It is possible that variables display some relation by chance. However, the sign can, of course, be computed even if the variables are related only by chance.
4. Wrong result: the computed sign is incorrect based on common sense and expert evaluation.

The four types of relations as described above were applied to the 190 comparisons of numerical vectors under study and categorized based on the six ranges of S (same ranges as appear in Table 1). The results are presented in Table 2[11].

Range of S	Strong Relation	Indirect Relation	No relation Expected	Wrong Result	Hard to Categorize
0.850-up	13	0	0	0	0
0.800-0.849	24	7	0	0	0
0.770-0.799	8	5	5	0	2
0.740-0.769	3	1	4	0	6
0.700-0.739	6	4	8	2	1
0.650-0.699	5	6	10	13	3

Table 2. Heuristic evaluation of 190 relations between variables

Following the heuristic evaluation of the economic/demographic relations under the study, it becomes apparent that relations having $S \geq 0.80$ are easy to interpret and do not violate our common sense understanding of economics and demographics. Therefore, it is reasonable to establish that:

RELIABILITY = 1 (for $S \geq 0.80$)

On the other hand, Table 2 clearly shows that the reliability for $0.65 \leq S < 0.70$ is very low since the amount of definitely wrong relations exceeds that of correct ones (strong and definite relations) substantially. Therefore:

RELIABILITY = 0 (for $S < 0.70$)

---

[11]Note: there is an additional column in the table (column 5) named "Hard to categorize". It is a column for cases, where it was too difficult to categorize cases into one of the four categories.

It is also clear (by observing the patterns reflected by Table 2) that the results are becoming generally more unreliable as S drops from 0.79 down to 0.70.

Therefore, the obvious conclusion is that it is necessary to establish a gradual function that will reflect the reliability of results as S drops below 0.80 down to 0.70. Based on the heuristic interpretation of all the results described above, one possible specification of the confidence level function is:

$$\begin{aligned}
&GRADE = 1 \quad for\ S \geq 0.80 \\
&GRADE = 0 \quad for\ S < 0.70 \\
&GRADE = \frac{S - 0.70}{0.80 - 0.70} = 10 * (S - 0.70) \quad for\ 0.70 \leq S < 0.80
\end{aligned} \tag{21}$$

$$\begin{aligned}
&DIST = 1 \quad for\ DIFF \geq 0.30 \\
&DIST = \frac{DIFF}{0.30} \quad for\ DIFF < 0.30
\end{aligned} \tag{22}$$

$$\begin{aligned}
&R = 1 \quad for\ RATIO \geq 1.50 \\
&R = \frac{RATIO - 1}{1.50 - 1.00} = 2 * (RATIO - 1) \quad for\ 1.00 \leq S < 1.50
\end{aligned} \tag{23}$$

Then

$$\text{RELIABILITY} = \text{GRADE} * \text{DIST} * \text{R} \tag{24}$$

Note: The cut-off points for DIST and R were selected based on Table 1 so that for $S \geq 0.80$, RELIABILITY = 1, as expected based on Table 2.

3 Soft Regression and Knowledge Discovery

In order to demonstrate how our system can be used to discover knowledge, we have chosen as a case study to perform economic modeling based on cross-national economic data published by the World Bank [15]. The data consists of measurements (observations) from 106 countries. Therefore, the numerical vectors used in this study consist of 106 elements (n = 106), where each element of the vector represents a measurement from a different country.

3.1. Defining the Goal

The goal here is to utilize the database [15] in order to compute the relationships among the various variables in the database, and compute the relative importance of each variable against others within the model.

3.2. Data Cleaning

When observing the database very closely, one can discover that some of the data presented in the database needs transformation or adjustment in order to fit logically into a given model. The following example illustrates the importance of allowing the user's intervention in assuring a more reasonable representation of the membership grades:

> The variable **Average Annual Rate of Growth of GNP per Capita,** which represents the rate of Economic Growth. It is reasonable to assign higher grades of membership in the fuzzy set of **Economic Growth** to countries where GNP/Capita increases more rapidly, and assign lower grades of membership to slower growing economies. However, the World Bank data used in this study contains almost two dozen countries which have experienced a negative average rate of growth. In other words, instead of experiencing economic growth, these countries have experienced economic decline. Therefore, based on common sense, the elements reflecting economic decline do not belong to the fuzzy set **Economic Growth**. Thus, instead of proportional projection of all elements of the numerical vector into the interval [0,1], it is more reasonable to assign $\mu = 0$ to all measurements reflecting economic decline. Otherwise, if $\mu = 0$ is assigned only to the smallest negative element of the vector, it will make countries with zero economic growth look successful in comparison. However, based on common sense, the cases of zero economic growth and the cases of economic decline do not belong to the fuzzy set of **Economic Growth**.

SOFT REGRESSION has a way to change the lower and upper bound of the fuzzy sets. In this way, all the data outside the boundaries will receive the value of 0 or 1. Also, some countries do not provide data regarding a particular variable. In this case, we change the entry to a special symbol that is ignored during the computation of the regression between the variables. Upon the completion of the cleaning stage, the user may define new variables using the editor available in the "Soft Regression" system.

3.3 Preparing the Data Set

In some cases, it is necessary to create new variables out of existing ones. The reason is that some existing variables do not fit into the model in their existing form based on common sense and in conjunction with other variables. The second reason is that the objectives of the model might require some transformation of the existing data so as to enable us to discover knowledge that we need, instead of generating knowledge that is useless to us. For example, assume that we are performing international marketing research. Let's assume that we are trying to market a regular consumer product that is not a necessity of life. In this case, one of the variables we will need in our model is the purchasing power of the population in various countries to purchase our product. For example, the variable such as the country's GDP (which represents a total combined income of that country) is not a correct variable to use because the average purchasing power of a given country with a relative large GDP can be small if that country has a very large population. Therefore, we will perform a transformation of some data in the data base: we will create a new variable (numerical vector): GDP per Capita, by dividing GDP by Population, and the new variable will reflect much more accurately the average purchasing power than the variable GDP.

At the end of this stage, the data set is cleaned and complete. Now the system can produce the correlation among the variables.

3.4. Data Mining

There are several steps in which SOFT REGRESSION system produces the results. First, it uses Equations [1] through [9], as required. In our case study, the system found that, for example, the variable "GDP per Capita" is related to the variable "High Education" with similarity 0.89. Next, the user specifies the dependent variable and the explanatory variables. Then, the system utilizes the method described in Section 2.5 in order to show how each of the explanatory variables is related to the dependent variable and its relative importance. For example: Let the model specification be:

GNP/Capita = f (*High Education, Secondary Education, Machinery & Transportation, Exports, Population Growth*)

The combined closeness of explanatory variables to the dependent variable is 0.949. The relative weights of the explanatory variables are:

Variable Name	RELIMP
High Education	0.335
Secondary Education	0.105
Machinery & Transportation	0.241
Exports	0.168
Population Growth	0.151

Table 3. Relative importance of explanatory variables

Finally, using the method described in Section 2.6, the system computes the significance of the variables in the model

Variable Name	S	DIFF	RATIO	RELIABILITY
High Education	0.89	0.50	2.25	$1*1*1=1$
Secondary Education	0.75	0.30	1.64	$\frac{0.75-0.7}{0.8-0.7}*1*1=0.5$
Machinery & Transportation	0.87	0.55	2.70	$1*1*1=1$
Exports	0.82	0.55	3.02	$1*1*1=1$
Population Growth	- 0.82	0.47	2.34	$1*1*1=1$

Table 4. Significance level of explanatory variables

As we can see, the model consists of four variables having reliability 1, and one variable with reliability 0.50. If the user feels that the variable having reliability of 0.50 is not reliable enough to be included in the model, then it is possible to specify the model to exclude that variable. Of course, the user can decide on any cut-off point of the reliability measure for inclusion/exclusion of variables. It is important to note that the system will retain consistency with respect to the variables that we retain in the model.

3.5. Final Report

The final report that is generated using SOFT REGRESSION has the capability to produce a graph where a node indicates a variable and the links display the strength of the relations among the variables. Also, tables are available to display the relationships between dependent variables and the specified explanatory variables.

4 Conclusion

In this chapter, a fuzzy modeling technique SOFT REGRESSION) was presented and evaluated. SOFT REGRESSION is a modeling tool equivalent to traditional regression modeling. It was demonstrated, both theoretically and with the help of a case study, that SOFT REGRESSION has several substantial advantages over the traditional regression based modeling tools, while no visible disadvantages have been detected.

References

[1] U. M. Fayyad, G. P. Shapiro and P. Smyth, "From Data Mining to Knowledge Discovery: An Overview", in *Advances in Knowledge Discovery and Data Mining*, U. Fayyad, et. al. Editors, AAAI Press/The MIT Press, 1996, pp. 1-34.

[2] W. J. Frawley, G. P. Shapiro and C. J. Matheus, "Knowledge Discovery in Databases: An Overview", in *Knowledge Discovery in Databases*, G. P. Shapiro, et. al. Editors, AAAI Press/The MIT Press, 1991, pp. 1-27.

[3] D. J. Hand, *Discrimination and Classification*, John Wiley and Sons, 1981.

[4] Sukesh K. Ghosh, *Econometrics: Theory and Application*, Prentice Hall, 1991.

[5] A. K. Jain, and R. C. Dubes, *Algorithms for Clustering Data*, Prentice Hall, 1988.

[6] R. Agrawal, H. Mannila, R. Srikant, H. Toivonen and A. I. Verkamo, "Fast Discovery of Association Rules", in *Advances in Knowledge Discovery and Data Mining*, U. Fayyad, et. al. Editors, AAAI Press/The MIT Press, 1996, pp. 307 – 328.

[7] R. Zembowicz and J. M. Zytkow, "From Contingency Tables to Various Forms of Knowledge in Databases", in *Advances in Knowledge Discovery and Data Mining*, U. Fayyad, et. al. Editors, AAAI Press/The MIT Press, 1996, pp. 329 - 352.

[8] D. Heckerman, "Bayesian Networks for Knowledge Discovery", in *Advances in Knowledge Discovery and Data Mining*, U. Fayyad, et. al. Editors, AAAI Press/ The MIT Press, 1996, pp. 273 - 306.

[9] C. Glymour, R. Scheines, P. Spirtes and K. Kelly, *Discovering Causal Structure*, Academic Press, 1987.

[10] M. Basseville and I. V. Nikiforov, *Detection of Abrupt Changes: Theory and Applications*, Prentice Hall, 1993.

[11] B. Kosko, *Neural Networks and Fuzzy Systems,* Prentice Hall, 1992.

[12] M. Schneider, E. Shnaider, A. Kandel and G. Chew, "Automatic Construction of FCMs", *Fuzzy sets and Systems*, Vol. 93, 1997, pp. 161-172.

[13] Shnaider E., M. Schneider and A. Kandel, 1997, "A Fuzzy Measure for Similarity of Numerical Vectors", *Fuzzy Economic Review*, Vol. II, No. 1, 1997, pp. 17 - 38.

[14] E. Shnaider and M. Schneider, "Fuzzy Tools for Economic Modeling", in *Uncertainty Logics: Applications in Economics and Management.* Proceedings of SIGEF'98 Congress, 1988.

[15] World Bank, *World Development Report 1992,* Oxford University Press, 1992.

Some Practical Applications of Soft Computing and Data Mining

Hung T. Nguyen[1], **Nadipuram R. Prasad**[2], **Vladik Kreinovich**[3], **and Habib Gassoumi**[2]

[1]Department of Mathematical Sciences

[2]Klipsch School of Electrical and Computer Engineering, New Mexico State University, Las Cruces, NM 88003-8001, USA,
emails {hunguyen,rprasad,hgassoum}@nmsu.edu

[3]Department of Computer Science, University of Texas at El Paso, El Paso, TX 79968, USA, email vladik@cs.utep.edu

Abstract. Traditional data mining techniques mainly deal with a search for patterns in traditional databases, where data consists of numbers and words. In many application areas, however, data is more complicated: real-life data is often obtained as an image from a camera rather than a few measurements. Furthermore, this image can also change dynamically. In this paper, we present several examples of how soft computing is related to mining such data.

Keywords. Data mining; soft computing; image analysis; cotton; tracking high-speed targets

1 Introduction

Traditional data mining techniques (see, e.g., [4, 6, 15, 18, 27, 28]) mainly deal with a search for patterns in traditional databases, where data consists of numbers and words. In many application areas, however, data is more complicated: real-life data is often obtained as an image from a camera (see, e.g., [2, 3]). Each image contains much more information than a typical data record, so we cannot simply use traditional methods to mine through image database (for new methods, see, e.g., [20]).

Another reason why real-life data is more complex than the data stored in traditional databases is that traditional databases (such as databases describing business transactions, purchases, etc.) deal mainly with rather slowly changing processes. For such processes, it is sufficient, for each quantity, to store its current value and to update this value periodically. In many real-life situations, however, we deal with a fast changing process. A numerical characteristic of such a process can no longer be characterized by a single number, but can only be described by a speedily changing function of time. In some practical cases, both these problems are present, i.e., we need to mine the database of dynamically changing images.

In this paper, we present several case studies of how soft computing is related to mining such data. Our first two case studies are analysis of images of cotton, both cotton in the field and ginned cotton. We use fuzzy, neural, and more traditional geometric techniques to detect and classify different types of trash in ginned cotton and different insects in the cotton field. Our third case study is an automated tracking system for tracking high-speed targets such as airplanes, missiles, etc. Here, we have an example of highly dynamical data, and moreover, data which is represented largely by images.

2 First Case Study: Classification of Trash in Ginned Cotton

2.1 A practical problem: brief description

The main use of cotton is in textile industry; for that purpose, we only need cotton fiber called *lint*. Mechanical harvesters collect fiber together with the seeds. To separate lint from the seeds and from other non-lint material, a special process called *ginning* is used. Ginned cotton consists primarily of lint, but some non-lint material (*trash*) is left. For the further textile processing, it is important to know how much trash of what type is left.

In principle, it is possible to detect the amount and type of trash by visual inspection, because trash is usually of different color than the whitish lint and is thus clearly visible. The problem with visual inspection is that the visual inspection of all 15 to 19 million bales of cotton annually produced in the USA is a very time-consuming and expensive process. It is therefore desirable to develop an automatic system for the analysis of trash in ginned cotton (see, e.g., [12, 13]).

2.2 The need for soft computing

In general, to automate expert skills, we can do two things:

- first, we can ask experts how they perform their tasks, and then try to formalize the resulting rules;
- second, we can record the expert classification, and then try to teach the automated system to follow the expert decisions on the given examples.

Experts usually formulate their rules by using words from a natural language like "small", "large", etc. Transforming such "fuzzy" rules into precise formulas is one of the main objectives of a special formalism called *fuzzy logic*; so, we must use fuzzy logic techniques. To make a system learn from examples of expert classification, we must use a universal learning technique, e.g., the technique of *neural networks*.

In many real-life situations, we have both expert rules *and* samples of expert decisions; we must therefore be able to combine the fuzzy technique of handling rules and the neural techniques of handling examples. To facilitate the combination of fuzzy and neural techniques (as well as several other intelligent techniques), an umbrella approach has been developed called *soft computing*. So, soft computing is necessary for automating expert skills.

2.3 The need for data mining

Traditional soft computing techniques for formalizing and automating expert skills work well only when the number n of input values $x_1, \ldots, x_n$ which determine the expert's decision is small. Indeed, in *fuzzy logic technique*, to elicit the expert rules, we usually select a few words like "small", "medium", "large" which describe each of the input quantities, and then ask the expert to describe his decision for all possible combination of such words, such as "x_1 is small x_2 is medium, ...". This elicitation procedure is feasible when n is small. For large n, however, this procedure is no longer feasible: even for three possible states of each variable, we need 3^n combinations of input values. When n is large (e.g., if the input is a picture described by $n \approx 10^6$ pixel values), this number of combinations is unrealistically large.

Similarly, to train a *neural network*, we normally need a number of examples to be at least as large as the square n^2 of the number n of input variables (see, e.g., [5] and references therein). This empirical fact can be easily understood. In the simplest possible case when the dependence of the decision y on the inputs x_i is linear, i.e., when $y = c_0 + c_1 x_1 + \ldots + c_n x_n$, we need at least $n+1$ examples to determine all $n+1$ coefficients c_i which describe the desired dependence. Neural networks describe, in general, non-linear dependencies. The simplest possible non-linear dependence is *quadratic*, when

$$y = c_0 + \sum_{i=1}^{n} c_i x_i + \sum_{i=1}^{n} \sum_{j=1}^{n} c_{ij} x_i x_j .$$

To describe the general quadratic dependence, we need $\approx n^2$ different coefficients c_i and c_{ij}; therefore, to determine all these coefficients, we need at least $\approx n^2$ different examples. When n is small, it is easy to record n^2 examples of the experts using their expertise. Alas, when n becomes large, e.g., when the input is an image with $n \approx 10^6$, the successful application of a neural network requires an unrealistic number of $n \approx 10^{12}$ examples.

Summarizing: when the num ber n of input variables is large, we cannot directly use traditional soft computing techniques. Therefore, instead of simply using all n input variables, we must find a smaller number of relevant *combinations* $y_1, \ldots, y_m$ of these input variables, and then use these combinations y_j as the new inputs. In other words, to be able to use soft computing techniques for automating expert skills, we must first use data *mining* to find relevant combinations of input variables.

In this section (and in the following section), we will show how this data mining can be performed for the problems of cotton analysis.

2.4 What we did: a brief overview

We started with a large sample of photos of the ginned cotton with different types of trash, and we asked the experts to classify the trash on these photos. As a result, we got a database of images with classified trash type. Our plan was to apply data mining techniques to this database, hopefully to find some dependencies, and then to fine-tune these dependencies:

- by testing them on other images,
- by consulting with the experts, and
- by trying to find a theoretical justification for these dependencies.

Since an important part of this database consists of images, we could not directly apply traditional data mining techniques [4, 6, 15, 18, 27, 28] which are more geared towards numerical data. To be able to apply these data mining techniques, we first computed, for every image, the values of the standard characteristics of a black and-white image which are described, e.g., in [19]. As a result, we got a numerical database. To this numerical database, we applied both statistical and neuro-fuzzy techniques (from [9]) for knowledge discovery in a database. After applying these techniques, we got a short list of characteristics which seem to be most relevant for our classification purpose.

To check this short list, we applied theoretical analysis to this problem. As a result, we got a reasonable theoretical explanation for both for the original classification and for the empirical short list of relevant image characteristics. This explanation was so good that we do not need to cite the results of preliminary data mining to explain this classification. The fact that we do not need these results does not mean, of course, that we should not have performed that data mining: without that data mining, we might not be able to find these theoretically justified results.

After this theoretical confirmation, we gained a certain confidence in our short list of relevant characteristics. In view of this confidence, we simplified our numerical database by retaining, for each image, only the values of the relevant numerical characteristics. To this simplified database, we again applied the neuro fuzzy data mining techniques described in [9], and, as a result, got a reasonably good trash classification algorithm.

In short, in our problem, we used a three-step approach:

- first, we apply preliminary data mining to the original (raw) data;
- second, we applied a theoretical analysis to check and justify the conclusions of the preliminary data mining;
- finally, after the conclusions have been theoretically confirmed, we used these conclusions to reduce the original database, and applied the data mining techniques to this reduced database.

In the first and third steps, we use well-known and well-documented techniques from [9]. The novel part of our approach is in the second (theoretical) step, and this is what we will be concentrating on in this section.

2.5 Towards formalization of the corresponding data mining problem

Since trash is clearly visible on the lint background, it is natural to take a photo of a cotton bale, and then run a computer program to analyze this photo. Our goal is to separate trash from lint; since trash is of different color than the lint, we can ignore the details about the intensities of different pixels and use a threshold on intensity to transform the original image into a black-and-white one: points in which the intensity is above the threshold are treated as white (i.e., as lint), and points in which the intensity is below the threshold are treated as black (i.e., as trash).

As a result, we get a black-and-white picture in which several pieces of trash are present on the white background. Pieces of trash can have complicated shapes. The user needs a simple classification of these shapes. A natural way of classifying different shapes is to describe several simple approximate shapes and then to classify a given piece of trash based on which simple shape it resembles most. So, to develop a good classification of trash in cotton, we need to find a good approximating family of sets.

Because of the large volume of cotton processing, even a small gain in classification quality can lead to a large economic benefit. It is therefore desirable to look not simply for a *good* approximating family of sets, but rather for a family, which is *optimal* in some reasonable sense.

Of course, the more parameters we allow, the better the approximation. So, the question can be reformulated as follows: for a given number of parameters (i.e., for a given dimension of approximating family), which is the best family? In this section, we use a geometric formalism developed in [11] and [25] to formalize and solve this problem.

2.6 Formalizing the problem

In this formalization, we will, in effect, follow [11] and [25].

The pieces of trash are usually smooth lines or areas with smooth boundaries, so it is reasonable to restrict us to families of sets with analytical boundaries. By definition, when we say that a piece of a boundary is analytical, we mean that it can be described by an equation $F(x, y) = 0$ for some analytical function

$$F(x, y) = a + bx + cy + dx^2 + exy + fy^2 + \cdots$$

So, in order to describe a family, we must describe the corresponding class of analytical functions $F(x, y)$.

Since we are interested in families of sets which are characterized by finitely many parameters (i.e., in finite-dimensional families of sets), it is natural to consider finite dimensional families of functions, i.e., families of the type

$$\{C_1 F_1(x, y) + \ldots + C_d F_d(x, y)\},$$

where $F_i(z)$ are given analytical functions, and $C_1, \ldots, C_d$ are arbitrary (real) constants. So, the question becomes: which of these families is the best? When we say "the best", we mean that on the set of all such families, there must be a relation $\geq$ describing which family is better or equal in quality. This relation must be transitive (if A is better than B, and B is better than C, then A is better than C).

This relation is not necessarily asymmetric, because we can have two approximating families of the same quality. However, we would like to require that this relation be *final* in the sense that it should define a unique *best* family A_{opt} (i.e., the unique family for which $\forall B(A_{opt} \geq B)$. Indeed, if none of the families is the best, then this criterion is of no use, so there should be *at least one* optimal family. If *several* different families are equally best, then we can use this ambiguity to optimize something else: e.g., if we have two families with the same approximating quality, then we choose the one which is easier to compute. As a result, the original criterion was not final: we get a new criterion $A \geq_{new} B$ if either A gives a better approximation, or if $A \sim_{old} B$ and A is easier to compute), for which the class of optimal families is narrower. We can repeat this procedure until we get a final criterion for which there is only one optimal family.

The exact shape depends on the choice of a starting point, on the orientation of the camera, and on the choice of the zoom. It is reasonable to require that if we change the starting point, the orientation, or the zoom, the relative quality of different approximating families should not change. In other words, it is reasonable to require that the relation $A \geq B$ should not change if shift, rotate, or scale the image; i.e., the relation $A \geq B$ should be shift-, rotation- and scale-invariant.

These requirements can be formalized as follows:

Definition 1. Let $d > 0$ be an integer. By a *d-dimensional family*, we mean a family A of all functions of the type

$$\{C_1 F_1(x, y) + \ldots + C_d F_d(x, y)\},$$

where $F_i(z)$ are given analytical functions, and $C_1, \ldots, C_d$ are arbitrary (real) constants. We say that a set S is *defined* by this family A if for some function $F \in A$, all points (x, y) from the border ∂S of the set S satisfy the equation $F(x, y) = 0$.

Definition 2.

- By an *optimality criterion*, we mean a transitive relation $\geq$ on the set of all d-dimensional families.
- We say that a criterion is *final* if there exists one and only one *optimal* family, i.e., a family A_{opt} for which $\forall B \left(A_{opt} \geq B\right)$.
- We say that a criterion $\geq$ is *shift*- (corr., *rotation*- and *scale*- invariant) if for every two families A and B, $A \geq B$ implies $TA \geq TB$, where TA is a shift (rotation, scaling) of the family A.

Proposition 1. *Let $d \geq 4$, let $\geq$ be a final optimality criterion which is shift-, rotation- and scale-invariant, and let A_{opt} be the corresponding optimal family. Then, the border of every set defined by this family A_{opt} is a straight line interval, a circle, or a circular arc.*

Proposition 1 was first proven in [11, 25]. For the convenience of readers who are mainly interested in practical results, the proofs of all propositions in this chapter are given in the Appendix.

2.7 Discussion

Among the shapes described by Proposition 1, the only shape which actually bounds a 2-D set is a circle (which bounds a disk). So, as a result of this proposition, we have the following trash shapes:

- straight line intervals,
- circular arcs, and
- disks.

When the disk is small, we can view it as a point, which leads us to the fourth possible approximate shape of cotton trash:

- points.

This classification is in perfect agreement with the existing empirical classification of trash into:

- *bark1* (approximately circular arcs),
- *bark2* (straight line segments),
- *leaf* (disks), and
- *pepper trash* (points).

The names of these types of trash come from their physical meaning, with the only exception of *pepper trash* which refers to broken or crushed pieces of leaf.

2.8 Implementation details: creating an image

We have used this geometric classification to develop a prototype system for classifying trash. In our system, images (640 x 480) are acquired using a 3-chip CCD Sony color camera. The imaging hardware consists of a Matrox IM-1280 imaging board and CLD acquisition board. The pixel resolution is 0.13 mm (0.005 inches).

The acquired images are flat field corrected for spatial illumination non-uniformity. Each acquired color image (RBG) is converted into hue, luma (intensity), and saturation (HLS) color space (see, e.g., [19]), and a threshold on intensity is used to create a black-and-white image.

2.9 Implementation details: selecting image characteristics

To classify trash, we selected several reasonable geometric characteristics from the list of standard characteristics of a black-and-white image described, e.g., [19].

2.9.1 First image characteristic – solidity – measures the image's convexity

First, we noticed that some of our shapes are convex sets (disks - leaves, points - pepper, and straight line segments - bark2), while some are not (circular arcs - bark1). By definition, a convex set is a set S whose convex hull $co(S)$ coincides with itself (i.e., $co(S) = S$); the closer the convex hull $co(S)$ to the set itself S, the more convex is this set S. Therefore, as a characteristic of convexity, one can use the ratio between the area A of the original set S (measured, e.g., by the total number of pixels in the set S) and the area of its convex hull $co(S)$. This ratio is equal to 1 for a convex set and is smaller than 1 for non-convex sets.

In computer imaging, the area of a convex hull is called the convex area, and the ratio of the area and the convex area is called the solidity of the set S. So, we expect that:

- for non-linear shapes such as bark1, solidity is much smaller than 1;
- while linear shapes such as bark2, leaf, and pepper trash, should have solidity close to 1.0.

The experimental analysis shows that, indeed, for bark1, solidity is typically less than 0.5, while for other types of trash, it is typically close to 1. Thus, solidity enables us to distinguish between bark1 and other trash types.

2.9.2 Second image characteristic – difference – measures the image's rotation invariance

Using solidity, we can distinguish between bark1 and other types of trash. To further distinguish between the three remaining types of trash, we can use the fact that our classification was based on invariance with respect to geometric transformations: shift, rotation, and scaling. It is therefore reasonable to check the invariance of the resulting shapes. Let us check these invariances one by one.

None of our trash shapes are exactly shift-invariant, so checking for this invariance does not help in distinguishing between different types of trash. Let us now consider rotation invariance. Bark2 (straight line segment) is not rotation-invariant, while leaf (circle) and pepper trash (point) are rotation-invariant. It is therefore desirable to find an image characteristic which will enable us to tell whether a given image is rotation-invariant; based on this characteristic, we will then be able to distinguish between bark2 and the remaining trash type (pepper and leaf).

In selecting the first characteristic, we used the area of the original image and the area of its convex hull. Neither of these two characteristics can distinguish between rotation-invariant and rotation-non-invariant shapes, because both the area A and the area of the convex hull are rotation-invariant. Instead, we can use a similar standard image characteristic which is *not* rotation-invariant: the area of the *bounding box*. The bounding box is defined as the smallest box (= rectangle parallel to coordinate axes) which contains the desired image. Its area is equal to the product $X_f \times Y_f$, where X_f and Y_f are *ferrets* - lengths of the image's projections on the corresponding axes.

In general, the area of the bounding box changes when we rotate the coordinate axes. It is therefore reasonable to take, as the second image characteristic, the difference E^{dif} between the original bounding box area and the bounding box area corresponding to the rotated coordinate system.

To finalize the selection of this characteristic, we must select the rotation angle. Some angles are not very useful. This angle should not be too large: e.g., rotation by 90^0 simply swaps x and y - axes without changing the bounding box and its area, so the corresponding difference is always equal to 0. Similarly, this angle cannot be too small: Indeed, real-life leaf and pepper trash shapes are only approximately rotation-invariant, so for these types, the difference E^{dif} is close to 0 (i.e., small) but, most probably, different from 0. If the rotation angle is small, then the rotated bounding box is close to the original one even for bark2; therefore, the two areas are close, and the difference E^{dif} between these two areas is small. Hence, for a small rotation angle, the difference E^{dif} will be small for all trash types, and we will not be able to use this characteristic to distinguish between different trash types.

Therefore, for the difference characteristic to be useful, it is important to select an appropriate rotation angle. Once again, we can formulate the problem of choosing an appropriate rotation angle as an optimization problem under an (arbitrary) reasonable optimality criterion. Before we formulate the result, let us make two comments. Since rotation by 90^0 leaves the bounding box area unchanged, it is sufficient to only consider *acute* angles, i.e., angles from 0 to $90^0 \left(=\frac{\pi}{2} \text{ radians}\right)$. It is reasonable to assume that the criterion does not change if we simply swap x and y axes. In geometric terms, this "swap" can be described as follows: the rotation angle can be defined, e.g., as the angle α between the original x-axis $0x$ and the new x-axes $0x'$. The result of swapping the original x-axis $0x$ is the original y-axis $0y$; so, the angle between the new x axis $0x'$ and the swapped original x axis is simply the angle between $0x'$ and $0y$, which is equal to $90^0 - \alpha$. Thus, in geometric terms, the swap means replacing an angle α by its complement $90^0 - \alpha$. Now, we are ready to formulate the result:

Definition 3.

- By an *optimality criterion*, we mean a transitive relation $\geq$ on the set [0, 90] of all acute angles.
- We say that a criterion is *final* if there exists one and only one *optimal* angle, i.e., an angle α_{opt} for which $\forall\beta\left(\alpha_{opt} \geq \beta\right)$.
- We say that a criterion $\geq$ is *swap-invariant* if for every two angles α and β, $\alpha \geq \beta$ implies $T(\alpha) \geq T(\beta)$, where $T(\alpha) = 90 - \alpha$.

Proposition 2. *Let $\geq$ be an arbitrary final optimality criterion which is swap-invariant. Then, the optimal angle α_{opt} is equal to 45^0.*

So, the optimal choice of the difference characteristic is the difference between the original bounding box area and the area of the bounding box after the rotation by 45^0.

Comments. We are checking rotation-invariance by using only one rotation. It is therefore quite possible that the image is not rotation-invariant (i.e., it is a straight line segment), but for the chosen angle, the bounding box areas are actually equal. However, this is only possible for a single rotation angle, and since the orientation of trash is random, this accidental coincidence will happen with a very small probability 0. So, with probability close to 1, the difference E^{dif} does enable us to distinguish between the shapes which are rotation-invariant (pepper and leaf) and which are not (bark2).

In general, the checking of rotation invariance is intended for distinguishing between bark2 and leaf or pepper; we assume that bark1 have already been classified. However, in reality, we may have intermediate situations in which a circular arc (bark1) is almost linear and so, bark1 (which is normally characterized by small solidity) is not easily distinguishable from bark2 (which is normally characterized by large solidity). For these situations of medium (intermediate) solidity, we can use the new difference characteristic E^{dif} to distinguish between bark1 (which is more rotation-invariant) and bark2 (which is less rotation invariant).

Alternative methods of checking rotation invariance are presented, e.g., in [10, 14].

2.9.3 Third image characteristic - area - distinguishes between points (pepper trash) and circles (leaves)

Using the first image characteristic (solidity), we can distinguish between bark1 and other types of trash (bark2, pepper, and leaf):

- low solidity means bark1, while

- larger values of solidity can mean one of the remaining three trash types.

So, if the solidity is low, we know that the trash is of type bark1. If the solidity is high, we can use the second image characteristic (difference) to distinguish between bark2 and pepper or leaf:

- large value of the difference means bark2, while
- small values of the difference mean that the trash is either pepper or leaf.

Hence, to complete the classification of trash type, the only remaining task is to separate pepper trash from leaf trash. From the invariance viewpoint, they are both rotation-invariant, and the difference between these two types is that pepper is scale-invariant, while leaf is not. Therefore, to distinguish between these two types, we can use the difference between, e.g., the area A of the original image and the area of the scaled image.

If we use scaling with a coefficient λ, then the area of the scaled image is equal to $\lambda^2 A$ and therefore, the desired difference is equal to $C A$, where we denoted $C = \lambda^2 - 1$. Thus:

- if the value of $C A$ is small, it is most probably pepper;
- if the value of $C A$ is large, then it is most probably leaf.

By appropriately changing which values we consider small and which values we consider large, we can always select $C = 1$. For this selection, the new difference characteristic is simply the area of the image. Therefore, as our third image characteristic, we select the image's area A.

This selection can be explained in common sense geometric terms, without using invariance:

- pepper trash is - approximately - a point, while
- leaf trash is - approximately - a circle.

A point is a degenerate circle, of radius 0 and of area 0. So, to distinguish between pepper and leaf trash, we can use the area A of the trash image. In other words, if we already know, from the values of the first two characteristics (solidity and difference), that the trash is either of pepper type or of leaf type, then we can use the third characteristic - area A - to distinguish between pepper trash and leaf trash:

- if the area is small $(A \approx 0)$, then the trash type is most probably pepper trash;
- if the area is not small, the trash is most probably a leaf.

2.10 Trash classification in terms of fuzzy rules

While describing the three characteristics, we showed natural rules which use the values of these characteristics to determine the trash type. These rules, however, cannot be directly implemented because they use words from natural language like "small", "large", etc. Specifically, we use two words "small" and "large" to describe the difference and the area, and three words "small", "medium", and "large" to describe solidity.

We therefore need fuzzy logic to formalize these rules. In this formalization, we used the Adaptive Network-Based Fuzzy Inference System ANFIS. In our case, we have 3 values for the first characteristic and 2 values each for the second and the third; thus, we have a total of $3 \times 2 \times 2 = 12$ possible combinations of characteristics, for each of which we know the trash type. We therefore formulated the corresponding 12 rules of the type "if solidity is large, difference is small, and area is small, then bark1", and used a neural network to adjust the shapes of the corresponding $3+2+2$ membership functions to achieve the best possible trash classification.

2.11 Practical Results

The resulting system achieves a 98% correct classification of trash - a much higher percentage than the previously known methods. A summary of the classification results is given in the following table. In this table, NN stands for the results of using a neural network trained on the data, FL for the results of using fuzzy logic-based C-means clustering, and New for the results of our new approach, which combines neuro-fuzzy approach from [9] with the theoretical analysis (for further details see, e.g., [21, 22]).

method	actual type	#	classified as bark1	classified as bark2	classified as leaf	classified as pepper	success rate
NN	bark1	4	4	0	0	0	93%
	bark2	2	1	0	0	1	
	leaf	9	0	1	5	3	
	pepper	90	0	0	1	89	
FL	bark1	4	0	1	2	1	87%
	bark2	2	0	1	0	1	
	leaf	9	0	0	0	9	
	pepper	90	0	0	0	90	
New	bark1	4	4	0	0	0	98%
	bark2	2	0	1	0	1	
	leaf	9	0	1	8	0	
	pepper	90	0	0	0	90	

3 Second Case Study: Classification of Insects in the Cotton Field

3.1 A practical problem: brief description

In addition to trash, cotton contains insects. Some of these insects destroy the cotton crop; to preserve the crop, farmers use insecticides. Among other crops, cotton is especially vulnerable to insects; as a result, worldwide, more insecticides are used on cotton than on any other crop. The problem is that it is often difficult to distinguish between harmful and harmless insects; as a result, insecticides are used even when only harmless insects are present, thus destroying the (often useful) insects and, in general, polluting the environment. It is therefore desirable to be able to distinguish between useful and harmful insects.

Expert entomologists can easily distinguish between harmful and harmless insects, but there are not enough experts to monitor every cotton field. It is therefore necessary to design an automated system which would analyze the image of a cotton sample and tell whether it contains harmful insects. Similarly, to the first case study, we need methods of *soft computing* to formalize expert rules, and methods of *data mining* to find the relevant combinations of input variables. Let us describe how these methods can be used in classifying insects.

3.2 What we did: a brief overview

Our approach to solving this problem was similar to the above solution to the trash classification problem.

We started with a large sample of photos of different insects, and we asked the experts to classify the insects on these photos. As a result, we got a database of classified insect images. We then computed, for every image, different geometric characteristics. To the resulting numerical database, we applied both statistical and neuro-fuzzy techniques (from [9]) for knowledge discovery in a database. After applying these techniques, we got a short list of characteristics which seem to be most relevant for our classification purpose. To check this short list, we applied theoretical analysis to this problem. After this theoretical check, we simplified our numerical database by retaining, for each image, only the values of the relevant numerical characteristics. To this simplified database, we again applied the neuro-fuzzy data mining techniques described in [9], and, as a result, got a reasonably good insect classification algorithm.

3.3 Formalization of the corresponding data mining problem. 1: We should use ellipses to approximate insect shapes

As in the first case study, we can use black-and-white images, and approximate the desired images (sets) by sets from a certain family. There are, however, two differences between the problem of classifying trash and the problem of classifying insects:

The first difference is that to classify trash, it was sufficient to use a very crude approximation by sets from a 4-parametric family. To classify insects, we need a more accurate approximation and thus, we need a larger family of approximating sets.

The second difference is that trash, by definition, may contain *pieces* of leaves, bark, etc., while the insects are usually viewed *completely*. Therefore, when classifying trash, we could use shapes for which the boundaries satisfied the equation $F(x, y) = 0$ but which contained only a part of all the points (x, y) which satisfy this equation: e.g., we considered a straight line segment, which is only a *piece* of a straight line $F(x, y) = a\,x + b\,y + c = 0$. For insects, we must consider only the shapes for which the corresponding equation $F(x, y) = 0$ bounds the whole image.

Definition 4. Let A be a *d-dimensional family*, i.e., a family A of all functions of the type

$$\{C_1 F_1(x, y) + \ldots + C_d F_d(x, y)\},$$

where $F_i(z)$ are given analytical functions, and $C_1, \ldots, C_d$ are arbitrary (real) constants. We say that a bounded set S is *defined as a whole* by a family A if for some function $F \in A$, the border ∂S of the set S coincides with the set of all points (x, y) for which $F(x, y) = 0$.

Proposition 3. Let $d \leq 6$, let $\geq$ be a final optimality criterion which is shift-, rotation- and scale-invariant, and let A_{opt} be the corresponding optimal family. Then, every bounded set defined as a whole by this family A_{opt} is an ellipse. Thus, we should use ellipses to approximate the insect shapes.

3.4 Formalization of the corresponding data mining problem. 2: The use of aspect ratio

According to our result, we must approximate the insect's shape by an ellipse. Since insects can destroy the crop, we must err on the side of caution, and use an ellipse which contains the actual insect shape S. To classify an insect, we should therefore use a characteristic of this approximating ellipse. What characteristic should we choose?

The type of an insect does not change if we simply shift or rotate the insect; thus, the characteristics used to classify the insect should not change if we simply shift or rotate the insect's image (and hence, shift or rotate the corresponding ellipse).

Similarly, the classification of an insect should not change if the insect simply *grows*. In the first approximation, this growth can be described as *scaling* $(x, y) \to (\lambda x, \lambda y)$, so our characteristic should not change with scaling.

(In the following text, we will show that for a more refined classification, we will need scale-dependent characteristics as well).

So, we want a characteristic of an ellipse, which does not change with shift, rotation, or scaling.

Definition 5.

- By a *characteristic* of an ellipse, we mean a function $J : \mathcal{E} \to R$ from the set $\mathcal{E}$ of all ellipses to the set R of real numbers.
- We say that a characteristic J is *shift*- (corr., *rotation*- and scale-*invariant*) if for every ellipse E, $J(E) = J(T(E))$, where $T(E)$ denotes a shift (rotation, scaling) of the ellipse E.
- An *aspect ratio* $a(E)$ is a ratio $\frac{D_{\max}}{D_{\min}}$ of the lengths of the major and minor axes of an ellipse.

It is easy to check that the aspect ratio is a shift-, rotation-, and scale-invariant characteristic of an ellipse. It turns out that it is, in effect, the only such characteristic:

Proposition 4. Let J be a characteristic of an ellipse which is shift-, rotation- and scale-invariant. Then there exists a function $f : R \to R$ for which $J(E) = f(a(E))$ for every ellipse E. Thus, if we know the aspect ratio, we can compute an arbitrary invariant characteristic of an ellipse. So, to classify an insect, we should use the aspect ratio of the approximating ellipse.

3.5 Formalization of the corresponding data mining problem. 3: Selected values of aspect ratio

3.5.1 Theoretical result

In the previous text, we took into consideration the fact that an insect grows; we represented this growth by a scaling transformation, i.e., a transformation which simply "blows up" the insect without changing its shape. In reality, the life of an insect can be divided into several stages. On each stage, the growth can be reasonably well described as scaling; however, the transition from one stage to another changes the shape. The harmlessness of an insect may drastically change from stage to stage, so, it is important not only to classify insects on a cotton field, but also to find out on what stage these insects are.

The transition from one stage to another can be described as a transformation $\vec{x} \to \vec{f}(\vec{x})$ which transforms the location $\vec{x} = (x, y)$ of the original point on a body (e.g., eye, leg, etc.), into its position $\vec{f}(\vec{x})$ on the next stage. In general, this transformation $\vec{f}(\vec{x})$ can be non-linear. To simplify this general expression, let us expand this function into Taylor series. Insects are small, so the coordinates $\vec{x}$ are small, hence quadratic terms in this expansion are also relatively small in comparison with the linear terms. Since we are approximating the insect's shape by an ellipse anyway (thus drastically distorting its shape), there is little sense in keeping these small quadratic terms. Therefore, it makes sense to assume that the transformation $\vec{x} \to \vec{f}(\vec{x})$ from one stage to another is linear.

A generic linear transformation can be described as a rotation and shift followed by contractions and dilatations along appropriately chosen (orthogonal) coordinates (see, e.g., Chapter 11, p. 49 from [1] or Theorem 5.42 from [26]). Since shifts and rotations do not change the shape, we can therefore assume, without losing generality, that the change in shape from one stage to another can be described by contractions and dilatations along the axes, i.e., by a transformation $x \to x' = \lambda_x x$, $y \to y' = \lambda_y y$ for some real numbers $\lambda_x > \lambda_y > 0$.

An insect starts as an extremely small point-size embryo; we can assume that the embryo is a small circle, i.e., an ellipse with an aspect ratio equal to 1, in which the minor and the major axes have the same length: $D_{\max} = D_{\min}$. To find the shape at the next stage, we must apply the above transformation. As a result, we get a new ellipse, with an aspect ratio $r = \frac{\lambda_x}{\lambda_y}$. One more application of the above transformation leads to the new ellipse with an aspect ratio r^2, then r^3, etc. We can therefore conclude the aspect ratios of the ellipses approximating to the actual insect shapes form a geometric progression 1, r, r^2, r^3, ...

3.5.2 Experimental testing of the theoretical result

To test this theoretical conclusion, we took the average aspect ratios r_i of the insects inhabiting cotton and alfalfa fields; if the above conclusion is correct, then each aspect ratio r_i has the form r^k for some integer k and therefore $\ln(r_i) = \ln(r)$. Indeed, the experimental data shows that all the values $\ln(r_i)$ are approximately proportional to whole multiples of some real number which can be therefore taken as $\ln(r)$. As a result, we got $r \approx 1.2$. The aspect ratios of different insects can be approximately described as q^k for integer values k:

- $k = 2$, aspect ratio $r^2 \approx 1.4$:
  - Stinkbug Adult (harmless) and
  - Hippodamia Lady Beetle Adult (harmless);
- $k = 3$, aspect ratio $r^3 \approx 1.7$:
  - Three-Corned Alfalfa Hopper (destructive);
  - Cucumber Beetle (destructive);
  - Collops Beetle (harmless);
- $k = 4$, aspect ratio $r^4 \approx 2.0$:
  - Big-Eyed Bug (harmless) and
  - Hippodamia Ladybug Larva (harmless);
- $k = 5$, aspect ratio $r^5 \approx 2.4$:
  - Assassin Bug (harmful to humans);
  - Lygus Adult (destructive);
  - Lacewing Larva (harmless);
- $k = 6$, aspect ratio $r^6 \approx 2.9$:
  - Nabid Adult (harmless);
  - Leaf Hopper (can be destructive);
- $k = 8$, aspect ratio $r^8 \approx 4$:
  - Grace Lace-Wing Adult (harmless).

We have six different values of k; for three of these values $(k = 2,\ k = 5, \text{ and } k = 8)$, we conclude that the corresponding insects are harmless. For three other values, to distinguish between harmless and harmful insects, we must consider other geometric characteristics.

3.5.3 Additional geometric characteristics

A natural idea is to use characteristics similar to the ones used to classify trash. The simplest geometric characteristic is the area A of the actual image; however, the area itself is not a good characteristic for insect classification because it increases when the insect grows: when an insect grows as $\vec{x} \to \lambda x$, the area increases by λ^2. Thus, the area itself characterizes not only the type of image but also the actual size of the insect of this particular type. Since we cannot use the area A directly, we must use area to define a new characteristic which is growth-invariant (i.e., scale-invariant) and thus, changes only from one specie to another, but not within the same species.

Our whole idea is to approximate the insect's shape with an ellipse, find the lengths D_{max} and D_{min} of the major and minor axes of the approximating ellipse, and then compute the ratio. Thus, for each image, we know the lengths D_{max} and D_{min}. As an insect grows $\vec{x} \to \lambda \vec{x}$, these lengths increase as $D_{max} \to \lambda D_{max}$ and $D_{min} \to D_{min} \lambda$. Since the area A of the shape increases as $A \to \lambda^2 A$, the ratio $\frac{A}{D_{max}^2}$ is scale-invariant. This ratio has a direct geometric sense: indeed, for a given D_{max}, this ratio attains the largest possible value when A is the largest possible, i.e., when:

- the area of the approximating ellipse is the largest possible for a given D_{max} and
- the image occupies the largest possible part of this approximating ellipse.

The second condition simply means that the image actually coincides with the approximating ellipse. For a fixed length D_{max} of the major axis, the area of the ellipse increases with D_{min}, so this area is the largest when D_{min} attains its largest possible value D_{max}, i.e., when this elliptical image is actually a round circle. Thus, the above ratio attains the largest possible value when the image is round; in view of this property, this ratio is called *roundness factor*.

For a circle, the area is equal to $A = \pi \frac{D^2}{4}$, and so the above roundness factor is equal to $\frac{\pi}{4}$. For manual analysis, it is convenient to "re-scale" the roundness factor in such a way that this maximum be equal to 1, in other words, it is convenient to consider the ratio $RF = \frac{(4A)}{\pi D_{max}^2}$.

3.5.4 Experimental use of roundness factor

This characteristic enables us to distinguish between several harmful and harmless insects:

- For $k = 5$,
  - harmful Assassin Bug has $RF \approx 0.25$, while
  - destructive Lygus Adult and harmless Lacewing Larva both have $RF \approx 0.36$
- For $k = 6$, we get a full distinction:
  - for harmless Habid Adult, $RF \approx 0.32$; while
  - for possibly destructive Leaf Hopper, $RF \approx 0.28$.

In both cases, we have a similar geometric phenomenon:

- harmless insects are more round (have larger values of the roundness factor), while
- harmful insects are less round (have smaller of the roundness factor).

For $k = 3$, all three species have approximately the same value of roundness factor $RF \approx 0.5$; so, to distinguish between them, we need an additional characteristic.

Since scale-invariant characteristics cannot distinguish between these species, we must use scale-dependent characteristics. It turns out that for these insects, the size (characterized, e.g., by the area A itself) can distinguish between harmless and harmful insects:

- harmless insects (Collops Beetle) are typically smaller ($A \approx 1{,}000$ pixels), while
- harmful insects are usually larger: for Three-Corned Alfalfa Hopper, $A \approx 2{,}000$ pixels ,and for Cucumber Beetle, $A \approx 3{,}000$ pixels .

3.6 Practical Results

By using aspect ratio, roundness factor, and area, we get an almost perfect insect classification; the only exception is that it is difficult to distinguish between destructive Lygus Adult and harmless Lacewing Larva.

While describing the three characteristics, we showed natural rules which use the values of these characteristics to determine the insect type. These rules, however, are difficult to implement directly because they use words from natural language like "small", "large", etc. We therefore need fuzzy logic to formalize these rules. In this formalization, we used the Adaptive Network-Based Fuzzy Inference System ANFIS (similar to trash classification). The resulting systems achieves an almost 100% correct classification of insects - a much higher percentage than previously known methods. The following table provides one example per each insect type (for further details see, e.g., [7, 8]).

Insect Type	a (E)	RF	A	correct?
Assassin Bug	2.48	0.255	2380	Y
Big-Eyed Bug	2.06	0.497	220	Y
Collops Beetle	1.76	0.532	360	Y
Cucumber Beetle	1.70	0.516	980	Y
G L Wing Adult	4.50	0.183	3510	Y
H Lady Beetle Adult	1.44	0.655	550	Y
H Ladybug Larva	2.19	0.366	810	Y
Leaf Hopper	3.11	0.282	1870	Y
Lacewing Larva	2.50	0.350	720	Y
Lygus Adult	2.44	0.400	720	Y
Nabid Adult	2.80	0.316	1090	Y
Stinkbug Adult	1.40	0.658	1140	Y
T-C Alfalfa Hopper	1.61	0.509	650	Y

4 Third Case Study: Automated System for Tracking High-Speed Targets

4.1 A practical problem: brief description

As our third case study, we take an important control problem, and we show that soft computing methods and data mining can help in solving this problem.

In air traffic control and in military applications, it is necessary to track high-speed targets such as airplanes, missiles, etc. Typically, radar images are used for this tracking, but radar provides a very crude picture of the targets: typically, a distant target is seen as a blurred point; from this image, it is difficult to tell whether it is a plane at all, and what type of plane it is. This low resolution is caused by the physical fact that the angular size of the smallest visible detail is $\approx \frac{\lambda}{D}$, where λ is the wavelength and D is the antenna's diameter; a radar uses radiowaves, for which λ is reasonably large. To improve the quality of the target pictures, it is therefore necessary to switch to smaller wavelengths, e.g., to visible light.

Thus, to get a good quality picture of the target, we must use a rotating telescope. Since we are interested in fast-moving targets, the tracking telescope must rotate fast, so fast that a human operator is unable to control it. We therefore need an automatic controller for the tracking system.

4.2 The need for fuzzy control

The corresponding control problem is highly non-linear, so traditional control methods—which work well for linear or almost linear systems—cannot be efficiently applied. Therefore, we need non-linear control techniques. Typically, in non-linear control, we select a general expression for a non-linear controller, and then tune this expression in such a way as to get an efficient controller. There are many different general non-linear expressions which can be used (and which have been actually used) in this process.

Most of these expressions come from the mathematical analysis of this problem: e.g., from the known fact that an arbitrary function can be approximated within any given accuracy by a polynomial (e.g., for an analytical function, we can take the sum of the first several terms in the Taylor series expansion as the desired polynomial approximation). The main disadvantage of these expressions is that they are very formal, they lack an intuitive understanding which is extremely important in real-life control problems.

There is a class of non-linear expressions, however, which does not have this drawback: namely, the class of non-linear expressions which come from *fuzzy control* (see, e.g., [17]). The corresponding expressions are universal approximators in the sense that an arbitrary non-linear control function can be approximated, with any given accuracy, by an input-output function of an appropriate fuzzy controller. However, no matter how complex the resulting input-output function, the system can still be described by a system of understandable if-then rules formulated in terms of words from natural language. This understandability and transparency of a non-linear controller is, as we have mentioned, an extremely important advantage of fuzzy control. With this advantage in mind, in our research, we used fuzzy control for tracking high-speed targets.

4.3 The need for data mining

Most applications of fuzzy control deal with near-linear systems, in which we can achieve a reasonably good control by using a near-linear controller. The most practically used linear controller is a PID controller, in which, in order to maintain a certain trajectory $x_0(t)$ of the controlled system (called *plant*), the system uses, at each given moment of time t, a control value $u(t)$ which is equal to the linear combination of three quantities:

- the state error $P(t) = x(t) - x_0(t)$, i.e., the difference between the actual state $x(t)$ and the desired state $x_0(t)$;
- the integral $I(t)$ of the state error;
- the time derivative $D(t)$ of the state error.

In other words, in PID control, to determine the control value $u(t)$, we use three inputs $P(t)$, $I(t)$, and $D(t)$, and form a linear combination to produce the desired control value: $u(t) = K_P\, P(t) + K_I\, I(t) + K_D\, D(t)$.

Naturally, for near-linear systems, the typically used fuzzy control uses rules with the same three inputs. If we use three membership functions (e.g., "small", "medium", and "large") to describe each of the three inputs, then we have to have $3 \times 3 \times 3 = 27$ rules to describe the control values for all 27 possible combinations of the input values.

For a strongly non-linear system, PID control, in which the gains K_i are the same for all pieces of the plant's trajectory, is no longer efficient: if we choose the gains K_i which lead to reasonable control on one part of the trajectory, these gains often lead to a low quality control in different parts of it. It is therefore necessary to make the control $u(t)$ depending not only on the difference $P(t)$ and on its integral $I(t)$ and derivative $D(t)$, but also on the actual values of the trajectory, i.e., on the current position $x(t)$, the current velocity $\dot{x}(t)$, etc. Therefore, in formulating fuzzy rules for such strongly non-linear systems, it is reasonable, in addition to the original three inputs $P(t)$, $I(t)$, and $D(t)$, to provide extra inputs such as $x(t)$, $\dot{x}(t)$, etc.

Even if use only 3 fuzzy values for each of the inputs, and even if we use only 5 inputs, we already need a huge number of $3^5 = 243$ rules. For each rules, we need to tune at least one parameter, so we need at least 243 parameters. It is extremely difficult to tune in a rule base with that many parameters. To decrease the number of rules, we use the *data mining* technique: namely, instead of simply using all input variables, we find a smaller number of relevant *combinations* $y_1, \ldots, y_m$ of these input variables, and then use these combinations y_j as the new inputs. So, to be able to use soft computing techniques (namely, fuzzy control techniques) for automated tracking of high-speed targets, we must first use *data mining* to find relevant combinations of input variables.

4.4 How this data mining was done

We have already mentioned one relationship between soft computing and data mining: that in order to use the expert-formalizing fuzzy control methodology, we must use data mining. Let us show that this relationship works the other way around too: the expert's knowledge (naturally formulated in fuzzy terms) can help in solving the corresponding data mining problem.

4.4.1 Handling the first non-linearity

The first reason why the control problem is non-linear is that the control is different for different elevations of the telescope; e.g.:

- when the system is pointing straight up (i.e., its elevation is 90^0), it is very easy to rotate it;
- when the system is horizontal, its moment of inertia is much larger, and it is more difficult to rotate.

For a fixed elevation, we can reasonably expect that a linear controller, with

$$u(t) = K_P\, P(t) + K_I\, I(t) + K_D\, D(t) + K_x\, x(t) + K_v\, \dot{x}(t),$$

will work well. For different elevation angles, we can tune this linear controller, and find the appropriate values of gains. The resulting control can now be described by the following three fuzzy rules:

- for low elevations, use the gains K_i corresponding to elevation angle 0;
- for medium elevations, use the gains K_i corresponding to elevation angle 45^0;
- for high elevations, use the gains K_i corresponding to elevation angle 90^0.

As a result of applying fuzzy control methodology to these rules, we get, for different values of the elevation angle, different values of the gains K_i.

4.4.2 Handling the second and third non-linearities

The above idea takes care of the first non-linearity. Dependence on the elevation, however, is not the only reason why this control problem is non-linear. Another reason is related to the following fundamental problem of linearly controlled plants.

Our goal is tracking. Therefore, when we slightly deviate from the correct trajectory, we want the system to get back to it as fast as possible. So, for small values of the deviation $P(t)$, the gain coefficient K_P corresponding to $P(t)$ should be large.

On the other hand, when the deviation becomes large, the use of the large coefficient K_P will lead to an extremely strong force applied to the telescope, and, as a result, the telescope will overcompensate and get into wild oscillations before getting back. So, for large value of the deviation $P(t)$, we must use the control corresponding to the smaller coefficient K_P.

In other words, for an ideal control, instead of the term $K_P P(t)$ with a constant gain, we should have the term $K_P(P(t))P(t)$, in which the gain K_P changes with the absolute value of $P(t)$. Alternatively, we can describe this desired control by assuming that the gain is fixed (e.g., as the gain $K_P(0)$ which is optimal for small deviations), but this gain is multiplied not by the deviation $P(t)$ itself, but by a "re-scaled" deviation $P_{new}(t) = c(P(t))P(t)$, where $c(P) = \frac{K_P(P)}{K_P(0)}$.

For each fixed value of P, we can fine-tune the resulting control and find the optimal value of $K_P(P)$ and thus, of $c(P)$. We can thus get the values $c(P)$ for several different values of P, and then use a fuzzy control methodology to interpolation from these values to arbitrary values of P. It turns out that we can use the following rules:

- if the angle deviation P is negligible, then $c(P) = 1$;
- if the angle deviation P is small, then $c(P) = 0.7$;
- if the angle deviation P is medium, then $c(P) = 0.4$;
- if the angle deviation P is large, then $c(P) = 0.2$.

As a result of applying fuzzy control technique with these rules, we get a continuous function $c(P)$.

The third reason for non-linearity is the saturation of control. This non-linearity is taken care of by simply thresholding the corresponding inputs, so that each value above the threshold is replaced by this threshold.

The resulting hierarchical fuzzy control system is indeed very effective in tracking; see, e.g., [23, 24].

5 Conclusion

In many applications of soft computing, the number of input variables is so large that traditional soft computing techniques are no longer practically applicable. This happens, for example, in image processing, when the number of numerical inputs (i.e., the number of pixels in an image) can be astronomic; this also happens in processing highly dynamical data, when the number of numerical inputs (i.e., the number of moments of time) can also be large. In such situations, instead of simply using all input variables, we must find a smaller number of relevant *combinations* $y_1, ..., y_m$ of these input variables, and then use these combinations y_j as the new inputs. In other words, in such situations, to be able to use soft computing techniques, we must first use *data mining* to find relevant combinations of input variables. In this paper, we showed how the resulting combination of data mining and soft computing techniques can help to solve practical problems in cotton industry and in tracking high-speed targets.

Acknowledgements. This work was supported in part by NASA under cooperative agreement NCC5-209, by NSF grant No. DUE-9750858, by United Space Alliance, grant No. NAS 9-20000 (PWO C0C67713A6), by the Future Aerospace Science and Technology Program (FAST) Center for Structural Integrity of Aerospace Systems, effort sponsored by the Air Force Office of Scientific Research, Air Force Materiel Command, USAF, under grant number F49620-95-1-0518, and by the National Security Agency under Grant No. MDA904-98-1-0561. The authors are thankful to the anonymous referees for valuable comments.

References

[1] A. D. Aleksandrov, A. N. Kolmogorov, and M. A. Lavrentiev, *Mathematics, its content, methods, and meaning*, Vol. 2, American Mathematical Society, Providence, R.I., 1963.

[2] H. Bunke and P. S. P. Wang (eds.), *Handbook of Character Recognition and Document Image Analysis*, World Scientific, Singapore, 1997.

[3] H. Bunke, P. S. P. Wang, and H. S. Baird (eds.), *Document Image Analysis*, World Scientific, Singapore, 1994.

[4] K. J. Cios, W. Pedrycz, and R. Swiniarski, *Data Mining Methods for Knowledge Discovery*, Kluwer. Dordrecht, 1998.

[5] L. Fausett, *Fundamentals of Neural Networks*, Englewood Cliffs, New Jersey: Prentice-Hall, 1994.

[6] U. M. Fayyad, G. Piatetsky-Shapiro, P. Smyth, and R. Uthurusamy (eds.), *Advances in Knowledge Discovery and Data Mining*, MIT Press, Cambridge, MA, 1996.

[7] H. Gassoumi, J. J. Ellington, H. T. Nguyen, and N. R. Prasad, "A soft computing approach to insects classification in the cotton field", *Proceedings of the International Symposium on Medical Informatics and Fuzzy Technology MIF'99*, Hanoi, Vietnam, August 27-29, 1999, pp. 454-485.

[8] H. Gassoumi, J. J. Ellington, H. T. Nguyen, and N. R. Prasad, "Integrated pest management system", In: H. Mohanty and C. Baral (eds.), *Trends in Information Technology, Proceedings of the International Conference on Information Technology ICIT'99, Bhubaneswar, India, December 20-22, 1999*, Tata McGraw-Hill, New Delhi, 2000, pp. 126-131.

[9] J.-S. Jang, C.-T. Sun, and E.Mizutani, *Neuro-Fuzzy and Soft Computing: A Computational Approach to Learning and Machine Intelligence*, Prentice Hall, Upper Saddle River, NJ, 1997.

[10] X. Jiang, K. Yu, and H. Bunke, "Detection of rotational and involutional symmetries and congruity of polyhedra", *Visual Comput.*, 1996, Vol. 12, No. 4, pp. 193-201.

[11] V. Kreinovich and J. Wolff von Gudenberg, "An optimality criterion for arithmetic of complex sets", *Geombinatorics*, 2000 (to appear).

[12] M. A. Lieberman and R. B. Patil, "Clustering and neural networks to categorize cotton trash", *Optical Engineering*, 1994, Vol. 33, No. 5, pp. 1642-1653.

[13] M. A. Lieberman and R. B. Patil, "Evaluation of learning vector quantization to classify cotton trash", *Optical Engineering*, 1997, Vol. 36, No. 3, pp. 914-921.

[14] J. Llados, H. Bunke, and E. Marti, "Finding rotational symmetries by cyclic string matching",+ *Pattern Recognit. Lett.*, 1997, Vol. 18, No. 14, pp. 1435-1442.

[15] R. S. Michalski, M. Kubat, I. Bratko, and A. Bratko (eds.), *Machine Learning and Data Mining: Methods and Applications,* J. Wiley & Sons, New York, 1998.

[16] H. T. Nguyen and V. Kreinovich, *Applications of continuous mathematics to computer science*, Kluwer, Dordrecht, 1997.

[17] H. T. Nguyen and M. Sugeno (eds.), *Fuzzy Systems: Modeling and Control*, Kluwer, Boston, MA, 1998.

[18] L. Polkowski et al. (eds.), *Rough sets in knowledge discovery 1. Methodology and applications*, Physica-Verlag: Heidelberg, 1998 (Studies in Fuzziness and Soft Comput. Vol. 18).

[19] J. C. Russ, *The image processing handbook*, Boca Raton, FL, CRC Press, 1994.

[20] K. Shearer, H. Bunke, S. Venkatesh, and D. Kieronska, "Efficient graph matching for video indexing", in: J.-M. Jolion et al. (eds.), *Graph based representations in pattern recognition. Workshop, GbR '97, Lyon, France, April 17-18, 1997*, Wien: Springer: Wien, Comput. Suppl. 1998, Vol. 12, pp. 53-62.

[21] M. Siddaiah, M. A. Lieberman, S. E. Hughs, and N. R. Prasad, "A soft computing approach to classification of trash in ginned cotton", *Proceedings of the 8th International Fuzzy Systems Association World Congress IFSA'99}*, Taipei, Taiwan, August 17-20, 1999, pp. 151-155.

[22] M. Siddaiah, M. A. Lieberman, S. E. Hughs, and N. R. Prasad, "Identification of trash types in ginned cotton using neuro fuzzy techniques", *Proceedings of the 8th IEEE International Conference on Fuzzy Systems FUZZ-IEEE'99*, Seoul, Korea, August 22-25, 1999, Vol. 2, pp. 738-743.

[23] J. Stufflebaum, *An integrated systems approach to tagret tracking using hierarchical fuzzy control*, Ph.D. Dissertation, New Mexico State University, 1999.

[24] J. Stufflebaum and N. R. Prasad, "Hierarchical fuzzy control", *Proceedings of the 8th IEEE International Conference on Fuzzy Systems FUZZ-IEEE'99*, Seoul, Korea, August 22-25, 1999, Vol. 1, pp. 498-503.

[25] J. Wolff von Gudenberg and V. Kreinovich, "Candidate Sets for Complex Interval Arithmetic", In: H. Mohanty and C. Baral (eds.), *Trends in Information Technology, Proceedings of the International Conference on Information Technology ICIT'99, Bhubaneswar, India, December 20-22, 1999*, Tata McGraw-Hill, New Delhi, 2000, pp. 230-233.

[26] P. B. Yale, *Geometry and symmetry*, Dover, New York, 1988.

[27] Y.-Q. Zhang and A. Kandel, *Compensatory Genetic Fuzzy Neural Networks and Their Applications*, World Scientific, Singapore, 1998.

[28] N. Zhong, A. Skowron, and S. Ohsuga (eds.), *New directions in rough sets, data mining, and granular-soft computing, Proc. of the 7th international workshop, RSFDGrC '99, Yamaguchi, Japan, November 9-11, 1999. Proceedings*, Springer-Verlag Lecture Notes in Artificial Intelligence, Vol. 1711, Berlin, 1999.

Appendix: Proofs

Proof of Proposition 1

This proof is similar to the proofs used in [8] to justify different heuristic methods in soft computing (fuzzy, neural, etc.).

Let us first show that the optimal family A_{opt} is itself shift-, rotation-, and scale-invariant.

Indeed, let T be an arbitrary shift, rotation, or scaling. Since A_{opt} is optimal, for every other family B, we have $A_{opt} \geq T^{-1}B$ (where A^{-1} means the inverse transformation). Since the optimality criterion $\geq$ is invariant, we conclude $T A_{opt} \geq T\left(T^{-1}B\right) = B$. Since this is true for every family B, the family TA_{opt} is also optimal. But since our criterion is final, there is only one optimal family and therefore, $TA_{opt} = A_{opt}$. In other words, the optimal family is indeed invariant.

Let us now show that all functions from A_{opt} are polynomials.

Indeed, every function $F \in A_{opt}$ is analytical, i.e., can be represented as a Taylor series (sum of monomials). Let us combine together monomials $c\,x^a\,y^b$ of the same degree $a+b$; then we get

$$F(z) = F_0(z) + F_1(z) + \ldots + F_k(z) + \ldots,$$

where $F_k(z)$ is the sum of all monomials of degree k. Let us show, by induction over k, that for every k, the function $F_k(z)$ also belongs to A_{opt}.

Let us first prove that $F_0(z) \in A_{opt}$. Since the family A_{opt} is scale-invariant, we conclude that for every $\lambda > 0$, the function $F(\lambda\, z)$ also belongs to A_{opt}. For each term $F_k(z)$, we have $F(\lambda\, z) = \lambda^k\, F_k(z)$, so

$$F(\lambda z) = F_0(z) + \lambda F_1(z) + \ldots \in A_{opt}$$

When $\lambda \to 0$ we get $F(\lambda z) \to F_0(z)$. The family A_{opt} is finite-dimensional hence closed; so, the limit $F_0(z)$ also belongs to A_{opt}. The induction base is proven.

Let us now suppose that we have already proven that for all $k < s$, $F_k(z) \in A_{opt}$. Let us prove $F_s(z) \in A_{opt}$. For that, let us take

$$G(z) = F(z) - F_1(z) - \ldots - F_{s-1}(z).$$

We already know that $F_1, \ldots, F_{s-1} \in A_{opt}$; so, since A_{opt} is linear space, we conclude that

$$G(z) = F_s(z) + F_{s+1}(z) + \ldots \in A_{opt}$$

The family A_{opt} is scale-invariant, so, for every $\lambda > 0$, the function

$$G(\lambda z) = \lambda^s F_s(z) + \lambda^{s+1} F_{s+1}(z) + \cdots$$

also belongs to A_{opt}. Since A_{opt} is a linear space, the function

$$H_\lambda(z) = \lambda^{-s} G(\lambda z) = F_s(z) + \lambda F_{s+1}(z) + \lambda^2 F_{s+2}(z) \ldots$$

also belongs to A_{opt}.

When $\lambda \to 0$, we get $H_\lambda(z) \to F_s(z)$. The family A_{opt} is finite-dimensional hence closed; so, the limit $F_s(z)$ also belongs to A_{opt}. The induction is proven.

Now, monomials of different degree are linearly independent; therefore, if we have infinitely many non-zero terms $F_k(z)$, we would have infinitely many linearly independent functions in a finite-dimensional family A_{opt} - a contradiction. Thus, only finitely many monomials $F_k(z)$ are different from 0, and so, $F(z)$ is a sum of finitely many monomials, i.e., a polynomial.

Let us prove that if a function $F(x, y)$ belongs to A_{opt}, then its partial derivatives $F_{,x}(x, y)$ and $F_{,y}(x, y)$ also belong to A_{opt}.

Indeed, since the family A_{opt} is shift-invariant, for every $H > 0$, we get $F(x+h, y) \in A_{opt}$. Since this family is a linear space, we conclude that a linear combination $h^{-1}(F(x+h, y) - F(x, y))$ of two functions from A_{opt} also belongs to A_{opt}. Since the family A_{opt} is finite-dimensional, it is closed and therefore, the limit $F_{,x}(x, y)$ of such linear combinations also belongs to A_{opt}. ($F_{,y}$, the proof is similar).

Due to Parts 2 and 3 of this proof, if any polynomial from A_{opt} has a non-zero part F_k of degree $k > 0$, then it also has a non-zero part $\left((F_k)_{,x} \; or \; (F_k)_{,y}\right)$ of degree $k-1$. Similarly, it has non-zero parts of degrees $k-2$, ..., 1, 0.

So, in all cases, A_{opt} contains a non-zero constant and a non-zero linear function $F_1(x, y) = bx + cy$. We can now use the fact that the family A_{opt} is rotation-invariant; let T be a rotation which transforms (b, c) into the x-axis, then we conclude that

$$F_1(T z) = b' x \in A_{opt},$$

and hence $x \in A_{opt}$. Similarly, $y \in A_{opt}$. So, the family A_{opt} contains at least 3 linearly independent functions: a non-zero constant, x, and y.

If $d = 3$, then the 3-D family A_{opt} cannot contain anything else, and all the pieces of borders $F(x, y) = 0$ of all the sets defined by this family are straight lines.

If $d = 4$, then we cannot have any cubic or higher order terms in A_{opt}, because then, due to Part 3, we would have both this cubic part *and* a (linearly independent) quadratic part, and the total dimension of A_{opt} would be at least $3 + 2 = 5$. So, all functions from A_{opt} are quadratic. Since $A_{opt} = 4$, and the dimension of 0- and 1-D parts is 3, the dimension of possible parts of second degree is 1. Since A_{opt} is rotation-invariant, the quadratic part $d\,x^2 + e\,x\,y + f\,y^2$ must be also rotation-invariant (else, we would have two linearly independent quadratic terms in A_{opt}: the original expression and its rotated version). Thus, this quadratic part must be proportional to $x^2 + y^2$.

Hence, every function $F \in A_{opt}$ has the form

$$F(x, y) = a + b\,x + c\,y + d\,(x^2 + y^2),$$

and therefore, all the pieces of borders $F(x, y) = 0$ of all the sets defined by this family are either straight lines or circular arcs. Proposition 1 is proven.

Proof of Proposition 2

Similarly to Part 1 of the proof of Proposition 1, we can show that the optimal angle is swap-invariant, i.e., $\alpha_{opt} = T(\alpha_{opt})$. Therefore, $\alpha_{opt} = 90 - \alpha_{opt}$, hence $2\alpha_{opt} = 90$, and $\alpha_{opt} = 45$. The proposition is proven.

Proof of Proposition 3

While proving Proposition 1, we have already shown the following:

all the functions F from the optimal family A_{opt} are polynomials;

if a function $F(x, y)$ belongs to A_{opt}, then its partial derivatives $F_{,x}(x, y)$ and $F_{,y}(x, y)$ also belong to A_{opt}; and

the optimal family A_{opt} contains at least 3 linearly independent functions: a non-zero constant, x, and $\sim y$.

Let us now show that since $d \le 6$, we cannot have any quadratic (or higher order) terms in A_{opt}.

Indeed, in this case, due to Part 3 of Proposition 1, in addition to 3-dimensional linear part, A_{opt} would contain this quadratic part, a (linearly independent) cubic part, *and* a (linearly independent) quadratic part, and the total dimension d of A_{opt} would be at least $d = 3 + d_2 + d_3 + d_4 \ldots$, where d_2 is the dimension of the quadratic part, d_3 is the dimension of the cubic part, etc. We have $d_2 \ge 1$, $d_3 \ge 1$, and $d_4 \ge 1$, so, if we had $d_3 > 1$, we would have

$$d = 3 + d_2 + d_3 + d_4 + \ldots > 3 + 1 + 1 + 1 = 6,$$

Since we assumed that $d \leq 6$ this is impossible and thus, $d_3 \leq 1$, i.e., $d_2 = 1$. Since A_{opt} is rotation-invariant, the cubic part $a\,x^3 + b\,x^2\,y + c\,x\,y^2 + d\,y^3$ must be also rotation-invariant (else, we would have two linearly independent cubic terms in A_{opt}: the original expression and its rotated version). However, it is known that there are no rotation-invariant cubic terms (actually, every rotation-invariant polynomial is a polynomial in $x^2 + y^2$, and is, therefore, of even order). Thus, quadratic terms are indeed impossible.

Since quadratic and higher order terms are impossible, every polynomial $F \in A_{opt}$ is either cubic or quadratic. Let us prove that for a cubic polynomial

$$F(x, y) = F_0(x, y) + F_1(x, y) + F_2(x, y) + F_3(x, y)$$

with a non-degenerate cubic part $F_3(x, y)$, the equation $F(x, y) = 0$ does not form a boundary of any bounded set at all.

Indeed, since $F_3 \neq 0$, there exists a point $z = (x, y)$ for which $F_3(x, y) \neq 0$. Without losing generality, we can assume that $F_3(z) > 0$. Let us take a new point $N \cdot z = (N \cdot x, N \cdot y)$, where N is a positive integer. For this new point, we have

$$F(N\,z) = F_0(z) + N\,F_1(z) + N^2\,F_2(z) + N^3\,F_3(z)$$

and hence,

$$\frac{F(N\,z)}{N^3} = N^{-3} \cdot F_0(z) + N^{-2}\,F_1(z) + N^{-1}\,F_2(z) + F_3(z)$$

When $N \to \infty$, we have $F(N\,z)/N^3 \to F_3(z) > 0$ and therefore, for all sufficiently large N, we have $F(N\,z)/N^3 > 0$ and thence, $F(N\,z) > 0$.

Similarly, we have

$$F(-N\,z) = F_0(z) - N\,F_1(z) + N^2\,F_2(z) - N^3 F_3(z)$$

hence,

$$\frac{F(-N\,z)}{N^3} = N^{-3}F_0(z) - N^{-2}F_1(z) + N^{-1}F_2(z) - F_3(z)$$

When $N \to \infty$, we have $F(-N\,z)/N^3 \to F_3(z) < 0$ and therefore, for all sufficiently large N, we have $F(-N\,z)/N^3 < 0$ and thence, $F(N\,z) < 0$.

Both points $N\,z$ and $-N\,z$ belong to the same circle with a center in 0 and radius $N\|z\|$ (where $\|z\| = \sqrt{x^2 + y^2}$. Thus, on this circle, there are two points for which the function $F(z)$ take values of different signs. Since this function $F(z)$ is continuous, it attains a 0 value somewhere on this circle. Thus, for arbitrarily large N, a circle of radius $N\|z\|$ contains a point z' for which $F(z') = 0$. Hence, the set of all the point for which $F(x, y) = 0$ is not bounded and therefore, cannot form a boundary of a bounded set.

Thus, if a bounded set defined as a whole by the optimal family A_{opt}, then the corresponding function $F(x, y)$ cannot be cubic and, therefore, it has to be quadratic. The only bounded set bounded by a

set $F(x, y) = 0$ for a quadratic function F is an ellipse. The proposition is proven.

Proof of Proposition 4

Let J be an invariant characteristic of an ellipse. It is well known that we can shift an arbitrary ellipse E so that its center coincides with the origin $(0, 0)$ of the coordinate system, and then rotate it in such a way that the major axis of the ellipse will lie on the coordinate axis $0x$, and its minor axis on the coordinate line $0y$. As a result, we get a new ellipse E_1 which is obtained from the original ellipse E by a combination T of shift and rotation: $E_1 = T(E)$. Since the characteristic J is invariant, shift and rotation do not change its value, so $J(E_1) = J(E)$. Shift and rotation preserve the axes of the ellipse, so for the new ellipse E_1, the lengths D_{max} and D_{min} of the ellipse's axes are the same as for the original ellipse E.

We can now scale E_1 by applying a scaling $x \to x / D_{min}$. After this scaling, we get a new ellipse E_2 which is (similarly to E_1) aligned with the coordinate axes;

the length of the axes of the new ellipse E_2 are equal to D_{max} / D_{min} and 1. Since the characteristic J is scale-invariant, we have $J(E_2) = J(E_1)$; since we already know that $J(E_1) = J(E)$, we conclude that $J(E_2) = J(E)$.

For the ellipse E_2, we know its orientation, and we know the lengths of its minor axis (1) and of its major axis (D_{max} / D_{min}). This information uniquely determines the ellipse; therefore, if we know the aspect ratio D_{max} / D_{min}, we can uniquely determine the ellipse E_2 and hence, the value $J(E_2) = J(E)$. Thus, the value $J(E)$ indeed depends only on the aspect ratio. The proposition is proven.

Intelligent Mining in Image Databases, with Applications to Satellite Imaging and to Web Search

Stephen Gibson[1,2], Vladik Kreinovich[1,2] , Luc Longpre[1], Brian Penn[2], and Scott A. Starks[2]

[1]Department of Computer Science and [2]NASA Pan-American Center for Earth and Environmental Sciences (PACES)

University of Texas at El Paso 500 W. University, El Paso, TX 79968, USA.

Contact email: vladik@cs.utep.edu

Abstract. An important part of our knowledge is in the form of images. For example, a large amount of geophysical and environmental data comes from satellite photos, a large amount of the information stored on the Web is in the form of images, etc. It is therefore desirable to use this image information in data mining. Unfortunately, most existing data mining techniques have been designed for mining numerical data and are thus not well suited for image databases. Hence, new methods are needed for image mining. In this paper, we show how data mining can be used to find common patterns in several images.

1 Introduction

1.1 It is necessary to apply data mining to images

An important part of our knowledge is in the form of images. For example, a large amount of geophysical and environmental data comes from satellite photos, a large amount of the information stored on the Web is in the form of images, etc. It is therefore desirable to use this image information in data mining. Unfortunately, most existing data mining techniques (see, e.g., [2, 3, 10, 12, 15, 16]) have been designed for mining numerical data and are thus not well suited for image databases; so, new methods are needed for image mining. An important part of image mining is finding common patterns in several images. It is difficult to uncover such a pattern, and it is difficult to automatically check whether a new image contains such a pattern. There exist (crisp) FFT-based methods for solving these problems, but often, they fail to detect a clearly visible pattern.

One possibility to find patterns uncovered by the existing FFT-based methods is to use alternative techniques, e.g., techniques based on string matching (see, e.g., [1, 9]) or graph techniques (see, e.g., [14]). These new techniques are a must in the situations where the FFT-based techniques do not work well. On the other hand, for situations where the FFT-based methods already work reasonably well, and we are only seeking an improvement, we do not want to completely replace these methods with methods based on alternative techniques, because such a replacement may worsen the already reasonable pattern matching performance. In such situations, instead of *replacing* the FFT-based methods with radically new ones, we would rather improve the existing FFT-based methods by *adding* new ideas to the main idea of FFT-based image processing.

In this paper, we show how the existing methods can be improved. We start with reasonable "expert rules" which describe possible improvements, and describe possible formalizations of these expert rules. Then, we use a group-theoretic technique to find the optimal formalization. It is known that symmetry-based techniques are indeed useful in image processing (see, e.g., [5, 9]). Our specific group-theoretic techniques have been successfully used to make choices in fuzzy, neural, and genetic methodologies that turned out to be empirically optimal [11]. The resulting new pattern-finding and pattern-checking methods are illustrated on two examples:

- analysis of satellite images and
- search for a known pattern (e.g., a known text) in web images.

1.2 First case study: Mosaicing satellite imaging

Satellite photos provide a good description of geographic areas. Often, we are interested in an area that is covered by several satellite photos, so we need to combine (*mosaic*) these photos into a single image. The problem is that we do not know the exact orientation of the satellite-based camera, so the photos may be shifted and rotated with respect to each other, and we do not know the exact values of these shifts and rotations. Therefore, to mosaic two images, we must find the relative shift and rotation between them. At present, mosaicing of satellite images is performed manually, by trial and error. This trial-and-error procedure is difficult to automate: for $n \times n$ images, where n can be from 1,000 to 6,000, we have n^2 possible shifts, which, together with $\approx n$ possible rotations and $\approx n$ possible scalings, make for an impossible number of $\approx n^4 \left(\geq 10^{12}\right)$ possible image comparisons. It is therefore necessary to come up with time-saving mosaicing algorithms.

1.3 Second case study: Searching for a pattern in a web image

A similar problem occurs when we search images stored on the web. We may want to find all images which contain a certain pattern (e.g., a certain text), but this pattern may be scaled differently in different web images. So, we must be able to mosaic two images:

- the image which contains the desired pattern, and
- the image which is stored on the web.

We must be able to find the relative shift, rotation, and scaling between the two images. One particular case of this problem is searching for text in web images. The growing popularity of the World Wide Web also means increasing security risks. As the World Wide Web has become an affordable way for different political groups to reach a broad audience it is becoming harder to monitor all these web sites for their content. While numerous web search tools can be used to automatically monitor plain text in web pages, search for text in graphical images is still a considerable challenge. This fact is used by designers of such web pages who "hide" their text by placing it inside of graphical images, avoiding detection from regular search engines. At present, the only known way to find all occurrences of suspicious words like "terror" in images is to use character recognition to find and read all the text in all the images. Performing character recognition is a computationally intensive task that has to be performed for every image. It is therefore desirable to develop faster algorithms for detecting text in web pages.

1.4 The existing FFT-based mosaicing algorithms

To decrease the mosaicing time, researchers have proposed methods based on Fast Fourier Transform (FFT). The best of the known FFT-based mosaicing algorithms is presented in [13]. The main ideas behind FFT-based mosaicing in general and this algorithm in particular are as follows.

1.4.1 The simplest case: shift detection in the absence of noise

Let us first consider the case when two images differ only by shift. It is known that if two images $I_1(\vec{x})$ and $I_2(\vec{x})$ differ only by shift, i.e., if $I_2(\vec{x}) = I_1(\vec{x}+\vec{a})$ for some (unknown) shift $\vec{a}$, then their Fourier transforms

$$F_i(\vec{\omega}) = \frac{1}{2\pi}\iint I(\vec{x})\, e^{-2\pi i\left(\vec{x}\,\vec{\omega}\right)}\,dx\,dy$$

are related by the following formula:

$$F_2(\vec{\omega}) = e^{2\pi i\left(\vec{\omega}\vec{a}\right)} F_1(\vec{\omega}) \tag{1}$$

Therefore, if the images are indeed obtained from each other by shift, then we have

$$M_2(\vec{\omega}) = M_1(\vec{\omega}), \tag{2}$$

where we denoted

$$M_i(\vec{\omega}) = \left| F_i(\vec{\omega}) \right| . \tag{3}$$

The actual value of the shift $\vec{a}$ can be obtained if we use the formula (1) to compute the value of the following ratio:

$$R(\vec{\omega}) = \frac{F_1^*(\vec{\omega}) F_2(\vec{\omega})}{\left| F_1^*(\vec{\omega}) F_2(\vec{\omega}) \right|} \tag{4}$$

Substituting (1) into (4), we get

$$R(\vec{\omega}) = e^{2\pi i\left(\vec{\omega}\vec{a}\right)} \tag{5}$$

Therefore, the inverse Fourier transform $P(\vec{x})$ of this ratio is equal to the delta-function $\delta\left(\vec{x} - \vec{a}\right)$. In other words, in the ideal no-noise situation, this inverse Fourier transform $P(\vec{x})$ is equal to 0 everywhere except for the point $\vec{x} = \vec{a}$; so, from $P(\vec{x})$, we can easily determine the desired shift by using the following algorithm:

- first, we apply FFT to the original images $I_1(\vec{x})$ and $I_2(\vec{x})$ and compute their Fourier transforms $F_1(\omega)$ and $F_2(\omega)$;
- on the second step, we compute the ratio (4);
- on the third step, we apply the inverse FFT to the ratio $R(\vec{\omega})$ and compute its inverse Fourier transform $P(\vec{x})$;

- finally, on the fourth step, we determine the desired shift $\vec{a}$ as the only value $\vec{a}$ for which $P(\vec{a}) \neq 0$.

In the presence of noise, we expect the values of $P(\vec{x})$ to be slightly different from the delta-function, but still, the value $\left|P(\vec{a})\right|$ should be much larger than all the other values of this function. So, to determine the shift $\vec{a}$ we can use the same algorithm as above but with a different final step:

- on the fourth step, we determine the desired shift $\vec{a}$ as the point for which $P(\vec{x})$ takes the largest possible value.

1.4.2 Reducing rotation and scaling to shift

If, in addition to shift, we also have rotation and scaling, then the absolute values $M_i(\vec{\omega})$ of the corresponding Fourier transforms are not equal, but differ from each by the corresponding rotation and scaling. If we go from Cartesian to polar coordinates (r, θ) in the $\vec{\omega}$-plane, then rotation by an angle θ_0 is described by a simple shift-like formula $\theta \to \theta + \theta_0$. In these same coordinates, scaling is also simple, but not shift-like: $r \to \lambda r$. If we go to *log-polar* coordinates (ρ, θ), where $\rho = \log(r)$, then scaling also becomes shift-like: $\rho \to \rho + b$, where $b = \log(\lambda)$. So, in log-polar coordinates, both rotation and scaling are described by a shift.

In view of the above reduction, in order to determine the rotation and scaling between M_1 and M_2, we can do the following:

- transform both images from the original Cartesian coordinates to log-polar coordinates;
- use the above FFT-based algorithm to determine the corresponding shift $(\theta_0, \log(\lambda))$;
- from the corresponding "shift" values, reconstruct the rotation angle θ_0 and the scaling coefficient λ.

The main computational problem with the transformation to log-polar coordinates is that we need values $M(\xi,\eta)$ on a rectangular grid in log-polar space $(\log(\rho),\theta)$, but computing $(\log(\rho),\theta)$ for the original grid points leads to points outside that grid. So, we need interpolation to find the values $M(\xi,\eta)$ on the desired grid. One possibility is to use *bilinear* interpolation. Let (x, y) be a rectangular point corresponding to the desired grid point $(\log(\rho),\theta)$ i.e.,

$$x = e^{\log(\rho)} \cos(\theta), \quad y = e^{\log(\rho)} \sin(\theta)$$

To find the value $M(x, y)$, we look at the intensities $M_{j,k}$, $M_{j+1,k}$, $M_{j,k+1}$, and

$M_{j+1,k+1}$ of the four grid points (j,k), $(j+1,k)$, $(j,k+1)$, and $(j+1,k+1)$

surrounding (x, y). Then, we can interpolate $M(x, y)$ as follows:

$M(x, y)=(1-t)(1-u)M_{jk} + t(1-u)M_{j+k,k} + (1-t)uM_{j,k+1} + tuM_{j+1,k+1}$,

where t is a fractional part of x and u is a fractional part of y.

1.4.3 Final algorithm: determining shift, rotation, and scaling

- First, we apply FFT to the original images $I_1(\vec{x})$ and $I_2(\vec{x})$ and compute their Fourier transforms $F_1(\omega)$ and $F_2(\omega)$.
- Then, we compute the absolute values $M_1(\vec{\omega}) = |F_1(\vec{\omega})|$ and $M_2(\vec{\omega}) = |F_2(\vec{\omega})|$ of these Fourier transforms.
- By applying the above algorithm and scaling detection algorithm to the functions $M_1(\omega)$ and $M_2(\omega)$, we can determine the rotation angle θ_0 and the scaling coefficient λ.
- Now, we can apply the corresponding rotation and scaling to one of the original images, e.g., to the first image $I_1(\vec{x})$. As a result, we get a new image $\tilde{I}_1(\vec{x})$.
- Since we rotated and re-scaled one of the images, the images $\tilde{I}_1(\vec{x})$ and $I_2(\vec{x})$ are already aligned in terms of rotation and scaling, and the only difference between them is in an (unknown) shift. So, we can again apply the

above described FFT-based algorithm for determining shift: this time, actually to determine shift.

As a result, we get the desired values of shift, rotation, and scaling; hence, we get the desired mosaicing.

1.5 Problems with the existing FFT-based algorithm

In many real life situations, this algorithm works well. However, when we tried to implement this algorithm on several test images, we encountered the following two problems:

- In some cases, we could not complete the algorithm because of a "division by zero" error message.
- In some other cases, although the algorithm worked, the resulting rotation angle was reconstructed with a large inaccuracy even for images with no noise added. For example, when we compared two simple 64×64 pixel images which were obtained from each other by an exact rotation, the inaccuracy in reconstructing the rotation angle was sometimes as high as 1.5 degrees. Sometimes we do not get any reconstruction at all.

It is therefore necessary to modify the above algorithm to avoid these two problems. In this paper, we describe the desired improvement of this algorithm. The details are given in [4].

2 Analysis of the problems

2.1 "Divide by zero" problem: analysis

2.1.1 Experimental analysis

In order to avoid the above problems, we must first find out what causes these problems. Let us describe the result of our analysis. The first problem that we analyzed was the problem of dividing by zero. This problem did not occur for images used in [6], but it did occur in some of our images. In order to find out what causes this problem, we first tried to find something in common between the different images in which this problem occurred. It turns out that, in our tests, this problem occurs exclusively in simple images. This observation explains why this problem was never encountered before: because the algorithm was always tested on rather complex, real-life image.

If all we wanted to do was mosaic satellite images, then we would not have to worry about this problem, because it occurs only in simple images. However, since one of our major application areas is detecting text in web images, and web images are often very simple, this problem becomes more important.

2.1.2 Theoretical analysis

The "division by zero" error comes from computing the expression (4), when one of one of the values $F_i(\vec{\omega})$ of the Fourier transforms is equal to 0. In this case, both the numerator and the denominator of (4) become equal to 0, so we have a 0/0 problem. In general, a Fourier transform $F(\vec{\omega})$ of an image $I(\vec{x})$ is a linear combination of the image's intensity values $I(\vec{x})$ at different pixels $\vec{x}$ with the complex coefficients depending on $\vec{x}$ and $\vec{\omega}$. To get zero, we need these terms to exactly compensate each other.

For a complex image, especially for a real-life image, the values $I(\vec{x})$ corresponding to different pixels $\vec{x}$ are different and unrelated, so it is unlikely that they will add up to exactly zero. However, for a simple image, the values $I(\vec{x})$ can be described by a simple formula, and the intensity values $I(\vec{x})$ corresponding to different pixels $\vec{x}$ are closely related. It is therefore quite possible that, for simple images, with these related values, we get $F(\vec{\omega})$ for some $\vec{\omega}$.

2.1.3 Example

This possibility can be illustrated by a simple two-pixel image, in which two neighboring pixels $-x_0$ and x_0 on both sides of the central point 0 have equal intensity: $I(x)=I_0\,\delta(x-x_0)+I_0\,\delta(x+x_0)$. The Fourier transform of this image is equal to $2I_0\cos(2\pi\xi x_0)$, and for certain values ξ, we get division by 0. In a discrete case, we see that division by zero occurs when one of the images has a unit intensity equally distributed between two neighboring points, e.g., if the intensities are 0, 0, 0, 0, 0, 0, 0, 0.5, 0.5, 0, 0, 0, 0, 0, 0, 0 .

2.2 Accuracy problem: analysis

In the FFT algorithm, we determine the shift as the point $\vec{x}$ *on the grid* for which $|P(\vec{x})|$ attains the largest possible value. The actual values of rotation angle θ_0

and log-scaling $\log(\lambda)$ may *not* be *exactly on the grid*. As a result, when we use the FFT-based shift-detection algorithm to determine rotation and scaling, we do not determine them exactly. Hence, the alignment made by these approximate values of rotation angle and scaling is not exact. For noisy images, the additional distortion produced by this mis-alignment often prevents the shift-detecting algorithm from finding the shift between the images I_1 and I_2. To decrease this distortion, we would like to be able to find a more accurate estimate of the shift, even when its actual value is not from the grid.

3 The new mosaicing algorithm

3.1 Main idea

We have mentioned that in the existing algorithm, we determine the shift as the point $\vec{x}$ on a grid for which $\left|P(\vec{x})\right|$ attains the largest possible value. To improve the accuracy of mosaicing, it is desirable we would like to be able to find a more accurate estimate of the shift, even when its actual value is not from the grid. In 1-D case, if the function $\left|P(\vec{x})\right|$ has a large maximum at a point a and is equal to 0 for all $x \neq a$, then, of course, the actual value of the shift is a. However, if the value $\left|P(\vec{x})\right|$ is large for two sequential points x_1 and x_2, then probably the actual shift is somewhere between x_1 and x_2. In other words, the actual shift should be equal to $x = \omega_1 x_1 + \omega_2 x_2$ for some weights $\omega_1 + \omega_2$. The larger $|P(x_i)|$, the closer the actual shift point to x_i; so, the larger the weight ω_i should be.

3.2 Toward formalizing this idea

The above idea is formulated in terms of words from natural language, like "large". Let us formalize this idea. We have already mentioned that the larger $\left|P(x_i)\right|$, the closer the actual shift point to x_i; so, the larger the weight ω_i should be. At first glance, it therefore seems reasonable to take $\omega_i = f\left(\left|P(x_i)\right|\right)$ for some monotonically increasing function $f(z)$. For this choice, however, we cannot guarantee that $\omega_1 + \omega_2 = 1$.

A natural way to avoid the above problem is to *normalize* these weights, i.e., to take

$$x=\frac{f\left(\left|P(x_1)\right|\right)x_1+f\left(\left|P(x_2)\right|\right)x_2}{f\left(\left|P(x_1)\right|\right)+f\left(\left|P(x_2)\right|\right)}. \tag{6}$$

In a 2-D case, we can similarly take two points x_1, x_2, y_1, y_2 in each of the grid's directions, and use the sums of the corresponding values $f\left(\left|P\right|\right)$ as the weights:

$$x=\frac{\omega_{x_1}x_1+\omega_{x_2}x_2}{\omega_{x_1}+\omega_{x_2}}; \tag{7}$$

$$y=\frac{\omega_{y_1}y_1+\omega_{y_2}y_2}{\omega_{y_1}+\omega_{y_2}} \tag{8}$$

where

$$\omega_{x_i}=f\left(\left|P(x_i, y_1)\right|\right)+f\left(\left|P(x_i, y_2)\right|\right); \tag{9}$$

$$\omega_{y_i}=f\left(\left|P(x_1, y_i)\right|\right)+f\left(\left|P(x_2, y_i)\right|\right); \tag{10}$$

To finalize this formalization, we must select a function $f(z)$. This selection is very important, because numerical experiments show that different choices lead to drastically different efficiency of the resulting method; so, to increase the algorithm's efficiency, we would like to choose the best possible function $f(z)$.

What do we mean by "the best" ? It is not so difficult to come up with different criteria for choosing a function $f(z)$:

- We may want to choose the function $f(z)$ for which the resulting location error is, on average, the smallest possible: $P(f)\to\min$ (i.e., for which the *quality of the answer* is, on average, the best).
- We may also want to choose the function $f(z)$ for which the *average computation time* $C(f)$ is the smallest (average in the sense of some reasonable probability distribution on the set of all problems).

At first glance, the situation seems hopeless: we cannot estimate these numerical criteria even for a single function $f(z)$, so it may look like we therefore cannot undertake an even more ambitious task of finding the *optimal* function $f(z)$. Hopefully, the situation is not as hopeless as it may seem, because there is a symmetry-based formalism (actively used in the foundations of fuzzy, neural, genetic computations, see, e.g., [11]) which will enable us to find the optimal function $f(z)$. (Our application will be mathematically similar to the optimal choice of a non-linear scaling function in genetic algorithms [8, 11]).

Before we make a formal definition, let us make two comments.

- The first comment is that our goal is to find the weights. The weights are always non-negative numbers, so the function $f(z)$ must also take only non-negative values.
- The second comment is that all we want from the function $f(z)$ is the weights. These probabilities are computed according to the formulas (6 - 8). From these expressions (6 - 8), one can easily see that if we multiply all the values of this function $f(z)$ by an arbitrary constant C, i.e., if we consider a new function $\tilde{f}(z) = C f(z)$, then this new function will lead (after the normalization involved in (6 - 8)), to exactly the same values of the weights. Thus, whether we choose $f(z)$ or $\tilde{f}(z) = C f(z)$, does not matter. So, what we are really choosing is not a *single* function $f(z)$, but a *family* of functions $\{C f(z)\}$ (characterized by a parameter $C > 0$).

In the following text, we will denote families of functions by capital letters, such as F, F', G, etc.

3.3 Towards an optimality criterion

Traditionally, optimality criteria are *numerical*, i.e., to every family F, we assign some value $J(F)$ expressing its quality, and choose a family for which this value is minimal (i.e., when $J(F) \le J(G)$ for every other alternative G). However, it is not necessary to restrict ourselves to such numeric criteria only. For example, if we have several different families F that have the same average location error $P(F)$, we can choose between them the one that has the minimal computational time $C(F)$. In this case, the actual criterion that we use to compare two families is not numeric, but more complicated: A family F_1 is better than the family F_2 if and only if either $P(F_1) < P(F_2)$, or $P(F_1) = P(F_2)$ and $C(F_1) < C(F_2)$. The only thing that a criterion *must* do is to allow us, for every pair of families (F_1, F_2), to make one of the following conclusions:

- the first family is better with respect to this criterion (we'll denote it by $F_1 > F_2$, or $F_2 < F_1$);
- with respect to the given criterion, the second family is better $(F_2 > F_1)$;
- with respect to this criterion, the two families have the same quality (we'll denote it by $F_1 \sim F_2$);
- this criterion does not allow us to compare the two families.

Of course, it is necessary to demand that these choices be consistent. For example, if $F_1 > F_2$ and $F_2 > F_3$ then $F_1 > F_3$.

A natural demand is that this criterion must choose a *unique* optimal family (i.e., a family that is better with respect to this criterion than any other family). The reason for this demand is very simple. If a criterion *does not choose* any family at all, then it is of no use. If *several* different families are the best according to this criterion, then we still have the problem of choosing the best among them. Therefore, we need some additional criterion for that choice, as in the above example: If several families F_1, F_2, ... turn out to have the same average location error $(P\ (F_1) = P\ (F_2) = \ldots)$, we can choose among them a family with minimal computation time $(C(F_i) \to \min)$. So what we actually do in this case is abandon that criterion for which there were several "best" families, and consider a new "composite" criterion instead: F_1 is better than F_2 according to this new criterion if either it was better according to the old criterion, or they had the same quality according to the old criterion and F_1 is better than F_2 according to the additional criterion. In other words, if a criterion does not allow us to choose a unique best family, it means that this criterion is not final. We must modify it until we come to a final criterion that will have that property.

The exact mathematical form of a function $f(z)$ depends on the exact choice of units for measuring length. If we replace this unit by a new unit that is λ times larger, then the same physical value that was previously described by a numerical value $I(x, y)$ will now be described, in the new units, by new numerical $\tilde{I}(x, y) = I\left(\frac{x}{\lambda}, \frac{y}{\lambda}\right)$, and the corresponding Fourier transform of the ratio will change to $\tilde{P}(x, y) = \frac{P(x, y)}{\lambda}$. So, for $J\left(\vec{x}\right) = \left|P\left(\vec{x}\right)\right|$, we will have

$\tilde{J}\left(\vec{x}\right)=\frac{J\left(\vec{x}\right)}{\lambda}$. How will the expression for $f(z)$ change if we use the new units? In terms of $\tilde{J}\left(\vec{x}\right)$, we have $J\left(\vec{x}\right)=\lambda\,\tilde{J}\left(\vec{x}\right)$. Thus, if we change the measuring unit for $J\left(\vec{x}\right)$, the same weight $\omega\left(\vec{x}\right)\sim f\left(J\left(\vec{x}\right)\right)$ that was originally represented by a function $f(z)$, will be described, in the new units, as $\omega\left(\vec{x}\right)\sim f\left(\lambda\,\tilde{J}\left(\vec{x}\right)\right)$, i.e., as $\omega\left(\vec{x}\right)\sim \tilde{f}\left(\tilde{J}\left(\vec{x}\right)\right)$, where $\tilde{f}(z)=f(\lambda z)$. There is no reason why one choice of unit should be preferable to the other. Therefore, it is reasonable to assume that the relative quality of different families should not change if we simply change the units, i.e., if the family F is better than a family G, then the transformed family $\tilde{F}$ should also be better than the family $\tilde{G}$. We will now formalize the preceding discussion.

3.4 Definition and the main result

Definition 1. Let $f(z)$ be a differentiable strictly increasing function from real numbers to non-negative real numbers. By a *family* that corresponds to this function $f(z)$, we mean a family of all functions of the type $\tilde{f}(z)=C\,f(z)$, where $C>0$ is an arbitrary positive real number. (Two families are considered *equal* if they coincide, i.e., consist of the same functions.)

In the following text, we will denote the set of all possible families by Φ.

Definition 2. By an *optimality criterion*, we mean a consistent pair $(<,\sim)$ of relations on the set Φ of all alternatives which satisfies the following conditions, for every $F, G, H \in \Phi$:

(1) if $F<G$ and $G<H$ then $F<H$;

(2) $F\sim F$;

(3) if $F\sim G$ then $G\sim F$;

(4) if $F \sim G$ and $G \sim H$ then $F \sim H$;

(5) if $F < G$ and $G < H$ then $F < H$;

(6) if $F \sim G$ and $G < H$ then $F < H$;

(7) if $F < G$ and $G \neq H$ then $F \neq H$;

Comment. The intended meaning of these relations is as follows:

- $F < G$ means that with respect to a given criterion, G is better than F;
- $F \sim G$ means that with respect to a given criterion, F and G are of the same quality.

Under this interpretation, conditions (1)-(7) have simple intuitive meaning; e.g., (1) means that if G is better than F, and H is better than G, then H is better than F.

Definition 3.

- We say that an alternative F is *optimal* (or *best*) with respect to a criterion $(<,\sim)$ if for every other alternative G either $F > G$ or $F \sim G$.
- We say that a criterion is *final* if there exists an optimal alternative, and this optimal alternative is unique.

Definition 4. Let λ be a positive real number.

- By a λ*-rescaling* of a function $f(x)$ we mean a function $\tilde{f}(x) = f(\lambda x)$.
- By a λ*-rescaling* $R_\lambda(F)$ of a family of functions F we mean the family consisting of λ*-rescalings* of all functions from F.

Definition 5. We say that an optimality criterion on Φ is *unit-invariant* if for every two families F and G and for every number $\lambda > 0$, the following two conditions are true:

i) if F is better than G in the sense of this criterion (i.e., $F > G$), then $R_\lambda(F) > R_\lambda(G)$;

ii) if F is equivalent to G in the sense of this criterion (i.e., $F \sim G$), then $R_\lambda(F) \sim R_\lambda(G)$.

Theorem 1. *If a family F is optimal in the sense of some optimality criterion that is final and unit-invariant, then every function $f(z)$ from this family F has the form $C z^{\alpha}$ for some real numbers C and α.*

This theorem was, in effect, proven in [7, 11]. For the reader's convenience, the proof is given in the Appendix.

3.5 Tuning the resulting algorithm

The above theorem shows that $f(z) = z^{\alpha}$, but it does not tell which value α we should choose. To determine the optimal value of α, we analyzed several different images and came up with the following experimental conclusion:

- on the first stage, when we determine rotation and scaling, the optimal value of α is $\alpha_r \approx 1.55$;
- on the second stage, on which we determine the shift, the optimal value of α is $\alpha_s \approx 0.65$.

For these values, we indeed get a pretty good mosaicing.

4 The optimal choice of 0 / 0

4.1 Main idea

In the previous section, we showed the optimal solution to the problem of fractional shifts. To complete the description of an optimal FFT-based algorithm, we must find an optimal solution to the first (0 / 0) problem. In principle, we can choose an arbitrary complex number as 0 / 0. Which is the best choice? In solving this problem, we will use the same theoretical approach as in the previous section: similarly to that section, it is difficult to formulate a numerical criterion for choosing z. So, we will assume that there is a final optimality criterion on the set of all complex numbers, and we will look for the number which is best with respect to this criterion. Similarly to the previous section, we can formulate natural invariance requirements for this criterion. Namely, the value 0 / 0 comes from the ratio (4). We have already mentioned that if we shift I_1, then the value of $F_1\left(\vec{\omega}\right)$ gets multiplied by $e^{2\pi i\left(\vec{\omega}\,\vec{a}\right)}$. Thus, the ratio z determined by the formula (4) gets changed to $z \to z e^{i\theta}$ where $\theta = 2\pi\left(\vec{\omega}\,\vec{a}\right)$.

The decision of which value of 0 / 0 is the best should be universal, and it should not change with an additional shift of I_1. Therefore, it makes sense to assume that the optimality criterion should not change if we apply the transformation (11). Now, we are ready for the formal definitions:

Definition 6. We say that an optimality criterion on the set C of all complex numbers is invariant if for every two complex numbers z and z' and for every real number $\theta > 0$, the following two conditions are true:

i) if z is better than z' in the sense of this criterion (i.e., $z > z'$), then $z e^{i\theta} > z' e^{i\theta}$.

ii) if z is equivalent to z' in the sense of this criterion (i.e., $z \sim z'$), then $z e^{i\theta} \sim z' e^{i\theta}$.

Theorem 2. *If a number z is optimal in the sense of some optimality criterion that is final and invariant, then $z = 0$.*

To test this theoretical conclusion, we tested our algorithm, for different values of $z = 0/0$, on the simple 2-pixel image described above. For this image, the error with which we can determine the shift is indeed the smallest for $z = 0$.

5 Summarizing: new algorithm

Combining the above results, we come up with the following new modification of the FFT-based algorithm:

5.1 The simplest case: shift detection

- First, we apply FFT to the original images $I_1\left(\vec{x}\right)$ and $I_2\left(\vec{x}\right)$ and compute their Fourier transforms $F_1(\omega)$ and $F_2(\omega)$.
- On the second step, we compute the ratio $R\left(\vec{\omega}\right)$ by using formula (4); if the denominator is 0, then we take the ratio to be equal to 0 too.
- On the third step, we apply the inverse FFT to the ratio $R\left(\vec{\omega}\right)$ and compute its inverse Fourier transform $P\left(\vec{x}\right)$.
- Finally, on the fourth step, we do the following:
- we find the point $\vec{x} = (x_1, y_1)$ for which $\left|P\left(\vec{x}\right)\right|$ takes the largest possible value;
- then, among 4 points $(x_1 \pm 1,\ y_1 \pm 1)$, we select a point $(x_2,\ y_2)$ for which the value $|P(x_2,\ y_2)|$ is the largest;
- after that, we apply the formulas (7 - 10) with $f(z) = z^{\alpha}$ and $\alpha = 0.65$ to find the coordinates (x, y) of the shift.

5.2 Final algorithm: determining shift, rotation, and scaling

- First, we apply FFT to the original images $I_1\left(\vec{x}\right)$ and $I_2\left(\vec{x}\right)$ and compute their Fourier transforms $F_1(\omega)$ and $F_2(\omega)$.

- Then, we compute the absolute values $M_1\left(\vec{\omega}\right)=\left|F_1\left(\vec{\omega}\right)\right|$ and $M_2\left(\vec{\omega}\right)=\left|F_2\left(\vec{\omega}\right)\right|$ of these Fourier transforms.

- We transform both "images" $M_i\left(\vec{\omega}\right)$ from the original Cartesian coordinates to log-polar coordinates.
- Then, we use the above FFT-based algorithm, with $\alpha = 1.55$, to determine the corresponding shift $(\theta_0, \log(\lambda))$.
- From the corresponding "shift" values, we reconstruct the rotation angle θ_0 and the scaling coefficient λ.
- Now, we apply the corresponding rotation and scaling to one of the original images, e.g., to the first image $I_1\left(\vec{x}\right)$. As a result, we get a new image $\tilde{I}_1\left(\vec{x}\right)$.

- Since we rotated and re-scaled one of the images, the images $\tilde{I}_1\left(\vec{x}\right)$ and $I_2\left(\vec{x}\right)$ are already aligned in terms of rotation and scaling, and the only difference between them is in an (unknown) shift. So, we can again apply the our new FFT-based algorithm for determining shift: this time, actually to determine shift.

As a result, we get the desired values of shift, rotation, and scaling; hence, we get the desired mosaicing.

6 Experimental testing of the new algorithm

We ran three series of tests:

- First, we checked whether the resulting algorithm indeed solves the problems of the original FFT-based method, i.e., that its accuracy is better and its applicability is wider.
- Second, we tested this algorithm on two overlapping satellite images to see how well the algorithm works with images that have different shading and substantial noise.
- Finally, we applied this algorithm to find text in images.

In all three series, we got good mosaicing results.

We started with an image of sheet music from Beethoven's Moonlight Sonata. This image was chosen because it contains several repeated sequences of notes, and even visually, it is difficult to properly align the two shifted images. We then shifted, rotated, and scaled this image. In creating the new images, we used all possible combinations of shift, no-shift, rotation, no-rotation, scaling, no-scaling, giving us a total of 7 images.

We then used both the original FFT-based algorithm and our new algorithm to compare the original image with each of the seven transforms. The results are given in the following table.

A second set of tests have been performed on a pair of satellite images in order to demonstrate the robustness of this algorithm with regard to noise and shading differences. We also test the limits as to how much two images must overlap in order for the program to detect the similarities and properly mosaic the images.

These two images are actually subscenes from two overlapping photos P33R37 and P34R37 taken from a Landsat satellite over southern New Mexico. The resolution is 30 meters meaning that each pixel represents the average intensity for a 30 by 30 meter area. The Landsat sensors detect eight different bands of light simultaneously, only some of which are composed of visible light frequencies.

	Angle (degrees)	Scale	Relative shift (pixels)
actual	0.00	1.000	(20.0,-10.0)
reconstructed (old)	180.00	1.000	(22.0,19.0)
reconstructed (new)	-0.02	1.000	(20.1,-10.0)
actual	0.00	1.176	(0.0,0.0)
reconstructed (old)	0.00	1.207	(0.0,0.0)
reconstructed (new)	0.15	1.210	(0.5,0.5)
actual	0.00	1.176	(-5.0,-13.0)
reconstructed (old)	0.00	1.207	(-5.0,-13.0)
reconstructed (new)	0.15	1.210	(-4.5,-12.5)
actual	-10.00	1.000	(0.0,0.0)
reconstructed (old)	170.16	1.000	(72.0,-89.0)
reconstructed (new)	-10.00	1.000	(0.0,0.0)
actual	-10.00	1.000	(22.0,5.0)
reconstructed (old)	170.16	1.000	(71.0,-84.0)
reconstructed (new)	-9.92	1.000	(23.2,4.2)
actual	-10.00	1.176	(0.0,0.0)
reconstructed (old)	-9.84	1.207	(0.0,0.0)
reconstructed (new)	-9.95	1.210	(0.5,-0.5)
actual	-10.00	1.176	(-11.0,13.0)
reconstructed (old)	-9.84	1.207	(-12.0,12.0)
reconstructed (new)	-9.96	1.210	(-12.5,11.5)

The images used here are made up of only the blue band, which have been converted to 256 grayscale images. The images were taken on different days at different times of the year. Although there is no apparent snow or clouds in either image, the shading and some of the ground features differ slightly.

These images are about one quarter the size of the original satellite photos. The first has 3171 columns and 2768 rows of pixels while the other is 3026 x 3214. Because these images are so large and only overlap by about 20%, we have taken

512 x 512 pixel sub images from the overlapping part of these sub images in order to conduct this test. Only one such sub image was taken from image P33R37 while eight were taken from P34R37. Each sub image taken from P34R37 overlaps the original sub image from P33R37 by a different percentage starting with approximately 100% and going down to 30%. The results of reconstructing shift, rotation, and scaling are as follows:

	Overlap (%)	Angle	Relative shift
actual	100	-0.85	(-0.5, -1.5)
reconstructed		-0.84	(-0.6, -1.5)
actual	90	-0.85	(25.5, 24.5)
reconstructed		-0.83	(21.5, 24.3)
actual	80	-0.85	(53.5, 52.5)
reconstructed		-0.84	(49.5, 51.6)
actual	70	-0.85	(83.5, 82.5)
reconstructed		-0.84	(79.6, 81.5)
actual	60	-0.85	(115.5, 114.5)
reconstructed		-0.82	(110.6, 114.4)
actual	50	-0.85	(149.5, 148.5)
reconstructed		-0.86	(146.5, 145.7)
actual	40	-0.85	(187.5, 186.5)
reconstructed		-0.83	(179.4, 183.7)
actual	30	-0.85	(230.5, 229.5)
reconstructed		-90.00	(-1.0, -102.0)

We got good reconstruction for at least 40% overlap. When the image overlap is near 100%, the algorithm is accurate to within 0,1 pixels and 0.01 degrees. From 90% overlap down to 40% overlap, the accuracy stays fairly consistent, within 5 pixels and 0.03 degrees, with one exception of 0.3 degrees variance.

In the last set of tests, we used our new algorithm to locate a given text string in a complex image. One important application of this is government agencies trying to find covert messages on web pages. For this application, texts are horizontal, so we are only looking for a shift.

Here, as a first image, we took the text on a white background, for the second image we took our original sheet music image and put our text on top of it. For a shifted test, we got perfect reconstruction:

	Relative shift
actual	(-59, -128)
reconstructed	(-59, -128)

7 Conclusion

In many application areas, several images cover a single area and, therefore, it is important to mosaic them into a single image. For that, we need to properly shift, rotate, and re-scale the component images. Several FFT-based algorithms have been proposed for such mosaicing. Sometimes, however, these algorithms do not work well: for some simple images, these methods do not work at all, while for some more complicated images, the resulting mosaicing accuracy is very low.

We have developed and tested an optimal FFT-based mosaicing algorithm. This algorithm works well on all kinds of images including man-made images, satellite photos, and detection of text in images. In particular, this algorithm works well on the images on which the previously known algorithms failed.

Acknowledgements

This work was supported in part by NASA under cooperative agreement NCC5-209, by NSF grants No. DUE-9750858 and CDA-9522207, by United Space Alliance, grant No. NAS 9-20000 (PWO C0C67713A6), by the Future Aerospace Science and Technology Program (FAST) Center for Structural Integrity of Aerospace Systems, effort sponsored by the Air Force Office of Scientific Research, Air Force Materiel Command, USAF, under grant number F49620-95-1-0518, and by the National Security Agency under Grant No. MDA904-98-1-0561. The authors are thankful to the anonymous referees for valuable suggestions.

References

[1] H. Bunke and M. Zumbuehl, "Acquisition of 2D shape models from scenes with overlapping objects using string matching", *Pattern Anal. Appl.*, 1999, Vol. 2, No. 1, pp. 2-9.

[2] K. J. Cios, W. Pedrycz, and R. Swiniarski, *Data Mining Methods for Knowledge Discovery*, Kluwer. Dordrecht, 1998.

[3] U. M. Fayyad, G. Piatetsky-Shapiro, P. Smyth, and R. Uthurusamy (eds.), *Advances in Knowledge Discovery and Data Mining*, MIT Press, Cambridge, MA, 1996.

[4] S. Gibson, *An optimal FFT-based algorithm for mosaicing images*, Master Thesis, Department of Computer Science, University of Texas at El Paso, December 1999.

[5] X. Jiang, K. Yu, and H. Bunke, "Detection of rotational and involutional symmetries and congruity of polyhedra", *Visual Comput.*, 1996, Vol. 12, No. 4, pp. 193-201.

[6] L. T. Koczy, V. Kreinovich, Y. Mendoza, H. T. Nguyen, and H. Schulte, "Towards Mathematical Foundations of Information Retrieval: Dependence of Website's Relevance on the Number of Occurrences of a Queried Word", *Proceedings of the Joint Conferences in Information Sciences JCIS'2000}*, Atlantic City, NJ, February 27-March 3, 2000 (to appear).

[7] O. Kosheleva, L. Longpre, and R. Osegueda, "Detecting Known Non-Smooth Structures in Images: Fuzzy and Probabilistic Methods, with Applications to Medical Imaging, Non-Destructive Testing, and Detecting Text on Web Pages", *Proceedings of The Eighth International Fuzzy Systems Association World Congress IFSA'99*, Taipei, Taiwan, August 17-20, 1999, pp. 269-273.

[8] V. Kreinovich, C. Quintana, and O. Fuentes. "Genetic algorithms: what fitness scaling is optimal?" Cybernetics and Systems: an International Journal, 1993, Vol. 24, No. 1, pp. 9-26.

[9] J. Llados, H. Bunke, and E. Marti, "Finding rotational symmetries by cyclic string matching", *Pattern Recognit. Lett.*, 1997, Vol. 18, No. 14, pp. 1435-1442.

[10] R. S. Michalski, M. Kubat, I. Bratko, and A. Bratko (eds.), *Machine Learning and Data Mining: Methods and Applications,* J. Wiley & Sons, New York, 1998.

[11] H. T. Nguyen and V. Kreinovich, *Applications of continuous mathematics to computer science*, Kluwer, Dordrecht, 1997.

[12] L. Polkowski et al. (eds.), *Rough sets in knowledge discovery 1. Methodology and applications*, Physica-Verlag: Heidelberg, 1998 (Studies in Fuzziness and Soft Comput. Vol. 18).

[13] B. S. Reddy and B. N. Chatterji, "An FFT-Based Technique for Translation, Rotation, and Scale-Invariant Image Registration," *IEEE Transactions on Image Processing*, 1996, Vol. 5, No. 8, pp. 1266-1271.

[14] K. Shearer, H. Bunke, S. Venkatesh, and D. Kieronska, "Efficient graph matching for video indexing", in: J.-M. Jolion et al. (eds.), *Graph based representations in pattern recognition. Workshop, GbR '97, Lyon, France, April 17-18, 1997*, Wien: Springer: Wien, Comput. Suppl. 1998, Vol. 12, pp. 53-62.

[15] Y.-Q. Zhang and A. Kandel, *Compensatory Genetic Fuzzy Neural Networks and Their Applications*, World Scientific, Singapore, 1998.

[16] N. Zhong, A. Skowron, and S. Ohsuga (eds.), *New directions in rough sets, data mining, and granular-soft computing, Proc. of the 7th international workshop, RSFDGrC '99, Yamaguchi, Japan, November 9-11, 1999. Proceedings*, Springer-Verlag Lecture Notes in Artificial Intelligence, Vol. 1711, Berlin, 1999

Appendix: Proofs

Proof of Theorem 1

This proof is based on the following lemma:

Lemma. *If an optimality criterion is final and unit-invariant, then the optimal family* F_{opt} *is also unit-invariant, i.e.,* $R_\lambda(F_{opt}) = F_{opt}$ *for every number* λ.

Proof of the Lemma. Since the optimality criterion is final, there exists a unique family F_{opt} that is optimal with respect to this criterion, i.e., for every other F:

- either $F_{opt} > F$,
- or $F_{opt} \sim F$

To prove that $F_{opt} = R_\lambda(F_{opt})$, we will first show that the re-scaled family $R_\lambda(F_{opt})$ is also optimal, i.e., that for every family F:

- either $R_\lambda(F_{opt}) > F$,
- or $R_\lambda(F_{opt}) \sim F$

If we prove this optimality, then the desired equality will follow from the fact that our optimality criterion is final and therefore, there is only one optimal family (so, since the families F_{opt} and $R_\lambda(F_{opt})$ are both optimal, they must be the same family).

Let us show that $R_\lambda(F_{opt})$ is indeed optimal. How can we, e.g., prove that $R_\lambda(F_{opt}) > F$? Since the optimality criterion is unit-invariant, the desired relation is equivalent to $F_{opt} > R_{\lambda^{-1}}(F)$. Similarly, the relation $R_\lambda(F_{opt}) \sim F$ is equivalent to $F_{opt} \sim R_{\lambda^{-1}}(F)$.

These two equivalences allow us to complete the proof of the lemma. Indeed, since F_{opt} is optimal, we have one of the two possibilities:

- either $F_{opt} > R_{\lambda^{-1}}(F)$,
- or $F_{opt} \sim R_{\lambda^{-1}}(F)$.

In the first case, we have $R_\lambda(F_{opt}) > F$; in the second case, we have $R_\lambda(F_{opt}) \sim F$.

Thus, whatever family F we take, we always have:

- either $R_\lambda(F_{opt}) > F$,
- or $R_\lambda(F_{opt}) \sim F$

Hence, $R_\lambda(F_{opt})$ is indeed optimal and thence, $R_\lambda(F_{opt}) = F_{opt}$. The lemma is proven.

Let us now prove the theorem. Since the criterion is final, there exists an optimal family $F_{opt} = \{C\, f(z)\}$. Due to the lemma, the optimal family is unit-invariant.

From unit-invariance, it follows that for every λ, there exists a real number $A(\lambda)$ for which $f(\lambda z) = A(\lambda) f(z)$. Since the function $f(z)$ is differentiable, we can conclude that the ratio

$$A(\lambda) = \frac{f(\lambda z)}{f(z)}$$

is differentiable as well. Thus, we can differentiate both sides of the above equation with respect to λ, and substitute $\lambda = 1$. As a result, we get the following differential equation for the unknown function $f(z)$:

$$z \frac{d f}{d z} = \alpha f$$

where by α, we denoted the value of the derivative

$$\frac{dA}{d\lambda}$$

taken at $\lambda = 1$. Moving terms $d z$ and z to the right-hand side and all the term containing f to the left-hand side, we conclude that

$$\frac{d f}{f} = \alpha \frac{d z}{z}.$$

Integrating both sides of this equation, we conclude that $\ln(f) = \alpha \ln(z) + C$ for some constant C, and therefore, that $f(z) = const\ z^{\alpha}$. The theorem is proven.

Proof of Theorem 2

This proof is based on the following lemma:

Lemma. If an optimality criterion is final and invariant, then the optimal value z_{opt} is also invariant, i.e., $z_{opt} = z_{opt} e^{i\theta}$ for every real number θ.

Proof of the Lemma. Since the optimality criterion is final, there exists a unique complex number z_{opt} that is optimal with respect to this criterion, i.e., for every other z,

- either $z_{opt} > z$,
- or $z_{opt} \sim z$.

To prove that $z_{opt} = z_{opt} e^{i\theta}$, we will first show that the $z_{opt} e^{i\theta}$ is also optimal, i.e., that for every number z:

- either $z_{opt} e^{i\theta} > z$,
- or $z_{opt} e^{i\theta} \sim z$

If we prove this optimality, then the desired equality will follow from the fact that our optimality criterion is final and therefore, there is only one optimal number (so, since the numbers z_{opt} and $z_{opt}\, e^{i\theta}$ are both optimal, they must be the same number).

Let us show that $z_{opt}\, e^{i\theta}$ is indeed optimal. How can we, e.g., prove that $z_{opt}\, e^{i\theta} > z$? Since the optimality criterion is invariant, the desired relation is equivalent to $z_{opt} > z\, e^{-i\theta}$. Similarly, the relation $z_{opt}\, e^{i\theta} \sim z$ is equivalent $z_{opt} \sim z\, e^{-i\theta}$.

These two equivalences allow us to complete the proof of the lemma. Indeed, since z_{opt} is optimal, we have one of the two possibilities:

- either $z_{opt} > z\, e^{-i\theta}$,
- or $z_{opt} \sim z\, e^{-i\theta}$

In the first case, we have $z_{opt}\, e^{i\theta} > z$; in the second case, we have $z_{opt}\, e^{i\theta} \sim z$.

Thus, whatever number z we take, we always have:

- either $z_{opt}\, e^{i\theta} > z$,
- or $z_{opt} \sim z\, e^{-i\theta}$.

Hence, $z_{opt}\, e^{i\theta}$ is indeed optimal and thence, $z_{opt}\, e^{i\theta} = z_{opt}$. The lemma is proven.

Let us now prove the theorem. Since the criterion is final, there exists an optimal number z_{opt}. Due to the lemma, the optimal family is invariant. So, $z_{opt} \cdot e^{i\theta} = z_{opt}$ for every real number θ. In particular, for $\theta = \pi$, we have $e^{i\theta} = -1$ and hence $z_{opt} = z_{opt}$, i.e., $z_{opt} = 0$. The theorem is proven.

Fuzzy Genetic Modeling and Forecasting for Nonlinear Time Series

Berlin Wu

Department of Mathematical Sciences ,National Chengchi University, Taiwan

Abstract. This paper presents a new approach to genetic–based modeling for nonlinear time series analysis. The research is based on the concepts of evolution theory as well as natural selection, and hence is called "genetic modeling". In order to find a predictive model from the nonlinear time series, we make use of 'survival of the fittest' principle of evolution. Through the process of genetic evolution, the AIC criteria are used as the performance measure, and the membership functions of the best-fitting models are the performance index of a chromosome. An empirical example shows that the genetic model can effectively find an intuitive model for nonlinear time series, especially when structure changes occur.

Keywords. Nonlinear time series, Genetic modeling, Leading models, Membership function.

1 Introduction

One weakness of many proposed models for time series is the assumption of having no structure changes during the whole dynamic process. In the real economic society, it is very difficult to construct an appropriate model that can honestly explain the trend of an underlying time series, such as exchange rates or stock indices. Two fundamental questions that often arise are: (1) does there exist an appropriate statistical model that can account for this underlying process, and (2) does the dynamic process agree with a single linear or nonlinear equation? (Need we use more than one equation, e.g. threshold model, to fit the time series?)

As a result, a priori selection of a model for a time series from a model-base system becomes an important procedure, occurring before model construction (see Wu, 1995). If a model family is correctly chosen a priori, model construction procedures such as parameter estimation, diagnosis and forecasting will make sense. But if the underlying time series demonstrates certain structure changes, it is necessary to detect those change points or change periods before modeling the whole process. Otherwise, using the traditional techniques for model construction we may not get a *good model* for the nonlinear time series.

In nonlinear time series analysis, a number of methods for detecting change points during structure identification have been proposed in the literature. In reality, we find that the structure of a time series changes gradually. The change points can exhibit characteristics of fuzziness and heredity. Many patterns of change structure exhibit certain kinds of duration, those phenomena should not be treated as a mere sudden change at a fixed time.

The problem of change point detection in a time series has been examined by many researchers. For instance, Tsay (1990) proposed some procedures for detecting outliers, level shifts, and variance changes in a univariate time series. The procedures he suggested are particularly useful and relatively easy to implement. Balke (1993) pointed out that Tsay's procedures do not always perform satisfactorily when level shifts are present. Inclan and Tiao (1994) proposed an iterative procedure to detect variance changes based on a centered version of the cumulative sums of squares presented by Brown, Durbin, and Evans (1975).

Some testing statistics dealing with change point detection include: MPAGE (Modified PAGE) proposed by Page (1955), and CUSUM (Cumulative Sum) proposed by Hinkley (1971). Hsu (1979, 1982) investigated the detection of a variance shift at an unknown point in a sequence of independent observations, focusing on the detection of points of change one at a time because of the heavy computational burden. Worsley (1986) used ML methods to test a change in mean for a sequence of independent exponential random variables. Sastri, Flores and Valdes (1989) presented a performance comparison for six time-series change detection procedures. Recently, Rukhin (1997) studied the classical change-point estimation problem in the Bayesian setting, i.e. the point estimation of the change –point parameter is considered after the data has been observed and the change-point is known to occur.

However, those detection techniques are based on the assumption that the underlying time series exhibits an abrupt change. In dealing with the time series with switching regimes, however, we must consider the change period instead of the change point. Since many patterns of structure change in time series exhibit a certain kind of duration, those phenomena should not be treated as a mere sudden turning at a certain time, cf. Wu and Chen (1999). For instance: (i) the exchange rate may go up or down gradually after a new financial policy performs. (ii) a national monetary supply of M_1 or M_2 may change their trend at different period of time according to the national economic conditions. In fact, the semantics of the term "change point" is vague or uncertain (interested readers may refer to any popular dictionary such as Webster's New Dictionary).

In this research, we make use of an integrated procedure to detect change periods for a nonlinear time series and construct a genetic model. Firstly, we choose certain initial gene models from a model-base and give the number of generations from the data. Then, we calculate the degree of membership for each gene models in each generation under an objective function. After deciding the memberships of the current population's fitness, we examine the evolution trend and choose the *leading model* from all generations. Finally, we determine the change periods by checking whether other candidate models have replaced the leading model. The modeling process we perform will be called *Genetic Modeling*. This change period detecting method will be called *Genetic Detecting*. The simulation and empirical results showed that our *Genetic Detecting* is an efficient and realistic procedure in detecting structure change in a time series. When the change is gradual, our model construction procedure demonstrated a superior explanation as well as prediction.

2 Genetic Modeling

The Genetic Algorithm (GA) proposed by Holland (1970) bases a derivative-free stochastic optimization method on the concepts of natural selection and evolutionary processes. Evolution theory stressed the fact that the existence of all living things is based on the rule of *survival of the fittest*. Darwin suggested that new breeds or classes of living things come into existence through the processes of reproduction, crossover, and mutation among existing organisms. The concepts of evolution theory have been translated into algorithms to search for solutions to problems in a more *natural* way.

In the following material, we show how evolutionary concepts and natural selection are used in the nonlinear time series analysis. Applying to the classical evolution theory into the analysis of real data, we may view the dynamic processes of a nonlinear time series as a result of heredity of certain gene models. Hence, if we partition the whole time series into N generation, and examine each generation with degree of fitness we may capture some heredity property through evolution.

Our procedure of our method is to choose initial gene models from a model-base and examine the heredity property through the generations. Since the ARIMA model family demonstrates a very good property in explaining the short-term stochastic process, we will choose five basic ARMA models: AR (1), AR (2), MA (1), MA (2), and ARMA (1, 1) as our initial gene models. The ARMA models can be found in the regular time series textbook, for example, Box and Jenkins (1976), or Brockwell and Davis (1996). For a time series $\{X_t; t = 1, 2, \ldots n\}$, the general ARMA (p, q) model is

$$X_t = \phi_1 X_{t-1} + \ldots + \phi_p X_{t-p} + \varepsilon_t - \theta_1 \varepsilon_{t-1} - \ldots - \theta_q \varepsilon_{t-q};$$

where $\varepsilon_t \sim WN(0, \sigma_\varepsilon^2)$, $\phi_i, \theta_j, i = 1, \ldots, p;\ j = 1, \ldots, q$ are the parameters of X_{t-i} and θ_{t-j}; p, q are orders of ARMA model.

The well-known *AIC* criterion is used as our adaptive measurement for the gene models, where $AIC = n \ln \hat{\sigma}_\varepsilon^2 + 2(p+q)$, and n is the degree of freedom for the fitted model. That is, the best appropriate model was chosen according to the *AIC* criteria.

2.1 Membership of fitness

For each generation, in order to measure the degree of fitness for gene models, we need to define '*degree of fitness*'. The membership of fitness is a useful tool, which can help us find a leading model through the evolution.

Definition 2.1 Membership of fitness for gene models

Let $\{C_1, C_2, \ldots, C_k\}$ be the k gene models. Let A_{ij} be the AIC value of the jth ($j = 1, 2, \ldots k$) gene model in the ith ($i = 1, 2, \ldots, N$) generation and $A_i = \min_{1 \le j \le k} \{A_{ij}\}$.

Then the membership of fitness for each gene model written by M_{ij} is defined as

$$M_{ij} = 1 - \frac{A_{ij} - A_i}{\sum_{j=1}^{k} (A_{ij} - A_i)}. \tag{2.1}$$

Example 2.1 Let X_t follow an AR (1) process with $X_t = 5 + 0.5X_{t-1} + \varepsilon_t$; $\varepsilon_t \sim N(0, 1)$. With a problem size of 250 simulated data, the data was separated into 6 generations. Suppose we choose 5 initial gene models AR (1), AR (2), MA (1), MA (2) and ARMA (1, 1) from the ARMA (p, q) family. Then, we fit each generation by these five gene models respectively. The *AIC* values for 5 candidate models in 6 generations are illustrated at Table 2.1.

Models	AR (1)	AR (2)	MA (1)	MA (2)	ARIMA (1 0 1)
Generation 1	23.99	26.44	27.81	28.03	26.44
Generation 2	5.08	7.59	7.77	9.65	7.56
Generation 3	1.91	4.50	2.44	4.56	4.79
Generation 4	14.30	16.83	15.62	18.16	16.77
Generation 5	1.91	4.79	1.83	4.71	3.06
Generation 6	-1.80	1.02	-0.33	0.60	1.03

Table 2.1. AIC values for 5 candidate models in 6 generation

We calculate the *AIC* value for each gene model and then apply equation (2.1) to compute the membership of gene models for the first generation.

$$\sum_{j=1}^{5}(A_{1j}-A_{1})=$$

$$(23.99-23.99)+(26.44-23.99)+(27.81-23.99)+(28.03-23.99)+(26.44-23.99)$$

$$=12.76$$

$$M_{11}=1-\frac{A_{11}-A_{1}}{\sum_{j=1}^{5}A_{1j}-A_{1}}=1-\frac{23.99-23.99}{12.76}=1,$$

$$M_{12}=1-\frac{A_{12}-A_{1}}{\sum_{j=1}^{5}A_{1j}-A_{1}}=1-\frac{26.44-23.99}{12.76}=0.81,$$

$$M_{13}=1-\frac{A_{13}-A_{1}}{\sum_{j=1}^{5}A_{1j}-A_{1}}=1-\frac{27.81-23.99}{12.76}=0.70,$$

$$M_{14}=1-\frac{A_{14}-A_{1}}{\sum_{j=1}^{5}A_{1j}-A_{1}}=1-\frac{28.03-23.99}{12.76}=0.68,$$

$$M_{15}=1-\frac{A_{15}-A_{1}}{\sum_{j=1}^{5}A_{1j}-A_{1}}=1-\frac{26.44-23.99}{12.76}=0.81.$$

Table 2.2 shows the result for the membership of best-fitted model for all six generations.

Gene Models	AR (1)	AR (2)	MA (1)	MA (2)	ARMA (1, 1)
Generation 1	1.00	0.81	0.70	0.68	0.81
Generation 2	1.00	0.80	0.78	0.63	0.80
Generation 3	1.00	0.00	0.94	0.69	0.67
Generation 4	1.00	0.95	0.97	0.62	0.96
Generation 5	0.99	0.59	1.00	0.60	0.83
Generation 6	1.00	0.70	0.85	0.75	0.70

Table 2.2. Memberships for 5 candidate models in 6 generation

From Table 2.2, we find that the smaller the *AIC* value is, the larger the membership is. That is, the fittest model will account for the simulated data fairly. Therefore, we will choose the highest membership function as our best-fitted model.

2.2 The leading model

After calculating the membership of fitness for gene models at each generation, we are going to find the leading model, which dominates the underlying dynamic process. Traditionally, we use the *AIC* criterion as our decision rule to choose the most appropriate model for the underlying time series. In this in this research, we select the most appropriate models not only by the minimum *AIC* value, but also those models that converges to within a neighborhood of the minimum *AIC*. Thus, the most appropriate model may not be unique. All models which approach the minimum *AIC* value are selected as the most appropriate models.

If we examine the most appropriate models through whole generations, we may find certain regulations among them. One way is to look at the outcome number of the most appropriated for each gene model. If the frequency of the most appropriate model reaches a confidence level $\lambda, 0.5 < \lambda < 1$, then we can say that this gene model can account for the time series fairly. Definitions 2.2 and 2.3 give the precise definitions for the above idea. Under the significant α-level, we claim that a leading model is one that takes the highest frequency for the most appropriated in all generations.

Definition 2.2 Most appropriate models under the significant α -level

Let A (i) be the fuzzy set of gene models at the $i^{th\ generation}$. Given the significant level $\alpha\,(0<\alpha<1)$, the most appropriate models $A(i)$ at the generation i are defined by $A_{\alpha}(i) = \{A(x) \mid A(i;x) \geq 1-\alpha,\ x \in U\}$

Example 2.2 From Table 2.1 of Example 2.1 the fuzzy set of $A_{\alpha}(5)$ at the 5th generation can be written as:

$$A_{\alpha}(5) = \frac{0.99}{AR(1)} + \frac{0.59}{AR(2)} + \frac{1}{MA(1)} + \frac{0.60}{MA(2)} + \frac{0.83}{ARMA(1,1)}.$$

Under the significance level $\alpha = 0.1$, we get $A_{0.1}(5) = \{C_1, C_3\}$. Hence, at the 5th generation, there are two most appropriate models: AR (1) and MA (1).

In order to choose a leading model for a nonlinear time series, we propose the following:

Definition 2.3 The leading model

Let $\{X_t, t = 1, 2, ..., m\}$ be a time series, C = { C_j : j = 1, 2, ..., k } be the set of gene models and $S(j) = \frac{1}{N}\sum_{i=1}^{N} n_i(j)$ (where N is the number of generation, $n_i(j) = 1$ if the jth gene model belongs to A_{α}, and the $n_i(j)$=0 otherwise) be the frequency of the gene model C_j being chosen as a most appropriate model at each generation. Given a confidence level $\lambda\ (0.5<\lambda<1)$, if max{S (j), j = 1 , ..., k} = S (l) $\geq \lambda$, then we say that the lth gene model is the leading model for time series $\{X_t\}$.

Example 2.3 From Table 2.1 of Example 2.1, we find the AR(1) model has the maximum memberships of the 5 gene models in the first generation . By Definition 2.2, under the significance level $\alpha = 0.1$, we have $A_{0.1}(j) = 0.9$. Hence $n_1(1) = 1$, $n_1(2) = n_1(3) = n_1(4) = n_1(5) = 0$.

Similarly, the best-fitted models at the 5th generation are AR (1) and MA (1). Hence denote $n_5(1) = n_5(3) = 1$ and $n_5(2) = n_5(4) = n_5(5) = 0$. Similarly, we can get the following Table 2.3

Gene Models	AR (1)	AR (2)	MA (1)	MA (2)	ARMA (1, 1)
Generation 1	1	0	0	0	0
Generation 2	1	0	0	0	0
Generation 3	1	0	1	0	0
Generation 4	1	1	1	0	1
Generation 5	1	0	1	0	0
Generation 6	1	0	0	0	0
S (j)	1	1 / 6	3 / 6	0	1 / 6

Table 2.3. The $n_i(j)$ values for 6 generation in Example 2.1

Obviously, if we choose the confidence level $\lambda = 0.9$, then $S(1) = 1 > 0.9$, which indicates that the AR (1) is the leading model for this time series.

2.3 An integrated genetic modeling process

By observing the evolution of a time series though N generations, we can find the memberships of candidate models as well as the leading model. On the other hand, if there exists a change for the leading model, we may also say that the underlying time series has occurred a structure change.

In this section, we propose a detector for the change period identification. The main idea is that if the membership of the leading model at the ith generation is less than A_α, it means that in the last generation another model became the best-fitted model. Naturally, the underlying time series encountered a structure change. We can say that the change period occurred at this generation. The following procedure demonstrates the identification and decision steps.

Algorithm for identification of change periods of a time series

(1) Take the set of the gene models $C = \{ C_j : j = 1, 2, \ldots, k \}$ and separate the time series into k generations

(2) Choose an adaptive function, and calculate the membership of fitness M_{ij} for each gene model j and each generation i.

(3) *Under the significance level* α *and the fuzzy set* A_{α} *(* $i = 1, 2, \ldots, N$*), decide the* $n_{l}(j)$, $n_{l}(j) = 1$ *if* C_{j} *belongs to the most appropriate model* $A_{\alpha}(i)$ *at the generation l, otherwise* $n_{l}(j) = 0$.

(4) *Calculating the frequency of* $S(j)$*. Under the confidence level* $\lambda \in (0,1)$*, if there exist j such that* $S(j) \geq \lambda$*, then the leading model is assigned to the* j^{th} *gene model, go to step 6; otherwise go to step 5.*

(5) *The time series exhibits a very unstable process, it may be a random walk, a chaotic time series or encounters too many intervention from outside system.*

(6) *Stop.*

2.4 Combined forecasting with gene models

After identifying the leading model, we can forecast this nonlinear time series. Let $f_{1,t}, f_{2,t}, \ldots, f_{k,t}$ be the forecasting values after t steps from the gene models $C_1, C_2, \ldots, C_k$ respectively. We assume that the conditional expectation of the variable being forecasted is a linear combination of the available forecasts. Thus when combining the individual forecasts $f_{1,t}, f_{2,t}, \ldots, f_{k,t}$, a single combined forecast F_t is produced according to equation (2.2)

$$F_t = w_1 f_{1,t} + w_2 f_{2,t} + \ldots + w_1 f_{k,t}, \text{ where } w_j = \frac{S(j)}{\sum_{j=1}^{k} S(j)}, \ j = 1, \ldots, k. \tag{2.2}$$

Clearly, this forecasting by weighted memberships combination in general will be more reasonable and efficient than the average forecasting of equal weight.

3 Simulation Studies

Time series data of 450 time steps was generated from three models, see model (3.1), (3.2) and (3.3). An AR (1) process with three different noise terms is shown in Figure 3.1. An ARCH (1) process with three different variances is shown in Figure 3.2. In Figure 3.3, an ARMA (1, 2) process with three different moving average noises terms is shown.

$$X_t = \begin{cases} 5 + 0.8X_{t-1} + \varepsilon_t & ,\varepsilon_t \sim N(0,\ 0.1) \quad \text{if} \quad 1 \le t \le 150 \\ 5 + 0.8X_{t-1} + \varepsilon_t & ,\varepsilon_t \sim N(0,\ 0.45) \quad \text{if} \quad 151 \le t \le 300 \\ 5 + 0.8X_{t-1} + \varepsilon_t & ,\varepsilon_t \sim N(0,\ 1.25) \quad \text{if} \quad 301 \le t \le 450 \end{cases} \tag{3.1}$$

$$X_t = \begin{cases} \sigma_t\varepsilon_t\ ,\sigma_t^2 = 5 + 0.5X_{t-1}^2\ , & \varepsilon_t \sim N(0,\ 1) \quad \text{if} \quad 1 \le t \le 150 \\ \sigma_t\varepsilon_t\ ,\sigma_t^2 = 5 + 0.2X_{t-1}^2\ , & \varepsilon_t \sim N(0,\ 1) \quad \text{if} \quad 151 \le t \le 300 \\ \sigma_t\varepsilon_t\ ,\sigma_t^2 = 10 + 0.6X_{t-1}^2\ , & \varepsilon_t \sim N(0,\ 1) \quad \text{if} \quad 301 \le t \le 450 \end{cases} \tag{3.2}$$

$$X_t = \begin{cases} 0.1 + X_{t-1} + \varepsilon_t - 0.8\varepsilon_{t-1} & ,\ \varepsilon_t \sim N(0,1) \quad \text{if} \quad 1 \le t \le 180 \\ 0.1 + X_{t-1} + \varepsilon_t - 0.1\varepsilon_{t-1} - 0.5\varepsilon_{t-2} & ,\ \varepsilon_t \sim N(0,1) \quad \text{if} \quad 181 \le t \le 200 \\ 0.1 + X_{t-1} + \varepsilon_t - 0.8\varepsilon_{t-1} & ,\ \varepsilon_t \sim N(0,1) \quad \text{if} \quad 201 \le t \le 300 \\ 0.1 + X_{t-1} + \varepsilon_t - 0.2\varepsilon_{t-1} - 0.7\varepsilon_{t-2} & ,\ \varepsilon_t \sim N(0,\ 1) \quad \text{if} \quad 301 \le t \le 320 \\ 0.1 + X_{t-1} + \varepsilon_t - 0.8\varepsilon_{t-1} & ,\ \varepsilon_t \sim N(0,1) \quad \text{if} \quad 321 \le t \le 450 \end{cases} \tag{3.3}$$

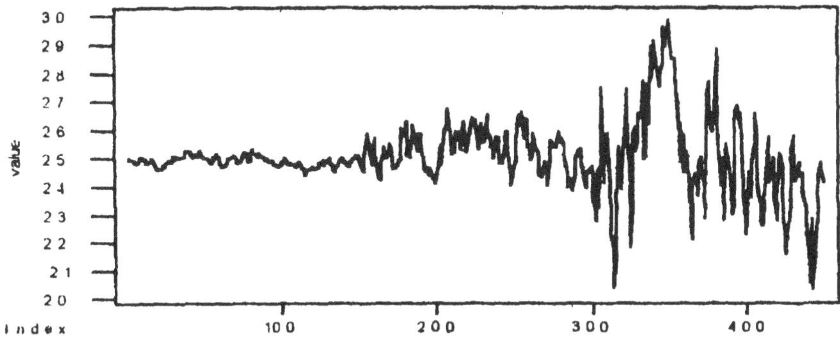

Figure 3.1. Trend for the time series model (3.1) (mean = 25.61 SD = 1.26)

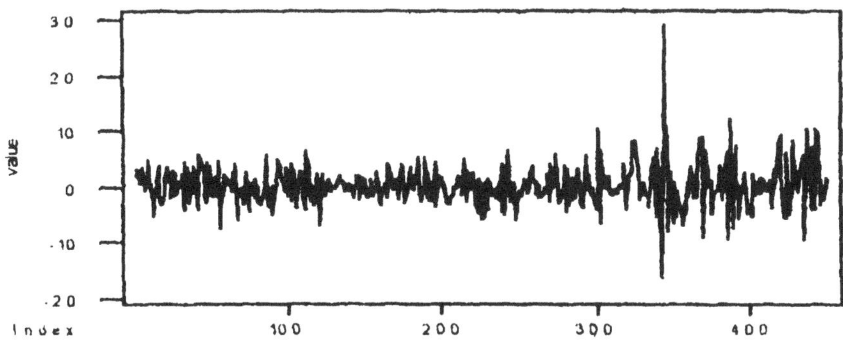

Figure 3.2. Trend for the time series model (3.2) (mean = 0.41, SD = 3.72)

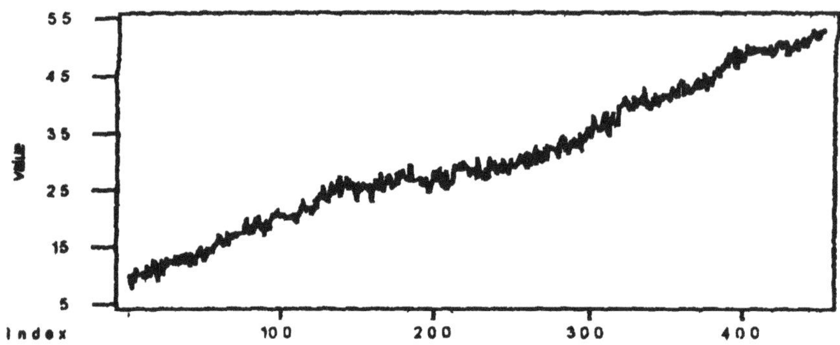

Figure 3.3. Trend for the time series model (3.3) (mean = 30.42, SD = 12.09)

From the above figures, we can see that the data originate from certain type of nonlinear process. In model (3.1) and (3.2), it fluctuates along a constant mean, while the data in model (3.3) illustrates an upward trend.

3.1 Genetic modeling analysis

Firstly, we separate these time series into 11 generations. In order to emphasize the heredity concept, we let each generation have 10 points overlapped. That is, the last 10 data points at the ith generation are the same as the first 10 points of $(i + 1)$ generation. Using to the techniques we discussed above, we find the following result.

For the model (3.1), we choose AR (1) □AR (2) □MA (1) □MA (2) □ARIMA (1 0 1) as our gene models. According to the AIC value, we calculate each membership for candidate models, as well as the $n_t(j)$ values with the significance level $\alpha = 0.1$, which were shown in Table 3.1. Under the confidence level $\lambda = 0.8$, since $S(1) = 0.82 > 0.8$, we say that AR (1) is the leading model for the time series (3.1).

The leading model AR(1) has $n_t(j) = 0$ at the 4th and 8th generations, showing that the leading model at these generations are not the best-fitted model. According to the identification and decision algorithm, the 4th and the 8th generation are changing periods. These generations correspond to time periods 120-170 and 180-330.

That is at the period with the data 120~170 and 180~330. This coincides with the original model (3.1).

	AR (1)	AR (2)	MA (1)	MA (2)	ARIMA (101)
1	1.00 (1)	0.89 (0)	0.68 (0)	0.70 (0)	0.76 (0)
2	1.00 (1)	0.76 (0)	0.76 (0)	0.745 (0)	0.75 (0)
3	1.00 (1)	0.95 (1)	0.51 (0)	0.63 (0)	0.92 (1)
4	0.64 (0)	0.79 (0)	1.00 (1)	0.83 (0)	0.78 (0)
5	1.00 (1)	0.82 (0)	0.57 (0)	0.82 (0)	0.82 (0)
6	1.00 (1)	0.81 (0)	0.70 (0)	0.76 (0)	0.77 (0)
7	1.00 (1)	0.89 (0)	0.53 (0)	0.74 (0)	0.87 (0)
8	0.46 (0)	0.81 (0)	0.90 (1)	0.95 (1)	0.89 (1)
9	1.00 (1)	0.95 (1)	0.43 (0)	0.69 (0)	0.96 (1)
10	0.91 (1)	0.80 (0)	0.46 (0)	1.00 (1)	0.81 (0)
11	1.00 (1)	0.86 (0)	0.50 (0)	0.80 (0)	0.86 (0)
S (j)	0.82	0.18	0.18	0.18	0.27

Table 3.1 Memberships and $n_i(j)$ values for model (3.1)

By equation (2.2), since $\sum_{j=1}^{5} S(j) = 0.82 + 0.18 + 0.18 + 0.18 + 0.27 = 1.63$,

and

$$w_1 = \frac{0.82}{1.63} = 0.5031, w_2 = \frac{0.18}{1.63} = 0.1104, w_3 = \frac{0.18}{1.63} = 0.1104$$

$w_4 = \frac{0.18}{1.63} = 0.1104$, $w_5 = \frac{0.27}{1.63} = 0.1656$, hence the combined forecasting F_t is

$$F_t = 0.5031 f_{1,t} + 0.1104 f_{2,t} + 0.1104 f_{3,t} + 0.1104 f_{4,t} + 0.1656 f_{5,t}$$

For the model (3.2), we calculate each membership for the gene models as well as the $n_i(j)$ value with the significance level $\alpha = 0.1$, which were shown in Table 3.2. Under the confidence level $\lambda = 0.8$, with S (2) and S (4) both equal to 0.55, we find that there does not exist a leading model for the time series (3.2). The time series exhibits characteristics of a very unstable process. In fact, the underlying data came from an ARCH (1) process, and our conclusion is thus very reasonable.

	AR(1)	AR(2)	MA(1)	MA(2)	ARIMA(101)
1	0.91 (1)	0.89 (0)	0.91 (1)	0.75 (0)	1.00 (1)
2	1.00 (1)	0.79 (0)	0.98 (1)	0.74 (0)	0.74 (0)
3	0.88 (0)	0.91 (1)	0.90 (1)	0.82 (0)	1.00 (1)
4	0.98 (1)	0.82 (0)	1.00 (1)	0.84 (0)	0.79 (0)
5	0.95 (1)	0.69 (0)	1.00 (1)	0.75 (0)	0.73 (0)
6	0.73 (0)	0.96 (1)	0.69 (0)	0.82 (0)	1.00 (1)
7	1.00 (1)	0.75 (0)	0.92 (1)	0.72 (0)	0.84 (0)
8	0.76 (0)	0.93 (1)	0.66 (0)	1.00 (1)	0.72 (0)
9	0.74 (0)	0.98 (1)	0.78 (0)	1.00 (1)	0.88 (1)
10	0.69 (0)	1.00 (1)	0.75 (0)	0.89 (0)	0.80 (0)
11	0.82 (0)	0.81 (0)	0.85 (0)	0.80 (0)	1.00 (1)
S(j)	0.45	0.45	0.55	0.18	0.45

Table 3.2 Memberships and $n_i(j)$ values for model (3.2)

By equation (2.2), since $\sum_{j=1}^{5} S(j) = 0.45 + 0.45 + 0.55 + 0.18 + 0.45 = 2.08$,

and

$w_1 = \frac{0.45}{2.08} = 0.2163$, $w_2 = \frac{0.45}{2.08} = 0.2163$, $w_3 = \frac{0.55}{2.08} = 0.2644$,

$w_4 = \frac{0.18}{2.08} = 0.0865$, $w_5 = \frac{0.45}{2.08} = 0.2163$, hence the combined forecasting F_t is $F_t = 0.2163 f_{1,t} + 0.2163 f_{2,t} + 0.2644 f_{3,t} + 0.0865 f_{4,t} + 0.2163 f_{5,t}$.

For the model (3.3), we differentiate the underlying time series with first order, and then separate it into 11 generations. Since the AR (1) model does not work in the model fitting for this process, we choose AR (2), MA (1), MA (2), ARMA (1, 1) as our gene models. Table 3.3 shows the membership for candidate models as well as the $n_t(j)$ values with the significance level α = 0.1. Under the confidence level $\lambda = 0.8$, since S (1) = 0.82 > 0.8, we say that MA (1) is the leading model for the time series (3.3).

	AR (2)	MA (1)	MA (2)	ARIMA (101)
1	0.36 (0)	0.98 (1)	0.82 (0)	1.00 (1)
2	0.35 (0)	1.00 (1)	0.89 (0)	0.85 (0)
3	0.76 (0)	1.00 (1)	0.72 (0)	0.69 (0)
4	0.49 (0)	1.00 (1)	0.81 (0)	0.79 (0)
5	0.39 (0)	0.78 (0)	0.99 (1)	1.00 (1)
6	0.28 (0)	0.93 (1)	0.97 (1)	1.00 (1)
7	0.24 (0)	1.00 (1)	0.93 (1)	0.93 (1)
8	0.43 (0)	0.70 (0)	0.97 (1)	1.00 (1)
9	0.32 (0)	1.00 (1)	0.92 (1)	0.93 (1)
10	0.55 (0)	1.00 (1)	0.80 (0)	0.81 (0)
11	0.65 (0)	1.00 (1)	0.76 (0)	0.74(0)
S (j)	0	0.82	0.45	0.55

Table 3.3 Memberships and $n_t(j)$ values for model (3.3)

By equation (2.2), since $\sum_{j=1}^{4} S(j) = 0 + 0.82 + 0.45 + 0.55 = 1.82$, and $w_1 = 0$,

$w_2 = \frac{0.82}{1.82} = 0.4505$, $w_3 = \frac{0.45}{1.82} = 0.2473$, $w_4 = \frac{0.55}{1.82} = 0.3022$, hence the combined forecasting F_t is

$$F_t = 0.4505 f_{2,t} + 0.2473 f_{3,t} + 0.3022 f_{4,t}.$$

4 An empirical application for Taiwan Business Cycle

Figure 4.1 is a plot of the Index of monthly Taiwan business cycle from November 1987 to February 1997. This data comes from the Council of Economic Planning and Development, Taiwan. It exhibits several non-regular business cycles in the 112 time series as well as structural changes. The non-regularity of business monitors makes the analysis of this time series very difficult. Figure 4.1 presents a large fluctuation and it is difficult to construct a suitable model. Hence, we firstly inspect the tendency of the Taiwan Business Monitors in Figure 4.1. From the large fluctuations during the whole period, we have strong confidence that there exists some structure changes..

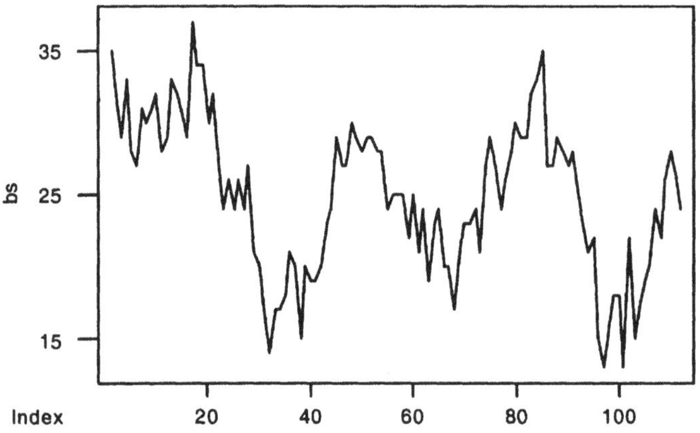

Figure 4.1. Index of Taiwan Business Cycle

The pattern in Figure 4.1 roughly exhibits about 6 periods, so we separate the time series into 6 generations. For the heredity reason, we let each generation have 4 points overlapping. That is, the last 4 data points in the ith generation are the first data points in the (i + 1) generation. We choose AR (1), AR (2), MA (1), MA (2) and ARMA (1, 1) as our gene models, and AIC as our adaptive function. According to the techniques we discuss above and for the significance level α = 0.1, we illustrate the result in Table 4.1.

	AR (1)	AR (2)	MA (1)	MA (2)	ARIMA(1 01)
1	1.00 (1)	0.91 (0)	0.69 (0)	0.70 (0)	0.76 (0)
2	1.00 (1)	0.79 (0)	0.76 (0)	0.77 (0)	0.74 (0)
3	1.00 (1)	0.96 (1)	0.51 (0)	0.64 (0)	0.93 (1)
4	0.68 (0)	0.79 (0)	1.00 (1)	0.83 (0)	0.78 (0)
5	1.00 (1)	0.80 (0)	0.57 (0)	0.84 (0)	0.81 (0)
6	1.00 (1)	0.81 (0)	0.70 (0)	0.76 (0)	0.79 (0)
S (j)	0.83	0.17	0.17	0	0.17

Table 4.1 Memberships and $n_t(j)$ values for Taiwan Business Cycle

Under the confidence level $\lambda = 0.8$, since $S(1) = 0.83 > 0.8$, we say that AR (1) is the leading model for the Taiwan Business Cycle.

The leading model AR (1) has the $n_t(j)$ value 0 at the 4th generation, it shows that the leading model at this generation are not the best-fitted model. According to the identification and decision algorithm, the 4th generation is a changing periods. That is at the period with the data 61~80 (from November 1991 to February 1993). At this period, the business index follows a MA(1) process.

In fact, the world faced with the Persian Gulf crisis that caused the petroleum problems at November 1990 (Survey Data, 1990). In the meantime, Taiwan's stock market was pounded; the real growth rate and public investment declined. All the harmful factors caused the Taiwan Business Cycle to show prosperity. The business cycle index showed the stable growth in February 1994 (Survey Data, 1994). On the other hand, the Taiwan economy became boomed from the growth in the employment rate, the prosperity of trade with foreign nations, the huge trade volume of the stock market, the increased orders in manufacturing, and the stable consumer price index. Therefore, the year before November 1990 and the year after February 1994 had prosperous business cycles.

Finally, by equation (2.2), since

$$\sum_{j=1}^{5} S(j) = 0.83 + 0.17 + 0.17 + 0 + 0.17 = 1.34, \text{ and}$$

$$w_1 = \frac{0.83}{1.34} = 0.6194,\ w_2 = \frac{0.17}{1.34} = 0.1269,\ w_3 = \frac{0.17}{1.34} = 0.1269,\ w_4 = 0,$$

$$w_5 = \frac{0.17}{1.34} = 0.1269.$$

Hence the combined forecasting F_t is

$$F_t = 0.6194 f_{1,t} + 0.1269 f_{2,t} + 0.1269 f_{3,t} + 0.1269 f_{5,t} .$$

5 Conclusion

There are many studies about the problem of model construction for nonlinear time series. Some of them are only suitable for uncorrelated observations or special cases. Some of them have too strong assumptions that could not be easily reached. The weakness of the model-based philosophy of Box-Jenkins modeling clearly resides in the impossibility of satisfying the stationary and linearity assumptions. Unlike the traditional methods, genetic modeling applies the concept of evolution theory to detect structure changes and dynamic heredity. This research liberates us from the model-based selection procedure and no assumption of the sample data will be made. Moreover, through the fuzzy identification procedure, the genetic modeling process will help us to detect a change period and/or change point for a nonlinear time series.

Finally, in spite of the robust forecasting performance for the genetic modeling, there remain some problems for further studies. For example:

(I) In this research, we only use basic ARIMA models as our gene models. In order to get a more extended result, we may include TAR, bilinear or ARCH into our gene model base.

(II) The convergence of the algorithm for classification and the proposed statistics have not been well proved, although the algorithms and the proposed statistics are known as fuzzy decision criteria. This needs further investigation.

(III) To find an efficient test of the outliers as well as the change period that make the structural change.

(IV) To find a more comprehensive adaptive function than *AIC*.

However, in order to give the popular questions, such as *duration of a business cycle*, *when do turning points occur*, and *combined forecasting*, a satisfied answer, we believe the current genetic modeling process suggested in this paper will be a worthwhile approach, and will stimulate more future empirical work in the nonlinear time series analysis.

References

[1] Andel, J.(1993). A time series model with suddenly changing parameters. *Journal of Time Series Analysis.* **14**(2), 111-123.

[2] Balke, N. S. (1993). Detecting level shifts in time series. *Journal of Business and Economic Statistics.* 11(1), 81-92.

[3] Barry, D. and Hartigan, J. A. (1993). A Bayesian analysis for change point problems. *Journal of the American Statistical Association.* **88**(421), 309-319.

[4] Bleany, M.(1990). Some comparisons of the relative power of simple tests for Structure Change in Regression Models. *Journal of Forecasting.* **9**, 437-444.

[5] Box, G. E. P. and Jenkins, G. M. (1976). *Time Series Analysis, Forecasting, and Control.* Holden-Day, San Francisco.

[6] Brockwell, P. and Davis, R. (1996). *Introduction to Time Series and Forecasting*. Springer-Verlag: New York.

[7] Brown, R., Dubin, J., and Evans, J. (1975). Techniques for testing the constancy of regression relationships over time. *Journal of the Royal Statistical Society*, Ser. B, **37**, 149-163.

[8] Chow, G. C.(1960). Testing for equality between sets of coefficients in two linear regressions. *Econometrica.* **28,** 291-605.

[9] De Gooijer, J. G. and K. Kumar. (1992). Some recent developments in nonlinear time series modeling, testing, and forecasting. *International Journal of Forecasting.* **8,** 135-156.

[10] Hinkey, D. V. (1971). Inference about the change point from cumulative sum test. *Biometry.* **26**, 279-284.

[11] Holland, J. H. (1975). Adaptation in Natural and Artificial Systems, University of Michigan Press, Ann Arbor.

[12] Hsu,D.A(1979), Detecting shifts of parameter in gamma sequences, with applications to stock price and air traffic flow analysis. *Journal of the American Statistical Association.* **74**, 31-40.

[13] Hsu, D. A. (1982), A Bayesian robust detection of shift in the risk structure of stock market returns. *Journal of the American Statistical Association.* **77**, 29-39.

[14] Inclan, C. & Tiao, G. C. (1994). Use of cumulative sums of squares for retrospective detection of changes of variance. *Journal of the American Statistical Association.* **89**(427), 913-924.

[15] Inclan, C. and Tiao,G.C.(1994). Use of cumulative sum of squares for retrospective detection of changes of variances. *Journal of the American Statistical Association.* **74**, 913-923.

[16] Kao, C. & Ross, S. L. (1995). A CUSUM test in the linear regression model with serially correlated disturbances. *Econometric Reviews.* 14(3), 331-346.

[17] Koza, J. R.(1994). Genetic Programming II: Automatic Discovery of Reusable Programs. MIT Press.

[18] Loraschi, A., Tettamani, A.,Tomassini, M. and Verda, P.(1995). Distributed genetic algorithms with an application to portfolio selection problem. *Artificial Neural Networks and Genetic Algorithms*, Edited by Pearson, N.C, Steele, N. C . and Al-Brett, R.F., Springer-Verlag , 384-387.

[19] Mitchell, M .(1996) . *An Introduction to Genetic Algorithms.* Cambridge , MA: MIT Press.

[20] Nyblom, J.(1989). Testing for the constancy of parameters over time. *Journal of the American Statistical Association.* **844**, 223-230.

[21] Page, E. S. (1955). A test for change in a parameter occurring at an unknown point. *Biometricka.* **42**, 523-527.

[22] Ploberger, W. and W. Kramer. (1992). The CUSUM-test with OLS Residuals. *Econometrica.* **60**, 271-285.

[23] Rukhin, A. (1997). Change-point estimation under Asymmetric loss. *Statistics & Decisions,* **15**, 141-163.

[24] Saatri, T., Flores, B., and Valdes, J. (1989). Detecting points of change in time series, *Computers Open Res.* **16**, 271-293.

[25] Tsay, R, S. (1991). Detecting and Modeling Non-linearity in Univariate Time Series Analysis. *Statistica Sinica.* **1**(2),431-451.

[26] Tsay, R. S. (1990). Testing and modeling threshold autoregressive processes. *Journal of the American Statistical Association.* **84**, 231-240.

[27] Weiss, A. A.(1986). ARCH and bilinear time series models: compares and combination. *Journal of Business and Economic Statistics.* **4**, 59-70.

[28] Wosley, K. J. (1986). Confidence regions and tests for a change-point in a sequence of exponential family random variables. *Biometrika.* **73**, 91-104.

[29] Wu, B.(1994). Identification Environment and Robust Forecasting for Nonlinear Time Series. *Computational Economics.* **7**, 37-53.

[30] Wu, B. (1995). Model-free forecasting for nonlinear time series: with application in exchange rates. *Computational Statistics and Data Analysis.* **19**, 433-459.

[31] Wu, B. and Chen, M. (1999). Use fuzzy statistical methods in change periods detection. *Applied Mathematics and Computation.* **99**, 241-254.

GPSR Compliance
The European Union's (EU) General Product Safety Regulation (GPSR) is a set of rules that requires consumer products to be safe and our obligations to ensure this.

If you have any concerns about our products, you can contact us on

ProductSafety@springernature.com

In case Publisher is established outside the EU, the EU authorized representative is:

Springer Nature Customer Service Center GmbH
Europaplatz 3
69115 Heidelberg, Germany

www.ingramcontent.com/pod-product-compliance
Ingram Content Group UK Ltd.
Pitfield, Milton Keynes, MK11 3LW, UK
UKHW061705190726
13853UKWH00008B/2414
* 9 7 8 3 6 6 2 0 0 3 5 8 9 *